Don Grant

Praise for *Bound Together*

"Given the avalanche of books on globalization it is reasonable to assume that for now the subject has been exhausted. This assumption crumbles after one reads Nayan Chanda's masterful analysis and discovers that this gifted writer has added a new and important layer to our understanding of why and how we are all 'Bound Together.' A must read."
  —Moisés Naim, editor in chief, *Foreign Policy*

"*Bound Together* is destined to be a classic book for the twenty-first century. Author Nayan Chanda has combined deep and far-ranging scholarship with a journalist's touch for storytelling to craft an enthralling narrative of humankind from our birth in Africa to our addiction to the Internet. Chanda is a true global citizen. His book should be read in every home, school, business, and embassy in the world, and become a vital part of our common intellectual heritage."
  —Ambassador Derek Shearer, Stuart Chevalier Professor of Diplomacy and World Affairs and Director of Global Affairs, Occidental College

"Chanda's account of globalization is a breath of fresh air. His treatment of the topic, from its origins with the first humans out of Africa to its most recent appearance in financial markets, is comprehensive, informed, and judicious. Refreshingly personal and humorous, it is probably the best single-volume work on world/global history now available, and a must for all students of the subject. Along the way, India, for example, becomes as much a focus as Europe in the overall story."
  —Bruce Mazlish, professor of history emeritus, MIT

"It is, in my view, a wonderful read—incredibly informative, insightful, and written with energy, eloquence, and simplicity. The themes are fresh and the organization especially interesting. Some of the great strengths of the book are the way he relates history to the present, the global perspective throughout, the broader-than-economics focus, and the way he describes the overlap of forces that have led to the world we now live in. My guess is that this book will be widely read and have a special place on any bookshelf that contains works on globalization."
  —Jeffrey Garten, former dean and Juan Trippe Professor in the Practice of International Trade, Finance, and Business, Yale School of Management

Bound Together

Bound Together

How Traders, Preachers, Adventurers, and
Warriors Shaped Globalization

Nayan Chanda

Yale University Press

New Haven and London

A Caravan book. For more information, visit www.caravanbooks.org

Set in Adobe Garamond and Stone Sans types by The Composing Room of
Michigan, Inc.
Printed in the United States of America.

Library of Congress Cataloging-in-Publication Data

Chanda, Nayan.
  Bound together : how traders, preachers, adventurers, and warriors shaped
globalization / Nayan Chanda.
     p.   cm.
  Includes bibliographical references and index.
  ISBN 978-0-300-11201-6 (clothbound : alk. paper)
  1. Social evolution.   2. Commerce—History.   3. Intercultural communication—History.   4. Culture diffusion—History.   5. Globalization—History.
I. Title.   II. Title: How traders, preachers, adventurers, and warriors shaped
globalization.   III. Title: Traders, preachers, adventurers, and warriors shaped
globalization.
  HM626.C45 2007
  303.48′209—dc22

                                                              2007000430

A catalogue record for this book is available from the British Library.

♾™ The paper in this book meets the guidelines for permanence and durability
of the Committee on Production Guidelines for Book Longevity of the Council
on Library Resources.

10 9 8 7 6 5 4 3 2 1

To the memory of my parents
and
To my other parents, Amarjit and Bhagwant

Contents

Introduction

A few days after my wife and I had moved into our home in New Haven, Connecticut, an electrician came to fix some electrical outlets that weren't working. Jerry was middle-aged and friendly, and he asked me what I did at Yale. When I mentioned my affiliation with the Yale Center for the Study of Globalization, he seemed stunned, as if I had just confessed to being a charter member of a Colombian drug cartel. "Oh! God help you," he muttered. Puzzled, I asked what was wrong. Jerry was clearly surprised to meet someone who he thought actually worked *for* globalization. "Isn't it true that globalization destroys the rain forest?" he asked by way of explanation. My protestation that the closest I had ventured to the Amazon was to order a few books did little to help my standing.

But Jerry's reaction had raised important questions. What precisely is globalization, and why is it accused of damaging the rain forest? It seems to have appeared out of nowhere, and now it is everywhere. Almost every problem—even extraordinary developments—has been laid at the door of this phenomenon called globalization. Its role in damaging rain forests is perhaps the easiest to understand. Forests are being cleared mainly to create farmland for the world's growing population. Rising international trade and the growing demand for construction materials and furniture have brought traders and loggers into the act. To answer Jerry's concerns, I thought it was important to understand who the globalizers are, what they are doing and why, and how long they have been at it.

Since the word *globalization* appeared in the dictionary, its meaning has undergone a massive transformation. Just two of the dozens of definitions of *globalization* illustrate the problem in grappling with this phenomenon. Writing in the *Encyclopedia Britannica,* Jeffrey L. Watson defines *globalization* in cultural terms—as "the process by which the experience of everyday life, marked by the diffusion of commodities and ideas, can foster a standardization of cultural expressions around the world." The official World Bank definition of *globalization* is stated, not surprisingly, in purely economic terms, as the "freedom and ability of individuals and firms to initiate voluntary economic transactions with residents of other countries."[1] Left-wing critics, echoing Karl Marx's observation about the "werewolfish hunger" of capitalism reaching the four corners of the world, see globalization as synonymous with expansionist and exploitative capitalism. Looking at globalization through the prism of business and economics helps one to understand the Internet, the mobile phone, and the cable TV-connected world we inhabit, but it does not explain how human life was globalized long before capitalism was formulated or electricity invented.

Many recent books, notably Thomas L. Friedman's *The World Is Flat,* have explained how mobile capital, trade, and technology have created today's instantaneously connected, interdependent world. Economic historians like Kevin O'Rourke and John G. Williamson have shown how the transportation revolution in the late nineteenth century kicked off large-scale trade and migration, laying the foundation for the current era of globalization. In fact, in their view, globalization began when large-scale trading brought about a convergence of commodity prices all over the world. But globalization defined in strictly economic terms leaves unexplained the myriad instances of global connectedness and indeed convergence that appeared long before the steamship.

The term *globalization* emerged because the visibility of our globally connected life called for a word to sum up the phenomenon of this interconnectedness. But if one looked under the hood of our daily existence, one could see a multitude of threads that connect us to faraway places from an ancient time. Without looking into the past, how does one explain that almost everything—from the cells in our bodies to everyday objects in our lives—carries within itself the imprints of a long journey? Why in that first instance did human beings leave Africa and become a globalized species? Most of what we eat, drink, or use originated somewhere else than where we find these objects today. Almost everything we associate with a nation or take pride in as our own is connected with another part of the world, however remotely. Today's capitalist business model can explain why Starbucks coffee—an iconic symbol of globalization—is sold in thousands of locations around the world or why Japan's Canon camera is a globally recognized brand. But the economic definition leaves other questions unanswered. How, for example, did the coffee bean, grown first only in Ethiopia, end up in our cups after a journey through Java and Colombia? How did the name of the Bodhisattva *Avalokiteswar,* translated into Chinese as *Guanyin* and in Japanese as *Kwanon,* inspire the Japanese brand name for a camera?

Endless other questions point to deeper processes at play. How is the same gene mutation found in three people living in continents thousands of miles apart? How did Islam, born in the deserts of Arabia, win over a billion converts in the world? How did Europeans learn to play the violin with a bowstring—made of Mongolian horsehair? Or, for that matter, how did the ninth-century Arab mathematician al-Khwarizimi lend his name to the algorithms that now run the world of information? How did the economic model of growing sugarcane with slave labor, developed in the eastern Mediterranean, reach the Caribbean? Why was there no fiery *kimchi* in Korea before Christopher Columbus found chili pepper plants in the New World? How did the United States currency get its name from a German silver-mining town? Why are the grapes that yielded the first barrel of wine in California called mission grapes? How did the Chinese paper-making technology reach the West and end up producing the stock for the book you are reading? The questions are as varied as they are unending, and they go to the heart of the all-embracing phenomenon of global interconnectedness. The economic definition of globalization cannot explain why an electrician in New Haven cared about the Brazilian rain forest or how global awareness of such issues has arisen. As we shall see in Chapter 8, the story of how the word *globalization* emerged is directly linked to the visibility of growing integration of the world. The term *globalization,* reflecting awareness of these global connections, grew out of the very process it describes—a process that has worked silently for millennia without having been given a name.

This book attempts to show that globalization stems, among other things, from a basic human urge to seek a better and more fulfilling life and that it has been driven by many actors who can be classified, for the sake of simplicity, as traders, preachers, adventurers, and warriors. These globalizers left their original habitats in the pursuit of a more enriching life or to fulfill their personal ambitions. In so doing, they not only carried products, ideas, and technology across borders, but with increased interconnectedness they created what Roland Robertson calls "intensification of consciousness of the world as a whole."[2] Despite his distaste for "globalization," electrician Jerry's concern for the health of the planet squarely places him among the globally aware who are themselves a product of an intensely interconnected world. Literally, of course, one cannot talk of such global connections until the first circumnavigation of the globe by Ferdinand Magellan in 1519. However, in the broad sense of expanding the known world—which the Greeks called *oikumene*—and linking the fate of geographically separated communities, globalization, as a trend, has been with us since the beginning of history. The same forces, sometimes with different names, are at work today in connecting the world ever faster and tighter. Multinational companies, nongovernmental organizations, activists, migrants, and tourists have been continuing the process of integration that began thousands of years ago.

This book is thus the result of a personal quest for an understanding of, if not answers to, some simple questions: Who are the globalizers, and how does one explain the global origins of everything that surrounds us? My search for the answers to many such questions altered my understanding of globalization, and the way I look at it today is quite different from when I started out. I have tried to understand the origin and transformation of goods and ideas as they travel the world from where they started, looking at the global voyage of commodities and concepts. In order to grasp the forces that have spurred various global journeys, I have focused on a selected set of commodities and ideas as examples of a broader trend. I have tried to identify the main actors and their motivations. To appreciate the trajectory of these actors—traders, preachers, adventurers, and warriors—and the goods and ideas they have carried, I have looked at them over a millennial canvas. My story of globalization begins with the journey of anatomically modern humans out of Africa some fifty thousand years ago. Out of the necessity for survival, these people were the first adventurers who over generations moved on, occupying the inhabitable areas of the earth, and taking divergent paths before settling down and reconnecting with other dispersed human communities. I have abandoned the conventional format of presenting a linear history of a particular people or territory and have tried instead to trace the growing connections and interdependence through the action of these four actors. A brief chronology of the role played by the four actors is given on pages 321–330.

I have benefited from the works of the pioneers in the field of global history, such as William McNeill, the historian of *longue durée* Fernand Braudel, world system historian Immanuel Wallerstein, and cultural historians Bruce Mazlish, Philip D. Curtin, and Jerry Bentley. The works of other authors, such as Jared Diamond's *Guns, Germs, and Steel* and Robert P. Clark's *Global Imperative: An Interpretive History of the Spread of Humankind,* have helped me to frame the rise of global awareness in a long-term perspective. A host of other books and articles that have aided me in weaving this narrative are acknowledged in the endnotes. Researching this book for more than six years has been an exhilarating journey of discovery. Apart from satisfying my curiosity about how the world got globalized, this long-range perspective of the process will, I believe, help others to understand the forces at work in the present phase of globalization. The same human desire for a better life and greater security that prompted traders to brave the waves, the same political ambition of warriors to occupy foreign lands, the same urge for preachers to set out to convert others to their ideas of the good, and the same drive of adventurers to seek new lands and opportunities are still working to shrink the world. Many more have joined the different categories: migrants and tourists have replaced the adventurers of the past, and NGOs espousing human rights, the environment, and many other causes have joined the traditional preachers of faith. By the exponential growth in their numbers, consumers have emerged as the newest category of globalizers. In a way, each one of us is a participant and an actor in this process in our various roles. A huge exception has been a third of the world's population, who desperately want to join in the globalized network as traders, migrants, and consumers but are prevented by global rules and by the hand they have been dealt. The big differences that mark the globalization of the early years with that of the present are in the *velocity* with which products and ideas are transferred, the ever-growing *volume* of consumers and products and their *variety,* and the resultant increase in the *visibility* of the process. It is this growing visibility of the process that has shown in sharp relief the warts and all of globalization. This is not to deny the totally new developments that globalization has brought. For the first time, the innovation and production of goods and the delivery of services are being done in real time across the continents, bringing unprecedented opportunity to the prepared and challenge to the unready.

If one accepts the essential continuity of the forces that have created the increasingly integrated world, one cannot but see globalization as an unstoppable process. History has chronicled how the various calamities resulting from close integration—from the ravages of Black Death to the collapse of the so-called First Globalization (1870–1914) in the conflagration of World War I—have periodically interrupted the process, but no event or cataclysm has been able to end it. An appreciation of the motives that have propelled globalization for so long would perhaps better enable us to prevent major calamities and attempt to shape the flow, however marginally.

The first chapter, "The African Beginning," traces the initial globalization of the human species, when in the late Ice Age, a tiny group of our ancestors walked out of Africa in search of better food and security. In fifty thousand years of wandering along ocean coasts and chasing game across Central Asia, they finally settled on all the continents. Along the way, they changed their pigmentation and facial features, and developed different languages and cultures as well. The period of divergence came to a close with the end of the Ice Age. Traders, preachers, soldiers, and adventurers from the emerging urban civilizations of the Levant, India, and China began connecting with one another, launching the process of globalization.

Chapter 2, "From Camel Commerce to E-Commerce," traces the growth of trade from the dawn of human civilization to the present, showing how it has connected an increasingly wider part of the world through a web of commerce. Along with growing trade and expanding merchandise, the means of transportation—from camel caravans to sails powered by the monsoon winds, and from steamboats to container ships and Internet shopping—has continually speeded up. Indian handloom weavers, who once supplied textiles to the world, literally perished because of the Industrial Revolution. Their place in the global economic order has been taken by the workers in India's call centers and the software programmers who are connecting to the world over fiber-optic cables—tying the world ever more tightly.

Chapter 3, "The World Inside," takes a closer look at three everyday products that emerged from global trade and contain within them the story of global interconnectedness. Cotton, originally grown in India, spread to the world before being supplanted by American cotton. Coffee, known only to the Arab world at one stage, has conquered the globe, providing employment to millions of people whose ancestors never saw a coffee bean. The most powerful tool of today's globalization, the microchip, which has fueled the information revolution and now powers almost all industrial products, grew out of evolving ideas of mathematics and physics that span a thousand years and three continents.

Chapter 4, "Preachers' World," explores the role that religious preachers played in reaching out and connecting with different human communities. The result of their proselytizing zeal is the domination of the world by three major religions. Buddhist pilgrims and preachers took their faith to distant corners, in the process transforming the world's art, culture, and society. Christian missionaries and Islamic preachers, often backed by the sword, have converted millions in foreign lands. In the modern period, a new kind of secular missionary has joined to link the world even more closely—in the name of the environment and various causes from feeding the hungry to stopping the violation of human rights.

Chapter 5, "World in Motion," tells the story of adventurers whose curiosity to discover what lay behind the next mountain or the next island has been a key factor in connecting a geographically separated world. From the Carthaginian commander Hanno, who sailed down Africa's west coast in 500 BCE to the fourteenth-century Moroccan traveler Ibn Battuta, and from Marco Polo to Ferdinand Magellan, countless adventurers have widened the horizon and helped to create the integrated world of today. Millions of migrants have left home in search of a better life, and millions of eager tourists, helped by modern transport, have built ever thickening bridges linking the globe.

Chapter 6, "The Imperial Weave," traces the role of ambitious rulers, the warriors whose universalist aspirations and search for power and glory have taken them to distant lands. From Alexander the Great to Genghis Khan, ambitious men have brought lands and populations under their control, creating a varied gene pool and diffusing cultures. Political edifices built by imperial rulers—from the Romans to the British Empire—promoted legal and linguistic unity and the exchange of plant and animal species across the globe.

Chapter 7, "Slaves, Germs, and Trojan Horses," explores the dark underbelly of expanding global connections. As more and more traders, preachers, soldiers, and adventurers have spread out across the world, they have also brought serious problems in their wake. Right from the beginning, they turned war prisoners and captured humans from other lands into slaves. The European discovery of the New World took slavery to a new height in the process, creating multiracial societies in many parts of the Americas. From the plague pathogen carried by traders on the silk route and the smallpox and flu viruses borne by the conquistadors to the SARS virus flying around the world with tourists, global connection has brought its share of disasters. In recent times, writers of malicious computer viruses have exploited their high-speed fiber-optic connections to disrupt and destroy computer operations around the planet.

Chapter 8, "Globalization: From Buzzword to Curse," examines how, with the growing awareness about the interconnected world, from its timid entry into the English vocabulary in 1961, the word *globalization* has grown into a buzzword. A survey of electronic databases since the 1970s shows that the use of the word grew rapidly in the 1990s, when deregulation and technological advances drove worldwide trading and investment. The word's meaning and usage has changed in tandem with the economic problems spawned by the process of globalization. The changing appreciation of the value of globalization can be seen in the eclipse of the word by a more evocative and worrisome word: outsourcing.

Chapter 9, "Who's Afraid of Globalization?" explores how, despite the economic growth and prosperity brought about by faster economic integration, globalization has emerged as a toxic word for some people. Protesters from Seattle to Cancún and Genoa to Hong Kong have dogged meetings of the World Trade Organization (WTO) and Group of Eight (G8) nations, complaining about undemocratic institutions and unfair policies. The gathering speed of trade and communication that has opened up labor markets to the multitudes of China and India now has economists and politicians worried about the future impact of globalization on industrial economies.

The final chapter, "The Road Ahead," offers a summary of the process of globalization and looks at its troubled future. Globalization has created an integrated world in which many have been lifted from poverty, but the speeding pace of globalization has left nearly a third of the world's population by the wayside. The global challenge ahead will be somehow to bring into the fold the excluded populations and encourage large developing nations such as China and India to carry on with their open-door policies while stanching the rising nationalist and protectionist tide in the developed West.

The drive to integrate the globe, gathering speed since the adventurous journey out of Africa eons ago, will be hard to stop. But given how closely our fate is intertwined, even a temporary derailment now could be more costly than when it was tried before the Great Depression. The stakes are much higher in a hyperconnected world.

Bound Together

Chapter 1 The African Beginning

"Look, they are returning and they have bought something truly amazing! Trees heavy with fresh incense ready to plant. Ebonine, precious ivory, baboons, monkeys and dogs, countless Leopard skins, even slaves and children. Nothing like this has ever happened to another king of Egypt."
—*Queen Hatshepsut exclaiming on the return of the Egyptian expedition to Punt (Africa) on the walls of her temple (1473–58 BCE)*

In some telling of history, imagination provides the context for a truer meaning underneath. To begin understanding the story of globalization, there is hardly a more apt opening phrase than the familiar fairy tale opening, "Once upon a time," followed by a tale that, as recorded here, is part imagination, part reality.

Once upon a time there was a village in a place called Duniya. It was a village on the edge of the forest where the sun shone on the tall grass and the undulating hills. Life was hard, but there were enough roots to dig, nuts to gather, and gazelles or hares to hunt. For shelter,

---

The "White Lady of the Brandberg," a rock painting in Namibia from 2000–1000 BCE. Drawing courtesy Rock Art Research Institute, South Africa

there were caves or overhanging rocks. But the countryside around the village began to change. The sun got hotter and the air drier. There was less and less food as animals perished from drought or left the area in search of water. Villagers, too, chose to follow the herds to stay near food. As they trudged along, they broke into groups. Some headed north following the animals, others moved toward the ocean. The exodus increasingly separated the groups moving farther and farther away from one another. It was an endless walk. As they walked, some settled in places that looked bountiful, others moved on in the direction that promised food and security. Thousands of years passed.

In their endless, slow wandering through icebound plains, windswept steppes, and snow-capped mountains, the villagers lost their sunburned look. Gradually their hair and eyes changed colors, and even their faces and body shapes were transformed. After two thousand generations of wandering, nobody knew where the original village in Duniya was. In their dispersed habitats, the people spread over the vast land, separated by mountains, deserts, and the rising ocean that submerged an earlier land bridge. They spoke a variety of tongues, wore diverse clothes, and ate different foods. Then one day a trader walked over the hill and discovered another human settlement, other people who spoke a different language and fashioned new and interesting tools. Trading between the separated villages took off. A preacher, too, ventured out from another of the many villages that now dotted Duniya, hoping to teach others about his god. In yet another village an ambitious chief assembled a small army to extend his control over other villages, in the hope of building an empire. There were also intrepid villagers, curious about what lay behind the mountain at the edge of their village or at the other side of the blue waters. They set forth to see what they could see, and they returned with stories about the amazing plants, animals, and treasures that lay on distant shores.

Thousands of years and thousands of generations passed. Some villages were no longer villages but bustling towns and cities. People had invented all sorts of devices that allowed them to go from one village to another faster than on horseback. They had built ships that carried huge amounts of goods from one place in Duniya to another. The population had grown to billions from the original few hundred who had left the drought-stricken village three thousand generations ago. The masses now traveled, migrated in search of jobs, and bought and sold goods from far and wide. Nobody remembered the name of the village of their origins or how their ancestors had lived. But every day they knew more about the many villages and towns that now dotted Duniya. They could taste different foods, listen to music they had not heard before, and, thanks to a magical box in their homes, even see what was happening in other parts of Duniya. This was duniyaization, they concluded. Many loved this new life, but some were upset to learn that people in other parts of Duniya led far more comfortable lives. Others complained that villagers from a distant place, who looked different and spoke other languages, were arriving in their towns and taking jobs. Cheap products from other places were filling up their store shelves, and local factories were closing down. If this is duniyaization, we will have none of it, they said. But nobody knew how to control this growing surge of connections that had linked all the descendants of one village thousands of years ago and continued to bring them closer. They did not know that they were once all from the same village.

It's no fantasy. Just call that metaphorical village Africa and replace Duniya with what it means in Arabic, Hindi, or Hausa—the world—and what you get in a nutshell is the story of globalization. Of course, there was no village until humans settled down to plant and harvest crops. But comparing the African continent to a metaphorical village is not so far-fetched. Africa may be a vast land that is home to nearly a billion people today, but our human ancestors who walked out of Africa so long ago may have numbered just two thousand, the size of a hamlet. One estimate puts the number of migrants out of Africa at no more than 150 people, the typical size of a hunter-gatherer population.[1] These early adventurers may have had wanderlust, but they ventured out of their known habitat mainly for survival. Those who stayed on survived by moving to more hospitable parts of Africa. The five billion inhabitants of today's non-African Duniya are descendants of those villagers who walked out of Africa. They are increasingly interconnected and, for better or for worse, interdependent. *Homo sapiens*—the anatomically modern humans who emerged in Africa—is the first mammalian species that has voluntarily spread itself out to every corner of the globe and begun what we have come to call globalization. In the sixty thousand years since that early journey out of Africa, humanity has diverged. The physical differences among humans that form the basis of what we call "race" were forged in this period of great divergence by geography, climate, and natural selection. As we shall see, the multihued great human diasporas from Africa, which sprang up in different latitudes and longitudes of the globe, organized themselves in distinct communities and began reconnecting with long-separated cousins across oceans and mountains.

This process of reconnection—driven by adventurers, traders, preachers, and warriors—has grown thicker and faster with each passing year, integrating the world more tightly than ever. The beginning of the twenty-first century marks an ironic turning of the full circle for the "out of Africa" adventurers. Thousands of destitute and jobless Africans are again on the move as migrants. In a desperate attempt to find a better life in Europe and the Middle East, they are trudging across forbidding deserts and risking life on perilous journeys. Unlike our ancestors of sixty thousand years ago, today's Africans are not walking along the Yemeni coast or trudging north through the Nile and Jordan valleys to the erstwhile unknown world of the Mediterranean and beyond. From the Atlantic coast of Senegal and Mauritania, they are boarding fishing boats, cramming into hulls in the hope of a better life across nine hundred miles of water. Their immediate destination: the Canary Islands, stepping-stone to the European Union. It is not just that Africans are again leaving the continent in search of a better life. The sight that often greets the fully clothed African immigrants wading ashore beaches of the Canary Islands compounds the irony: the "naturist" European bathers soaking in the sun are in the same state of undress as when our ancestors left Africa.

Other desperate people from Ethiopia—humanity's cradle land—and Somalia are taking to the ocean in the hope of reaching Yemen and beyond. Globalization continues. In this chapter we will see how the urge to find a safer, better life turned some of our human ancestors into adventurers and set them on a journey that marked the first step in the globalization of our species. It would take more than forty thousand years for human settlements to emerge and the process of connecting with one another to take off. But the same motivations that drive greater and greater integration today have been with us from the day humans formed sedentary communities.

THE HIDDEN STORY OF A JOURNEY

How do we know that we all are originally from Africa? Twenty years ago the proposition was mostly guesswork. In his work on human evolution *The Descent of Man, and Selection in Relation to Sex* (1871), Charles Darwin suggested that because Africa was inhabited by humans' nearest allies, gorillas and chimpanzees, "it is somewhat more probable that our early progenitors lived on the African continent than elsewhere."[2] Although voluminous biological and paleoanthropological evidence gathered since this statement has fortified the evolutionary history of life on earth, it has been a long wait to validate Darwin's insight about Africa. Opportunity emerged with our new ability to look deep into our cells and decode the history written there. The first step was taken in 1953 when British scientist Francis S. Crick and his American colleague James D. Watson discovered the structure of DNA. "We've discovered the secret of life,"

Crick announced with justifiable pride.[3] With the discovery of the double helix structure of DNA—the complex molecules that transmit genetic information from generation to generation—we received the most powerful tool to dig into our ancestral history. As Watson wrote, "We find written in every individual's DNA sequences of a record of our ancestors' respective journeys."[4] Since these early days, sequencing DNA has gotten much easier, faster, and cheaper. With help from archaeologists, climatologists, and linguists, geneticists and paleoanthropologists have been able to reconstruct the histories of human populations—a reconstruction that was unimaginable only two decades ago.

The discovery of fossils of *Homo erectus* in Indonesia and China—the so-called Java and Peking men—showed that the ancestors of *Homo sapiens*, or anatomically modern humans, had begun to travel and colonize Asia and the Old World about two million years ago. The dedicated work of paleoanthropologists like Louis and Mary Leakey in the 1950s and a slew of researchers in the following thirty years established that ancestors of modern humans lived in East Africa's Rift Valley.[5] The remains of a hundred-thousand-year-old *Homo sapiens* were found in Israel, but that species met a biological dead-end, blocked perhaps by the more robust Neanderthals who then inhabited the area. Amazingly, so far the only other remains of modern man dating back to forty-six thousand years have been found in Australia. Did these anatomically modern humans—*Homo sapiens*—have multiple origins, or did they evolve as a single species in Africa? The first intriguing evidence that those fossil finds in Africa were, not just the earliest humans, but our direct ancestors, came to light, not in some ancient fossils, but in the history contained in cells of modern women. This startling discovery was built on the earlier discovery of the structure of DNA. By analyzing the DNA of living humans from different parts of the world, geneticists can reconstruct the movement of their ancestors and track the prehistoric human colonization of the world. We now know that around sixty thousand years ago, a small group of people—as few as perhaps one hundred fifty to two thousand people from present-day East Africa—walked out.[6] Over the next fifty thousand or so years they moved, slowly occupying the Fertile Crescent, Asia, Australia, and Europe and finally moving across the Beringia land bridge to the American continent. The rising waters at the end of the Ice Age separated the Americas from the Asian continent. It was not until Christopher Columbus's encounter with the Arawak on the shores of San Salvador in 1492 that the long-separated human cousins from Africa would meet each other.[7] More about that later. First, we will see how our ancestors succeeded in making humans the first truly globalized species.

A MOTHER IN AFRICA

The discovery that all humanity stems from the same common parents came in 1987. The New Zealand biochemist Allan Wilson and his American colleague Rebecca Cann reached this conclusion at the University of California, Berkeley, by looking into a so-far ignored part of human DNA. Wilson and Cann's team collected 147 samples of mitochondrial DNA from baby placentas donated by hospitals around the world. Unlike the DNA that is recombined as it is passed from one generation to the next, mitochondrial DNA (abbreviated mtDNA) has tiny parts that remain largely intact through the generations, altered only occasionally by mutations that become "genetic markers." MtDNA is maternally inherited, transmitted only from a mother to her offspring, and only daughters can pass it on to the next generation. The mtDNA leaves intact all the mutations that a daughter inherits from her maternal ancestors, thus allowing one to find the traces of the earliest mutation. Since the rate of mutation is roughly constant, the level of variation in mutations allows us to calculate the age of the family tree created by the mtDNA string passed down through the generations. The result of Wilson and Cann's research was a bombshell. Going down the human family tree of five geographic populations, they found that all five stemmed from "one woman who is postulated to have lived about 200,000 years ago, probably in Africa."[8] The press inevitably, if misleadingly, called her the "African Eve." She indeed was, as James Watson put it, "the great-great-great . . . grandmother of us all," who lived in Africa some two hundred thousand years ago.[9] Obviously, she was not the only woman alive at that time: she was just the luckiest because her progenies survived to populate the world, while the lines of descendants of other women became extinct.[10] Or, in genealogical terms, their lines suffered a "pedigree collapse."[11] Children of the three surviving lines of daughters—identified by mtDNA markers L1, L2, and L3—now populate the world. While the first two lines mostly account for the African female population, the non-African women of the world all carry in their cells the inheritance of the two daughters of L3 line—M and N. A scientist has given these lines the nicknames Manju and Nasrin based on the assumption of where the two mutations are likely to have occurred: India and the Middle East.

Our most recent common mother may have been African, but what about the father? Significant recent progress in elucidating the paternal Y-chromosome has filled in the gap. In a groundbreaking research paper in 2000, Italian geneticist Luigi Luca Cavalli-Sforza and his colleague Peter Underhill established that the Y chromosome that determines male sex also has an African ancestry.[12] Just as mtDNA is transmitted only from a mother to her children, the Y chromosome that is passed on from a father to his son also does not undergo the shuffling—or recombination—that the rest of the chromosomes do. But there are mutations just like mtDNA. The result is that the history of our fathers is carried in perpetuity by sons. Human ancestors who left Africa all carried in their cells either the African Adam's Y chromosome, which has been given the prosaic label "M168," or the mtDNA of one of the African Eve's daughters. Based on extensive study of the world's population, geneticists now say that the most recent common ancestor of us all left Africa just fifty thousand years ago.[13]

Wilson and Cann's thesis of the human out-of-Africa origin was, of course, not unchallenged by some anthropologists and geneticists. The school that believed in multiregional evolution of the modern human refused to accept a recent or unique origin of *Homo sapiens*. Its proponents argued that the abundant *Homo erectus* fossils found in China and other regions in East Asia (such as Peking Man and Java Man) demonstrate a continuity, and to these researchers it was evident that *Homo sapiens* emerged out of frequent gene exchanges between continental populations, since the earlier species *Homo erectus* came out of Africa about a million years ago. Besides, they argued, the archaeological evidence does not mesh with the out-of-Africa hypothesis, thus making this conclusion at best premature.[14] At least in the case of Chinese critics, one also suspects that the disclaimer about African origins may be linked to national pride about the antiquity of the Chinese civilization. However, as research in the migration of the human genome has continued to produce more and more evidence of African origins, the scientific opinion has increasingly tilted toward the out-of-Africa school. Some Chinese objections have been countered with a large new body of research based on a massive DNA database collected by both Chinese and international geneticists. In 1998 a consortium of seven major research groups from China and the United States, funded by the National Natural Science Foundation of China, conducted a DNA analysis of twenty-eight of China's official population groups and concluded that "modern humans originating in Africa constitute the majority of the current gene pool in East Asia."[15] Several other researchers, including Chinese, have since sampled a large number of Chinese from all over China and reached the same conclusion.[16] Interestingly, research on both mtDNA and the Y chromosome has shown evidence even in Africa of the early colonization by the original group within Africa. The remaining cousins left in East Africa also spread out to the interior of the continent in search of survival. A strong school of thought in

South Africa actually suggests the possibility that the ancestors of the Bushmen also are our ancestors and that the spread of those humans who all became our ancestors was from south to north. Whichever way they moved, their imprint is left in the DNA of the Bushmen or Khoisan of the Kalahari Desert and in certain pygmy tribes in the central African rain forest.[17]

The genome revolution and the discovery of the African Eve have sparked a new interest in finding one's roots. The dark-haired *New York Times* columnist Nicholas Kristof thought he knew who he was. His father came to the United States from Europe, so Kristof assumed himself to be of a typical American-European heritage. But he wanted to find out who he really was under the skin and learn more about his origins, and so he sent his DNA sample for analysis. He was in for a surprise. A mere two thousand generations ago his great-great-great-grandmother was an African, possibly from Ethiopia or Kenya. Under his white skin and Caucasian features, exclaimed Kristof, "I am African-American!" After the publication of his column he received a flood of e-mails. One particularly droll one read, "Welcome to the club. But look out while driving in New Jersey." However, the African continent alone cannot lay sole claim to Nicholas Kristof. The genetic markers found in his DNA showed he was also related to people who now inhabit Finland, Poland, Armenia, the Netherlands, Scotland, Israel, Germany, and Norway. "The [DNA] testing just underscored the degree to which we're all mongrels," Kristof told me.[18]

One trait of the human community makes it possible to track the genomic journey. Humans prefer to settle down in one place if conditions permit, but they are equally ready to migrate in search of a better life. The result has been that people who settled along the path of the human journey are marked by a lineage associated with geographic regions. The fact that humans have mostly practiced patrilocality—in which women come to their husband's homes after marriage—enables one to associate the Y chromosome with a particular location. Looking at my DNA, geneticists could tell I was from the Indian subcontinent. My M52 Y-chromosome, shared by a large number of Indians, was a giveaway. This ability has allowed geneticists and anthropologists to sketch out a better picture of when and how the progenies of the African Eve left the old continent and found themselves in their current habitat. DNA shows that this migration, spanning forty to fifty thousand years, came in successive waves, mostly in gentle ripples and sometimes in large swells. The Wilson team found that all the world populations they examined, except the African population, have multiple origins, implying that each region was colonized repeatedly.

THE BEACHCOMBER EXPRESS TO AUSTRALIA

The lack of archaeological evidence does not allow us to answer with certainty why our ancestors left Africa. Probably a dry spell of the late Ice Age shrank the forests and dried the savannas that provided game for the hunter-gatherer population. When a small group took the momentous step of crossing the Red Sea into the southern Arabian coast, the whole world was open. Following game herds up into the Middle East or following the shellfish beds around the Arabian Peninsula and on into India, the humans were launched on a journey that would result in populating the entire planet.

One of the most striking of those journeys was the arrival of the ancestral population from Africa to Australia in just seven hundred generations. Some have called this journey an "express train" to Australia. Of course, the ancestors did not know they were headed to Australia: they were just following food. But the eastward movement of generations of people along the Indian and Southeast Asian coasts brought them to a continent twelve thousand miles from their East African origins.

In a series of articles in *Science* in May 2006, a team of international geneticists and anthropologists showed that the dates of this human journey, as gleaned from the paternally inherited Y chromosome, are in broad agreement with the dates derived from the earlier Wilson study of mtDNA. The articles combined the genetic study with anthropological evidence to show that the oldest human remains found outside Africa and the Middle East, at Lake Mungo in southeast Australia dating from forty-six thousand years ago and in a Borneo cave of a thousand years earlier, could have reached their destinations by following a coastal route along the Indian Ocean. In the Andaman Islands, where the indigenous people have long been isolated, the researchers found mtDNA types that matched those of the known founder African group dating back sixty-five thousand years. Amazingly, the aboriginal population of the Andamans had unique markers not shared by the population of South or Southeast Asia, suggesting that they had lived in isolation since the initial penetration of the northern coastal areas of the Indian Ocean by anatomically modern humans migrating out of Africa fifty to seventy thousand years ago.[19] The investigation of an aboriginal Malaysian group, Orang Asli, or original people, who had also lived in isolation for a long period, showed similar DNA traces going back to Africa.

Although the coastal route taken by the descendants of the marker M130 had now been established, how quickly humans from Africa reached Australia remained an enigma. However, by analyzing the molecular dates of sampled mtDNA across the vast swath of territory from India to Australia, geneticist Vincent Macaulay and his colleagues were able to gauge the speed of population dispersal. An estimated distance of seventy-five hundred miles between India and southern Australia following the coastal routes was covered in some 150 generations. Life along the beaches perhaps was comfortable enough to lead to a fast rise in population and the need for part of the community to move on in search of food—at the remarkable rate of two miles a year. Compared to the Australia-bound express, Macaulay notes that the dispersal rate during the recolonization of Europe after the Ice Age was barely four-tenths of a mile a year.[20]

DINNER ON THE RED SEA

Because the rising sea levels after the Ice Age engulfed all archaeological evidence of this migration, paleontologists long despaired of finding evidence of the coastal journey. Then came a lucky break. In 1999 an international team of marine biologists, paleontologists, archaeologists, and geologists led by Robert C. Walter unearthed startling evidence of human habitation near the village of Abdur on Eritrea's Red Sea coast. Fortunately for science, a seismic event had pushed up the limestone reef that preserved the ancient treasure, dating back more than 125,000 years. The rock exposed by the seismic event contained the first concrete information about how the ancestors survived in the new environment of the sea. Scientists speculate that the extremely arid conditions— and shortage of food sources wrought by the glacial age—forced humans to move to the coastal areas to survive. In their beachcomber existence they not only survived, as can be determined from the fossilized midden from their meals, but ate well. They feasted not just on fruits of the sea—oysters, mussels, and crabs—but on meat as well. Scraped bones of large animals like elephants and rhinoceros were found in the same area, suggesting a rather exotic "surf and turf" diet.

In a paper in *Nature,* Walter and others excitedly concluded: "Together with similar, tentatively dated discoveries from South Africa, this is the earliest well-dated evidence for human adaptation to a coastal marine environment, heralding an expansion in the range and complexity of human behavior from one end of Africa to the other."[21] The date of the find suggests that the stone tools at the site overlap in time with the apparent transition from archaic to anatomically modern *Homo sapiens* in Africa. More important, the artifacts from the Abdur

Reef limestone suggest that a coastal existence was becoming common before a group launched their "beachcomber's express" to end up in Australia.[22]

Low sea levels during the last Ice Age permitted small groups of our ancestors to walk across a newly emerged land bridge on the Red Sea to the Arabian Sea coast in Yemen.[23] Some forty-eight thousand years later an Egyptian naval expedition would return, perhaps to the same area on the Red Sea, in the Egyptians' first encounter with Punt, as that part of Africa was then called. Expanding ice sheets over the northern hemisphere fifty thousand years ago would have lowered the sea level by around three hundred feet, with exposed seabed shortening the distance that now exists between Africa, India, and Southeast Asia. The geneticist Spencer Wells estimates that it would have exposed as much as 125 miles of land off the west coast of India and would have connected it to Sri Lanka with a land bridge.[24] One can speculate that the speed of the ancestors' journey along the coast may have accelerated with the development of stone tools and the availability of new plants and trees when they reached the tropical coastline of India. The abundance of the coconut tree in particular may have been a great boon. The flesh of the coconut provides nourishment, and its juice is a safe drink. Its leaves can be used to build a shelter against sun and rain, its copra to roll into rope, and its trunk to make rafts or dugouts. Tying logs together to make a raft has long been in practice in southern India. The Tamil name for such a boat, *kattumaran,* later morphed into *catamaran*. In any case, a low sea level would certainly have made the journey through the shallow Java Sea to Indonesia easy. Those arriving in Southeast Asia could have paddled across the shallow waters of the Timor Sea to arrive in Australia.[25] The fact that the first humans to arrive in Australia introduced the prehistoric dog the dingo to the continent suggests that they arrived by boat.[26]

MY AFRICAN GREAT-GRANDFATHER

All this news about an "express train" of migrants leaving Africa and reaching Australia in just about five thousand years intrigued me. Were my ancestors on that early train? And did they somehow get off in India? Fortunately, I was able to discover the answer through the Genographic Project launched in 2005 by National Geographic in collaboration with IBM. The ambitious project, directed by Texas-born Wells, seeks to map humanity's genetic journey through the ages: where we came from and how we got to where we live today. As part of the research, the project directors encourage people to participate by sending their DNA samples and providing information about their ancestors.

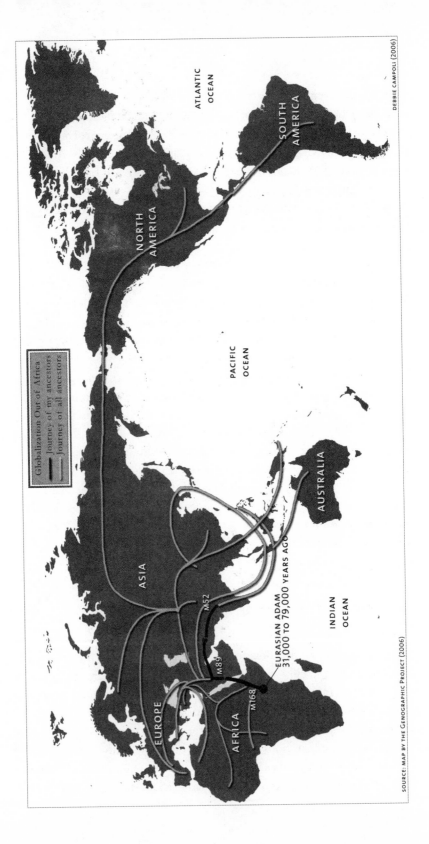

Globalization Out of Africa
— Journey of my ancestors
— Journey of all ancestors

ATLANTIC OCEAN

SOUTH AMERICA

NORTH AMERICA

PACIFIC OCEAN

AUSTRALIA

ASIA

M52

M89

EURASIAN ADAM
31,000 TO 79,000 YEARS AGO

M168

EUROPE

AFRICA

INDIAN OCEAN

SOURCE: MAP BY THE GENOGRAPHIC PROJECT (2006)

DEBBIE CAMPOLI (2006)

I ordered a participant kit, dutifully swabbed DNA from my cheeks, and mailed off the vials with just a serial number on them. After weeks of impatient waiting, I could access the results. The results were posted on the Web, and the lab that did the analysis knew me only as a serial number. But when I opened the report on the National Geographic Web site, logging in with my serial number, it told me straightaway that I was from India. My report claimed, "This lineage represents one of the very earliest pre-historic migrations into India, and today this line of descent is rarely found outside of India." The genetic group I belong to carries the three Y chromosome markers that immediately make me a blood relative, though distant, of millions of people who are now in the Middle East and Central Europe and hundreds of millions more in India. The Y chromosome traces left in my genome indicate that in the long line of my great-great-great-grandfathers, the last one had the Y chromosome marker M168. This marker also belonged to someone who lived in what is now Ethiopia. The part of the report that jumped out at me was this comment: "The very widely dispersed *M168* marker can be traced to an African man, who lived some 31,000 to 79,000 years ago, and is *the common ancestor of every non-African person living today.* His descendants migrated out of Africa and became the only lineage to survive away from humanity's home continent." Suddenly the aphorism from the *Panchatantra* I had heard growing up in India made sense: *Vasudhaiva kutumbakam,* "The whole world is a family."

Most interesting was the order of the markers in my Y chromosome—M168 to M89 to M201 to M52. It was like finding my family passport with stamps of the countries my ancestors passed through before reaching their final destination. As a medical researcher put it, "The people you've met and the places you've seen are in your genome."[27] The first station in this journey, like that of every non-African in the world, was someplace in today's Ethiopia. The DNA story recounts that at some point between thirty-one thousand to seventy-nine thousand years ago the progenies of the M168—we will call it the Grandpa marker—headed northeast. Perhaps the plains were becoming too crowded, and they left to seek new hunting grounds. A brief period of moist and favorable climate had expanded the ranges of such hunted animals at this time, so these nomadic peoples may have simply followed their food source, my report speculated. The next paternal marker, M89—we will call it the Levant marker—puts my ancestors in the same group that lived forty-five thousand years ago in northern Africa or the Middle East and formed part of a large inland migration of hunters who followed expanding grasslands and plentiful game to the Middle East, which was then much greener than today. This marker in my genome was a disappointment of sorts. My ancestors had not been on that "express train" to Australia, where all the travelers carried M130—the so-called Australia marker—the characteristic marker for the founder group that had branched off from Grandpa M168.[28]

Other genetic studies show that a small group of the Levant marker descendants moved north from the Middle East to Anatolia and the Balkans, trading familiar grasslands for forests and high country. While my ancestors crossed the Red Sea—perhaps at the narrowest point at Bab-al-Mandab, or the Gate of Grief—over to the Arabian Peninsula and eventually ended up in India, many people of M89 lineage remained in the Middle East. Others continued their movement and followed the grasslands through Iran to the vast steppes of Central Asia. Herds of buffalo, antelope, woolly mammoths, and other game probably enticed them to explore new grasslands. With much of the earth's water frozen in massive ice sheets, the era's vast steppes stretched from eastern France to Korea. The grassland hunters of the M89 lineage traveled both east and west along this steppe "superhighway" and eventually peopled much of Eurasia.

My genome report told me that my ancestors were in the larger group that veered east and continued their journey across today's Iran and Afghanistan. By then my ancestors had acquired a new and rather rare M201 lineage. The report said that M201 "first appeared in northern India's Indus valley, on the *M89* lineage, and subsequently dispersed during the past 10,000 to 20,000 years." It seems that some of my ancestors moved west to Anatolia and Central Europe, since the M201 lineage is found among people in that area.[29] But judging by the southern direction taken by my ancestors, they may have been among the founders of India's earliest Harappan civilization, which emerged five thousand years ago in the Indus River Valley. One can speculate whether the trade that developed in the third millennium BCE between the Sumerian civilization in the Fertile Crescent and the Indus Valley was or was not a continuation of a much earlier link. As we will see, the Indus and Euphrates-Tigris Valley trade was the beginning of a phenomenon that would eventually connect the whole world. The final marker in my Y chromosome—M52—was acquired when my ancestors reached western India. It seems that my ancestors liked what they found in India because, except for a small number of this marker showing up among coastal Southeast Asian populations, there is not much evidence of further movement by the progenies of the M52 marker. In the past twenty to thirty thousand years, M52 spread all over India, making it almost a national marker. A vast majority of people in India, especially in the south and east, carry this "India marker."[30] A second group of out-of-Africa time-walkers who joined India's gene pool reached India after a detour through Central Asia. They carried a different Eurasian marker—M20—that might offer a partial explanation for the striking physical variety between the populations of northern and southern India.

THE YELLOW EMPEROR'S BLACK MAMA

How did one group of migrants end up in Central Asia instead of sticking with the group that headed east? As geneticist Spencer Wells explains, the early human migration was not a conscious effort to move from one place to another. As they walked on the continuous belt of the Eurasian Steppe, they might simply have been following game further and further afield. Some forty thousand years ago, a new marker, M9, appeared on the Levant lineage—perhaps on the plains of Iran or South-Central Asia. The progenies of this marker, whom Wells calls the Eurasian clan, would expand their range to the ends of the earth in the next thirty thousand years. They soon encountered the biggest mountain ranges anyone had ever seen. As the bitter cold of the last Ice Age gripped the world, the Hindu Kush, Himalaya, and Tien Shan ranges would have proved a formidable barrier to the M9 clan. At this point somewhere in today's Tajikistan the migrants split, with one group heading south and the other north. The southern group, carrying a different marker, M20, ended up in India, forming a uniquely Indian genetic substratum. Their northern cousins, carrying the M45 marker, survived their journey through the Siberian freezer by hunting woolly mammoths and overwhelmingly populated Central Asia. "The Eurasian interior," Wells writes, "was a fairly brutal school for our ancestors. . . . During their sojourn on the steppes, modern humans developed highly specialized toolkits, including bone needles that allowed them to sew together animal skins into clothing that provided warmth at temperatures not unlike those on the moon, but still allowed the mobility necessary to hunt game such as reindeer and mammoth successfully."[31]

It would be the members of the M45 clan, hardened by their wintry ordeal, who would reach Siberia and be ready to walk across the Beringia snow to Alaska. But before reaching Siberia, some of the Eurasian–Central Asian members produced another line, M175, which headed into western China from southern Siberia. Around thirty-five thousand years ago the descendants of M175 and subsidiary markers largely populated Korea and northern China.

With the exception of such minorities as Uighur, Kazak, Kirghiz, and Hui Salar, who originated from Arab, Iranian, and Central Asian stock, a vast proportion of minorities in China carry the M175 or a derivative marker.[32] They now account for 60 to 90 percent of East Asian chromosomes. But before the Eurasian group showed up in China, the descendants of the original Australian express who got off the train, so to speak, in island Southeast Asia were making their moves.

For the story about how the Southeast Asian and other genetic groups came to coalesce in China, we turn to geneticist Li Jin and his students. They wanted to resolve once and for all the controversy about the origin of the Chinese population. Did they really evolve locally from the prehistoric Peking man? Chinese believe they are the descendants of the legendary Yellow Emperor, who unified the tribes of China in the third millennium. Jin and his students fanned out and collected DNA samples from ten thousand males. In all those Y chromosomes, not a single unusual one was found. "We looked," Jin later said. "It's just not there. Modern humans originated in Africa."[33] It seems that had the Yellow Emperor existed, he, too, had an African mother eons ago. Jin's data from the 163 populations across Southeast Asia, Oceania, East Asia, Siberia, and Central Asia also established the same case. Every individual carried the original Grandpa marker, M168, and the Australian express M130 marker.[34]

In 2000 Jin also offered conclusive evidence of the Southeast Asian provenance of the Chinese population. He surmised that the first entry of modern humans into the southern part of East Asia occurred about eighteen thousand to sixty thousand years ago. Both Y chromosome and mtDNA analysis of Southeast Asian samples revealed that the same seven main genetic groupings—called haplotypes—present in Southeast Asian descendants of the M130 lineage are also found in China. Peering at the genetic markers of today's Chinese population, geneticists can see that "the ancient evidence of a two-pronged settlement is still visible in the blood of today's Chinese."[35] Because the southern population had been there longer, the level of genetic variation is greater than among the people in the north. Anthropologists suspect that the genetic mixing that followed might account for the physical differences between northerners and southerners today. The northern Chinese tend to be paler and taller with smaller eyes and a more pronounced epicanthic fold. The southern Chinese are darker and broader, resembling more the peoples of Southeast Asia.[36]

Besides moving north to China and Siberia, Jin and colleagues found, the population moved in two other directions. One group seems to have island-hopped and reached the Pacific Islands, including Polynesia and Micronesia, and the other moved toward Taiwan.[37] These descendants of the same Grandpa chromosome would live in the splendid isolation of Australia and the Pacific for thousands of years before the arrival of Captain James Cook's tall sailing-ship. The sketches of the aborigines made by the visitors make them look as if they are from another world.

China and Southeast Asia turned out to be the holding area and later launching pad for migration to Japan. Sometime between twenty thousand and twelve thousand years ago, when a low sea level linked Japan to the Asian mainland, hunter-gatherers from Central Asia moved into northern Japan. An estimated three thousand people from the area between Tibet and the Altai Mountains in northwestern China walked to Japan and developed what came to be known as the Jomon culture. Rising sea levels cut Japan off from the Asian mainland for nearly ten thousand years, during which people in Southeast Asia and South China's river valleys developed agriculture. Rice farming spread to the Korean peninsula and the cold-resistant rice strain was developed. Some twenty-three hundred years ago people carrying the same genetic markers as Southeast Asians and Koreans sailed to the southern Japanese islands.[38] The farmer immigrants introduced wet rice culture, which spread throughout Japan and emerged as a marker of Japanese identity. In the twentieth century Japan would resist opening its rice market, claiming that Japanese-grown rice was unique!

After East Africa and the Levant, the Central Asian mountains and steppes were a major churning point for the human genome. Some thirty thousand years ago the Central Asian marker M45 led to the rise of another lineage, M173, who changed the northeastern direction of the journey so far and began moving westward across the steppes toward Europe. These migrants would form the bulk of present-day Europeans. Based on fossil evidence as well as on cave paintings in France, we know that reindeer of the cold tundra were then common in the steppes that extended to Germany and perhaps even France. The Eurasians who had by then been schooled in the coldest of Central Asian winters moved into Europe and in the course of a few thousand years populated a vast area. The Neanderthals—the archaic human form that shared mitochondrial genomes of modern humans and inhabited Europe and western Asia—ceded ground to modern humans.

Until very recently there has been no evidence that the Eurasian arrivals in-

terbred with the Neanderthals, nor is there evidence of a Neanderthal genocide.[39] It was believed that in the process of natural selection, modern humans
with the advantages of language, toolkits, intelligence, and social hunting skills
won.[40] There are also indications that over many areas of Europe the demise of
the Neanderthal populations may have coincided with the sudden onset of
much colder and drier climatic conditions. If, as current evidence suggests, the
new anatomically modern human populations were better equipped techno-
logically and culturally to deal with these severe glacial conditions, then, notes
researcher Paul Mellars, this could have delivered the coup de grace to the Neanderthals.[41] By about twenty-five thousand years ago the Neanderthals had
vanished, leaving our ancestors alone to roam the world. And as M52 did for Indians, M45 for Central Asians, and M175 for East Asians, so did the M173 lineage emerge as the terminal marker defining Europeans.

COMING TO AMERICA

The journey of people carrying the Central Asian marker was not finished.
Their progenies who had reached Siberia in pursuit of reindeer and woolly
mammoths would quietly slip into the last continent completely devoid of people, even of hominids. Although it is generally agreed that the first settlers to
North America came from Siberia, when they first arrived remains hotly debated. Ever since an eleven-thousand-year-old fluted stone blade lodged in a
mammoth bone was discovered in Clovis, New Mexico, in 1932, anthropologists have argued whether the Clovis people were the first to arrive from Asia.
That claim was shattered when even more ancient relics of human habitation
were found in the Meadowcroft Rock shelter in Pennsylvania and at Mon-
teverde in Chile. Exhaustive analysis of Native American DNA reveals that over
90 percent of Indians carry the Y chromosome of a man who has been dubbed
the Native American Adam.[42] He lived roughly 22,500 years ago and sprang
from the lineage that had lived in Siberia and Central Asia's Altai Mountain
range area. Only after the Ice Age began to recede some fifteen thousand
years ago was it possible for even the hardened veterans of Siberia to enter the
North American plains. Paleoclimatologists believe that an ice-free corridor
opened up east of the Rocky Mountains where the Canadian plains abut the
foothills.[43]

   From mtDNA analysis it seems that the number of maternal lineages was
small among the big-game hunters and settlers who trudged their way through
the Alaskan snow to the corridor. The women were all closely related.[44] But

once the group reached the Great Plains, the land and all the animals were theirs for the taking. Not only did the population explode, but successive waves of settlers made it to the American continent and soon spread out in all directions. About fourteen thousand years ago, the human journey begun so long ago in Ethiopia completed the conquest of the earth when Native Americans reached the southern tip of Chile. Like Pacific islanders, Native Americans would live in total isolation until Europeans sailed to their shores. Their long isolation from the gene flow in the Old World, as we will see, deprived them of immunity to many common diseases and brought calamity after their first encounter with the Europeans. Yet curiously, some typical genetic markers—termed haplogroup X—had reached America long before Columbus. Geneticists have been surprised to discover that Italian and Finnish populations share genetic links with some Native Americans. There is enough mutation on the marker to make it at least ten thousand years old and therefore not brought by Europeans who arrived after Columbus. How did this European marker reach the Americas? Given the walls of glaciers and ice sheets that covered the northern Atlantic, it would have been impossible for people to reach America by a northern route. That mystery remains to be solved by future geneticists.[45]

The ancient connections like the land bridge between Siberia and Alaska, between Japan and China, between continental Europe and Britain, and between Indonesian archipelago and mainland Southeast Asia all began drowning with the end of the Ice Age and rising oceans. Since the end of the Ice Age, the sea has generally risen about four hundred feet; and land so long covered under ice sheets has risen up to one hundred feet. The diversification of humanity that began as a centrifugal movement out of Africa fifty thousand years earlier peaked with the physical separation of much of the landmass they had covered. As historian David Christian put it, "With humans now settled throughout the world, this severing of ancient links threatened to divide humans into separate populations with separate histories."[46] What emerged instead were four world zones: Afro-Eurasian, Australia–New Guinea, American, and Pacific world zones. The interconnection among humans living in each zone—in their known universes—would grow and intensify, creating mini-globalizations until the age of Columbus would break the ocean barrier. The American continent, which had disappeared from the sight of the Old World, would reappear in 1492 with the exultant cry of "Tierra, tierra!" when in the pale moonlight the night watch on Columbus's *Santa Maria* spotted the contours of San Salvador.

One of the amazing things about this global journey is that it was undertaken almost entirely on foot, with occasional use of rafts or dugouts over waters. The horse was not domesticated until six thousand years ago and the camel only three thousand years ago, long after the exodus from Africa or the ancestors' arrival on South America's southern tip.[47] A tiny population of men and women walked to find a better life. Their children, grandchildren, and two thousand subsequent generations kept moving until they found a place to settle. While some continued a nomadic life—as do some thirty to forty million pastoralists all over the world even today—others settled down to a sedentary life of agriculture, fishing, and hunting. The forty or fifty thousand years that our human ancestors spent walking the length of the earth, experiencing the unimaginably harsh weather of the late Ice Age, have carved our bodies, altered our faces, and changed our pigmentation. The effect of the first globalization— the dispersal of humans around the globe—has been the emergence of a superficially diverse human species.

CHANGING COLOR

Two thousand generations after leaving the African savanna, the descendants who came to occupy different parts of the earth looked remarkably different from one another and spoke mutually incomprehensible languages. But nothing perhaps divides us humans more than the most superficial of changes that occurred in our body during those fifty millennia of journey—in morphological traits like skin color. It has become an important element in creating the category called "race." Although genetically all humans are 99.9 percent alike, that minute difference in our DNA that accounts for the visible difference of skin color throws a spoke in the wheel of the globalization wrought by the human species. However insignificant those differences may be in a string of three billion nucleotides, they nevertheless often correspond to a geographic area. Francis Collins, codiscoverer of DNA, says that genetic variations can be used to make a reasonably accurate prediction of geographic origins of an individual, at least if the individuals all came from the same part of the world.[48]

As the geneticist Luca Cavalli-Sforza put it, the diaspora of Africans to the rest of the world exposed them to a great variety of environments: from hot and humid or hot and dry surroundings, to which they were already accustomed, to temperate and chilly ones, including the coldest ones of the world, as in Siberia. "One can say that each ethnic group has been genetically engineered under the influence of the environments where it settled," Cavalli-Sforza wrote.[49]

The ancestors who walked out of Africa presumably were mostly dark-skinned and tall like present-day Ethiopians. The color of African skin is produced by melanin, the pigment produced by skin cells to prevent damage from the ultraviolet (UV) rays of the sun, particularly strong nearer to the equator. Because melanin acts as an effective sunscreen, it protects dark-skinned individuals from sunburn and skin cancer.[50] The sun's radiation destroys an essential nutrient, folic acid, connected with fertility, thus producing a lesser number of progenies and shaping evolution. But the human body's need for sunlight to synthesize vitamin D, an essential ingredient for calcium intake and strong bones, exerted a different pressure on humans as they moved to the northern hemisphere. There, under a weaker sun and with fewer sunny days, the natural selection process favored those with lighter skins. The people who lacked melanin could absorb more sunlight to make vitamin D. Indeed, mothers' greater need for vitamin D is believed to explain why in every population women's skin color is 3 to 4 percent lighter than men's.[51] The same process accounts for the lighter skin of the San people who moved to South Africa—a latitude where UV rays are of the same level as those of the Mediterranean. How does one explain the relatively dark skin of the Inuit, who live in the Arctic under layers of heavy clothing and with little sun? The answer appears to be that they have solved the problem of vitamin D deficiency with a mostly fish diet that is rich in vitamin D.[52]

CLIMATE'S SHAPING HAND

Body shapes also adjusted to the environment. Keeping the body cool through sweating in a hot climate and preserving heat in a cold climate became two key functions that determined body shape. In hot and humid climates like tropical forests, shorter people fared better because their bodies had a greater surface area for the evaporation of sweat compared to their bodies' volume and because they carried less body weight and produced less heat while hunting for game. The frizzy hair of the pygmies, for instance, also allows sweat to remain on the scalp longer and results in greater cooling. The tall and slender shape of the East African population also served the same purpose, since their maximum surface-area-to-volume-ratio better enabled them to cool off under a tropical sun.[53] Their relatively small head and slim shoulders also caught less of the sun's rays beating down at noon—the best time to hunt for animals that were resting in the shade.

The bitter cold of the last Ice Age that humans faced in Central Asia also left its mark. The flat face, short nose, and hooded eyes of the "Mongoloid" trait are believed to have been the result of our ancestors' Central Asian and Siberian passage. Cavalli-Sforza points out that the Mongoloid body, and particularly the head, tends to be round, increasing body volume. The reduced evaporative surface area of the skin in relation to body volume means that less heat is lost. The small nose has less likelihood of freezing, with narrow nostrils warming the air before it reaches the lungs. Fatty folds of skin protect the eyes from the cold Siberian air while acting as a visor against glare from snow. As we have seen, the group with M175 marker who survived the journey through the Central Asian freezer began moving to China and Korea some thirty-five thousand years ago. Of course, as Darwin speculated, other factors, such as particular tastes of individuals in "sex selection," could have been at play. Cavalli-Sforza suggests that it is very likely that some characteristics, such as eye color and shape, undergo sexual selection. The prevalence of the almond eye shape in East Asia may also be due to Darwinian selection. Some group is likely to have come to view this shape as attractive, leading to its proliferation.[54] Eyes with an epicanthic fold, notes Cavalli-Sforza, are also characteristic of the Bushmen of southern Africa and other African population groups. Similarly, the shape of the eye was probably diffused by sexual selection from northeastern Asia to warm and moist Southeast Asia. While wondering about the physical differences that arose among humans, it is useful to remember Cavalli-Sforza's words of caution: "We must also bear in mind that the genes that react to climate are those that influence *external features*. Adaptation of the body for the most part requires changes, because this is our interface with the outside world. *It is because they are external that these racial differences strike us so forcibly, and we automatically assume that differences of similar magnitude exist below the surface, in the rest of our genetic makeup. This is simply not so: the remainder of our genetic makeup hardly differs at all.*"[55]

Although the global journey has produced morphological changes among humans, the descendants from Africa have carried hidden in their cells mutations that would cause disease hundreds, even thousands of years later. Paul Plotz, a researcher who studies rare muscle diseases at the National Institutes of Health in Bethesda, Maryland, was intrigued to find a rare form of disease among unrelated African-Americans whose genome nonetheless showed a similar mutation. He teamed up with a historian to pursue the source of the mutation and concluded that it occurred some one thousand years ago among the Hausa tribe in Nigeria. Through a trading connection with the Ashanti people in present-day Ghana—which obviously involved genetic exchange—the mutation was passed to the Ashanti. All the American patients with the mutation had Ashanti ancestors who had been brought to the United States as slaves. Reports of the same disease mutation found in a Pakistani man also brought tantalizing evidence of Africa's slave-trade connection with South Asia.[56]

By ten thousand years ago the human race had reached virtually every continent except Antarctica and was poised for the beginning of a new era heralding a process that would eventually set human communities on the path of reconnection. Soon after 20,000 BCE global warming began, and after many ups and downs and a brief return to extreme cold and drought, the end of the Ice Age truly began by 10,000 BCE. As if on cue, everywhere on the planet the melting of the ice sheets was followed by the rise of agriculture and the emergence of settled communities of farmers that supported specialist craftworkers, priests, and chiefs. Those who remained hunter-gatherers mostly took to the pastoral life, emerging as the ambulatory connector between settled communities. With surplus agriculture arose towns, new crafts, and the production of commodities. Informal exchanges of earlier times developed into trade networks. The warfare that had been a constant feature of the hunter-gatherer life became more organized with the rise of states. Empire building soon followed. Essentially, the basic motivations that propelled humans to connect with others—the urge to profit by trading, the drive to spread religious belief, the desire to explore new lands, and the ambition to dominate others by armed might—all had been assembled by 6000 BCE to start the process we now call globalization.

ROOTS OF A FIG TREE

Climate change wrought a greening of the landscape, with trees sprouting on the Sahara and forest advancing on the cold steppes. Growing moisture and the creation of lakes and rivers allowed for the rise of larger population settlements along the banks and in turn the need to grow more food from the same area.[57] In a critical switch in the human mind, as Harvard archaeologist Ofer Bar-Yosef said, "people decided to intervene in nature and supply their own food rather than relying on what was provided by the gods."[58] From the banks of the Euphrates to the Yangtze Valley, agrarian communities sprouted. One reason that the hunters' nomadic life became less viable was that humans no longer had the options that beachcombers once had during their millennial journey east. They had moved on to the next beach when the food supply in an area dwindled. But twelve thousand years later, simply moving on may not have been an option, for it would have brought migrants into conflict with other people living in the area. Learning how to adapt seeds of wild grass to grow as crops and domesticating animals and fishing may have seemed an easier option. Although there is some evidence of the transfer of seeds of domesticated plants across distances, agriculture arose simultaneously in several parts of the world. It was in the Fertile Crescent region on the eastern shores of the Mediterranean that the earliest human settlers learned to exploit wild plants and animals. Wheat, barley, rye, chickpeas, lentils, sheep, goats, and pigs were all first grown or domesticated in this area before being diffused through the connected parts of the Old World. Wheat, first domesticated in what is now Turkey, spread to the Indus Valley and into China between six thousand and four thousand years ago.[59] China's Yangtze River basin saw the domestication of rice some 11,500 years ago, from where it spread southward.[60] Waves of agricultural migrants creating rice fields would ripple down Southeast Asia's river valleys all the way to Indonesia. The genetic trace of that ancient journey can still be found among today's population.

The rise of agrarian communities provided a rooted identity for the first time to groups of humans who floated across the land in search of edible roots, fruits, and nuts and game to hunt. Recent archaeological evidence shows that humans began putting down their roots literally by planting a garden—of fig trees. The discovery that the fig was the earliest plant to be domesticated by humans offers a tantalizing clue to the beginning of what can be called territorial loyalty and identity linked to the land. Excavating an ancient site in the Lower Jordan Valley north of Jericho, archaeologists came across burned figs. Analysis revealed that these nearly twelve-thousand-year-old figs were the earliest examples of a domesticated food-bearing plant.

A genetic mutation seems to have created a variety of fig that produced infertile fruit but could be easily domesticated because the cuttings developed roots more easily than those of any other fruit tree. Researchers reported that the figs were found stored with other vegetal staples such as wild barley, wild oat, and acorns, which indicates that the subsistence strategy of these early Neolithic farmers was a mixed exploitation of wild plants and initial fig domestication.[61] Since fig trees and later plants like olives and dates could take years before producing fruit, planting orchards could be seen as the first flag posts of identity for a people who had chosen a sedentary life.[62] Wheat and barley fields would follow. Until other discoveries push back the date of the domestication of crops, the planting of these domesticated figs can be considered the beginning of the agrarian phase of human evolution. Agriculture required humans to put down roots and finally halted the ceaseless dispersion across the globe. The olive, a plant that has become the icon for rootedness and identity in the Middle East, was not domesticated until five thousand years later.[63]

Initially, people tended and adopted species like the fig that grew where they had settled. Over time a range of other plants, and then animals, were integrated into their life. By 10,000 BCE sedentary cultures centered on crop growing and animal husbandry had taken shape across the broad arc of the Fertile Crescent. As in the Near East, Indus Valley, or Yangtze basin, the rise of human settlements identified with a specific geographic location was the first step in the rise of civilization, states, and empires. The earliest known people to practice sedentary agriculture in the Jordan Valley have been called the Natufians. In the millennia that followed, others emerged to occupy different parts of the Fertile Crescent: Sumerians, Akkadians, Assyrians, Hittites, Scythians, Canaanites, Philistines, Phoenicians, Hebrews, and many others.[64] Occupation of a particular territory came to be associated with a people for the occupation of which incessant wars were fought. How strongly possession of and association with land became part of one's identity and honor was summed up in the ultimatum that marked the beginning of catastrophic war in the Indian epic the *Mahabharata* of about 500 BCE: "We'll not cede land worth the point of a needle without war." Communities rose and transformed into principalities and kingdoms; they connected with other communities for the exchange of goods or by launching military attacks and occupying others' land. That process continued until the emergence of modern political structures.

NEW MIGRATION

Agriculture brought in its train four prime movers of growing interconnection: migration, trade, religion, and the conquering power of state. With an assured food supply from planted crops, populations grew, setting the stage for migration of people to other areas along with their tools and seeds. The urge to migrate in the postagrarian period was different from the earliest out-of-Africa exodus. It was not a journey in search of means of survival as it had been in the initial period. As one anthropologist explains, later migration was "a behavior [that was] typically performed by defined subgroups (often kin-recruited) with specific goals, targeted on known destinations and likely to use familiar routes."[65] It was a purposeful journey to find new land where a people could settle down with their old tools and planting skills. These early migrants looking for cultivable land also encountered other clusters of settled communities.

Apart from the economic "push" of negative stresses at home and the "pull" of the attraction of the new destination, a cultural-ideological factor may have prompted migration. The anthropologist David Anthony notes, "Among societies in which male statuses and roles were largely determined by success in war, and in which young males therefore actively sought opportunities for conflict, the cumulative effects of sustained glory-seeking raiding might lead to significant outward migration."[66] Whether through peaceful assimilation or violent occupation, the oecumene, or known world, expanded as did people's connections. Migrations moved like a stream finding its way and avoiding obstacles to reach the destination. The trail that was blazed eventually became a well-trodden path for more migration and trade. As we will see, these adventuring pioneers and migrants—grouped as adventurers in this book—emerged as a key actor of globalization. Short-distance migration that might have begun as a recurring response to localized resource shortages was soon to become a phenomenon spanning vast distances.

Although the cause of many waves of migrations remains in dispute, their impact has clearly been to create a web of relationships. For example, many linguists believe that the spread of the agricultural way of life from Anatolia played a key role in the diffusion of what is called Proto-Indo-European language over vast areas of Europe and Central and South Asia. According to one of the more widely accepted hypotheses, supported since by genetic and linguistic forensic analysis, early farmers searching for more land migrated from Turkey and Asia Minor to southeastern Europe in about 7000 BCE and spread the proto-Indo-European language that gave birth to eighty-seven languages—including Sanskrit, Greek, Latin, and Persian and eventually to such modern languages as English, French, Russian, and German.[67] Beside this "plow school" of explanation for the spread of Indo-European languages, another school offers the power of the sword as the explanation. This theory argues that Indo-European languages were spread by the ax-wielding horsemen invaders from the so-called Kurgan culture of present-day Ukraine.[68] According to this theory, a seminomadic group from the lower Volga region who had domesticated the horse migrated across the vast stretch of steppes from Europe to Central Asia and southward into present-day Turkey and Greece at a time when the warming climate favored their pastoralist economy. In the process, they or associated groups gained political control and ended up spreading their Indo-European languages and culture.[69]

The debate over what caused the spread of language continues, but there is no doubt that the domestication of the horse in 4000 BCE by the people living in the lower Volga-Dnieper region was a seminal development in connecting dispersed communities. Yet it was not until two millennia later that the horse made an appearance as a draft animal attached to wheeled carts. Late in history the horse would be the engine of Mongol imperial expansion and indeed the means of transportation well into the modern period. Horse-drawn streetcars served New York City until the late nineteenth century. David Anthony and colleagues' sleuthing of the bit mark on horse teeth fossils provided the evidence of the horse's early domestication. But as the researchers note in *Scientific American,* its immediate impact was remarkable:

> The acquisition of horses wrought a revolution in virtually every aspect of life of the Plains tribes. Riders could move two to three times farther and faster during a day than people on foot. Resources, enemies, allies and markets that had previously been beyond effective reach suddenly became attainable. Subsistence and economic survival in the dry grasslands, an uncertain and risky proposition for pedestrian hunters, became predictable and productive. Sedentary horticultural villagers whose river valley settlements had been the centers of population and economic productivity became vulnerable to lightning raids by mounted enemies who could not be pursued or punished.[70]

The horse helped migrant traders and soldiers establish connections with distant agrarian settlements that had been inconceivable earlier. As we will see, thanks to the horse, the vast steppes that spanned Eurasia were turned into an immense conveyer belt for the transmission of people, goods, and ideas.

THE TRADING CONNECTION

Agrarian communities also gave birth to the second actor of globalization: the trader. Foraging communities had already accomplished exchanges of produce, ritual exchanges over marriage, and other gift-giving traditions. The spread of agriculture gave the practice of exchange an important momentum because now people in one location regularly grew food crops or plants that they could sell or exchange with people who did not have them. How agriculture stimulated early trading can be seen in the archaeological finds in one of the world's earliest urban settlements, Çatal Höyük (7400–6000 BCE), in present-day Turkey. Located near two active volcanoes, Çatal Höyük operated a virtual monopoly on the trade in obsidian in the eastern Mediterranean and Levant.[71] Obsidian, a sharp-edged volcanic rock that could be used as a scythe, was an essential tool for harvesting crops. Many generations earlier, the beachcomber settlements on the Red Sea had used obsidian to pry open oysters. Food surpluses in other parts of Europe later led to the rise of specialized crafts like the mining of flint and turning it into ax-heads and other tools.[72] In exchange, settlements received many shells from the Red Sea and the Mediterranean, along with stones or materials of all kinds that craftsmen turned into tools and ceremonial objects or wove into fabrics.[73] The trading of agricultural goods among peoples on the heavily traveled routes linking Africa to the Mediterranean may have led to the rise of ancient towns like Jericho. River craft made of reed and animal hide sailed on the Euphrates and the Nile, and the cloth sail made its appearance by the fourth millennium BCE. In the fourth and third millennia, the Mesopotamian civilization emerged in the lower Tigris and Euphrates River Valley based on trade with neighboring areas of Syria and Anatolia that procured such items as metals, good timber, stone, and other exotic items. With time, the trade network expanded to the Persian Gulf and western India.[74] Mesopotamian barley fed the Gulf Arab population, who supplied copper for making weapons and tools. Exchanges of luxuries and gifts also became an important way of connecting with other communities and developing alliances among chiefs.[75] In search of frankincense, myrrh, ebony, and other exotic products, Egyptian pharaohs began to send trading expeditions to Punt, probably today's Eritrea (from where their ancestors had once walked out of Africa). To barter with the chiefs they took strings of beads, axes, daggers, bracelets, and wine and beer. The expeditions also brought back skins of giraffe and leopard and perhaps the first African slaves, pygmies who were made to dance for royalty. That first recorded encounter in the mid-third millennium between humans who had left Africa and those who stayed behind seems to have set the tone for what would happen to Africa in the millennia of broadening contacts that would follow. Ironically, many centuries later Arabs and Europeans brought almost identical products to buy slaves from Africa.[76]

The expeditions to Punt, conducted aboard large ships with sails and by donkey caravans, were already a huge advance in trading. As economies developed, the role of merchants and long-distance trade widened. Like drops of ink on wet paper, the trade-linked areas from Mesopotamia and Egypt kept spreading. As we will see in later chapters, the trade network by donkey caravans that debuted in Çatal Höyük and reached out from Mesopotamia to the Indus Valley and sub-Saharan Africa kept expanding. By the first century CE new blots of ink flowing from China and India and Southeast Asia had begun to overlap and merge with others, in the process diffusing ideas and culture. Trade would transform societies when a trading class would rise to challenge state power. With the expansion of long-distance exchanges, trading diasporas would emerge to connect communities even more closely.[77] Driven by traders—people who earned a living by exchange of goods and services or, in the modern parlance, businesspeople—the commercial network would continually expand, thicken, and accelerate to eventually encompass the globe in an ever-tightening web.

THE IMPERIAL DRIVE

The rise of agrarian society also led to the emergence of states, some of whose imperial ambitions proved to be the third key driver in connecting states within the Afro-Eurasian world zone and eventually with the other three zones. What began as isolated agrarian communities around towns like Çatal Höyük expanded over larger areas in the Fertile Crescent and Egypt as well as to the new grasslands of Sudan. In India's Indus Valley and Ganges plains and in China's Yellow River basin, agrarian communities grew and started coalescing. Whether forced by a strong leader or out of the necessity of managing an increasingly complex society, rudimentary state power came into existence.[78] About five thousand years ago, small city-states appeared in the Euphrates Valley and later in the Nile Valley. Nourished by agriculture in the Indus plains, urban civilization took shape in Mohenjo-Daro and Harappa. The territory of Mesopotamia between the Euphrates and Tigris rivers witnessed the rise of the first state when a desert tribe from today's Syria led by Sargon established the empire of Akkad (2340–230 BC). Sargon's conquests spanned the Mediterranean to the Persian Gulf—covering virtually all of the settled communities in the Levant except Egypt—making Akkad the world's first empire that sought to forge nations different in race, religion, and culture into a political weapon under one man's control.[79] Another key motive for imperial intervention was the control of resources. For instance, Sargon went to war to secure timber, a daily necessity lacking in Mesopotamia and Egypt.[80] His was the first state with a standing army, an administrative service, and organized trade. Perhaps in the first example of imperial pride at promoting trade, Sargon boasted that he brought the boats of Dilmun [modern-day Bahrain], Magan [in the Persian Gulf], and Meluhha [Harappa] to dock at the newly founded imperial center at Agade [probably at the confluence of the Tigris and Euphrates rivers].[81] Sargon defeated rival city-states, and instead of following the common policy of exacting ransom from the defeated population, he incorporated them into his empire. Indeed, as the historian Jean-Jacques Glassner writes, Akkadian imperialism exhibited new attitudes toward war, where warfare outside the zone of direct political control became an instituted economic activity driven by a search for booty and tribute in the form of corvée labor and military service.[82]

This approach to expanding a territorial and population base would be pursued by ambitious rulers through history, thus linking ever-wider areas of separate populations. The need to gather intelligence about potential threats and alliance building seen in Sargon's time also called for diplomacy. One of the earliest examples of a long-distance diplomatic mission was in 130 BCE, when an envoy of China's Han emperor traveled to the periphery of Persia in search of allies against nomadic tribes that periodically threatened China.[83]

By the beginning of second millennium BCE, the first "modern" state with its written legal code emerged in Babylon. The 282 laws of the Hammurabi Code on various personal and public aspects of life, including currency and trade, created a framework that would later inspire Roman law and its extension to diverse other populations of the empire.[84] The state's growing involvement in trade that would later become the norm was visible in one law: "If the merchant give, to an agent corn, wool, oil, or any sort of goods with which to trade, the agent shall write down the value and return (the money) to the merchant; the agent shall take a sealed receipt for the money which he shall give to the merchant."[85] Organizing and managing trade emerged as key functions of the emergent states in peacetime. The result was the creation of a web of long-distance exchanges encompassing the Eurasian zone with far-reaching impact on societies and cultures.

With the rise of more efficient means of transportation, especially horse and chariot warfare, and growth of a solid economic base, the size of the empires and their armies expanded. Political scientist Rein Taagepera has calculated that the area controlled by empires grew from 0.6 megameter (1 megameter = 100,000 km^2) under Sargon of Akkad to 3 megameters under the Mauryas in India, 4 megameters under the Roman Empire, 6 megameters under China's Han dynasty, and reached the maximum extent of a land empire under the Mongols with 25 megameters.[86] Humanity's growing mastery of the ocean and the age of exploration in the sixteenth century allowed for the first time in history the creation of the empires over which the sun never set. Economic exploitation, political control, and massive migration resulting from European empires created a dynamic of world integration that has rolled on despite periodic interruptions. As we will see, the imperial drive—embodied by the warriors for the purpose of this book—has played a major role in shaping today's interconnected world.

PREACHING THE FAITH

Religion as a set of symbolic forms and acts that give meaning to human existence has been a part of human life since the beginning. In the early millennia of the rise of agriculture, the cult of the Mother Goddess, the source of all fertility, emerged independently in agrarian societies. She was called Inana in Sumer, Ishtar in Babylon, Anat in Canaan, Isis in Egypt, and Aphrodite in Greece. We don't know what she was called in India, but terra-cotta figurines of the Mother Goddess have been found in the Indus Valley. As the agrarian civilization flourished and the power of the state grew, the state was increasingly associated with divinity. The success of the state was attributed to the blessings of the gods. The ruler was part of the divinity, and the god's imagined abode inspired the creation of temple towers such as Babylon's ziggurats. With the growing complexity of life, many more gods were imagined, and mythologies blossomed. Yet in early agrarian societies, religions tended to be local, and gods were invoked to protect local tribes or cities. The emergence of empires and expansion of trading networks brought within their folds different faiths and deities, enabling the concept of universal religion. Indeed, as David Christian notes, most of the universal religions appeared in the hub region between Mesopotamia and northern India. By the first millennium BCE, people's material progress seems also to have generated "an extremely negative evaluation of man and society and the exaltation of another realm of reality as alone true and infinitely valuable."[87] For Gautam Buddha, in sixth-century BCE India, life even in the palace meant endless cycles of suffering that could be ended only by the pursuit of a virtuous path. Buddhism, like Christianity and Islam that were to follow in half-millennium intervals, was a missionary faith. After Gautam attained the enlightenment to become the Buddha, he decided not to be content in his own bliss but to go forth and explain his way to the world. For the next forty-five years of his life he traveled all over the land preaching. That mission to spread the faith to the far corners of the world was later taken up by devout kings and monks. The commission that Jesus gave his disciples was not very different: "Go therefore and make disciples of all nations, baptizing them in the name of the Father and of the Son and of the Holy Spirit, and teaching them to obey everything that I have commanded you" (Matt. 28:19). The monotheistic Islamic faith that arose in seventh-century Arabia in response to the hedonism and corruption brought by trade was driven by messianic zeal in converting the nonbelievers. As we will see, in the centuries to come the prose-lytizing spirit of these universalist religions would emerge as the fourth prime mover in connecting the separate populations across the world, binding them more closely and shaping their lives. The spirit of the universality of the human condition that lies behind missionary activities would later be taken up by secular groups. Environmental and human rights advocates bring to their work convictions about helping humanity as a whole, tying our world even more firmly together.

This rather schematic account of the human journey from Africa to the world does not pretend to be even a summary of the vast movement. It is an attempt to grasp the main trends and identify the forces that propelled the growing interconnectedness of our world. The rest of the book will explore in detail, though with selective examples, how the human search for security and for a better and more fulfilling life has led men and women to migrate, engage in trade, journey to faraway places, and try to convert fellow human beings to their faith; how ambitions of greatness have inspired generations of rulers to invade distant lands and bring larger populations under one umbrella of an empire. I believe that the same basic motivations drive today's globalization. I have compared trade linkages to ink flowing on wet paper. They can also be seen as a series of ripples sent by rocks hurled on placid water, multiple connections spreading out from different human settlements reaching and merging with other ripples until the radiating lines form a huge worldwide pattern of connections. Over time, ripples have turned into waves. In a new out-of-Africa move, no doubt feeling the desperation of our ancestors from long ago, people board boats to cross the Atlantic and the Mediterranean, and tens of millions of migrants from other continents continue to flow to where they see hope for a better life. Adventurers of the past have been replaced by a new class of tourists. Caravan traders of the past have been succeeded by multinational companies transporting their goods on container ships. Another new actor pushing globalization today is the consumer, whose demand for cheaper and better goods and services is fueling the fire of global commerce. The likes of Amnesty International and Human Rights Watch have enlarged the scope of traditional preachers in reaching out to distant lands with their message of common good. Imperial ambitions of the past have been replaced by political ambition to spread democracy and human rights. Multinational forces are spread throughout the world, attempting to subjugate the "enemies of democracy" or maintain peace between warring nations. The result of all this has been to intertwine peoples' lives across the globe ever more intimately. The process of reconnecting the dispersed human community that started more than ten thousand years ago is stronger than ever, and thanks to technology it is continuously accelerating, binding us ever more tightly.

Chapter 2 From Camel Commerce to E-Commerce

Our Celestial Empire possesses all things in prolific abundance and lacks no product within its own borders. There was therefore no need to import the manufactures of outside barbarians in exchange for our own produce. But as the tea, silk and porcelain which the Celestial Empire produces, are absolute necessities to European nations and to yourselves, we have permitted, as a signal mark of favour, that foreign hongs [merchant firms] should be established at Canton, so that your wants might be supplied and your country thus participate in our beneficence.
—*Emperor Qian Long's letter to King George III, 1793*

In the spring of 2004, I was looking for an appropriate college graduation present for my son Ateesh and decided on an Apple iPod music player. I knew exactly what I wanted, so there was no need to drive to a shopping mall. Instead, I went directly to Apple Computer's Web site and placed my online order for the slick-looking player that would literally put thousands of songs in my son's palm. The site even allowed me to order his name engraved on the shiny metallic back.

Marco Polo lands at Ormuz, on the Persian Gulf. Illustration from Marco Polo, *Le Livre des merveilles du monde*, 1298; manuscript copy from 1410. Bibliothèque nationale de France

I chose the free delivery option. Since Apple Computer is based in California, I calculated that the iPod wouldn't take more than a few days to reach me on the East Coast. I was astonished by what followed. I received a confirmation e-mail within minutes of placing the order, with a tracking number for the item that allowed me to follow its progress. I idly checked the status of the shipment on the Web site for the carrier, Federal Express, and sat up with a jolt. The product was being shipped not from California but from Shanghai, China. During the next day and a half, I watched my computer screen with fascination as the iPod journeyed across the Pacific. Just as genetic markers in our DNA tell the story of our own journey, the bar code on the iPod package, scanned and tracked as it passed through various locations, told a remarkable tale of a shrunken world.

Within hours of receiving the order, Apple's Chinese employees had engraved Ateesh's name on the iPod and placed it and all its accessories in a small box. At 1:52 in the afternoon in Shanghai—exactly six hours and forty-five minutes after I received confirmation of my order—the personalized iPod left the Apple factory in a FedEx van for the sorting facility. Eight hours and nine minutes later, the package was on a plane leaving for Anchorage, Alaska. I tracked the iPod as it flew across the Pacific and landed at the FedEx hub at the airport in Indianapolis, Indiana, about midnight on the day after I placed the order. Wending its way through a maze of conveyor belts and ramps, examined by scanners and guided by robotic arms into containers with specific zip codes, traveling aboard vans and aircraft, Ateesh's personalized iPod landed on our New Haven doorstep barely forty hours after I had clicked "Buy." This gadget had traveled eight thousand miles in less than two days and was now sitting on our kitchen table. Human ancestors took thousands of years to make that journey from the Asian mainland to North America.

The back of the shiny white metal box, the size of a cigarette pack, said "Designed by Apple in California, Assembled in China." Getting a California-designed and Chinese-assembled music player delivered to my doorstep by an American courier company was of course only part of the story. The "made in" label did not reveal how many more countries' workers joined in making the iPod: The microdrive that was the heart of the machine was made by Hitachi in Japan, the controller chip was made in South Korea, the Sony battery was assembled in China, the stereo digital-to-analog converter was made by a company in Edinburgh, Scotland, the flash memory chip came from Japan, and the software on a chip that allows one to search for and play ten thousand songs was designed by programmers at PortalPlayer in India. By buying what I thought was this "American" product, I had actually become an unwitting participant in globalization, like millions of other consumers around the world. The biggest globalizer in this case was the American boy wonder Steve Jobs, the founder of Apple Computer. Jobs belongs to one of the four main categories of agents of globalization that I track in this book.

Jobs has been called many things, but few would call him a trader. These days, the term is reserved mainly for those intense men and women who sit at computer terminals and make loads of real money by buying and selling everything in a virtual world. But entrepreneur Jobs and his Apple Computer company fall in the broad category of agents of globalization I call "traders"—people who produce or carry products and services to consumers in distant parts of the planet and, in the process, have created an interconnected world. Perhaps it is hard to imagine this veritable rock star of the high-tech world as a modern incarnation of those traders in the early years of the Christian era who transported merchandise by camel caravans on the Silk Road or the Dutch traders who shipped cloves from Southeast Asia. But if one examines the essence of what they did—making profit by producing and transporting goods across borders—Jobs is one of them. Apple Computer also offers a good example of how traders have changed their strategies while doing essentially the same task: connecting people. Not only does Apple not own a shipping fleet, it does not even have a manufacturing plant. A music player designed by Jobs and his engineers in Cupertino, California, integrating the innovations and work of many others from Taiwan, South Korea, and India, was assembled in China, sold on the Internet, and delivered to my home by an American courier company. Yet Apple is driven to expand its market by the same profit motive that has inspired traders for millennia, with its profit enriching millions of people worldwide who own Apple shares.

In this chapter we will see many glimpses of what Adam Smith called the basic human instinct for "truck and trade" for profit, which has grown since the dawn of civilization and connects a widening part of the world through a web of commerce. Since the time humans settled in the Fertile Crescent, they have not stopped searching for different and better food, commodities, and toolmaking materials. To meet that social need and make profit through price arbitrage—buying low and selling high—came along a new class of people, traders. Ready to take the risk of long journeys and life abroad for profitable transactions, the traders and financiers emerged as the most important connectors. The means of transporting the fruits of trade have progressed from donkey and camel to sail and steamboats, from container ships and airplanes to fiber-optic cables. The modes of payment have evolved from barter, cowries, metal coin, paper money, and credit card to electronic bank transfers and online payment systems like PayPal. These developments enabled the speedy transportation of large quantities of goods, and the consumer base and the number of traders and entrepreneurs also grew. Multinational enterprises replaced individuals and groups of traders, all successors to one of the earliest examples, the English East India Company, founded in 1600. By a United Nations count, in 2003 there were sixty-three thousand multinational corporations in the world.[1] If one counted the shareholders of these businesses, the number of people promoting worldwide trade could be in the hundreds of millions. The difference between the camel caravan–borne "c-commerce" of the past and today's e-commerce, which delivered the Apple iPod to my door, is in the scale and speed of such transactions. Thus, it is not surprising that in the popular imagination, foreign trade has become synonymous with globalization.

But trading with strangers, as we saw in the last chapter, has been with us since the dawn of sedentary life in the Fertile Crescent. The most traded commodity among communities was the blade of obsidian—volcanic rock—that could be used as a knife to cut meat and a sickle to harvest grains. The evidence of this trade is scattered all over the Middle East and western Asia in the form of stone tools and seashells that were exchanged. However, the first written account of trade comes to us from the beginning of the second millennium BCE.

Both necessity and a taste for the exotic have led humans to engage in commerce. As agriculture developed and surplus food was available, a class of people, attracted by the prospect of profit and perhaps by a sense of adventure, became traveling merchants to look for goods and novelties that could be bought with gold or silver or bartered for whatever they had. Traders frequently worked with the sanction of the ruler and paid tax, as we have seen in ancient Mesopotamia. However, often the ruler himself took charge of trade to ensure a supply of luxuries and profit to be made from commercial transactions.

WHEN WILL WE HAVE A BIGGER HOUSE?

The fertile Tigris and Euphrates Valley produced enough food grain and wool to make cloth but completely lacked mineral resources needed to make bronze battle gear. The emergence of traders to carry out this necessary exchange has been recorded in four-thousand-year-old Mesopotamian clay tablets. By deciphering the cuneiform script in which details of commercial transactions and caravan trade were meticulously kept, archaeologists have allowed us to meet

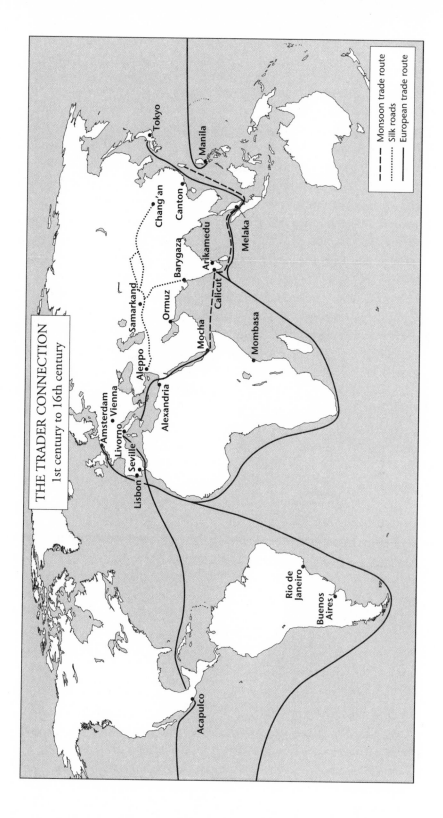

THE TRADER CONNECTION
1st century to 16th century

Amsterdam
Vienna
Livorno
Seville
Lisbon
Alexandria
Aleppo
Samarkand
Ormuz
Mocha
Barygaza
Chang'an
Arikamedu
Calicut
Canton
Tokyo
Manila
Melaka
Mombasa
Acapulco
Rio de Janeiro
Buenos Aires

Monsoon trade route
Silk roads
European trade route

our first globalizers: foreign traders and their financiers. We meet traders like Assur-idi, Su-Kubum, Salim-ahum, and Pusu-ken, who prospered by operating the caravan trade between the Assyrian capital and the entrepôt city of Kanis, in the Anatolian region of present-day Turkey. Long caravans, sometimes consisting of three hundred donkeys loaded with grain and wool, made the eight-hundred-mile journey, at the end of which most of the donkeys were sold and a smaller number were sent back to Assur carrying minerals, gold, and silver. The donkey caravans traveled at an average speed of almost twenty miles a day. A donkey could carry an average of two hundred pounds, limiting the quantity and type of goods that could be traded or the kind of terrain traversed.[2]

In what appears to be the first known trading diaspora, Assyrian merchants or their representatives lived in Kanis, away from their wives and families, and often took secondary wives. It is estimated that traders made approximately 100 percent profit on tin and 200 percent on textiles. The successful traders made enough money to build large houses and possess expensive lapis lazuli imported from Afghanistan. The trader Pusu-ken's wife, Lamassi, and her daughters worked at home to knit woolen clothes for export to Kanis. Lamassi wrote to her husband on a clay tablet. "Since you left, Salim-ahum [another trader] has already built a house double the size! When will we be able to do the same?" she asked.[3] Whether to make money to build a bigger house or just trying to avoid a high customs duty, Pusu-ken was caught with contraband goods and thrown in jail. One letter mentioned his being freed after making an unspecified "gift" to the crown prince of Kanis.[4]

The key player in the Assyrian trade was the wealthy entrepreneur, or *ummeânum,* who supplied the necessary capital and goods. As Louis Lawrence Orlin explains, "Ever concerned with finding markets for his surplus domestic goods, he supplied his itinerant employees with merchandise destined either for direct sale to native Anatolian consumers, for delivery to his agents or regional representative abroad."[5] The early venture capitalists would deliver orders not by computer but on clay tablets, the size of which had to be kept small in order to minimize weight for the long journeys. The focus on distance can be seen in the Assyrian correspondence of the period. A typical business communication written on a clay tablet addressed to Pusu-ken said:

> [Of] the tin and the textiles take [each] one half, and deposit the corresponding [amount in] silver yourselves—doing me a favor—and let the silver come to me with Inaja's caravan. Let not my heart be troubled!

If you do not take the tin and the textiles and [thus] do me no favor, sell it either for cash or on long terms or on short terms and act in my best interest.[6]

There was also trouble on the path of the donkey caravans that trekked the long distance from Assur to Kanis over rugged mountains and deserts. Traders periodically encountered attacks by bandits and suffered loss of animals. Such attacks were the standard perils of the long-distance trade over the ages. Concern over the speed of transport and the costs for delayed delivery has also preoccupied traders ever since. Even now, the insurance company Lloyd's charges higher premiums for ships that ply the pirate-infested waters of Southeast Asia. The desire to make more trips and deliver more goods has led traders to look continually for shorter routes and faster transport.

THE SHIP OF THE DESERT

Transport of higher capacity was pressed into service toward the beginning of the Christian era. Although the domestication of camels got under way between 3000 and 2000 BCE in the Horn of Africa, it was not until sometime between 500 BCE and 200 CE that the "North Arabian saddle" was invented and traders in the Arabian Peninsula could exploit the camel's ability to be a "ship of the desert." [7] Camels can travel approximately twenty miles in about six hours and carry about 550 pounds, twice as much as a horse or a mule. Since they foraged along the way, historian William McNeill notes, "In most Middle Eastern landscapes, where semi-arid wasteland abounded, caravans captured free energy just as sailing ships did. Thus caravans could often compete with ships on fairly even terms. They did so for about a thousand years, from the time when the arts of camel management became firmly established in the Middle East during the early Christian centuries until improvements in ship design and techniques of navigation changed the terms of competition after 1300 AD." [8]

The introduction of camels opened up new trade horizons. Camel caravans across the Central Asian deserts established the first direct connection between China, India, and the eastern Mediterranean. A series of trading routes linking oases and human habitations along the steppes and along the edge of the Taklimakan Desert and mountain valleys of Central Asia emerged. These were perhaps very natural passages through which small colonies of migrants out of Africa moved east, chasing game thirty to forty thousand years earlier. By the first century CE, foreign traders were present in small oasis towns fringing the Taklimakan, carrying silk and lacquerware to the Roman Empire and woolen and linen textiles, glass, coral, amber, and pearl to China. Because Chinese silk was the most prized commodity transported along the pathways, the nineteenth-century German geographer Baron Ferdinand von Richthofen gave this collection of routes the romantic name of the Silk Roads, or *Die Seidenstrassen,* popularly known today as the Silk Road.

For more than a millennium, this constantly shifting network of pathways served as the great connector between the Asian mainland, Europe, and sub-Saharan Africa. Through it the traders transported more than just the luxuries that European and Asian elites craved. For rulers, whether in China or India or other countries without pastures for horse-breeding, Central Asian horses became a prized export item on the Silk Road. They were not only the equivalent of luxury Mercedes Benz cars but were essential to building a powerful cavalry. China's Tang dynasty records show the government spent nearly a seventh of its annual revenue received from bolts of silk to import one hundred thousand horses.[9] In the eleventh century, Tibetan tribes who controlled major trade routes from Central Asia to China prospered by exchanging Chinese tea for Central Asian horses—at times trading twenty-two thousand horses a year. And of course, the Silk Road conveyed much more than goods. For more than a millennium the path that spanned three continents became a conveyor belt for the transmission of religions, art, philosophy, languages, technologies, germs, and genes.[10]

Trading on the Silk Road reached its peak during the thirteenth century, when the Mongol Empire presided over its entire length. The journey on the backs of double-humped Bactrian camels from Afghanistan to Peking took a year to complete on the average, but goods did get delivered.[11] A peaceful environment maintained by Mongol watchtowers and garrisons and the maintenance of caravansaries, or rest houses, along the route boosted the flow of merchandise. Traders carried wheat noodles and silk culture from China to Iran and Italy, both of which established profitable silk industries of their own. Chinese papermaking technology moved to Europe, providing the basis for book printing and the Renaissance.[12] Thanks to cobalt brought by traders from Iran, Ming ceramic workshops developed blue-and-white porcelain designs specifically for the Islamic market.[13]

In the second to fifth centuries, traders leading camel caravans opened up new population settlements in formerly unknown areas of sub-Saharan Africa. By the fourth century, gold from the sub-Saharan region was bartered for copper and date palms from North Africa. Date palms growing in abundance in the oases at the edge of the Sahara were profitably traded for gold. The caravan trade connection would later emerge as a cultural bridge when enthusiastic Muslim traders from North Africa carried the Islamic faith to Nigeria, Ghana, Senegal, and beyond. In the Senegambian language, the word *Muslim* became synonymous with trader.[14]

In the seventh and eighth centuries, China's Tang dynasty capital, Chang'an, now Xian, was the eastern terminus of the Silk Road. With a million inhabitants, it was not only the largest city in the world but, thanks to the presence of international traders and religious missionaries, the most cosmopolitan. The Silk Road and Chang'an also played a role in the spread of Buddhism, which we will explore later. At this point it is useful to note the city of Chang'an as a classic example of how traders connected the world's culture. Historian Valerie Hansen has described Chang'an's foreign quarters around the Western Market as a bustling place of world culture: "Non-Chinese residents built religious institutions dedicated to the religions of their homelands. The Persian-speaking merchants continued to worship at two kinds of temples devoted to religions they brought with them from Iran. Travelers from Syria embraced their own form of Christianity, Nestorianism."[15]

SOME SWEET WINE, DRIED FIGS, AND A SOPHIST

The boat was the form of transportation that opened up huge possibilities of long-distance connections. One item in great demand in the arid, alluvial plains of Mesopotamia was wood to build palaces, temples, and furniture, and it could be found on the shores of the eastern Mediterranean and in India. By the middle of the second millennium BCE, Phoenician traders had begun to use boats made of reed to float cedars from the north down the Euphrates to Lower Mesopotamia and bring hardwood, minerals, and precious stones from western India.[16] The riverine trade-based civilization of Mohenjo-daro and Harappa in the Indian subcontinent—with craftsmen making wooden boats and artisans turning precious stones, gold, silver, and ivory into ornaments, and cotton fiber into cloth—emerged as Mesopotamia's biggest trade partner.[17] We have seen the Akkadian ruler Sargon's boast that ships of Meluhha, the Sumerian name for South Asia, and other lands were docked in the quay of his capital on the Euphrates.[18] Exports from India were not just luxuries: even small monkeys from the subcontinent became popular pets for wealthy Mesopotamians!

The Phoenicians who inhabited the east coast of the Mediterranean—Sidon and Tyre in present-day Lebanon—were the first specialized merchants whose seafaring skill enabled them to spread their trading network throughout the Persian Gulf and the Mediterranean. Copper from Cyprus and cedar from Lebanon were transported throughout the Levant. The need to communicate with a variety of people led the Phoenicians to develop the alphabet in place of complex hieroglyphic and cuneiform writing. The known world expanded as population pressure at home and the search for wider markets led the Phoenicians to establish colonies on the North African coast, in Sicily, in Sardinia, and along the coast of Spain.

In the first millennium BCE, Greek traders followed in their footsteps, and Greek settlements spread throughout the eastern Mediterranean and the Black Sea coasts. Southern Italy and Sicily were so heavily colonized by the Greeks that the region came to be known as Magna Graecia, or Greater Greece.[19] Trade between the Mediterranean and India had developed enough in the third century BCE for the Indian king Bindusara to ask the Greek king Antiochus to send him "some sweet wine, dried figs, and a sophist."[20]

A FREE RIDE ACROSS THE INDIAN OCEAN

In the first century CE, the Roman Empire reached the Red Sea, and the door was fully opened to trade with India, the long-coveted source of exotic luxuries. We do not know the names of any traders, but a remarkable navigation and trading manual written in Greek by an anonymous author in the middle of the first century offers a detailed picture of the expansion of the "known world." In *The Periplus of the Erythraen Sea* (the circumnavigation of the sea that encompassed the Red Sea, Arabian Sea, and Indian Ocean), the author writes knowledgably of a journey down the African coast and along the Indian coastline all the way up to Bengal, beyond which lies the region of China.

He mentions the happy "discovery" of the southwest wind by a Greek or Egyptian navigator named Hippalos, by which ships leaving the mouth of the Red Sea in summer could ride most of the way to India's Malabar Coast and return in the winter when the wind blew in the opposite direction. This wind later came to be known as "monsoon," from the Arabic word for season, *mausim,* and Pliny later wrote how this discovery "and the thirst for gain brought India still nearer us."[21] Following the wind and currents drastically reduced the sailing time between India and Egypt—the eastern edge of the Roman Empire—from thirty months to three months for a round trip.[22] As one historian noted, the predictability of a homeward wind made the Indian Ocean the most benign environment in the world for long-range voyaging.[23] Until the introduction of steamships in 1780, the speed of transporting goods remained stable for seventeen hundred years.

This success in shortening the sailing time across some three thousand nautical miles of sea to India intensified contact and produced rising trade volume. The Greek geographer Strabo wrote: "Previously not twenty ships dared . . . peep outside the Straits [of Bab-el-Mandeb], but now great fleets are sent as far as India and the extremities of Ethiopia."[24] Compared to barely twenty ships a year before the discovery, now a merchant ship left Egypt for India almost every day of the season carrying tin, lead, wine, coral, glass, and gold and silver coins. The gain in shipping time and advances in building sturdy, hulled vessels to sail the open seas came at the same time that Rome had emerged as the hub of the "world economy."[25] The Roman elites accumulated enough wealth to indulge their taste for the exotic, and they were ready to invest in overseas trade and finance risky, long sea voyages. Luxuries from faraway places defined the power of the Roman Empire, and Rome had emerged as a consumer city par excellence, chic and cosmopolitan. As Grant Parker notes, "To Roman consumers, the actual existence of so distant a place, directly visited by so few people of note, was far less important than its impact on the imagination."[26] A special spice market was built in Rome, and the city's most glitzy street was named Via Piperatica, Pepper Street. The search for luxuries spread Roman trade far. Roman artifacts found in a Vietnamese port, including a gold medallion of the emperor Antonius Pius from 152 CE, showed the extent of Roman trade with Asia.[27]

The rising demand for luxuries probably drained the Roman treasury, which obtained its gold from Spain. It led the emperor Tiberius to complain to the Senate: "How shall we reform the taste for dress? How are we to deal with the particular articles of feminine vanity, and in particular with that rage for jewels and precious trinkets, which drains the empire of its wealth, and sends, in exchange for baubles, the money of the commonwealth to foreign nations, and even the enemies of Rome?"[28] Historians, however, doubt the authenticity of Tiberius's moralistic and, in modern parlance, protectionist accusation, pointing out that the Roman treasury collected a 25 percent customs duty on all imports. The complaint nevertheless points to the significance of Asian trade to the Roman economy.

COOL, FRAGRANT WINE FROM ITALY

Indeed, hoards of Roman imperial coins discovered in south India, and evidence of Indian traders' presence in ports on the Red Sea, bear testimony to the rising volume of this trade. As the elites of the Roman Empire consumed ever larger quantities of Indian spices—black pepper and ginger—along with ivory and silk, amphorae full of Italian and Greek wine, olive oil, and garum (fish sauce) were reaching India for Greek and Roman settlers and for the Indian aristocracy. A contemporary shipping document written on papyrus shows that just one shipment of ivory, textile, and aromatic herbs fetched a value large enough to buy 2,400 acres of the finest farmland in Egypt. One modest-sized ship of five hundred tons could carry 150 such consignments.[29] The most important Indian port for trading with Rome in the beginning of the Christian era was Arikamedu, on the southern coast of India, which received a large amount of Roman gold coin and vast quantities of Greek and Italian wine from the exchange. An ancient Tamil poem exulted in how one "increased the joy by giving to the girls of shining bangles, who everyday have taken in hands vessels beautified by gold, to drink the cool fragrant wine brought by the yavanas [westerners] in beautiful bowls."[30] Archaeologists have discovered that the fine wine produced on the Greek island of Kos was so famous that large amounts of what Elizabeth Will has called "factitious Italian-made Koan wine" was exported to India in typical Koan amphorae.[31] Since the amphorae are dated between the first and second centuries BCE, this must be some of the earliest evidence in the history of global trade of pushing an imitation product.

Other more serious ills of global trading were visible from the earliest times. Trading in slaves has been practiced since the third millennium, and trafficking in women was added at least at the beginning of the Christian era. As the author of the *Periplus* noted, among the merchandise exported to the Indian king of Barygaza, today's Broach, were "choice girls for the Royal Harem."[32] The fourteenth-century harem of rulers in Bengal reportedly boasted Chinese and "Roman" (European) concubines.[33] Given the rigor of travel across the vast ocean in primitive boats, the numbers of such human cargo were presumably small. Large-scale trafficking in slaves and women from Central Europe and Africa had to wait until large-scale caravans and ocean shipping had begun.

Trading with the monsoon winds transformed the Indian Ocean into a virtual lake, with ports and entrepôts sprouting on India's west coast, along the Red Sea, and on the east coast of Africa. Indian traders looking for profit also turned east, sailing to the uncharted waters of island Southeast Asia in search of gold and fragrant wood. An ancient Indian writer put down the stakes clearly: "Who goes to Java, never returns. If by chance he returns, then he brings back enough money to support seven generations of his family."[34] Rising monsoon-borne trade boosted the coastwise traffic around the Arabian Peninsula, lowering the freight rate and affecting the inland caravan trade. In the resulting shakeout of the caravan trade, one Arabian tribe, the Qurayish, seized whatever was left of the carrying trade and established a permanent settlement in the Mecca Valley around the year 400. Two centuries later a Qurayish trader would emerge as the Prophet Mohammed to turn the trading tribe into an incipient state and lay the foundation of an Islamic empire.[35]

The impact of the increasing Indian Ocean trade was visible in the following centuries with the rise of Sofala, Kilwa, Mogadishu, and Malindi as bustling ports with a growing population of Arab and Indian traders. Slaves, gold, ivory, fragrant wood, resin, and other exotic products that once attracted Queen Hatshepsut to dispatch an expedition down the Red Sea at the dawn of Egyptian civilization were made accessible not just to the wealthy in the Mediterranean but to the elites in faraway India and China. Chinese coins of the eighth and ninth centuries have been found on the East African coast at Mogadishu, at Kilwah, and on the Mafia Islands.[36] Philip D. Curtin says that Chinese sources mention slaves from Zenj, in sub-Saharan Africa, as early as the seventh century, and by the early twelfth century, most of the wealthy people of Canton were said to have possessed slaves from Africa. Thousands of slaves were taken to Persia to work in the saltpeter mines and to Iraq to clear the marshes.[37]

Linked by the Tigris to the Persian Gulf, the Abbasid capital of Baghdad rose to become the center of wealth and luxury as the terminus of eastern trade. As one Abbasid ruler proclaimed: "This is the Tigris; there is no obstacle between us and China; everything on the sea can come to us on it."[38] Indeed, ocean shipping to China and India by Arab sailors had become routine by the mid-ninth century, when ships sailed from the Gulf and the Red Sea for a year's round trip to China. As a ninth-century account of Baghdad put it, there was a continuous flow of merchandise of East and West, "from India, Sind, China, Tibet, the lands of the Turks, the Dailamites, the Khazars and Abyssinians." Silk, cinnamon, paper, ink, and ceramics from China; sandalwood, ebony, and coconut from India; fine textiles and papyrus from Egypt; paper from Samarkand; and prepared fruits and nuts from around the Muslim world all moved around the globe.[39]

Another town on the Persian Gulf, Siraf, rode the monsoon trade with Africa, India, and China to unprecedented prosperity. Trading inspired the growth of a range of professions: shipwrights, weavers, metalworkers, jewelers, and potters. As Jerry Bentley notes, "During the ninth century residents of Siraf built a great mosque and a bazaar, and they set their tables with porcelain imported from China."[40]

A large colony of Arab, European, and Jewish traders became established in the Chinese port city of Canton, known to Arabs as Khanfu. A contemporary account says that at the onset of the westerly return monsoon, large Arab ships laden with silk, fabrics, camphor, musk, and spices left Canton, "passing hundreds of craft of every shape and size from all parts of Asia."[41] Chinese documents of the seventh and eighth centuries list Persians, Indians, and Malaysians as owners of the visiting ships.

By the tenth and eleventh centuries, Arab traders and Indian artisans had set up a rudimentary supply-chain production involving ivory. The ivory from elephants found in India and Southeast Asia was more expensive and harder than African ivory. Arab traders along the African coast exported large quantities of elephant tusks to India, where artisans carved them into jewelry, ornaments, and religious icons for export to China and the Mediterranean.[42] In addition to the old trading favorite—spices—the Indian artisans' skill in making stone beads, weaving and dyeing cotton textiles, and manufacturing bronze artifacts and steel swords attracted foreign traders to India. India's early success in exports was built on the organization of ivory-carvers, goldsmiths, silversmiths, and a whole range of crafts into guilds, along with the development of an intricate system of financing and marketing by specialized individuals.

Travel required such a long time that trading diasporas grew almost as soon as long-distance trade began, as we have seen in Anatolia and in India's Arikamedu, near Pondicherry. As the volume of trade grew, the need for a layover of several months to avail of the monsoon became another reason for foreign traders to settle on India's Malabar Coast.[43] Arab, Persian, Armenian, and Jewish traders made up for a sizable part of the Calicut, Cranganore (known in Roman times as Muziris), and Quilon populations. So welcome were the foreign traders as the harbinger of prosperity that they were called *Mapilla*, or sons-in-law. By the time the Portuguese explorer Vasco da Gama landed in Calicut in 1498, *Mapilla* had come to mean exclusively the Muslim traders—descendants of Arab and Persian traders from the ninth century.[44] Clearly, traders had not only exchanged goods across oceans but enriched the host country's gene pool!

THE ARAB LATEEN SAIL AND CHINESE RUDDER

By the time the long wars of the Crusades had ended and Islam had regained control of Jerusalem, long-distance trading had been given a new impetus. Western Europeans who had come to the Levant as Crusaders to fight the Muslims returned home with a new taste for spices and other Asian luxuries, creating fresh demand for imports. As merchants sought improved means to meet the demand, the prosperous trading cities of Genoa and Venice combined technologies from around the world and instigated a major revolution in nautical technology that would enable stable, all-weather sailing. In 1104, Venice created its first public shipyard, the Arsenal, in which shipwrights would build a fleet of large, oared galleys, boosting trade to new heights. Unlike ships on the Indian Ocean, which could navigate essentially by following the direction of the monsoon wind and gazing at the stars, European ships had been restricted, especially in the fog-bound waters of the North Sea. Europeans now adopted the Arab "lateen sail"—a triangular sail fitted to a mast and a movable boom—which allowed them to achieve speed and sail close to the wind. They also adopted from the Chinese the use of the sternpost rudder, which enabled them to steer ships safely to port. Thanks to the abundance of hardwood from northern Europe, shipwrights could construct three-masted sailing ships—equipped with square, lateen, and staysails—to be used for ocean shipping.[45] Scholars disagree about whether the compass was introduced from China, which had known about the device since at least the ninth century. Whatever its origin, the compass, introduced to Europe in the late thirteenth century, made voyages safer and doubled the volume of trading as ships could now make two voyages a year from Mediterranean ports to the English Channel and the Levant.[46]

Chinese shipbuilders, too, made impressive advances. By the time Marco Polo sailed from China to India in 1292, Chinese-made ships were large enough to carry 1,520 to 1,860 tons and had multiple decks with private cabins. Two hundred years later, when Chinese admiral Zheng He sailed his fleet in the Indian Ocean, ship-building technology had advanced to create his nine-masted "treasure ships," four-hundred-foot-long vessels capable of carrying a crew of a thousand men. These impressive advances in Chinese marine technology, however, did not help Chinese exports much, since by an imperial fiat China turned inward soon after Zheng He's foray into the Indian Ocean. But together, technological improvements in shipping and the rising demand for spices in Europe quickened the tempo of voyages and widened trading connections. The historian James Burke has described how these innovations affected European commerce:

> The immediate effect of the spread of the lateen was to increase the number of voyages, since masters no longer had to wait for a favorable offshore wind before leaving port. The pace of trade quickened, and in consequence the size of ships increased, for as more and more cargo left harbor for more and more ports, it made sense to make one ship do the work of two. It saved money, and increased profit. . . .

The rudder gave the masters the necessary longitudinal control of their big ships, which in turn encouraged the merchants. . . . Together with the use of the combination of lateen and square sail, and the sternpost rudder, the compass altered the sailing schedule almost immediately. . . . With the aid of the compass, ships could sail under cloudy skies by day and night. The number of voyages doubled, and crews were kept in regular employment. This in turn encouraged the investors, and the number of voyages further increased.[47]

A JEWISH TRADER IN MALABAR

A fascinating glimpse into this rising volume of trade and wide dispersal of traders is offered by twelfth- and thirteenth-century documents preserved in a Cairo synagogue. Because Jewish custom forbade the desecration of papers in which the name "God" is written, hundreds of thousands of pages of commercial correspondence by Jewish traders were preserved in the synagogue's special vault known as the Geniza, offering historians a treasure trove of information. Thus, literally by the grace of God, we have come to know traders who sailed to distant shores—the Far East, India and Yemen, Egypt, Palestine and Syria, Tunisia and Morocco—and wrote about their commercial as well as personal concerns. They traded in textile, metals, flax, medicinal plants and preparations, spices and aromatics, and perfumes and incenses.

In the Geniza correspondence we meet Abraham Yiju, a Jewish merchant from Tunisia who ran a bronze factory on India's Malabar Coast, where his Indian employees turned copper, tin, and old bronze vessels sent from Aden and Spain into new vessels. Other objects such as iron, spices of all descriptions, and textiles also formed part of his shipment from India.

Even though large ships made regular sailings, danger was ever present, and so was the need for God's assistance. In a letter Yiju wrote to a client to give him bad news:

You, my master, may God make your honored position permanent, wrote that you kindly sold the silk and sent goods for its proceeds and that you sent them in the ships of *Rashmit*. I learned, however, that *Rashmit's* two ships were lost completely. May the H[oly one, be] he b[lessed], compensate me and you. Do not ask me, my master, how much I was affected by the loss of the cargo belonging to you. But the Creator will compensate you soon. In any case, there is no counsel against the decree of God.

All the "copper" [vessels, *nakas*], which you sent with Abu 'All, arrived, and the "table-bowl" also arrived. It was exactly as I wished—may God give you a good reward and undertake your recompensation (for only he is able to do it adequately).[48]

Yiju's and some twelve hundred other pieces of correspondence offer a picture of a globalized world in which traders took enormous risk in search of profit. While these traders made sizable gains, the long-distance trade shaped the personal lives of peoples in different continents. Yiju—after a sojourn of at least seventeen years in India, where he had bought the freedom of an Indian slave girl, Ashu, and married her—returned to Arabia with his only surviving child to marry her to his nephew.

While Yiju was in India, the Norman invasion of Tunisia had made his brother a destitute refugee. Yiju had a consolation: the fortune he had made as a trader in India could now help the family. In a letter to his brother in 1149 he wrote:

> This is to announce to you, my brother, that I have set out from India and arrived safely in Aden, may God protect it, with my belongings, life, and children well preserved. May God be thanked for this. *"O that men would praise the Lord for his goodness and for his miraculous deeds with the children of men."*
>
> Now I wish to let you know that I have enough to live on for all of us. May God, the exalted, let this money be a living for me and my children and be sufficient for you as well.[49]

Abraham Yiju was one of the many lucky foreign traders who made fortunes for their families to live on and in the process integrated the world. Thanks to the Silk Road and the booming Indian Ocean trade, an international trade economy developed, stretching all the way from northwestern Europe to China and generating unprecedented wealth in the process. The sea trade of Genoa in 1293 was three times as large as the revenue of the kingdom of France in the same year.[50] Of course, because this trade involved mostly luxury items for elites, it did not create the close interdependence that globalization has come to imply today. Yet parts of these countries' economies—a network of trading cities connected by overland or sea routes, with the hinterlands producing export items—became increasingly dependent on foreign trade. To some, trade brought unimaginable prosperity, to others exploitation and pain.

MELAKA'S HAND ON THE THROAT OF VENICE

As seafaring expanded, the lure of highly prized spices like cloves and nutmeg that grew only on some islands in the Indonesian archipelago started bringing Arab traders to Southeast Asia. The spread of pepper cultivation, which had been introduced to Southeast Asia from the Malabar Coast, also attracted traders from all over the Indian Ocean rim as well as China. By the fourteenth century, Arab and Gujarati Muslim trading enclaves dotted the northern shores of Sumatra and Java.[51] Prosperous and devout traders also had success in converting locals to Islam.

In 1409 a Malay prince, Parameswaram, sought to capitalize on the region's growing trade link by founding the city of Melaka at the site of a fishing village on the Strait of Malacca. With Muslim traders predominant in the region, he converted to Islam and led his citizens to do the same. Yet, mindful of the multinational and multifaith character of the traders who gathered in Melaka, he maintained strict neutrality. Because of his wise trader-friendly policy and low taxes, Melaka, or Malacca, became one of the most vibrant cosmopolitan cities in Southeast Asia. Situated at "the end of the monsoons," the winds that brought traders from the west on the southwest monsoon and those from Japan and China on the northeast monsoon, Malacca became the favorite entrepôt for swapping goods. Not surprisingly, within barely two decades of Vasco da Gama's arrival in the Indian Ocean, Malacca fell prey to the Portuguese gunboat. A Portuguese apothecary-turned-trader and diplomat named Tomé Pires left a lively account of a region that was totally integrated with world trade in his *Suma Oriental* (Eastern account, 1512). Pires estimated Melaka's population at forty to fifty thousand, with sixty-one "nations" represented in its trade and some eighty-four languages spoken at the port. He expressed admiration of the enormous profits foreign traders made by carrying goods back and forth between the Persian Gulf and Asia, writing: "Malacca is a city that was made for merchandise, fitter than any other in the world; the end of monsoons and the beginning of others. Malacca is surrounded and lies in the middle, and the trade and commerce between the different nations for a thousand leagues on every hand must come to Malacca. . . . Whoever is lord of Malacca has his hand on the throat of Venice."[52]

The power and prosperity of Melaka rose, not just from its geographical location as a stopping place halfway between India and China, but from the growing world demand for pepper. In the hundred years since the arrival of Portuguese, Spanish, Dutch, and British traders, international commerce and religious conversion had transformed spice-growing Southeast Asia. As historian Anthony Reid has observed, "New cities and states flourished, most Southeast Asians were brought within the ambit of scriptural and universal faiths, and large proportions of the population became dependent on international trade for their livelihood, their clothing and everyday necessities, and even their food."[53] This dependence would soon bring great tragedy and suffering to those who were killed by the thousands for their spice orchards or turned into slaves. Their story would be repeated all over the world in the years of European conquest and rise of commercial empires, and Chapter 7 explores more about the evil consequences of trade. For now, it may be useful to step back and look at the origins of the desire for spice that brought about the eventual Western European dominance of Asia. As we have seen, the desire for spices led to extensive trade during the Roman Empire. In 408, the Visigoths demanded a ransom in gold, silver, and pepper as a condition for halting their siege of Rome. After the empire fell, however, trade dropped off amid general economic and political insecurity. Spices, which had already drained the gold of the Roman Empire, became costlier. Then the rise of Islam—including the fall of Alexandria, the great entrepôt for transferring Asian spices from the Red Sea to the Mediterranean—dealt a heavy blow to trading. Amid the general scarcity and rising prices of spice, Venetian merchants struck a deal with the Muslims to emerge as the near-exclusive distributor of spice in Europe. Italian city-states played this role even during the Crusades of the late eleventh to thirteenth centuries, when Europeans' attempts to regain the Holy Land from the Muslims disrupted commerce. Spice, always precious, rose to a new level of social value as a luxury. When in 1194 the king of Scotland paid a visit to his fellow monarch Richard I of England, he received, among other tokens of hospitality, daily allotments of two pounds of pepper and four pounds of cinnamon.[54]

THE DEVIL TAKE YOU, WHAT BROUGHT YOU HERE?

The escalating consumer demand in Europe for Asian spices and the Christian monarchies' desperate desire to find a way to the source, while bypassing the Islamic traders in the Middle East, spurred exploration of new routes around Africa and the building of ships capable of undertaking hazardous journeys over vast distances of open ocean. Long-distance trade has always required daring and desire. In the fifteenth century, Portugal's Prince Henry the Navigator emerged as a pioneer in the search for a new route to Asia around Africa and took up the role Venice's Arsenal had played in the design of ships and navigational tools for longer sea voyages. In 1497 King Manuel I of Portugal authorized Vasco da Gama's voyage to India "in search of spices." Seeing da Gama's first messenger on shore in Calicut, a Muslim merchant from Tunis asked him in Spanish, "The devil take you, what brought you here?" His succinct reply: "We came to look for Christians and spices."[55]

The question was not out of place, for the hazards of travel were enormous. Between 1500 and 1634, Philip D. Curtin estimates, 28 percent of all ships that set out from Portugal bound for India were lost at sea. In their first voyages to Asia, da Gama and Cabral lost half their crew and more than half of their ships. But the lure of high profit kept the ships coming.[56] The Catalan monarchy of Portugal's neighbor Spain sponsored Christopher Columbus's effort to find a direct route to India across the Atlantic. The result of this effort was a sudden widening of the horizon. Within two decades of Columbus's serendipitous discovery of the New World, Ferdinand Magellan's crew (only 10 percent of whom survived) circumnavigated the world, creating for the first time truly global linkages. Trading on a worldwide scale took off, and the often blurry distinction between traders, explorers, missionaries, and conquerors grew fainter. But the ensuing scramble for resources, slaves, and new markets for the countries' own products connected the world ever more tightly. For the first time, all the continents were connected by direct shipping instead of a relay through a chain of intermediaries using boats, mule packs, and camel caravans.

The Portuguese establishment of beachheads in Goa in India, Melaka in Malaysia, and Macao in China in the sixteenth century created the framework of truly global trading. The availability of regular shipping to the East led to the rise of specialization—from Chinese porcelain to Indian diamonds. After Portuguese traders returned from Asia with fine China porcelain, the Portuguese king and his courtiers became the first to be infected by "the contagion of China-fancy," as Samuel Johnson caustically described it. By 1580 Lisbon's Rua Nova dos Mercadores alone had six shops for Chinese porcelain.[57] In response to the craze for porcelain, Western merchants imported at least seventy million pieces in the seventeenth and eighteenth centuries.[58]

From the mass of correspondence left by traders in European ports, we meet a successful Jewish diamond merchant in the Italian port of Livorno. Isaac Ergas of the trading house of Ergas and Silvera took customers' orders for diamonds from India's famous Golconda mines. Italian scholar Francesca Trivellato, who has studied the eighteenth-century Jewish traders of Livorno, says that customers placed specific orders. Much like I ordered my iPod from Apple, an Italian customer looking for a diamond would approach Ergas and deposit cash. Since the traders in India, who would supply the diamond, did not much care for Italian lire, Ergas and Silvera would ship Mediterranean coral beads. Some customers were lucky enough to place an order in time for the annual monsoon journey to India, and the coral shipment would be sent to Lisbon aboard British or Dutch vessels. There it would be transferred onto large-hulled carracks leaving for the yearlong journey to Goa. Hindu trading houses in Goa would assess the market value of the coral and accordingly send back diamonds of different sizes and qualities. If everything went well—and the ship did not sink in a storm—the customers received the diamonds a year or two later.[59]

The arrival of Portuguese and Dutch traders in the Arabian Sea opened the door for another specialty trade, coffee. Early in the eighteenth century, French trader Jean de la Roque led the first French ship around the Cape of Good Hope to Aden and Mocha. He undertook this dangerous yearlong voyage to get coffee beans from the source rather than at a high price from Turkish, Dutch, or English middlemen. His trip took two and half years to complete, but the profit he made on six hundred tons of coffee was worth his trouble. More important, perhaps, his ensuing book, *Voyage de l'Arabie heureuse* (1716), offered the first detailed description of the product that grew in Ethiopia and Yemen before it took over the world. Two decades after de la Roque's voyage to Mocha, a French captain would take a coffee plant to the Caribbean (for more on the story of coffee, see Chapter 3).

Not surprisingly, the transportation revolution that linked the continents created the conditions for the emergence of the first multinational trading company. The business venture that Assyrian traders ran from Anatolia in the third millennium BCE has been called the world's first multinational.[60] The definition of *multinational* as an enterprise with substantial foreign direct investment and engaged in trade intermediation between countries can certainly be applied in at least its embryonic form to enterprises such as those run by Pusu-ken, whom we met earlier in this chapter. But the formation of government-chartered trading monopolies, such as the English and Dutch East India Companies in the early 1600s, marked a new stage and presaged the rise of global companies. From some five hundred at the end of the seventeenth century, multinationals now number more than sixty-three thousand. The number of consumers has grown apace.

A major contribution to the soaring ocean trade came from relative latecomers to exploration, the Dutch. By the late sixteenth century, the Dutch had developed a cheap, general-purpose cargo vessel known as the *fluyt*, or flyboat. Shorn of gun platforms and armor plating, de rigueur for sailing in pirate-infested oceans, the lighter and more spacious fluyt, weighing just two to three hundred tons, could not only carry larger cargo but operate with a smaller crew. Fluyts sailed in safe waters or were accompanied by men-of-war. A well-equipped fluyt could complete a return journey from Europe to Asia in eight months.[61] To catch up with the Dutch, who dominated shipping, the British government financed and encouraged research into astronomy and terrestrial magnetism. That investment paid off with many innovations, especially the production of the first reliable maritime chronometer, which told navigators where they were in the open sea.

While other minor innovations shortened sailing times and enhanced sailing's safety by the end of the eighteenth century, the next big jump in speed came with the introduction of steam power. Without steam, even the speediest of British sailing ships of the mid-nineteenth century took 110 days for a return journey to Canton, and Jules Verne's imaginary trip around the world in eighty days was far away.[62] All that changed when in 1807 Robert Fulton invented the steamship. Freight costs dropped dramatically, and the volume of merchandise exchanged between major nations rose rapidly to an annual quantity of about eighty-eight million tons in the 1870s, up from twenty million tons in 1840. Over the same period, the value of trade among the most industrialized economies and the most remote or backward regions of the world grew about sixfold.[63]

Thanks to the larger size of vessels and faster turnaround time of steamships, British ocean freight rates plummeted by about 70 percent between 1840 and 1910. Worldwide real freight rates fell by 1.5 percent per annum between 1840 and 1910.[64] The falling costs were mirrored in the speed of sea routes worldwide.[65] The completion of the Suez Canal in 1869 removed the last land barrier between the Red Sea and the Mediterranean, cutting travel time by as much as two-thirds.[66] And the launching of the *Paraguay*, the first refrigerated ship, designed by French engineer Ferdinand Carré, in 1877 opened up a whole new area of long-distance trade: fresh food. Argentine beef and Australian leg of lamb could now be served for supper in Europe. As Kenneth Pomeranz has written:

> By vastly increasing the speed and volume of the carrying trade while dramatically slashing prices, railroads and steamships set into motion a conceptual revolution in time, space, and commodification. With steam, the Atlantic and Pacific shrank to ponds and continents to small principalities. . . . The global supermarket began taking shape in the nineteenth century. Luxuries no longer dominated the long-distance trade. Beef and mutton from Argentina, Uruguay, and the United States and wheat from Australia, the United States and India fed hungry European populations; Japanese mills mixed US, Indian and Chinese cotton.[67]

Forty-five years later the opening of Panama Canal brought the Pacific closer to the West, shortening the distance from New York to San Francisco by 60 percent and to Hong Kong by 30 percent. Not until the advent of air cargo would anything shrink the world as much as the Suez and Panama canals.

Even before Panama Canal was opened, another idea to boost shipping came from the serendipitous discovery of petroleum in Pennsylvania. From ancient times, oil oozing from shale in the earth had been used to light torches and lamps to illuminate the night. The first patent to refine this bounty of nature for other uses was granted by the British monarch in 1694 to three subjects who had found "a way to extract and make great quantityes of pitch, tarr, and oyle out of a sort of stone." Heavy oil that could be refined into petroleum was discovered by Edwin Laurentine Drake in 1859 when a well-drilling technique he had developed gushed forth heavy crude oil in Pennsylvania. Within half a century the internal combustion engine was invented, and by the 1970s giant oil tankers running on diesel fuel began lowering the cost of carrying crude and the cost of all freight.

A further drop to transportation costs was brought about by a North Carolina trucking entrepreneur named Malcolm McLean. His plan to put cargo-laden truck trailers on steamships led to the creation of the world's first container ship, the *Ideal-X*. On 26 April 1956, the *Ideal-X* was packed with fifty-eight containers in just eight hours, cutting the cost of freight by over 97 percent, to 15.8 cents a ton. This ushered in a new era in shipping that has continually lowered freight costs. The biggest of the container ships, nicknamed "monster ships," carry containers equivalent to twenty miles of trucks,[68] and a car can be delivered anywhere in the world for less than a five-hundred-dollar freight charge. Although container ships barely achieve a speed of more than twenty knots, the large size of the load each ship carries and the speed with which the containers can be loaded, unloaded, and seamlessly transferred from ship to truck or train have sharply brought down freight costs. It often now costs more to send a container by road one hundred miles from port to its final destination than it does to ship the container by sea from Shanghai to Rotterdam.

The maximum gain in speed, of course, came with the beginning of air-freight, the cost of which declined dramatically between the 1950s and 1980s. Especially significant was the introduction of the wide-bodied Boeing 747 Jumbo Jet in 1970, a cargo version of which began flying soon thereafter. The cost savings, however, were not just in freight but in the contraction of time. The less time a ship spends in loading and unloading its goods, the lower its port charges and demurrages and, eventually, the price of imported goods. Economists calculate that cost savings stemming from rapid transport between 1950 and 1998 were equivalent to reducing U.S. tariffs on manufacturing goods from 32 to 9 percent.[69]

FROM GOLD COINS TO PAYPAL

Faster and larger ships and aircraft were not the only factors in the gathering speed of delivery. The evolving medium of exchange—from bartering to cowries and from precious metals and letters promising gold and silver to plastic credit cards—has simplified and standardized transactions and boosted trade. Although metal had been used as money for more than two thousand years, not until the seventh century BCE did gold coins issued by Mediterranean states become the currency commonly accepted by traders all over the Mediterranean and Indian subcontinent. The silver Athenian coin with the head of the goddess Athena on one side and the bird associated with her—the owl—on the reverse were to traders then what Visa and MasterCard are today. The gold and silver coins later issued by the Roman Empire had an even greater reach, as traders traveled across the Indian Ocean to Southeast Asia and China. The Asians wanted few goods from the Mediterranean and, later, Europe in barter for their spices and textiles. They were willing to produce textiles to Roman specifications but invariably preferred gold and silver as payment.

Until the middle of the thirteenth century, when Italian city-states began to mint their own gold coins, the ones struck by the Byzantine Empire and Egypt continued to be an acceptable medium of exchange.[70] Nevertheless, the fall of the Roman Empire and the consequent rarity of Roman coins had an adverse effect on global trading, leading, for instance, to the decline of trade-reliant towns in far-off India.[71] Indian traders then turned their attentions to Southeast Asia, seeking new markets for their textiles. Several centuries later, the growing trade links with the spice-growing islands in Indonesia would allow Arab and European traders to use Indian ports as relay stations for the import of spices, exchanging them for Indian-made textiles. While glass beads and woolen cloth paid for some of their imports from India, the Europeans still needed precious metals to do business. The credit instrument by which the buyer promised to pay later also developed in the Indian subcontinent and the Middle East. The informal credit network, however, existed only between trading families, whether Christians, Jews, or Hindus, rather than unconnected individuals.[72]

The return to coinage, with Genoa, Florence, and Venice introducing gold coins in the late thirteenth century, gave international trade a new boost.[73] Trade impetus was dimmed, however, by the disaster wrought by the plague. As the ravages of the fourteenth-century Black Death faded, long-distance trade began gaining a new momentum from the increased availability of silver in Central Europe. Technological innovations involving pumping of mine shafts and chemical processes to separate silver in the mid-fifteenth century led to a silver mining boom. Silver mines in Japan also provided the Dutch traders the precious metal to conduct their business in Asia.

Increasing amounts of silver—especially from Germany—were spent by Venetian traders to purchase Syrian cotton for the German mills and Asian spices for European consumption.[74] The primacy of German-minted silver coins of that era is still being felt centuries later. The U.S. currency, the dollar, received its name from the vulgarization of the German silver coin *Joachim-staler*—in short, "thaler."

Although Columbus died a disappointed soul, having failed to find the golden-roofed houses of Cipangu in Japan, as described by Marco Polo, huge quantities of precious metal were soon found in Mexico and Peru. As one historian has put it, it was "almost free money."[75] Silver bullion from Mexico and Peru, mined by slave labor, soon began flowing to Asia as European merchants bought luxuries in quantities that they could not have imagined earlier. Throughout the first half of the seventeenth century, some 268 tons of silver were shipped to Europe every year, much of which was then shipped to the Baltic, the Levant, and Asia to buy goods. A century later, annual shipments of silver from the New World to Europe rose to five hundred tons, more than half of which was spent on importing spices, silk, porcelain, and other luxuries.[76] In 1621 a Portuguese merchant's account notes: "Silver wanders throughout all the world in its peregrinations before flocking to China, where it remains as if at its natural center."[77]

THE SILVER, TEXTILE, AND SPICE TRIANGLE

Gold mined by the Portuguese in Africa and, later, Brazil added to the world's trading. Between 1712 and 1755, some ten tons of gold were shipped to Lisbon every year and sent on their way to Asia to pay for exotic imports.[78] European traders who reached the Spice Islands found—to their surprise—that the natives who could supply them cloves, cardamom, nutmeg, and cinnamon cared little about silver but wanted cotton cloth. Soon a triangular trade emerged in which the Dutch and the British paid Indians in bullion for their handloom-woven cloth and bartered that cloth in Southeast Asia for spices for the home market. As one historian put it, Europeans now "linked the silver and gold mines of Mexico and Peru with the distant spice gardens and aromatic forests of Southeast Asia, via the markets of the Mediterranean and Atlantic seaboard."[79]

Venice's contribution to the growing international trade went beyond its

nautical innovations. Institutional innovations that undergird successful trading—from the development of banking to accountancy, foreign exchange, and
credit markets—gave Venice its preeminence. The fifteenth-century development of such credit instruments as bills of exchange, transferable bills, and the
legalization of interest collection in England and Holland accelerated trade
transactions. The English and Dutch East India Companies, for instance, began to work like banks, taking deposits in gold and silver from their employees
abroad, who were independently wealthy from their private business, and
promising to pay out the value of deposits back in the home country with interest. This ready availability of cash meant that companies could buy and ship
goods without waiting for silver bullion to arrive from London, Lisbon, or Amsterdam after a perilous year at sea.[80] However, with dwindling supplies of
silver and mercantilist concerns about reserves of precious metal by the late
eighteenth and early nineteenth centuries, paper money issued by sovereign
governments and bank notes became more common. The paper currencies further simplified business transactions. Problems arose only when wars broke
out. During the war between Napoleonic France and Europe in the late eighteenth and early nineteenth centuries, for example, the French government
stopped honoring bank notes promising gold.

A second round of impetus to international trade, however, came from the
New World—specifically from California—with the discovery of significant
gold deposits. Australia and its gold mines joined California soon after, and
enough precious metal to facilitate trade was pumped into the global market.
Because gold backed all paper money in the world—for instance, one U.S.
dollar was equivalent to 23.22 grains of pure gold—there was, in fact, a single
global currency. It is not surprising, then, that the years leading up to World
War I, during which the gold standard ended, are considered the "golden" age
of globalization in more than one sense. The outbreak of World War I saw governments suspending payment in gold, while hostilities across Europe and in
the Atlantic Ocean disrupted trade. The gold standard returned briefly in the
1920s, only to be discarded in the Great Depression years following the stock
market crash of 1929. By then, the world had become so interconnected with
trade and financial links that the misery that began on Wall Street quickly
spread to all of America's economic partners.

When the world later emerged from the horrors of World War II in 1945, a
new economic order was taking root. Resurgent America's dollar, pegged to
gold, became the new global currency. World trade was now denominated in
U.S. dollars, with all countries linking their currencies to the dollar. The credit

card, invented in the 1920s to encourage customers with accounts to shop, fill their cars at gas stations, and check into hotels without cash in hand, got a fresh lease on life. The booming American economy certainly encouraged this easy consumerism. The idea of a universal card that could be used for all purchases dawned on banker Frank X. McNamara in a moment of embarrassment during a business dinner at a trendy New York restaurant. When it came time to pay the bill, he realized he had forgotten his wallet. Entertaining business clients was one of the principal expenses for which one had to carry cash, so in 1950 McNamara launched the first universal credit card—the Diner's Club card—which was followed eight years later by American Express. The electronic network that emerged in the 1970s has since made transcontinental commerce a snap. Gold and silver have long since disappeared as currencies, but plastic cards bearing those same metallic colors have taken their place to lubricate global transactions.

FROM CLAY TABLET TO THE INTERNET

One major problem in buying and selling goods over long distances was the difficulty of communications. How could traders stay in touch with their trading partners and keep track of what is being bought and sold? In 5000 BCE the Sumerians, who lived in what is now Iraq, found a solution by inventing writing. A trader would use a small clay tablet and a cleft stick to write down the numbers of cattle being sold. The partner at the other end would break the clay container to read the tablet and verify the number of animals that had been delivered. Our Assyrian trader Pusu-ken communicated with his financier and his wife by using such clay tablets. Since then our ancestors have used papyrus, leather parchment, engraved bamboo, and paper to conduct business transactions. During the height of Mongol rule over China and Central Asia, postal stations were set up along the Silk Road to allow for the transcontinental delivery of information and business contracts. By the end of the twelfth century, Genghis Khan had set up a system of messenger posts extending from Europe to his capital of Ulaanbaatar, using homing pigeons as messengers. The trading diasporas such as the Jewish traders in Cairo or on India's Malabar Coast used their goods carriers to carry mail, remaining copies of which have been found in the Geniza in Cairo. In the eighteenth century, the French had developed a visual signaling system across long distances, using tall towers and movable arms.

From Roman times to Genghis Khan and Napoleon Bonaparte, however, long-distance messaging was generally for the exclusive use of the sovereign—

for maintaining control over far-flung territories and for conducting military operations. For nearly seven thousand years until the eventual invention of the telegraph, business information traveled only as fast as the speediest available transport could carry passengers and goods. Isaac Ergas, our eighteenth-century coral and diamond trader in Livorno, wrote numerous letters to his business partners in Lisbon, London, and Goa but had to wait a year or more to find out what price his coral shipments had fetched in those markets.

All that waiting ended in 1844 with the completion of the first telegraph line (*telegraph* literally means "writing over distance"). In his first test message over a wire from Baltimore to Washington, DC, painter-turned-inventor Samuel Morse aptly wrote, "What hath God wrought?" The small contraption of an electromagnet and copper wire and the messaging through dots and dashes of Morse code ushered in an information revolution that continues to bring the world ever closer together. "Since the discovery of Columbus," the *Times* of London wrote, "nothing has been done in any degree comparable to the vast enlargement which has thus been given to the sphere of human activity [by the telegraph]."[81] A telegraphic cable, wrote the brother of Atlantic cable pioneer Cyrus Field, "is a living, fleshy bond between severed portions of the human family."[82]

Like so many other inventions, the telegraph was quickly deployed in the service of commerce. European entrepreneur Paul Julius von Reuter was already operating a news operation for businessmen in the 1840s, disseminating closing stock prices collated from information flown in by homing pigeons from different cities.[83] Once the commercial telegraph became available, the vast majority of cables sent pertained to business, especially stock and commodity prices. For the first time, commodities prices—from minerals to corn and cotton—were available in real time. Information, combined with easy transportation via trains and steamships, enabled the emergence of a truly global market. The Chicago Board of Trade was founded as the wire reached the city in 1848. In 1867, a further boost in trade information took place with the invention of the stock ticker. A telegraph operator in New York, E. A. Callahan, devised a telegraph machine that automatically recorded changing stock prices on a continuous strip of paper. Five years later, the Western Union cable company had begun a system of telegraphic money orders, bringing consumers and traders even closer.

Steamships, which had been used primarily to ferry passengers between the United States and Europe, now had a different task. In what science fiction writer Arthur C. Clarke described as the Victorian equivalent of the Apollo space project, huge rolls of copper wire sheathed in water-resistant gutta-percha were laid across the Atlantic Ocean floor.[84] Gutta-percha rubber came from the British colony of Malaya. The introduction of the trans-Atlantic cable in 1866 accelerated business deals and sharply drove down prices. The would-be arbitrageurs in these markets previously had to place orders based on ten-day-old information that had arrived by steamboat, and their orders took another ten days to be executed. Now armed with real-time prices, transatlantic traders could execute buy-and-sell orders in a day. "The result," says Kevin O'Rourke, "was an immediate 69 per cent decline in mean absolute price differentials for identical assets between the two cities."[85] Telegraphic links soon extended across the Middle East to India, and to the far corners of Asia. In 1870, the British Indian Submarine Telegraph Company installed the first telegraph link between London and Bombay. Within a year, the same line extended to far-off Hong Kong. By the time World War I broke out, nine lines connected Europe to the Far East, some of which were disabled as they ran through hostile territory.

The telecommunications and transportation revolutions would give trading a huge boost as the traditional tariff barriers began coming down. With the repeal of the British Corn Law in 1846 and the Navigation Acts in 1849 that restricted foreign shipping, an age of free trade was ushered in that lasted until the 1870s. In 1860 Britain signed treaties for freer trade with France and other European countries, and because they had "most-favored nation" clauses all countries could benefit from bilateral liberalization. However, facing competition from American grain producers, Europe began to raise tariff barriers. Trade protectionism grew steadily until World War I and the Great Depression ended nineteenth-century globalization.

MELAKA TO MEMPHIS

The telegraphic revolution was followed in 1876 by Alexander Graham Bell's funnel-like device called the telephone—literally "sound over distance." Unlike the telegraph, however, undersea telephone lines would not be laid for another eighty years. Radio telephones were available to call London from New York, but a three-minute call would have cost $458 in today's money.

The American Telephone and Telegraph Company (AT&T) set up the first transatlantic telephone system in 1956; a transpacific cable to Japan and Hong Kong followed a year later. In 1989, another transatlantic cable was laid to connect North America with South Africa—linking the New World to the continent from which humans began their journey fifty thousand years earlier. Technological advances notwithstanding, the number of people who could telephone between New York and London at any given moment in 1983 was only 4,200. A member of this select group first had to book a call and then wait for hours to get a connection, for which a hefty price was charged. Later, trade speeded up with the introduction of the fax machine by Xerox in 1966. The Magnafax Telecopier weighed in at a hefty thirty-seven pounds and could transmit one page in about six minutes. From invoices to designs, all kinds of text communications could now be sent across the globe in minutes to expedite business deals and production processes. Now a fashion designer on New York's Madison Avenue could sketch a dress and send product specifications to the manager of a garment factory in Shenzhen, China, in real time. Also in 1966, an American consortium developed ASCII (American Standard Code for Information Interchange) code, immediately adopted all over the world and enabling the transmission of texts and numbers over phone lines at lightning speed.

The electronic revolution swept the world. In the mid-1960s a Yale undergraduate named Fred Smith wrote a paper on how the power of the computer could be harnessed to deliver packages overnight. The germ of Smith's idea took shape in 1970 when he started a company he named Federal Express. Using computerized tracking of parcels and a small fleet of jets, the company began serving American cities. On its first night, it delivered just 186 packages. The company now operates all over the world, delivering an average of three million packages a day—everything from the tiny iPod that I ordered to automobile engines and even human organs for transplant.

The sprawling FedEx (that's how they list themselves in the phone book and in their logo) hub in Memphis, Tennessee, is like a modern-day version of Melaka, a port for transshipping goods from all over the world. In fifteenth-century Melaka, as we have seen, traders carrying different commodities spent months buying and bartering before making the journey home on the return monsoon. The sultan provided the elephants to carry sacks of spices and other commodities from the individual trader's warehouse to the dock. In modern-day Melaka it was different. On one night at the FedEx hub in Memphis, I watched thousands of packages from all over the world whizzing by on conveyor belts before being directed by robotic arms to their destination containers. The witching hour is 2:07 AM. Every night at this time, a silence descends upon the cavernous hall at the center of the FedEx hub. By this time each day, the three million packages have been sorted, registered, processed, and readied for loading onto 150 waiting aircraft. Each plane in this airborne armada of FedEx jets then roars down the runway and melts into the Tennessee night sky.

That evening in Memphis I watched robotic bar code scanners at work sorting millions of packages to their destination. Each package bore a seemingly insignificant rectangle of black vertical lines—the outcome of a modest new technology, the bar code, or Universal Product Code, that made a quiet debut in U.S. grocery stores on 26 June 1974. Today, more than five million bar-coded products are scanned and sold all over the world.[86] Sensors housed in store shelves can now read the bar codes on boxes of shoes, shirts, or shampoo, and automatically alert suppliers when stocks run low, allowing replenishments to arrive quickly without the need for costly inventories.

The most dramatic transformation in trade since the birth of the telegraph came with the electronics revolution—particularly the personal computer and the World Wide Web. In 1976, a brilliant twenty-one-year-old college dropout named Steve Jobs who dreamed of becoming a millionaire assembled the first personal computer from a kit. A year later Apple Computer was founded, launching the PC (Personal Computer) revolution. In the 1980s, IBM (International Business Machines) picked up the flag, turning what once was an electronic toy for hobbyists into a powerful tool of productivity for individuals. By the 1990s the Internet emerged to link the PCs worldwide, ushering in the closest connections between human communities since before the ancestors left Africa and dispersed.

The method of recording business transactions has evolved from Sumerian clay tablets to tablet PCs by way of quill and parchment paper, typewriters and computer keyboards. From word processing, spreadsheet, and database management to myriad other software, packages were developed that simplified and accelerated all aspects of business. The ever-increasing processing power of the personal computer and its steadily falling price—following closely on the heels of financial deregulation in the mid-1980s—provided an unprecedented momentum to global business. Millions of computers around the world could now be connected through telephone networks. But how would they speak to one another? British physicist Tim Berners-Lee came up with the solution. Berners-Lee had taken a consulting job at the renowned European particle physics laboratory CERN, and he wrote a program in order to remember the connections among various people, computers, and projects at his lab. He remembers wondering:

> *Suppose all the information stored on computers everywhere were linked,* I thought. *Suppose I could program my computer to create a space in which anything could be linked to anything.* All the bits of information in every computer at CERN, and on the planet, would be available to me and to anyone else. There would be a single, global information space.

Once a bit of information in that space was labeled with an address, I could tell my computer to get it. By being able to reference anything with equal ease, a computer could represent associations between things that might seem unrelated but somehow did, in fact, share a relationship. A web of information would form.[87]

The solution he came up with to link everything was a hypertext markup language (HTML) that all the computers programmed in different languages could understand and a browser that could seamlessly read, write, and transfer text, image, and sound from computers located in different places. Ten years after he had begun toying with the notion of connecting everything, Berners-Lee wrote a client program—a point-and-click browser-editor—and called it the World Wide Web. The rest is history. Other scientists invented a way of sending electronic mail from one computer to another. By 2006, close to a billion people—a sixth of the world's population—were connected to the Internet. In 2001 Jobs, by then a multimillionaire, hit the headlines again with the launch of a pocket-size music player, the iPod. It took the consumer world by storm, selling a staggering 32 billion machines in 2005. The downloading of music online by iPod users all over the world enabled them to enjoy millions of songs they would otherwise not have known about, much less heard. My order of an iPod for my son also meant jobs for factory workers in China, Japan, South Korea, and Malaysia, to name a few. They produced the components that went into the guts of the machine.

NEW MONSOON WIND

The rise of the Internet came hand in hand with fiber-optic communication. The laser—a narrow, unidirectional beam of light—and the success in manufacturing fiber-optic cable that could carry information through pulses of light revolutionized communication. Thin strands of fiberglass that allowed laser beams to carry sound and images at, well, the speed of light to far corners of the globe ushered in a new era of affordable, instantaneous communication. While mid-nineteenth-century telegraph operators could transmit perhaps four or five dots and dashes of Samuel Morse's code per second, fast processors and fiber-optic cable in the late twentieth century could communicate at speeds of up to 1 gigabit, or 1,000,000,000 separate 1s and 0s, every second. The contents of the entire *Encyclopaedia Britannica* could be transmitted in the blink of an eye.

After the first transatlantic fiber-optic cable was laid in 1988, some 37,800 simultaneous calls could be made. New cables subsequently laid in the mid-1990s were capable of carrying more traffic than the entire previous network of submarine cables combined.[88] In 1996, the number of simultaneous calls that could be made between Europe and North America was 1.3 million, and to Asia, nearly a million. Add to that the new capacity opened up by more than 150 communication satellites launched since the mid-1960s, and you have the ability of connecting to another million callers worldwide.

Businesses wasted no time in seizing upon these new opportunities. The Chicago Stock Exchange started to allow after-hours trading in 1999, giving birth to the twenty-four-hour marketplace.[89] Sitting at a computer terminal linked by telephone or high-speed cable, you can buy and sell stocks and bonds from anywhere in the world. Adding foreign exchange to the existing trade in commodities, the world saw a sevenfold rise in currency trading between 1983 and 1992, up to $160 billion.[90] Over the next decade, riding on the high-speed network, forex trading doubled to a trillion dollars a day—a sum that can be measured in stacks of hundred dollar bills 120 miles high, dwarfing Mount Everest.[91]

The rise of the Internet helped spawn a new type of trader like N. R. Narayana Murthy, the cofounder of India's leading software company, Infosys Technologies. Diminutive, bespectacled Murthy was a brilliant software engineer who came from a poor family. Frustrated at writing routine code in his first job out of college, Murthy and six programmer friends created Infosys in 1981. "We were huddled together in a small room in Bombay," he reminisced, "in the hope of creating a brighter future for ourselves, for the Indian society and, perhaps, we dreamed, even for the world."[92] The company would sell its service to clients by writing customized software programs. Facing bureaucratic hurdles and a lack of computer connectivity in India of the 1980s, Murthy developed a "body-shopping" model. He and his colleagues would travel to the sites of foreign clients, write the codes, and return home with cash.

Murthy is one of many entrepreneurs who are products as well as promoters of globalization. Murthy told me that although he faced great resistance from bureaucrats and material hurdles such as the lack of infrastructure, he recognized the paradigm shift brought about by globalization. High-speed connections could eliminate the need for body-shopping, and services could be provided without leaving one's computer terminal. He saw globalization, he says, "as sourcing capital from where it is cheapest, sourcing talent from where it is best available, producing where it is most cost effective and selling where the markets are without being constrained by national boundaries." India's liberal economic reform in the 1990s opened up its telecommunication sector and removed those constraints while the cost of communications fell. Not unlike the first-century discovery of the monsoon winds that increasingly brought traders to India's spice coast, the computer and communications revolution opened the way to the outsourcing of services and an electronic-based model of global delivery. The thicket of fiber-optic cables laid along ocean beds during the dot-com boom of the late 1990s and the subsequent bust led to plummeting costs. Indian and Singaporean firms were among the biggest beneficiaries of the fire sale by bankrupt fiber-optic network owners. As a result, the Asian companies were able to acquire the virtually brand-new optical information highways at discounts of 95 percent or more.[93] India's telecom giant VSNL (Videsh Sanchar Nigam, Ltd.) acquired the old AT&T undersea fiber-optic cable network from bankrupt Tyco for just $130 million. It had cost the original owners $3 billion to develop.[94]

During a visit to the sprawling Infosys campus in Bangalore, I saw firsthand what this new monsoon wind of fiber optics meant for business. It was a long-distance trade, offering service where distance itself was irrelevant. In a cavernous hall capable of seating two hundred, a huge, wall-size TV screen brought together clients and engineers face-to-face live from different corners of the world to discuss the various products Infosys can deliver. In another air-conditioned hall across the leafy campus, scores of programmers sat at computer terminals, linked to their clients' mainframes in Frankfurt, London, and New York. They were fine-tuning multimillion-dollar software applications that they had developed for their foreign clients continents away. Major Fortune 500 global corporations are now clients, and a company that was founded in 1981 with $250 capital had in early 2006 market capitalization of about $22 billion.

The fiber-optic cable and inexpensive voice-over Internet telephony (VOIP) have stimulated new entrepreneurs in countries like Senegal and established a whole new connection between Europe and the African continent. Senegal, which until recently exported mainly peanuts, now exports service by its educated young people over the Internet. At the blue-carpeted office of the Premium Contact Center International (PCCI) call center in Dakar, young men and women sit before banks of glowing computer screens, murmuring softly into the telephones. The French callers at the other end of the line don't realize that their calls are being answered twenty-five hundred miles away on another continent. Working for French companies, the Senegalese staff is selling washing machines, doing customer surveys, and answering queries about the Internet. "We launched our operation by offering a price 20 to 40 percent cheaper than in France," says Abdoulaye Sarre, the soft-spoken CEO of the company in his large air-conditioned office. The call center service offers French customers savings and the Senegalese staff a whole new career in client counseling with higher than average salaries.

In the nearly five thousand years since humans began to exchange obsidian and clothes, the number of traders and the varieties of goods they ship across borders have grown—spectacularly. From Assyrian Pusu-ken to Jewish Abraham Yiju and from Tomé Pires to Jean de la Roque and from Steve Jobs to Narayana Murthy, merchants have continuously expanded their wares, reached wider markets, and integrated the world. The urge for profit has led them to seek faster and higher capacity forms of transportation and rapid, accurate means of payment. The rise of personal computers with ever-accelerating processing power, combined with the warp speed of fiber-optic telecommunications, effectively eliminated distance in one fell swoop, laying the foundation for a new type of business and industry in which geography was no longer a factor. Thousands of e-commerce sites—from Amazon to Travelocity—mushroomed to cater to customers who preferred to shop for books, electronics, and even holiday packages from the comfort of their own homes and offices. A new derivation of a quintessentially "old" business was born in 1995 with eBay, the global Internet flea market. Like their bazaar merchant ancestors, ordinary people could now sell their used appliances, vintage movie posters, and trinkets to a globally interlinked community of potential highest bidders. The introduction of the online payment system PayPal as an intermediary between bank and the vendor meant that anyone, anywhere in the world with a bank or credit card account could make a bid for an old book or a camera that you were ready to discard.

The ease with which I could buy the iPod—assembled from components of many countries and delivered by a Federal Express courier to my home in New Haven in less than forty-eight hours—is but a small example of the global marketplace that has evolved over thousands of years. Most of the manufactured goods that we buy today are, as Martin Kenney puts it, "the end result of an elaborately choreographed transnational odyssey."[95] Meanwhile, the emergence of a seamless international payment and clearing system—which allowed me to pay for the iPod by personal credit card—has dismantled an obstacle that had hampered traders from the Roman times to the British and Dutch East India Companies. When it came time to transport my newly purchased commodity, there was no need to go out in search of a camel driver or the owner of a Dutch fluyt or wait for the monsoon wind. I needed none of those things to obtain a product manufactured thousands of miles away because I had a personal computer, an Internet connection, a credit card, and a home address for free delivery by a white FedEx van.

VOYAGE
de
ABIE HEUREUSE.

Chapter 3 The World Inside

Whatever we understand and enjoy in human products instantly becomes ours, wherever they might have their origin.
—*Rabindranath Tagore, letter to C. F. Andrews, 13 March 1921*

Since the birth of Seattle some 150 years ago, the Emerald City had never witnessed violence of the kind that descended upon its streets in November 1999. Ever since the city along the blue waters of the Pacific was chosen to host the first summit of the World Trade Organization, the organizers knew there might be trouble. Protesters of all stripes from all over the world—from trade union members to students, agriculturalists to environmentalists—had been planning to gather in Seattle to take a stand against globalization. They wanted to make it clear to the Clinton administration, the proud host of the event, that the globalization it was promoting through free trade was hurting people. The relentless pressure to open markets in developing countries was helping rich multinationals but harming everybody and

French coffee traders in Mocha, Yemen, 1710. Illustration from Jean de la Roque, *Voyage de l'Arabie heureuse* (Amsterdam: Steenhower, 1716)

everything else. Workers in developed countries were losing jobs that ended up on sweatshop floors in countries like China and Indonesia. In the drive for corporate profit the rain forests of the world were disappearing, and companies trawling the oceans for ever-larger catches were threatening sea turtles with extinction. What better place to show the protesters' anger than Seattle, the home of America's most powerful globalizing corporations—Boeing, Microsoft, and Starbucks?

Seattle authorities and federal officials knew that the protesters were planning a fifty-thousand-strong "mobilization against globalization" to "Shut Down Sea-Town." They had gathered thousands of law enforcement agents to hold the demonstrators back from the conference hall where world leaders and WTO officials would meet. But they had not foreseen what would hit them on the evening before the summit was to begin.

One of the memorable scenes of mayhem that gripped the city and forced the cancellation of the meeting played out not at the entrance of the Washington State Convention and Trade Center, which was cleared by Darth Vader–like policemen with teargas guns and pepper spray, but in the city's business district. As millions of television viewers saw in the little drama on their screens, a young man picked up a trash can and hurled it against the glass door of a Starbucks coffee shop. An elderly woman passerby scolded the young man, saying, "Stop it. You're making fools of our country and our city." "It's self-defense," the protester shouted back. "What are you defending yourself against? The window?" the woman exclaimed in amazement.[1]

The vandalism shown on prime-time national television on the day Seattle became a war zone was an embarrassment for thousands of serious critics of globalization. But the massive protests that led to the cancellation of the WTO meeting nevertheless put the world on notice about what the demonstrators saw as the unacceptable inequity of globalization. Organizations like Global Exchange that took part in the Seattle protest had been urging Starbucks and other major coffee wholesalers to purchase coffee from small producers at a fair-trade price without success. The gap between the suggested fair-trade price of $1.50 a pound and the 50 cents companies actually pay for a pound of coffee beans, they argued, results in an obscene profit for big companies and spells penury for small producers.

The WTO Seattle summit is remembered for the destruction of Starbucks franchises and shops of other multinational companies, but the protesters who took part in the demonstrations included a wide range of workers, farmers, students, and professionals with a variety of grievances. There were American workers—from steel mills to textile factories—who protested "dumping" by low-cost producers and environmental and human rights organizations who opposed polluting practices and the exploitation of foreign workers like coffee growers in Asia and Latin America.

The protest in Seattle, in fact, underlines the double-edged nature of globalization. Centuries of long-distance trade involving basic commodities have literally woven the world closer together. Cotton grown in one place was turned into clothing in another; backbreaking labor by coffee pickers in Kenya produced hefty profits for coffee retailers in New York and London. Basic human sympathy for poorly paid workers and small local producers bound the world even more closely. People felt for the unfortunate growers of coffee in distant lands. They were also angered by companies who were "stealing" American jobs to send them to sweatshops in the developing world. The U.S. textile industry's largest labor union, UNITE, was in Seattle in full force to voice its protest against WTO for encouraging the overseas flow. Of course, the communications revolution that allowed the dramatic images of rioting in Seattle to be projected on millions of screens worldwide created a global awareness about the antiglobalization movement that was itself a product of globalization. In this chapter we will see how everyday commodities like the clothes we wear, the coffee we drink, and the ubiquitous microchip that powers the Information Age all have grown out of the interconnectedness brought about by millennia of trade contacts, military conquests, and explorations of the physical world. As cotton, coffee, and microchips have spread, the world's interdependence and interconnectedness have grown. The protests in Seattle over the loss of American cotton textile jobs were in many ways a continuation of the anger and despair felt by weavers in Britain who attacked the East India Company's office in the seventeenth century and the silent deaths of Indian weavers deprived of their livelihood by the Industrial Revolution and British tariffs a century later. As coffee spread from its original home in the Horn of Africa, it too aroused similar passions among both the drinkers and the denouncers of the dark brew—from Islamic ulemas, Christian priests, sultans, and even housewives fed up with absent husbands engrossed in coffeehouses. Of course, the reasons for their various angers were different from those of the vandals attacking Starbucks cafés in Seattle. But the sacking of coffee shops in Istanbul in the sixteenth century by the Ottoman security force did not enjoy the worldwide publicity accorded to the Seattle protests via satellite television and the Internet. The tiny sliver of silicon in all electronic gadgets—the microchip—is the culprit that helped to turn the antiglobalization protests into a worldwide phenomenon.

But the microchip itself is a product of millennia of exploration and global interaction. Invented by two Americans, the microchip is in fact "made everywhere." As we shall see, everyday commodities like cotton, coffee, and the microchip all carry within them the story of how agents of globalization brought about the world's interconnectedness. To paraphrase the slogan that Intel slaps on its ubiquitous logo—"Intel Inside"—cotton, coffee, and microchips all have the World Inside.

COTTON MORE LIQUID THAN MONEY

Our ancestors tried animal hide and hair, tree bark, woven grass, and various vegetable fibers to cover themselves, but in the end cotton won out. Botanists say that the genus *Gossypium*—which now literally provides the fabric of our lives, from shirts to shoelaces—developed independently in both the Old and the New World. This species, however, was not known outside North America until Columbus's voyages. It has since spread around the world and now constitutes 90 percent of cotton production. Yet for the first four thousand years of human history in the Old World, cotton was a valuable commodity associated mainly with India and Egypt.

Wild cotton (the word derives from the Arabic *qoton*) was domesticated in the Indus River Valley in the Indian subcontinent sometime between 2300 and 1760 BCE. Indian skill in weaving cotton cloth and dyeing fabric with fast color was quickly discovered by neighbors who began sending boats and camel caravans to procure the cloth in exchange for gold, silver, and precious stones. With the discovery of the monsoon wind in the first century CE, oceangoing vessels joined the existing caravan trading with India.

Although a variety of cotton was known in China in the first century BCE, the traditional textile industry in China serving mass demand was based on hemp fiber. Not until the tenth century CE did cotton, introduced from India through Southeast Asia, become an important Chinese cash crop.[2] Large-scale cotton cloth production began in China in the fourteenth to fifteenth centuries, and from the Yangtze Basin, cotton culture spread to Korea and Japan.[3] However, from the beginning silk used by the royal elite remained China's principal export. Indians, in contrast, developed technologies like vegetable dyes with fast color and print designs with wood blocks to produce exportable cotton fabrics. They also mastered the art of ginning the cotton (cleaning the seeds from the fibers), spinning the fibers into thread, and weaving cloth on handlooms made of bamboo and wood. Once the fiber was introduced and the basic technology spread, however, others joined in developing it further. There are indications that the Indian spinning wheel made popular by Mahatma Gandhi as the symbol of India's self-reliance during the anticolonial struggle may have been introduced from Persia in the thirteenth century. *Charkha,* the Hindi word for the spinning wheel, is of Persian origin.[4]

Along with domesticated cotton, weaving technology also spread from India. Mark Elvin, who studies the history of Chinese technology, writes that in China "the introduction of cotton brought with it, perhaps from India, the cotton gin, while a spinning wheel with multiple spindles and driven by foot treadle was soon invented."[5] By the time of the Song dynasty (960–1279) cotton weaving was sufficiently developed for Chinese boats to use canvas sails.[6] By the seventeenth and eighteenth centuries cotton weaving had emerged as the largest industry in China. Thousands of peasant households bought raw cotton daily from the market to spin or weave it for supplementary cash—often in order to pay tax.

As early as the year 600, cotton was introduced from India to Iraq, and from there it spread to Syria, Cyprus, Sicily, Tunisia, Morocco, Spain, and eventually Egypt.[7] By the tenth century Arabs had taken cotton cultivation further west to Portugal. However, despite the extensive spread of cotton in the first millennium, cloth was woven mostly for home consumption and for supplementary cash income. High-quality cotton cloth was still imported. During the holy Islamic pilgrimage of hajj the great annual cloth market was held in Jidda and Mecca, and the bulk of the textile sold there continued to come from Egypt and India.[8] Until the Industrial Revolution, Indian-made textiles remained the biggest major manufacturing export in the world. Cotton textile was the main engine behind India's accounting for nearly 25 percent of the world's gross domestic product in 1700. The crown has since passed to China. But textile import remained a near-monopoly for India until the twentieth century, when China acquired textile mills that could produce large volumes of cloth with its abundant labor.

Although India's cotton textiles had been a coveted item of trade in the Red Sea, Arabian Sea, and Indian Ocean trade since Roman times, Europeans discovered Indian cotton only after Vasco da Gama blazed the trail for shipping trade with Asia in 1498. Even then, the Portuguese were more interested in intricately embroidered cotton quilts from Bengal than in cloth for items of clothing. Among the gifts King Henry of Portugal sent to the sultan of Morocco were "embroidered bedspreads of Bengal."[9] But soon the Dutch and the British who arrived in Asia to buy spices realized that the currency needed to make those purchases was Indian cotton textile. The Dutch also exported Indian checkered and indigo-dyed blue fabrics to Africa to buy slaves to be dispatched to the New World. The Indian blue cotton textile used to clothe the slaves came to be known as the "cloth of sorrow."[10]

Europeans, who for centuries had been clad entirely in linen and wool (except for the rich, who wore silk), at last discovered cotton. Light, washable chintz with bright and fast color became a rage. Indian cotton manufacturing boomed, even though its spinning and weaving technology had remained essentially the same for centuries. It boomed simply because more and more workers were pressed into growing cotton and producing cloth. Specializations did develop, but in only the variety of fabrics and designs. In Gujarat and the Coromandel Coast entire villages specialized in textile production. Workers were given material or cash advances to supply specified quantities of piece goods in a stipulated time. Cotton spun on single spinning wheels at village homes was carried on caravans of bullock carts to workshops housing hundreds of handlooms in coastal towns and ports, from where finished textiles were exported to Europe. Apart from the fine quality of the cloth, the biggest attraction of Indian fabric was its vibrant color and designs. Indians had mastered the art of creating bright vegetable dyes that did not fade with washing. Seeing the burgeoning demand, Indian producers were quick to adapt to European and Asian tastes for design and color.[11] Foreign buyers from Indonesia to Nigeria would supply designs with local motifs and patterns that traders would take back to the Indian village weavers for delivery in the following season.[12]

SHUN THE THREAD OF INFIDELS

The protocapitalist production system developed in India—which was very similar to the "putting out" system developed in Europe (in which merchant clothiers engaged farmers to process and weave wool they owned)—could be scaled up to meet growing demand. So high was the demand for Indian textiles that Britain had a constant trade deficit, not unlike what the Roman historian Pliny complained about some seventeen hundred years earlier.[13] Between 1710 and 1759 the East India Company imported goods, mostly cotton, worth nine million pounds and exported twenty-six million pounds' worth of bullion.[14] Gemelli Careri, an Italian traveler who visited India in 1695, claimed that all the gold and silver that circulated in the world eventually found its resting place in the Mogul Empire. Of the estimated seventeen thousand tons of silver taken out of the New World in the sixteenth century, some six thousand tons ended up in India to pay for European imports.[15] At the peak of this trade, in the early eighteenth century, India annually exported thirty million yards of fine and coarse textiles to the world.[16] Indian domination of textile alarmed Britain's silk and wool weavers. In Roman times moral reasons (such as horror at flimsy, lascivious cloths worn by ladies) had been invoked to ban the import of silk. Centuries later, some Britons found religious piety to be a good reason for banning imports of cotton. In *England Treasure by Forraign Trade* (1664), Thomas Mun exhorted pious Christians not to wear cotton fabrics manufactured by infidels.[17] Protests and workers' riots eventually led Britain to impose the Calico Act of 1701, a partial ban on the import and wearing of Indian textiles. Protests continued, however. One center of agitation against the scourge of Indian cotton fabrics was Spitalfields, a town where many Huguenots, who had earlier fled persecution of Protestants in France, had set up looms to weave silk. As one historical account puts it:

> The growing fashion for wearing Indian calicoes and printed linen was the cause of serious disturbances in 1719. On 13 June a mob of about 4,000 Spitalfields weavers paraded the streets of the City attacking all females whom they could find wearing Indian calicoes or linens, and sousing them with ink, aqua fortis, and other fluids. The Lord Mayor obtained the assistance of the Trained Bands to suppress the rioters, two of whom were secured by the Horse Grenadiers and lodged in the Marshalsea Prison. As soon as the Guards left, the mob re-assembled, the weavers tearing all the calico gowns they could meet with.[18]

In 1721 Britain passed a second Calico Act banning cotton textiles of all kinds, but this only fired up smuggling. The obvious answer to the popularity of Indian calico was to begin producing the same fabric locally, but that turned out to be problematic. Since European wages were six times higher than Indian wages, the European-made cloth could not compete with Indian imports. The search for technology to reduce the need for labor led to a series of inventions and finally to the opening of a water-powered cotton spinning mill in Cromford in 1771. The Industrial Revolution was launched. The town of Lancashire emerged as the symbol of the new industrial age with its "dark satanic mills," and its marketing capital, Manchester, became "the first global industrial city—the 'Cottonopolis'—of an industrial system whose tentacles spread across the globe."[19] Although many workers were still needed to work with the machines, the speed and volume of production eliminated the cheap labor advantage so far enjoyed by India. In just fourteen years (1814–28) India's cotton piece goods exports to Britain dropped by two-thirds, and mass-produced

British textile exports to India, backed by tariff policy, rose more than five times.[20] For the first time in its history India was importing what the mass of its citizenry wore. Tens of thousands of Indian villagers engaged in textile businesses lost their livelihood. As the governor-general of India William Bentinck wrote in a confidential report in 1835, "The misery [of the weavers] hardly finds a parallel in the history of commerce. The bones of the cotton-weavers are bleaching the plains of India."[21]

KING COTTON AND HIS SLAVES

The Industrial Revolution had the opposite effect on American cotton farmers, who simply could not supply enough cotton for British mills. The painstakingly slow process of manually removing seeds from the raw fiber constrained the quantity of cotton that could be exported. A chance invention by a Yale graduate on holiday at a Georgia cotton plantation during the spring of 1793 removed that obstacle. Eli Whitney's hand-operated cotton gin meant that one laborer could produce fifty pounds of cleaned cotton a day. The accelerated process gave a dramatic tenfold boost to American cotton export in the year after Whitney's invention. In the following two decades cotton export grew from 1.6 million pounds to 35 million pounds. Rising demand for cotton spurred by the cotton gin made cotton the king. Cotton cultivation expanded virtually to the exclusion of other crops. And so grew the African slave population, especially as women were now preferred for their supposed nimbleness in plucking cotton. Between 1800 and 1810 the number of slaves in the United States increased by a third, and then by another third in the next decade. The changing gender composition had the effect of making the American slave population the largest in the hemisphere.[22] When, decades later, calls to abolish slavery intensified, a staunch supporter, Senator James H. Hammond, famously declared before the U.S. Senate on 4 March 1858: "You dare not make war upon cotton! No power on earth dares make war upon it. Cotton is king."

The senator was wrong on one count: soon thereafter the American Civil War did end slavery. And yet the shortages caused by the war propelled King Cotton's march across the globe. Mill owners' search for alternative sources led directly to a renewed demand for cotton from India and to the introduction of American upland cotton in Egypt and Brazil. The American Civil War became a landmark in Egyptian history as during the war years 40 percent of Lower

Egypt's fertile land was converted to cotton. But when the Civil War ended, the windfall of the new growers soon turned into misery as cotton prices fell. In places like Brazil, natural calamity combined with the cotton crisis resulted, by some accounts, in the death of half a million people through starvation and disease. Although historians disagree as to how much the fall in world market prices affected cultivators, historian of cotton Sven Beckert notes that "at the very least, world market integration increased the economic uncertainty faced by people in remote corners of the world. Their incomes, and quite literally their survival, were newly linked to global price fluctuations over which they had little control."[23] The protesters in Seattle showed how the globalization of cotton was having a very different impact on America a century and half later: while American cotton farmers, fattened by government subsidies, stayed home, American textile mill workers were on the streets protesting the threat to their jobs from imports. There were no protesters from Mali to raise their voice against the export of heavily subsidized U.S. cotton.

Cotton cultivation today has moved beyond these traditional growers to become a major cash crop in African nations—where it was introduced by European colonial rulers. Cotton exports represent about 30 percent of export earnings for countries in West and Central Africa, where some ten million farmers depend on cotton for their livelihood. As we shall see, the threat to their livelihood from American cotton subsidies would later bring antiglobalization sentiment to a boil and scuttle trade talks. Before returning to the cotton growers, let us follow the story of how the cotton-powered Industrial Revolution connected the world.

The growth of American cotton also signaled a beginning of the decline of British textile hegemony. In the late eighteenth century, an apprentice at the Arkwright water mill named Samuel Slater bypassed a British prohibition against technology exports and memorized the technical details of the mill before sailing to America. In 1793 Slater built the first successful American cotton mill in Pawtucket, Rhode Island. The world's textile manufacturing crown soon passed to America, thanks to its abundant cotton supply, string of inventions, and superior management. After mechanization of the production of cloth came the mechanization of tailoring and garment manufacturing. In 1755 the British government issued the first patent for a needle to be used for mechanical sewing. It was not until a hundred years later that the first sewing machines were commercialized in the United States by entrepreneur Isaac Singer, using technology developed by Elias Howe, who had filed for a patent in 1846.

An earlier attempt to patent a sewing machine in France had run into trouble. The inventor, a French tailor, Barthélemy Thimonnier, was almost killed by an angry mob of fellow tailors who torched his garment factory out of fear of losing their jobs.[24] Thimonnier was left penniless after the arson, but his American counterparts fared better. Howe and Singer became millionaires. By the mid-nineteenth century the production of ready-made garments got its start with the sewing of uniforms for sailors.[25]

From the use of raw energy resources like waterpower and coal, the United States moved to more efficient processed energy—of the internal combustion engine and electricity. In consequence, tasks like spinning and weaving processes were speeded up. The technology of garment manufacturing, however, has remained fundamentally the same. The hand-cranked and foot-pedaled sewing machines have been replaced by electric-powered machines with multiple stitching capacities, but individual garments still have to be sewn manually. It is thus not surprising that garment manufacturing has emerged as one of the highest employing sectors of the modern economy. And it has offered opportunity for emerging economies to join in the worldwide supply chain in different parts of the operation, from spinning thread to stitching buttons. In 2000, China employed six million people in the textile and garment sector, followed by one and a half million in India and eight hundred thousand in the United States.[26]

In search of cheaper labor, the American textile industry has continually moved south—from New England to North Carolina to the Caribbean and eventually across the Pacific to the hungry emerging economies. Wages range from an hourly ten dollars in the United States to twenty cents in China and Vietnam. These low wages still opened the door out of grinding poverty in rural China or Thailand. But human rights and labor groups in the West and the demonstrators in Seattle charged that corporate-led globalization was stocking America's malls with produce from sweatshops.

THE SUPPLY CHAIN AND SWEATSHOPS

Since the 1960s, textile production and garment manufacturing jobs have indeed shifted increasingly to developing nations like China, India, Bangladesh, and Sri Lanka. Developing countries doubled their share of world clothes exports from 30 percent in the early 1970s to over 60 percent by the mid-1990s.[27] The MFA (Multi-Fiber Arrangement), a complex system of quotas given to nearly fifty countries, was developed in 1974 to protect the developed countries' garment sectors from the competition of low-wage countries. It had the effect of constraining traditionally big exporters and giving smaller countries an entry into the global market—an unintended spreading of global growth. By forcing garment suppliers to diversify their sourcing, the quota system helped create a larger and more complex global supply chain. A pioneer in the field of "dispersed manufacturing" is the Hong Kong-based apparel company Li and Fung. The yarn may be procured from South Korea, woven and dyed in Taiwan, then shipped to whichever country had the requisite quota—Sri Lanka, Cambodia, or the Philippines—for stitching clothes and fitting with zippers made by a Japanese company. The label on the finished trousers may read "Made in Cambodia," but the pants are truly a global product.[28] The quota system has also had the effect of parceling out earnings from textiles to many countries as the various tasks in the supply chain were distributed. By the end of 2004 some forty million people worldwide, mostly in developing countries, were involved in the $350 billion garment trade. Countries like Bangladesh, once renowned for producing the world's finest muslin, would have been left out of the world market. Thanks to the quota system, however, Bangladesh's exports of garments have risen from about 4 percent of total exports in 1983–84 to about 76 percent in 1999–2000. Its garment exports have generated employment for one and a half million workers, mostly women.

This is not to say that the MFA system did not have serious problems. The quota system—in which the label of origin became the key commodity—resulted in countless shenanigans by enterprising exporters. Given the value of the label "Made in the USA," a little island in the Pacific, American Samoa, became a hot spot for textile exporters like Daewoosa who brought in cheap labor to sew garments for J. C. Penney, Sears, and MV Sport. Stories of the physical abuse of workers, withholding of wages, and unhealthy housing and food came to light when some Vietnamese women workers escaped from the factory premises to tell their tale.[29] World Bank and IMF economists estimate that barriers to textiles and clothing trade have cost developing countries forty billion dollars in lost export revenues and deprived them of twenty-seven million jobs—or thirty-five jobs for every one saved in rich nations.

The end of the quota in January 2005, however, threatened protected developed-country workers as well as any small gains made by poor countries through "quota-hopping." China's huge textile production capacity had long outstripped its meager quota and led Chinese exporters to set up operations in countries with quotas. As the quota ended, hundreds of modern textile mills were rising in China to leverage its low wages, rising technical skill, and state-of-the-art transportation and communication infrastructure, raising the fear that it could gobble up as much as 50 percent of the U.S. market from its current estimated 10 to 15 percent.[30] India, which was long held back by quotas, could increase its share of world textile market from 4 percent in 2002 to 17 percent. Other countries feared that world importers' shifting to China would throw thousands of their workers out of employment. According to one dire projection, some thirty million jobs worldwide may be threatened.[31]

The end of the quota, though, promised lower prices for consumers who had been forced to pay higher prices for quota-limited imports. As a report in the *Financial Times* put it, "The annual cost to U.S. consumers has been put at $70 billion and has fallen hardest on poor families, which spend a relatively large share of income on clothing. Each job saved by quotas in the U.S. industry is estimated to have cost consumers an average of $170,000."[32] Perhaps American taxpayers would have been willing to pay that price to keep the remaining twenty-five thousand U.S. garment workers employed. In any case, it was not an argument that would carry any weight with the workers who went to Seattle to protest. Although the fallout from the end of the quota for poor countries was less severe than predicted, the surge in Chinese exports to the United States and Europe beginning in January 2005 brought a fresh howl of protest from local industry and labor. Using a safeguard provision of the WTO, both the United States and the European Union capped Chinese exports for three years. The Seattle protesters' cause received another reprieve, pausing the march of globalization. But if one is to believe a U.S. Department of Agriculture analyst's forecast, at the current rate of job loss in the textile and apparel sector, there would not be a textile industry in the United States by 2014.[33]

GAMBOLING GOATS

The demonstrators who trashed Starbucks stores in Seattle would have perhaps been gladdened by the news six years later that Ethiopia, the original home of coffee, had been spared the presence of the hated chain. Instead, a knock-off coffeehouse with Starbucks-inspired decor opened in Addis Ababa, with workers in Starbucks-like green aprons serving café latte at a fifth of Starbucks's regular international price.[34] The coffee shop is called Kaldi in memory of the legendary goatherd who is said to have discovered the power of caffeine in an unknown red bean. Starbucks, the much hated poster child of globalization, is in fact the latest in many incarnations of coffee as it has traveled the world beyond the hills of Ethiopia.

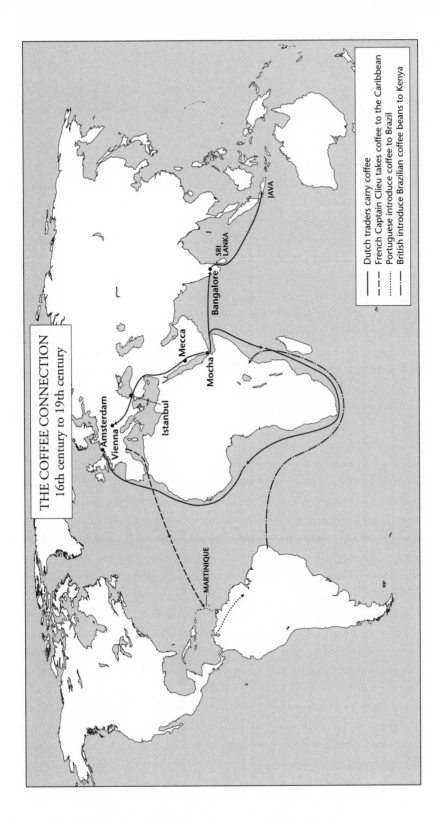

THE COFFEE CONNECTION
16th century to 19th century

Amsterdam
Vienna
Istanbul
Mecca
Mocha
Bangalore
SRI LANKA
JAVA
MARTINIQUE

Dutch traders carry coffee
French Captain Clieu takes coffee to the Caribbean
Portuguese introduce coffee to Brazil
British introduce Brazilian coffee beans to Kenya

Despite the name *Coffea arabica,* the coffee shrub originally grew wild in the Ethiopian hills. It gained fame when it was domesticated and planted in Yemen in the fifteenth century. According to the legend, though, once upon a time it was discovered by the goatherd Kaldi in the southwestern province of Kaffa. When Kaldi went to gather his flock of goats late one afternoon he found them in an unusually excited state, prancing around, butting heads, and not keen to return home. Tasting the red berries they had been consuming, he found out why. The berries gave a pleasurable tingling sensation from his tongue throughout his body.[35] Some scholars maintain that the name *coffee* comes from the name of the province—Kaffa—where coffee was found.[36] Where the goatherd found the beans is also disputed. According to the version of the goat story told by Heinrich Eduard Jacob in *Coffee: The Epic of a Commodity,* the discovery of the brew is related to Islam in Yemen. The imam of the Shehodet Monastery in Yemen undertook to investigate the strange behavior of goats that the goatherd reported. He brewed the roasted kernel of the strange berry that the goatherd said had "bewitched" the goats. "Within a few moments, the imam of Shehodet Monastery," Jacob writes, "was as if in a spell. He was in a state of intoxication differing from all other intoxication hitherto known to his people. The imam, being indeed a fervent Moslem, had had no experience of drunkenness. . . . Now, . . . though he had almost ceased to be aware of his body, his mind was unusually active, cheerful and alert. He was not merely thinking; his thoughts had become concretely visible." Soon the imam was serving the black, bitter drink to devout Sufis before their midnight prayer.[37] In his version of the story, Jean de la Roque, the French trader who voyaged to Yemen to buy coffee, describes the ceremony of drinking coffee that preceded the long night of prayer. "The coffee was contained in a vessel of red clay, and they [dervishes] received it very respectfully at the hands of their superior, who poured it out for them himself into the cups."[38]

Gratefully, they called it "k'hawah"—the invigorating drink.[39] The dark brew seems to have reminded the Sufis of wine, and hence the Arabic word for "wine" was applied to the drink. The Turks called it *qahveh,* and the word was eventually pronounced variously as *kauve* or *cauve,* from which evolved the French *café,* and the English *coffee.* Within less than six hundred years a prayer aid has been turned into a multibillion-dollar business employing twenty million families in fifty countries and giving flavored kicks to hundreds of millions: it is a summary of the story of globalization. Starbucks, founded in 1971, alone operated and licensed more than ten thousand coffee shops in more than thirty countries in 2006. On some American university campuses Starbucks stalls are set up next to the library to help students stay awake during their long toil, not unlike the dervishes in Yemen's Shehodet Monastery.

Whatever the precise date of the discovery, by the thirteenth century Arabian coffeehouses serving the drink, known as *kaveh kanes,* had become popular—even in Mecca. Perhaps because of its very name, "Islamic wine," coffee faced a challenge from the zealous young viceroy of Mecca, who shut down coffeehouses because of their evil effects on society. The coffee drinkers played music until late at night and even rioted when challenged to stop their activities. "It is recorded," Jacob wrote, "that many of the women forsook their husbands from jealousy of coffee, since he who sat awake enjoying the stimulation of the draught had no desire to lie down beside his wife."[40] But the sultan at Cairo, the viceroy's boss and a habitual coffee drinker, asked him to rescind the order. Coffee, after all, was favored by devout Muslims, since it "produced the necessary wakefulness for the nightly devotional exercises."[41] The news of the defeat suffered by the enemy of coffee in Mecca was carried by returning pilgrims to all the parts of the Islamic world.[42] An Islamic holy man was quoted as saying: "He who dies with some Kahwa (coffee) in his body enters not into hell-fire." Another saying told the faithful that "when taken with a righteous intention and devotion and genuine religious conviction, coffee-drinking leads to the enjoyment of hidden mysteries."[43]

Coffee drinking took hold in the Islamic world, and its success in the Ottoman Empire forever associated the drink in the European mind with the luxury and exoticism of the East. Although a stimulant, it had no socially negative effect like the wine that Islam outlawed. Coffee beans could be transported easily and kept fresh. Most important, coffee provided a focus for social gathering at all hours like nothing else. Yet the drink's name recalling wine and its association with Islam periodically made it fall foul of both Christian and Muslim religious authorities.

SATAN'S DELICIOUS DRINK

Coffee's global journey began with the Ottoman conquest of Yemen in the sixteenth century, which opened up the empire to this new drink. In 1554 a businessman from Aleppo teamed up with another from Damascus to open the first coffeehouse in Istanbul. The phenomenon caught fire. Soon gentlemen of leisure, men seeking distraction, and professors and poets flocked to the coffeehouses. They read, played backgammon, and listened to poetry but did not much frequent the mosque. Half-jokingly, they were called the *mekteb-i-irfan* (school of knowledge). As Ralph S. Hattox notes in his history of coffee, the coffeehouse not only served as entertainment but injected something entirely new into Muslim society. The coffeehouse gave everyone an opportunity "to get out of the house" at all hours and created new social habits that had not been possible before.[44] It was a habit that has spread to many societies in the world after conquering Europe.

The fascination with this bitter drink in Italy proved a cause for concern among pious Christians. In 1592 Pope Clement VIII was called on to resolve a dispute among clergy over the growing addiction to this "Islamic wine" among Christians. Before giving his verdict the pope took a sip and exclaimed: "Why, this Satan's drink is so delicious that it would be a pity to let the infidels have exclusive use of it. We shall cheat Satan by baptizing it."[45] Since wine and beer happened to be the most common—and safe—beverages at the time in Europe, coffee's utility in sobering people up was not insignificant either. Despite the pope's approval, though, in the seventeenth century the Ethiopian Church prohibited Christians from drinking coffee or smoking tobacco (which had been introduced from the New World) because they were associated with Muslims and pagans.[46] But coffee drinking took off in Europe.

Although coffee withstood the early challenge from Islamic clerics in Cairo, it was never completely out of the woods. Periodically, zealous ulemas would rail against the evil drink that kept men engaged in pleasure and away from prayer. Calling coffeehouses in Istanbul worse than wine rooms, Muslim jurists and religious scholars urged the young Sultan Murad IV to shut them down in the early seventeenth century. Coffeehouses numbered in the thousands and were more than places for immoral chat, poetry reading, and gambling—they were places of antigovernment chatter and intrigue. Murad IV visited the Istanbul coffeehouses in disguise and didn't at all like what he saw. In 1640 the city's coffeehouses were torn down and their owners jailed.[47] Yet the ban did not last long. Not only did smoke-filled cafés return, but drinking Turkish-style coffee became all the rage in Europe.

A Turkish Jew named Jacob opened the first coffeehouse in Christian Europe in Oxford in 1650. Coffee's voyage to the Continent was in part a serendipitous outcome of difficulties faced by British and Dutch East India Company traders in Persia. Flourishing coffeehouses in Iran like those in Istanbul were closed by the shah on the advice of his imams, who were annoyed that menfolk were whiling away their time telling bawdy tales in coffee shops instead of going to the mosque. The Dutch and British traders tried to save their investment by shipping their unsold coffee stock to England, thus kicking off a new craze that started with Jacob's coffeehouse in Oxford. Frequented by students, professors, and intellectuals, coffeehouses earned the nickname "penny university," where for a pence-worth of coffee one gained knowledge. Coffee was still being drunk Islamic style—a strong black brew with sugar. Thanks to the rising volume of sugar produced by slave colonies in the Caribbean, where it was introduced by Christopher Columbus, sugar was no longer a luxury item for the rich. Lactose-tolerant Europeans soon found a way of adding nutritional milk to the brew.[48] Credit for mixing coffee with milk goes to the Viennese, who started their first coffeehouse, the Blue Bottle, using sacks of coffee abandoned by Turkish soldiers who failed to capture Vienna in the siege of 1638. Legend has it that an Italian named Marco d'Aviano, a Capuchin monk in Vienna, came up with the idea of mixing cream and honey with coffee to alleviate its bitterness. Grateful Viennese named the brown drink *cappuccino* in tribute to its resemblance to the color of the monk's robes.

In France, where the Sun King, Louis XIV, thanks to a gift of coffee plant from the Dutch, had been brewing his own coffee—grown in Europe's first greenhouse, the Jardin des plantes at Versailles—coffee became a rage with the arrival of the Ottoman ambassador to his court in 1669. Ambassador Suleiman Aga became the envoy of coffee extraordinaire. According to a later English account in 1851, Aga wowed Parisian women with his coffee, grace, and exoticism.

> If a Frenchman, in a similar case, to please the ladies, had presented to them his black and bitter liquor, he would be rendered for ever ridiculous. But the beverage was served by a Turk—a gallant Turk—and this was sufficient to give it inestimable value. Besides, before the palate could judge, the eyes were seduced by the display of elegance and neatness which accompanied it,—by those brilliant porcelain cups into which it was poured,—by napkins with gold fringes on which it was served to the ladies; add to this the furniture, the dresses, and the foreign customs, the strangeness of addressing the host through an interpreter,—being seated on the ground on tiles, &c., and you will allow that there was more than enough to turn the heads of French women.[49]

As coffee and all that went with it became the rage, high-society Parisians began affecting the Turkish style of wearing turbans and billowing caftans and lolling on rugs and cushions. From a mere drink, coffee was turned into a lifestyle. From fashionable coffee salons to the café as hothouse for intellectuals, the drink for Yemeni Sufi had crossed over to the culture of Europe. More than what coffee you drank, which cafés you frequented told one who you were. In 1689 Paris saw the opening of its first café—Le Procope—and the emergence of café culture that has forever linked Parisian intellectual life to this drink. Voltaire was reputed to be a regular at Le Procope, where he drank eighty cups a day.[50] The Left Bank café and habitual hangout of intellectual giants like Jean-Paul Sartre, Le Coupole, is now a landmark.

The fast spread of coffeehouses in Europe and the growing demand for the fashionable drink could not be met by the coffee shipments that came from the Yemeni port of Mocha. As with the practice of countries with precious commodities for export, Yemen's sultan had imposed restrictions: he prohibited the export of coffee beans unless they were boiled or roasted. Coffee-crazed Europeans found a way around it. They colonized land where rain was abundant. The first known case of successful coffee smuggling, though, is credited to Baba Budan, an Indian pilgrim to Mecca, who at the beginning of the seventeenth century managed to take out a few uncooked beans and started a plantation in south India. Dutch traders soon followed suit. They planted coffee in Ceylon and in the Indonesian island of Java.

In France, the coffee rage was lucrative for the trader Jean de la Roque's Company of the Indies, which enjoyed a monopoly on the French coffee trade with Yemen. The company was therefore alarmed to learn that French colonial authorities on the Caribbean island of Martinique were plotting to send a spy to Yemen to spirit away coffee seeds. A solution was soon found.

COFFEE BEANS WITH LOVE

Coffee's journey to the Caribbean is a celebrated tale of heroism and sacrifice. In 1723 a French army captain, Gabriel Mathieu de Clieu, was charged with bringing a single coffee plant to Martinique. It was the same variety of an arabica coffee plant that the Dutch had once given Louis XIV. The story told to this day in Martinique, and which historians consider plausible, is that when Clieu's ship was caught in the doldrums during its harrowing voyage across the Atlantic, he used his meager ration of drinking water to keep the single plant alive.[51] That sole sapling marked the introduction of coffee to the New World. In less than a decade two million coffee shrubs covered Martinique's hillsides. By 1732 the Company of the Indies relented and agreed that the Caribbean coffee could land in French ports, as long as it was exclusively for re-export.

Even in their South American territories the French and Dutch followed the

Yemeni practice of forbidding the export of live seeds. Long frustrated by their failure to get the golden plant, the Portuguese finally found an opportunity in 1727, when a neutral Portuguese Brazilian official was invited to mediate a border dispute between the governors of French and Dutch Guiana. Francisco de Melho Palheta quickly agreed, but his interest lay more in finding a way to sneak out coffee seeds than in adjudicating a territorial spat. A quick but passionate affair with the wife of the French governor offered Palheta the ideal opportunity. According to Heinrich Jacob, at a banquet and under the gaze of her unsuspecting husband, the governor's wife gave him a huge bouquet. Concealed in its interior was a handful of ripe coffee berries. Palheta sailed off with his treasure, and Brazil was launched on its course to become the world's largest coffee producer. By 1750, the coffee that intrigued and enchanted Islamic mystics in Yemen had circumnavigated the globe, growing on five continents. In one of the great ironies of history, in 1893 coffee seeds from Brazil were introduced to the British colony of Kenya and Tanzania—not far from where the famed goatherd discovered the bean almost a thousand years before.[52]

The romantic story of the Franco-Portuguese origin of coffee in Brazil may be apocryphal, but the plant does seem to have been introduced in Brazil from neighboring French Guiana. What followed was the rise of coffee as the country's most important export and the cause of one of the most brutal chapters in Brazil's history. A fungus infestation is reported to have struck coffee in Ceylon and Java, giving Brazilian coffee the opportunity to rise. The transatlantic slave trade conducted by the Portuguese had been going on since the sixteenth century as more and more labor was needed in Brazil to dig the mines and plant sugar, cocoa, and tobacco. Ironically, at just about the time coffee arrived in Brazil, its colonial government had bowed to British pressure and announced the abolition of slavery. Yet a sharp rise in demand for labor to clear land and to plant, nurture, and harvest coffee saw the growth of the slave trade as never before. The British minister in Rio de Janeiro reported in the late 1830s that imports of slaves into Brazil had reached "fearful and impressive" levels. Economic prosperity in Europe and the rise in demand for coffee, sugar, and cocoa translated into ever-expanding coffee frontiers in Brazil. Brazil is coffee (*O Brasil é o café*), so the saying went, and coffee was slavery. Illegal trade was now responsible for landing more than forty-five thousand African slaves every year.[53] Coffee plantations also brought about a demographic change in the slave trade. Slave buyers on the coffee plantations preferred young slaves to adult men and women, perhaps because they were more agile in moving through coffee shrubs picking ripe fruits. Between two-thirds and three-quarters of coffee plantation slaves were boys. By 1870, when slavery was finally abolished, there were 1.5 million slaves in Brazil, most on coffee plantations.[54] Emancipation of the slaves gave a new fillip to emigration from Europe as Italians, Portuguese, Spanish, Germans, Russians, and even Japanese began entering Brazil to work on coffee plantations, although the first two groups alone accounted for about 60 to 70 percent of the immigrants.[55]

Coffee also wreaked havoc in Asia. The lucrative coffee trade fueled colonial expansion in Southeast Asia and the use of forced labor to produce the golden crop. Dutch traders introduced coffee in West Java in 1707, and local aristocrats enthusiastically joined the craze in planting the shrub. They grew and supplied coffee to the Dutch traders, leading to Indonesia's emergence as one of the world's major coffee producers. As a result Java, like Mocha before it, entered the world vocabulary of coffee. By 1725 the coffee boom had peaked in Europe, and prices dropped to a level that progressively excluded independent growers. Even though this fall-off in world coffee prices resulted from a glut in production, European companies were not about to accept a decline in profit. Backed by military force, the Dutch East India Company began a practice (later followed by the British) of forcing locals to deliver coffee and other produce. Local rulers used corvée labor by their subjects to fulfill the delivery quota. The vicissitude of fluctuating coffee prices in the world market was also passed on to the growers. The Dutch practice of forcing growers to expand coffee production when the price was high and demanding its reduction whenever the price fell proved disastrous for farmers, leading ultimately to what might be called the first antiglobalization war—the Java War of 1810–11.[56]

HUNGER KILLER

The nineteenth century saw coffee transformed from a specialty drink for the elite to a mass commodity. By the end of the eighteenth century, women commonly sold café au lait for two cents per earthenware pot on Paris street corners. As a contemporary account put it, the workmen "have found more economy, more sustenance, more flavour in this foodstuff than in any other. As a result they drank prodigious quantities saying that it generally sustains them until the evening."[57] Not surprisingly, some have seen coffee as a tool in the exploitation of workers during the rise of capitalism. Sidney Mintz describes soft drugs like coffee, sugar, tea, and chocolate as "proletarian hunger killers." He writes, "As more and more disinherited rural people gathered in Europe's cities and industrial production spread, tea and sugar came to satisfy people who were hungry anyway. The sweet calories were welcome, the hot drink itself made a cold meal seem warm, and the stimulant cheered the ill, the ill-fed, the overworked, the very young, the elderly."[58]

The reduction of shipping costs, growth of income in the United States and Europe, and expanding urbanization turned coffee into a universal drink for the then developing West. In response to the growing demand, coffee plantations spread—bringing in their wake the inevitable boom and bust.

The dark side of the global coffee boom in terms of slavery and corvée labor has largely passed, but some twenty million coffee growers in the world today live with the vagaries of price fluctuations brought on by bad weather, pests, and overproduction. Coffee is now grown mostly by small growers around the world. In faraway places like New York's Coffee Exchange, traders determine whether they will earn a decent price for their beans or be forced to sell them below cost. If weather in Brazil, the world's largest producer, is forecast to be good, coffee prices worldwide head south. Conversely, growers elsewhere cheer when bad weather in Brazil pushes prices up. Because the green beans cannot be stored for long, stockpiling coffee is no solution for dealing with price fluctuations. Back in 1938, in response to the Brazilian government's plea for a solution to bean surpluses, the Swiss company Nestlé developed a freeze-drying process that could preserve ground coffee and instantly turn the powdered coffee into a drink with the addition of hot water.

Since the 1960s, however, per capita coffee consumption has been declining, and the burden of falling prices is—as always—passed on to the farmer (not unlike the era of the Dutch East India Company). From a high of about $1.20 per pound in 1998, the average price a grower gets has dropped to less than 50 cents.[59] Technological innovations in Brazil and Vietnam helped both countries double production since 1997, generating a glut and a subsequent collapse in coffee prices. In 2002, the World Bank calculated that six hundred thousand jobs were lost in Central America alone because of coffee farms cutting their workforces or going out of business. Nothing perhaps demonstrates more dramatically the change of fortune brought about by globalization than the impact on Ethiopia, where coffee originated. Some fifteen million Ethiopians depend in part on the coffee economy, which also brings about two-thirds of the country's export earnings. Collapsing prices brought export revenue losses of almost $300 million in 2000–2001, an amount equivalent to half the country's total annual export earnings.[60]

The four giant roasters and retailers—Procter and Gamble, Kraft Foods,

Sara Lee, and Nestlé—which together control 40 percent of the world's coffee, have benefited from the falling prices. They have passed on some of the lower price to consumers but have also fattened their margins considerably. Prices paid to growers have plunged more than 80 percent since 1997, but average retail prices for ground roast coffee in American cities have fallen only 27 to 37 percent.[61] The companies that have done well in this downturn are specialty boutique retailers like Starbucks that charge customers up to five dollars for a cup of coffee—of which barely one penny goes to the farmer.

A Holland-based consortium of NGOs took action to stem this apparent exploitation by lobbying industry to offer poor farmers a safety net. The consortium had the support of the British aid organization Oxfam, which has been involved in fair-trade movements to help third world producers. In 1997 this loose consortium of concerned NGOs, including Oxfam, came together to form Fairtrade Labelling Organizations International, which offered certification to mainstream coffee roasters and retailers if they paid a floor price of $1.26 cents per pound to poor growers and their co-ops.

The U.S.-based Global Exchange has meanwhile been campaigning to pressure major retailers to buy a portion of their beans from certified Fairtrade growers. Although the specialty retailer Starbucks uses only 1 percent of the world's coffee supply, its global brand image has made the company the lightning rod of Seattle-like protests. Since three coffee lovers founded the company in 1971, Starbucks has grown into a major international icon, with some ten thousand cafés worldwide, including more than a hundred locations in the world's biggest tea-drinking nation, China. In an unconscious replay of the Turkish ambassador Suleiman Aga's fancy coffee parties in Paris, Starbucks has managed to turn drinking coffee into a statement about lifestyle. Thanks to its marketing genius Starbucks has turned a common drink into an experience, a "cool" thing for millions of young people worldwide, and it has racked up billions in revenue in the process. The company selling varieties of coffee with fancy names has emerged, like Coke, McDonald's, and Nike, as an icon of American-dominated globalization. Its success also has brought the poverty and exploitation of coffee growers into the limelight. If the past opposition to coffee concerned the drinkers and their activities in the café, critics today object to the meager payment the coffee farmers get. Under pressure from lobby groups in 2001, Starbucks pledged to purchase a million pounds—just 1 percent of its imports—of Fairtrade coffee over an eighteen-month period. After initially resisting the same pressures, Procter and Gamble, the maker of Folgers, also agreed to buy Fairtrade certified coffee.

These small victories for fair trade, however, cannot mask the depth of the crisis caused by global overproduction. The amount of coffee sold at fair-trade prices was just too small to make any overall difference. Governments in coffee-growing countries have difficulty forcing farmers to cut coffee production and switch to other crops. In countries like Peru and Colombia, many farmers are turning to growing coca and other drug crops; others continue growing the only thing—coffee—they have been producing for generations. The televised act of "self-defense" performed by protesters at Starbucks in Seattle may have thrown the spotlight on a global crisis, but it did little else.

CAFÉ AU CHIP

Just a year after Seattle, Starbucks scored a major coup in 2000 by bringing its brand of coffee to the country that gave the world another addictive caffeine-based hot drink: tea. Amid protests by nationalist-minded Chinese, a Starbucks café opened right in the heart of the five-hundred-year-old Forbidden City compound in Beijing. Located unobtrusively inside a nondescript shed, the café was not your typical Starbucks. But the political symbolism of the American company's arrival in the historic palace compound of Chinese power was unmistakable. "This is no different from slapping China's 1.2 billion people and 5,000-year traditional culture in the face," fulminated a Chinese journal. But Starbucks's advance was unstoppable.[62] In the autumn of 2003 I watched a clutch of American tourists milling around the Starbucks counter, savoring the familiar taste of latte from home. Not many Chinese customers were in evidence. At three dollars a cup, which for most Chinese represents a day's wage, it was not a feasible option even if they wanted to switch from their oolong.

Back in the States, however, Starbucks had embarked on another strategy to attract more customers: offering a Café au Wi-Fi. In August 2002 the company launched a program to provide wireless (Wireless Fidelity or Wi-Fi) Internet connections to customers, hoping to turn Starbucks outlets into a transitional space between office and home. Four years later, that strategy to attract customers by lifestyle choice had expanded to music and video. Customers could sip a Frappuccino while downloading music from the company's playlist onto their MP3 players and ordering their favorite DVDs. Starbucks's idea seems to have caught on with other shops. Many cafés all over the world now serve a hot cuppa while customers surf on their laptops. The marriage of some of the world's most globalized products—coffee, consumer electronics, and the Internet—is indeed a perfect match made in the marketplace.

The big difference among these globalized products lies in their origins and in how they came to spread worldwide. Coffee shrubs grew on the hills of Ethiopia and Yemen for centuries before humans discovered their use and eventually spread coffee production and consumption worldwide. The electronic accoutrements of today's Starbucks clients—computers, iPods, PDAs, cameras, and videos—all carry deep inside them perhaps the most ubiquitous product of globalization: the microchip. Not only computers or consumer electronics but almost any machine we use today has embedded intelligence contained in logic or memory chips. The 1959 invention by two American scientists, Jack Kilby and Robert Noyce, turned a sliver of silicon into a calculating machine, revolutionizing life on the planet. In less than fifty years the chip or semiconductor has accelerated every aspect of life like nothing else in human history. The domestication of the camel and horse, the mastery of the monsoon wind, and the invention of steam and internal combustion engines and the telegraph have been stages in the long but slowly developing interconnectedness we call globalization. Yet today's vertiginous speed of global connection owes it to that invention for which Kilby won the Nobel Prize in 2000. (Noyce had died a year earlier.) The Nobel committee recognized Kilby's brilliance in embedding transistors in a silicon wafer. The microchip Kilby and Noyce launched is responsible for all the four aspects of modern interconnectedness that distinguish our period from past globalization: velocity, volume, variety, and visibility of transfers.

As with any other invention, however, the microchip is the fruition of a millennium of ideas and experiments from different parts of the world merging in a stream to unleash the enormous power of the electron to perform logic and calculation. It is both a product of the globalization of ideas and an incredible vehicle pushing global connections. A computer comprises hundreds of parts, but the core or heart of it is an inch-or-so-wide sliver of the etched silicon chip—the central processing unit (CPU)—that sits snugly on a green motherboard. When powered up, it performs calculations and follows logical steps that allow me to write this text, surf the Net, download music from the Web, or drive my car with a fuel efficiency unthinkable decades ago. On 20 July 1969 astronaut Neil A. Armstrong set foot on the lunar soil in what was considered a huge step for humankind. But that step was enabled by unsung heroes: the low-powered, high-speed microchips that made the billions of calculations necessary for the *Apollo* rocket to reach the moon. The speed of calculation since then has grown exponentially. Take Intel's Pentium 4 processor, which now runs many personal computers. If your feet were as fast as that processor, you could walk to the moon and back in less than a second.[63] It is beyond the scope of this brief history to relate how the advance of mathematics and the invention of electrical energy and material to control the flow of current to perform calculations and instruct other machines came about and led to the creation of the microchip. But we can sketch the long-term effort by scientists, mathematicians, and thinkers from all over the world, who can be classified as adventurers. Whereas adventurers of yore expanded geographic knowledge, these new explorers stepped out of the box of existing knowledge and connected the world with this super-fast tool of globalization. One can paraphrase Intel's slogan about the ubiquity of its processors—Intel Inside—and say that the innards of Intel's or any other maker's microprocessor carry the thinking and tinkering of the world's scientific explorers. They do indeed carry the "World Inside."

Like cotton and coffee, the microchip or microprocessor is both the product and the promoter of globalization. But unlike them, this tiny brain behind today's machines is invisible. Even if one dismantles a computer or an iPod, one would find only a sealed container holding a minutely etched silicon wafer made in the United States, Japan, Taiwan, or South Korea. That would tell you only where it was designed or in which fabrication facility it was cut out of a silicon wafer. It does not reveal how many millennia of thoughts and inventions by countless people from all over the world lie behind that tiny computer brain.

JOSTLING WITH ZERO

Counting one's possessions, from heads of cattle to baskets of grain, has been one of humans' earliest impulses. One of the first things people did, as can be seen in the clay tablets of Mesopotamia, was to count. Numerals were developed, in the case of Mesopotamia by units of sixty, and the place of zero in the number was marked by two wedge symbols etched on unbaked clay. There was yet no idea of zero as a number. The brilliant Greek civilization had developed geometry to measure but had not focused on the concept of zero as a numeral. In the *Almagest,* written circa 130, Ptolemy used the Babylonian numeral system based on sixty and for the first time employed the symbol zero as an empty placeholder. But it was Indian astronomers (who had learned from the Greeks) who carried forward the abstract thinking about what they called *sunya,* or emptiness. "The Yavanas [Greeks] are barbarians," wrote an ancient Indian author of the *Gargi Samhita,* "yet the science of astronomy originated with them, and for this they must be reverenced like gods." That reverence was shown in the works of the seventh-century Indian astronomer and mathematician Brahmagupta, who picked up where the Greeks left off. He used the symbol zero and tried to answer many questions raised by the concept of zero as a numeral and not just a placeholder. Translated into Arabic, the concept reached scientists in Baghdad, then the biggest seat of learning in the Middle East.[64] Two hundred years later a Persian mathematician in Baghdad, Mohammed ibn Musa al-Khwarizmi, used what he called Hindu numerals to work on equations that equaled zero, or what has come to be known as algebra.[65] He also developed quick methods for multiplying and dividing numbers that came to be known as algorithms (from the corrupted Latin transcription of his name, Algoritmi). Al-Khwarizmi called zero "sifr," literally translating the Sanskrit word *sunya,* from which the word *cipher* is derived. Even al-Khwarizmi's ninth-century algebra (the term *algebra* is derived from the title of his famous book *Al-Jabr wa-al-Muqabilah*) remained unknown to the West until it reached the Moorish Spain, a culture that Jacob Bronowski has called "a kind of bazaar of knowledge."[66] But for a long time the zero was not widely used. In the early thirteenth century, the Italian mathematician Fibonacci, a thoroughly Arabized merchant who had studied accounting methods in North Africa, popularized al-Khwarizmi's concept in his *Liber Abaci* (Book of the abacus). The next great mathematician to use zero was French philosopher René Descartes, the founder of the Cartesian coordinate system. Although the zero was gaining currency in Europe, it would not be until the 1600s that the English physicist Sir Isaac Newton and German philosopher Gottfried Wilhelm Leibniz would take the final step in coming to grips with zero. Understanding zero led to the birth of calculus, without which there wouldn't have been modern physics, engineering, the microchip, or for that matter much of economics and finance. Another figure whose work contributed tremendously in developing the logic that would power microchips was the British mathematician George Boole. In *Investigation into the Laws of Thought* (1854) he developed the new science of symbolic logic that came to be known as Boolean logic—in which all decisions could be reduced to yes or no and true or false. This binary logic would later be a perfect fit for performing logical action with the help of the on-off switch of a transistor.

THALES' AMBER

Understanding of the material world and its laws grew hand in hand with the progress of mathematics, and the speed of the diffusion of knowledge accelerated with the printing press. Thales of Miletus (600 BCE), a Greek philosopher and one of the founders of Greek scientific thought, was the first to observe the phenomenon of static electrical charge. He noticed that if amber was rubbed against fur it became charged and attracted smaller objects such as hair. Several hundred years later the Chinese independently discovered magnetism in some rocks and built a crude compass for use by sailors. It took several hundred more years for the compass to reach Europe. The fascination of English scientist William Gilbert with the device that allowed British naval expansion and conquest led him to experiment with amber and other lodestones. Was there a magnetic mountain in the pole that would pull out all the nails of a ship if it approached? Would a magnetic compass malfunction if there was garlic nearby—as many believed? In a treatise on magnetism Gilbert answered these questions and coined the term *electricity* from the Greek word for amber. The next major step was the development of a method to generate an electrical charge—in the so-called Leyden jar (1745)—by Dutch physicist Pieter van Musschenbroek of the University of Leiden. The idea of the battery was born. A London bookworm named Michael Faraday who studied physics and chemistry discovered electromagnetic induction—generating electricity by manipulating wires and magnets—and his invention in 1831 paved the way for the electrical generator and motor and transformer. In 1873 a French papermaker in the French Alps attached his water turbine to a dynamo, creating the first hydropower. A decade later the invention of the steam turbine freed electricity generation from the need to be close to a water source and hooked up the energy of coal to produce electricity. The rise of regular transatlantic shipping, the telegraph, and increasing travel helped to bring about the frequent and growing exchange of scientific knowledge between the continents.

In 1883, when electricity had already been in use for some time, a team of scientists led by Thomas A. Edison, the inventor of the lightbulb, discovered yet another character of electricity—its ability to flow across a metal plate. The discovered phenomenon, called the Edison effect, led to the creation of the cathode ray tube that now resides inside television and other video terminals. In 1897, on the other side of the Atlantic, Cambridge physicist J. J. Thomson discovered what that mysterious current really was. By mathematically calculating the speed of this unseen power shooting through the metal and glass, he realized it had to be something smaller than one-thousandth the size of a hydrogen atom—which was the smallest possible object. This tiniest of objects, which Thomson called a "corpuscle," later came to be known as the electron that universally exists in all atoms. Following Thomson's discovery of electrons, another British scientist, J. A. Fleming, established that the flow of electrons could be switched on and off faster than any mechanical switch. This discovery led to the invention of diodes and dependable radio transmission. The ball was then taken up by an American in New York, Lee De Forest, who invented another type of vacuum bulb that could amplify the electron flow. With that capacity electrical waves could bridge distances without losing their potency, and the radio was born.

The discovery of these vacuum bulbs that are able to switch on and off quickly—ten thousand times a second—and to amplify signal created capabilities that laid the foundations for building computers. At first vacuum bulbs were used in building radio sets and radars for the army during World War II. The first Philips radio that my father bought in the late 1950s was a thing of endless fascination for me. Through air vents in the back of the radio I could see the tubes flickering with an orange glow as a disembodied voice emanated from the set along with a hissing sound. A major problem with these devices using vacuum bulbs was the enormous amount of power they consumed and the heat they generated. Comparably, the first digital computer capable of making fast calculations was built in the 1930s by the University of Pennsylvania's ENIAC (Electronic Numerical Integrator and Computer). The computer occupied a whole room and used eighteen thousand vacuum bulbs. Their soft glow would attract moths, causing short circuits. That's when the need for "debugging" a computer arose, and the word has stayed ever since, even though the discovery of solid-state transistors eliminated the moth menace.[67] The work of Danish scientist Niels Bohr in the early 1940s explored the atomic structure of materials and established that just as planets revolve around the sun, in all atoms electrons swirl around a nucleus. Different electronic characters of different materials determined which materials were good or bad conductors of electrons. Copper was good and wood was bad. Then scientists discovered other materials like germanium or silicon that fell in-between: they were "semi-conductors." Since they were borderline performers in conducting—or carrying—electrons, scientists found ways of changing their chemical composition to make lab-grown semi-conductors resist transmission or speed it up and amplify.

In 1947 three scientists at Bell Laboratories—John Bardeen, Walter Brattain, and William Shockley—invented ways for these semi-conductors to perform the same task as the vacuum tubes: amplify electronic signals and switch on and off even twenty times faster than the vacuum tubes. The transistors consumed so little power that for the first time portable radios, hearing aids, and other electric devices could be run on batteries. Within seven years the world's first fully transistorized radio—the Regency—went on sale. It was a big hit during the 1954 Christmas season. Three months earlier nineteen-year-old Elvis Presley had cut his first record.[68] The age of Rock 'n Roll was launched with the transistor radio, which sold over one hundred thousand units in the first year. The mass production of transistorized radios and televisions shrank the world more than ever before. The invention of the transistor came well after scientists on both sides of the Atlantic had foreseen how a fast on-off switch could be used to calculate binary numbers created by combinations of ones and zeroes. One British and one Hungarian scientist simultaneously came up with the idea of using binary mathematics to solve different problems.

The brilliant British scientist Alan M. Turing foresaw in a paper in 1937 that "it is possible to invent a single machine which can be used to compute any computable sequence."[69] The exigency of breaking German secret code during World War II led to the development of the first large-scale use of electronic switching. A computer named Colossus, started in 1943 in Britain's Bletchley Park, put to use Turing's statistical theory to break the famous German Enigma code. Hungarian-born John von Neumann arrived in Princeton, New Jersey, in 1930 to join the Institute of Advanced Studies. Inspired by the power of the new ENIAC computer in Philadelphia, which could zip through repetitive computation at an unprecedented speed, Von Neumann saw a future in which computing machines were widely used with universal application. He was joined by Turing in setting out the general architecture of an electronic computer to take data and instructions, process them, and report the answer to the user. Since computer calculations could be performed by switches flipping from on to off and back again, Turing wrote, it was natural enough to assign the value 1 to on and 0 to off, and handle all mathematics with only those two digits. As T. R. Reid has since put it, "It was human genius on the part of Von Neumann, Turing and others like them that figured out how to use binary numbers and binary math to turn inert chain of electronic switches into a powerful computational tool."[70] They also designed a complete system of logic that permits machines to make decisions and comparisons and thus work through complex patterns, or "programs," for manipulating words or numbers.

COLOSSUS TO MICROCHIP

While the program to run on fast on-off switches was being developed, the available machines were the size of Colossus and ENIAC. The challenge was what scientists called "the numbers barrier" or the "tyranny of numbers." To have the transistors carry out more instructions, other components like diodes, resistors, capacitors, and wires linking thousands of transistors were needed. One bypassed this problem by spreading the entangling wires and transistors out in a room like vacuum tubes were dispersed in ENIAC. Just as Colossus was developed in response to the challenge of the German war machine, the making of the microchip got its push from the Cold War. American defense contractors who were making rockets and missiles pressed U.S. manufacturers to come up with small, low-power-consuming transistors that could be fitted into the Minuteman missile. The need was urgent because Russia's launch of Sputnik, the first man-made satellite, in October 1957 had dramatically exposed the "missile gap." Sputnik demonstrated that the Soviets had an intercontinental ballistic missile capable of hitting the United States.

In less than two years, two American engineers, Jack Kilby of Texas Instruments (TI) and Robert Noyce of Fairchild Semiconductor, came up with the solution. They independently hit upon the ideas that led to the creation of the first microchip, or integrated circuit. The six-foot-six-inch-tall Kilby, nicknamed "gentle giant" after he achieved fame, grew up in rural Kansas and was an avid ham radio operator at fourteen. He failed his entrance exam to MIT but got his engineering degrees from Midwestern universities and went on to receive sixty patents for his inventions. The most important of his inventions came within months of his joining TI as he grappled with the task of building circuits with large numbers of transistors and other components. His idea of a monolith, making all of the three components—transistors, capacitors, and resistors—out of the silicon crystal half the size of a paper clip, was the brilliant solution.[71] Kilby himself later acknowledged that the idea of integrated circuit design occurred to a number of people in various parts of the world. He wrote: "In the early 1950's, another Englishman, Geoff Dummer, suggested that it was possible to foresee a time when all electronics would be made as a single block."[72] Kilby came up with practical ways to realize that dream. Kilby's coinventor Noyce, who was hired by his hero, William Shockley, one of the transistor's Nobel Prize–winning inventors, was also working on the same problem as Kilby and reached the same conclusion. Searching for an unencumbered way to place many transistors together, Noyce independently came up with the idea of integrating the circuits on a single chip. Additionally, he found a way out of entangling wires with what was called planar technology—using photolithography to etch circuits on silicon wafers.

While the defense contractors were fitting the microchip in the nose of Minuteman missiles, the integrated circuit made its civilian debut before the Electronic Society at the New York Coliseum on 24 March 1959. Launching the product, the president of Texas Instruments said that Kilby's invention would prove to be the most important and most lucrative technological development since the silicon transistor. But the press virtually ignored the arrival of this epoch-making technology. It was hard to see what this buglike thing made of silicon wafer could do. Just as the transistor caught people's imagination with the launch of pocket radios, Texas Instruments needed a consumer product that would dramatize the value of the new technology. What better than turning a typewriter-sized calculator into a slim box that would fit in a shirt pocket? TI knew that it had no expertise in consumer products, and just as it had turned to an outside company to produce the transistor radio, it had to find a partner to make a splash with the microchip. In what turned out to be a momentous decision for future U.S.-Japanese technology cooperation, TI teamed up with a consumer electronic company in Japan, Canon, to launch the Pocketronic—a 1.8-pound box that printed out the results of calculations on a strip of paper. Compared to the available desktop calculator costing two thousand dollars, it was a bargain at four hundred. "At the supermarket," an American industry magazine breathlessly reported, "the new calculator will help your wife find the best unit price bargains. At the lumberyard, they'll help you decide which combination of plywood, lumber and hardboard would be least expensive for your project."[73] The next logical step that fully launched the information revolution came out of the partnership between Japanese manufacturing and American innovation.

In July 1968, Noyce and Gordon Moore, who had both left Fairchild Semiconductor to found Intel (the name combines *integrated* and *electronics*), staked their fortune on developing a chip with a large number of transistors. Such a chip could be turned into a memory storage device, something all computers needed no matter their function. Shortly after the launch of Intel, Noyce had been to see a Japanese semiconductor pioneer, Tadashi Sasaki of Sharp Corporation, in the hope of getting business for his struggling new company. Sasaki had worked with Noyce when Noyce was with Fairchild and was eager to help.

Because Sharp was locked in a contract with another company for the design of the semiconductor, Sasaki asked his old college-mate Yoshio Kojima of the new calculator manufacturer Busicom to place an order with Intel. In June 1969, three Busicom employees showed up at Intel's office in Santa Clara, California, to describe the work they wanted done. Busicom put up sixty thousand dollars to cover design and engineering costs with a commitment to purchase the integrated circuits.[74] Although Intel's main interest was in developing the memory chip, to meet its client's order its engineers began developing a large-scale integrated chip with a central processing unit and other chips containing enough transistors and circuitry to perform all the necessary functions. By 1971, when Intel was ready with the microprocessor, called 4004, Busicom had gone bust. But in the bargain, the Japanese plan to build a programmable calculator helped Intel to launch a computer on a chip. Intel bought back its rights to the microprocessor and the half-inch-long chip packed with 2,300 transistors and as much computing power as the thirty-ton ENIAC that had launched the computer revolution.

Microchips continue to shrink in size, packing in more and more transistors—a billion by the beginning of the twenty-first century—and performing an unimaginable number of calculations per second.[75] They have enabled a mesh of fiber-optic cables and overhead satellites to link the planet instantaneously. As the world moves toward the greater embedding of radio frequency identification (RFID) chips in all products in stores, in personal identity cards, even in cattle and pets, the globalization of man-made products takes on a whole new dimension. As Von Neumann and Turing foresaw, with the help of programming, that tiny device could process any data. Because of the information that it was able to carry and the speed with which it connected the world, the microchip now occupies a central place in the process of globalization.

That role is not simply in connecting people more quickly and with greater ease. While Intel and other chip makers have switched to "fables manufacturing"—undertaking the increasingly costly task of designing complex semiconductors—the actual production of the wafer has been taken up by Taiwan, South Korea, and other countries. This division of labor in producing one of modern technology's critical components has increased global interdependence to an unprecedented extent. In 1999, a severe earthquake hit Taiwan, halting production at the twenty-eight wafer production facilities responsible for manufacturing more than half of the world's semiconductors and raising worldwide fears of a chip shortage. Fortunately for the global economy, the chip manufacturers recovered quickly, suffering only a minor shortfall in production. But the threat of disruption stemming from the quake-prone parts of the Pacific hangs over the increasingly globalized economy like the sword of Damocles. The drive to diversify sources of chip production continues. In 2006, Intel announced a billion-dollar microchip assembly and testing plant in Vietnam. With its low-cost economy and educated labor force, Vietnam has joined the invisible chain-link fence of wafers connecting manufacturers across the globe. Intel's investment also had the unintended consequence of reuniting people. The young son of a U.S. embassy employee, Than Trong Phuc was airlifted off the roof of the embassy in Saigon in April 1975. Thirty years later, he returned as Intel's country manager for Vietnam.

Meanwhile microchips and electronic media continue to help antiglobalization protesters to carry their messages with multiple and faster means. During another WTO meeting in 2003, protesters organized a peer-to-peer video-sharing service to transmit broadcast-quality video of the protests to television stations and other activists. They also set up wireless networks to stream over the Internet audio recordings of antiglobalization speeches.[76] In fact, information processed by microchip is the single most important factor that distinguishes today's globalization from the slowly growing interconnection and interdependence of the past.

The demonstrators in Seattle who railed against the exploitation of textile workers and coffee growers and denounced the evil effects of globalization by using their personal computers and the World Wide Web were unwitting participants in the long-running process that they thought they despised.

Chapter 4 Preachers' World

Go forth, O monks, for the good of the many, for the happiness of the many, out of compassion for the world; for the good, the gain and the welfare of gods and men. Let not two go the same way. Teach, O monks, the Dharma, good in the beginning, good in the middle, good in the ending.
—*The Buddha to his first sixty disciples, 2,500 years ago*

As on every day of the week, a multiethnic crowd gathered outside the heavy glass doors of the Empire State Building. An Italian family, a Brazilian, an elderly Indian couple, teenage schoolchildren from Kansas—they had been milling outside on the Fifth Avenue entrance, waiting for their turn to ride the elevator to the 86th Floor Observatory. After the World Trade Center towers were felled by the terrorist attack on 11 September 2001, the needle-topped building that soars skyward 1,454 feet regained its former glory as New York's tallest building. Tens of thousands of people from all over the world go there

The Chinese monk Xuanzang returns to Chang'an in 645, carrying more than six hundred Buddhist texts. Fujita Art Museum, Osaka to take in vistas of the sprawling city from the building atop which King Kong famously clutched Fay Wray, and more recently Naomi Watts, in his hand and fought off air assaults to dislodge him. On the morning of 1 April 2005, the crowd queuing in the Empire State Building lobby was unaware of a quiet celebration taking place thirty-four floors up in the headquarters of Human Rights Watch. Similarly unaware were those whose fates were being determined, at least in part, by the missionary-like activities of the secular human-rights organization: the pitiful African refugees in Darfur, huddling inside flimsy plastic shelters wilting under a scorching sun.

When Richard Dicker in his crumpled tweed jacket walked through the glass door of the office, many grinning, happy colleagues waited to shake his hand. As director of the Human Rights Watch's International Justice Program, Dicker had spent months lobbying diplomats in their United Nations offices. The efforts of people like him to alert the world to the tragedy unfolding in Darfur had worked. The seemingly unmovable United Nations had finally agreed to what human rights organizations like Human Rights Watch had been urging for months. But it had been a roller coaster. When the U.N. members had assembled in the Security Council chamber for informal consultations on Darfur the day before, chances did not look good. They looked even worse when at six o'clock they broke off to go to a Brazilian restaurant in TriBeCa. It was a dinner for the Brazilian ambassador, whose term as head of the Security Council was ending that day. Dicker had been hanging out in the corridor the whole day and was dispirited that diplomats showed little outrage about reports of rapes and murders. "My god! What a scandal! [People are being raped and murdered and] they're doing the samba down in some restaurant."[1]

More than two hundred thousand people have been killed and almost two million have been forcefully displaced from their homes in the past three years of civil war in the Darfur region of the North African state of Sudan. Civilians have been killed and driven out of their homes in an "ethnic cleansing" by the government-backed Arab Janjaweed militia. Although the Bush administration and the U.S. Congress had declared this to be genocide, the United Nations had not. Millions of people fleeing the ethnic cleansing were huddled in camps, unable to return to their homes and farms due to continuing attacks, rape, and looting by the Janjaweed. The Sudanese government flatly denied, contrary to incontrovertible evidence, that genocide was taking place and ignored repeated calls by Western governments to stop the violence.

Dicker lobbied the U.N. Security Council to refer the Darfur violence to the newly established International Criminal Court (ICC). Precisely to suppress such acts, in 1998 some 121 nations had voted for a treaty establishing the court. The United States, which had first signed and then unsigned the ICC treaty, blocked the Security Council's attempts to refer Darfur to the court. If the meeting of 31 March had failed, the momentum built by Human Rights Watch and others would have been lost.

Yet it turned out that the dinner was not all fun and samba. Bowing to the pressure of media campaigns and allies, not to mention the pressure of Christian organizations, the U.S. government decided to back away from its veto threat. While the principals of the major delegations, including Secretary of State Condoleezza Rice and Foreign Secretary Jack Straw of Britain—undertook many phone consultations, thorny issues remained to be worked out. The relaxed atmosphere of a restaurant enabled some last-minute haggling and negotiation to take place. The diplomats returned to the United Nations after dinner, and by eleven o'clock it was announced that they had voted to send the Darfur case to the ICC. Reporters thronging outside the meeting room besieged an elated Dicker for comment on the major development. The resolution not only provided hope that the violence in Darfur would end, but the U.S. abstention was good news for the future of the International Criminal Court.

At Human Rights Watch's Empire State Building office, Dicker told me, "There was a real sense of accomplishment, not gloating, and even more fundamentally that this was a step that would offer real protection to the people of Darfur. It signaled to Sudan that those most responsible for mass murder in western Sudan could find themselves facing arrest warrants from an international court." Reviewing the situation, Dicker said, "The killing didn't stop but it dropped dramatically." He paused a moment and added, "the struggle to protect the people of Darfur goes on."[2]

Why am I telling the story of people like Richard Dicker and his colleagues who continue to fight to save the people of Darfur? They are the newest incarnation of missionaries, in the broadest sense of the term, agents of globalization who have been a historical force in reconnecting dispersed human communities. These secular missionaries do travel the world not to preach religious sermons but to unite the world around one agenda: protecting the life, liberty, and freedoms of all humans. Human Rights Watch director Kenneth Roth, who like Dicker demurs at being called a missionary, gave up a lucrative legal practice to work to defend human rights. "Unlike the missionary who is looking to convert individuals," Roth told me, "the human rights activist is looking to convert governments."[3] Human rights activists don't evangelize about a higher power, and they don't tell people how to lead their lives, but they do try to convince other cultures to share their outrage or sense of morality. They ask governments to build a human rights culture within the society and a political space so that people can defend their own rights. And in this effort, they spare no government. From the mighty American government to tin-pot dictators, human rights activists regularly shame governments in an attempt to defend individuals worldwide. This chapter will offer a sketch of how faith and people's desire to convert fellow human beings to their convictions have spurred countless missionaries to travel to far corners of the world, encouraged traders living in foreign lands to double as preachers, and, unfortunately, motivated warriors to wield their swords to win converts and eliminate those who refused. As the traders have used evolving ever-faster transportation technology to spread their networks, missionaries have accompanied them. Now, greater public awareness of human conditions around the world and a growing consciousness about the unity of the human species have brought into existence new types of missionaries. Their faiths center on saving all the species on earth, protecting the environment, and nurturing human life and dignity. Modern travel, media, and communication have enabled them to spread their messages faster and reach out to people in different parts of the world. The net result of the action of these missionaries—old and new—has been to bind humankind with thicker webs of religious faith and secular convictions and to shrink the world.

HAVE FAITH WILL TRAVEL

In Chapter 1 we saw the rise of early religion in sedentary communities. Humans sought protection from the wrath of nature by praying to the sky god and the gods of small and big things. The power of those gods was local. The gods spoke only the language of the people, and local priests were the intermediaries through whom the gods made their wishes clear. The notion that there was one god who created life on earth was commonplace, but he or she was remote. There arose a host of other lesser gods who could be approached for good health and help with a variety of specific problems. Then there were gods of the sun and the moon, the god of love, a god of writing and divination, just to mention a few. Depending on from where they emerged, they had different names.

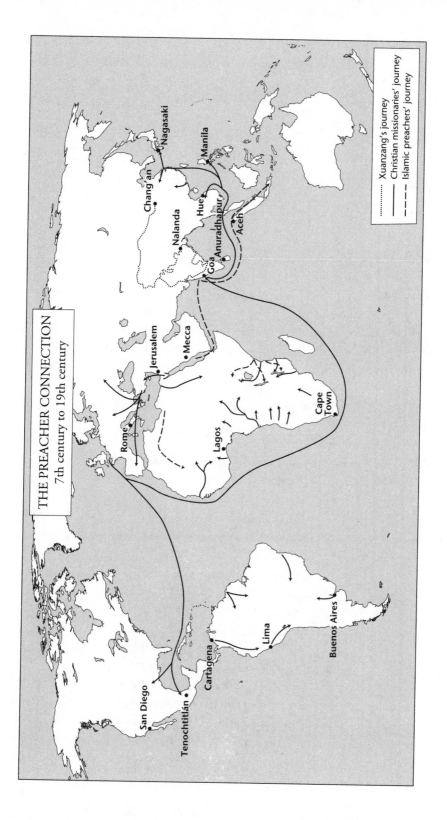

THE PREACHER CONNECTION
7th century to 19th century

Xuanzang's journey
Christian missionaries' journey
Islamic preachers' journey

Nagasaki
Manila
Chang'an
Nalanda
Hue
Anuradhapur
Goa
Aceh
Jerusalem
Mecca
Rome
Lagos
Cape Town
San Diego
Tenochtitlán
Cartagena
Lima
Buenos Aires

Lesser gods were embodied in particular trees, stones, rivers, and mountains. Traders venturing out of their localities had to leave their local protective spirits behind.

The rise of monotheistic religion, centered on the belief in one god for all, could unshackle humans from their animistic local gods. Freed from local settings, religion could travel and become global, and yet a god could be personal. The sole exception among the emerging universal religions was Buddhism, which did not have a god. The Buddha taught that people's suffering was universal and that the path to salvation was the same for each—engendering a belief system that could appeal to human beings no matter where they were located, what language they spoke, or what they ate. A faith that did not call for worshipping any object or local gods was perfectly suited for the life of itinerant traders. Not surprisingly, the most enthusiastic devotees of Buddhism were found among traders. The Christian and Islamic faiths, with their message of a single deity, were also eminently portable concepts. And both faiths assumed that they would be the only religion for all humanity. The notion of the universality of humanity under one God has since evolved to embrace human rights and issues from ecology to environment that are believed to affect all humankind. We will see how spreading the Christian faith in the New World raised thorny questions of human rights among conscientious missionaries. That concept has evolved and has been embraced by nongovernmental organizations that campaign for universal human rights.

New York–based Human Rights Watch is an example of these new breed of missionaries. The organization owes its existence to the West's concern about human rights abuse in the former Soviet Union and its satellites. As part of the Helsinki Accord to bring about détente, Helsinki Watch was formed in 1978. Realizing that abusing citizens' rights was not just limited to the Soviets, the organization set up Americas Watch to monitor human rights in the western hemisphere. Middle East Watch performed the same function for that part of the world. In 1988 the various regional committees were united under the umbrella of Human Rights Watch. With its staff of 150 lawyers, journalists, academics, and country experts of many nationalities, and its offices in Brussels, London, Moscow, Hong Kong, Los Angeles, San Francisco, Tashkent, Toronto, and Washington, the body has emerged as one of the leading defenders of weak individuals all over the world. Funded by private donation and motivated by humanitarian passion, members of NGOs like Human Rights Watch have gone out to the world as the new missionaries and through their work have connected the world.

As we noted earlier, distinctions among the traders, adventurers, preachers, and warriors—the agents of globalization—were often blurry. Traders often sought to proselytize, as did adventurers; warriors not only secured territories for their sovereigns and merchants but actively sought new souls to be converted, sometimes forcing people to adopt a new faith. To varying degrees, missionary zeal to convert others was often the impetus, or the pretext, to venture beyond one's own known world.

The sociologist Max Weber defined missionary religion as one that raises the spreading of the truth and the conversion of the unbelievers to the rank of "a sacred duty." He said that the believer's spirit "is not satisfied until it has carried its message to every human soul, till what it believes to be the truth is accepted as the truth by all members of the human family."[4] This definition is applicable not only to great monotheistic proselytizing religions like Christianity and Islam but to universal human rights, which Nobel laureate Eli Wiesel has called the "secular religion" of our time. Wiesel defined human rights as an application of the idea that "the other is not my enemy. The other is my ally, my kin, my friend. And whatever happens to that other involves me. . . . I have no right to stand by whenever the other is being humiliated."[5] Similar idealistic fervor has led activists to launch campaigns to stop global warming, protect whales and other endangered species, or fight AIDS. The activists are as passionate in their dedication to these causes as many religious preachers. Their untiring efforts to spread their messages and shape the world in the image of their deeply held beliefs are comparable to religious proselytizers.

The profound urge to show people the "true path" continues, although the pace of work today is much faster than ever and the geographic reach is truly global. Camel caravans, sailing ships, and steamers have been replaced by jet planes. Wood-block-printed texts and Johannes Gutenberg's movable type have been joined by radio, television, and the Internet as means of preaching the gospel. One can even indulge in missionary activities without leaving home. Nobel laureate Jody Williams campaigned for a world free of landmines from her kitchen with a fax machine, a computer, and a phone line.

Thanks to "preachers" like Williams and her dedicated band of multinational colleagues, a movement to ban landmines, launched in 1992, in just five years persuaded 122 countries to sign a mine ban treaty (Convention on the Prohibition of the Use, Stockpiling, Production and Transfer of Anti-Personnel Mines and on Their Destruction), thus eliminating a scourge that has killed hundreds of thousands of people in some eighty countries in past decades. Even after wars have ended, the mines claim between fifteen thousand and twenty thousand casualties every year. The treaty will ensure that no new landmines are planted and that existing mines are destroyed. In 1997 Williams and the International Campaign to Ban Landmines received the Nobel Peace Prize for their work. Williams and her colleagues were only the visible tip of the iceberg. Tens of thousands like them all over the world were crossing borders to resolve humanitarian problems that affect us all.

Work by millions of preachers and missionaries—in both the conventional and the unconventional sense—has created global communities of Christians, Muslims, and Buddhists and a growing civil society. Obviously, the emergence of globe-spanning religious communities has not been the handiwork of missionaries alone. Much of the conversion in the early phases of history was achieved by the sword. Nor was the motive always spiritual. The conversion of those called heathens and infidels served more often than not as means to a more selfish end—from building empires to acquiring new resources and markets.

The material greed lurking behind Christian attempts to recover the Holy Land during the Crusades was hardly a secret. Perhaps the most striking example of this greed was the sacking of Constantinople in 1204 by soldiers of the Fourth Crusade. "Never since the creation of the world had so much booty been taken from a city," wrote a contemporary chronicler. "No one could possibly count the piles of gold, silver, jewels or the bales of precious materials."[6] The sixteenth-century Spanish expeditions to South America were ostensibly to convince the Incas to accept the true God. Asked about his failure to convert the natives of Peru, the conquistador Francisco Pizarro was frank: "I have not come for any such reasons: I have come to take away from them their gold."[7] When a Spanish expedition was ordered to sail with God's blessings from Mexico to the spice-rich Philippines, the commander explained that the "the main purposes of this expedition are the conversion of the natives and the discovery of a safe route back to Nueva España, that the kingdom may increase and profit from trade and by other legitimate means."[8] In the name of winning new converts to the faith, tens of thousands were tortured and killed, continents colonized, and massive amounts of resources transferred to the metropolitan countries.

LOOKING FOR GOLD

For all the horror it visited upon people over the long span of history, missionary activity had the effect of shrinking the world. The spread of these proselytizing faiths brought dispersed communities into contact, both peaceful and violent. Preachers enriched languages of their converts, introduced printing technology, and transformed cultures for better or for worse. If the world today looks more homogenous than at any time in the past it is because a vast number of people have come to embrace the great religions that streamed out of the foothills of the Himalayas and deserts of the Middle East. In the remotest corner of the planet you will find a mosque, a church, or a temple. To appreciate the significance of preachers and missionaries in making the world smaller, you have to imagine a world in which Buddhism is practiced in just a little corner of India, and Christianity and Islam remain the faiths of the Arabian Desert. For a significant period of history, religious proselytizing has been associated with such violence and cruelty that it is hard to imagine anything positive arising out of connections made by missionary efforts. Yet like all human efforts to connect with others, missionary activities have had unintended consequences that have shaped human lives and influenced cultures in far corners of the world. Monasteries have served as repositories of human knowledge that could be shared, and the spreading of faith has led to the efflorescence of literature and art and inspired the creation of thousands of monuments—from the stunning architecture of La Mezquita, or Grand Mosque, in Cordoba to the magnificent temples of Angkor Wat.

Proselytization has always been based on the conviction of the universal applicability of faith. Whether it was Buddhism, Christianity, or Islam, its teachings were believed to be good for humankind as a whole. The spread of universalistic religion in creating a global consciousness can be seen in a tenth-century mural in the Mogao Caves of Dunhuang, China. In a dark cave hewn into a mountainside lies a gigantic reclining figure of the Buddha surrounded by mourners of different nationalities. The mourners are painted with infinite precision, showing their different origins, varied garments, and distinctive headdresses as they stand grief-stricken at the death of the Buddha. Some are weeping, some beating their chests, and one even thrusts a long sword in his chest. This painting, drawn more than fifteen hundred years after the Buddha's passing, must be one of the earliest metaphorical representations of global grief—humanity in all its diversity united in mourning for a teacher from a different land. That the Buddha looked different, lived in India long before, and spoke a different tongue did not matter to the devotees of many races. His message was universal and timeless. The artist easily imagined the grief that the Buddha's passing would have caused, even though at the time of his actual death the rulers of Tibet, China, and the kingdoms of Central Asian would not have known who the Buddha was, much less mourn his passing. The anachronism of the painting, obviously meant to show devotion rather than represent reality, is in sharp contrast to the speed that characterizes global awareness in our era. It took eighteen months for the news of Joan of Arc's death to reach Constantinople and three months for the news of that city's fall to the Turks in 1453 to reach all of Europe.[9] Thanks to satellite television and the Internet, everyone was instantly aware of Princess Diana's death and shared in the grief of Pope John Paul II's passing. The day after the terrorist attacks on New York and Washington killed more than three thousand people, students in Tehran held candlelight vigils for the victims. This global awareness about human fate, as we will see, has been growing for a long time, and the transmission of global concerns has become increasingly faster. The connections began slowly, however, with missionaries like China's Xuanzang, who walked for months along thousands of miles of tracks across desolate landscape to reach India, where the Buddha was born.

A prince in a small kingdom in northern India, Siddhartha Gautam was troubled by the suffering he saw around him and furtively left the palace to become an ascetic. After years of wandering he sat down to meditate on the means of salvation from the suffering of human life. On the forty-ninth day of meditation, on a full moon night in the spring of 623 BCE Siddhartha received *bodhi,* or enlightenment. He gave his first sermon to five disciples. His universalistic message about the cause of human suffering and the path to salvation caught people's imagination. The later Christian concept of a "suffering savior" appears to have reached India in the first century CE—some seven hundred years after the Buddha lived—to inspire Buddhist scholars to develop the idea of the Maitreya, a bodhisattva who will come to save the world and who will redress humanity through his suffering.[10] Descendants of the Greeks who settled in the kingdom of Gandhara, in today's Pakistan and Afghanistan, soon replaced the symbolic images of the Buddha, such as his footprints on stone or a lotus, with Greek-inspired lifelike depictions. A new Buddhist Mahayana sect shed some of the earlier severity of the faith, based on abstinence and sacrifice. It allowed the worship of Buddha's images and the earning of merit through devotion and offerings. Within the next thousand years, Buddhist preachers set out on the Silk Road and on boats hugging the coast of the Bay of Bengal and the South China Sea and succeeded in converting people from Sogdiana, in today's eastern Iran and central Asia, to Japan and Vietnam.

The Mauryan emperor Aśoka, whose army brought vast parts of India under his rule by the force of arms in the third century BCE, embraced Buddhism and used his imperial authority to spread the religion. He sent his own son Mahinda, who had become a monk, as ambassador preacher to the court of Sri Lanka.[11] Mahinda undertook what he termed *dhammavijaya,* a religious conquest, dispatching large numbers of Buddhist missionaries abroad to the kings of Egypt, Macedonia, and several Hellenistic kingdoms in the Mediterranean. Some 250 years before the Christian era, filaments of connections were being laid among people around common themes of human suffering and salvation, and those links grew and spread eastward. In the first century CE, the first imperial Chinese convert to Buddhism, the Han emperor Mingdi, invited two Indian monks, Dharmaraksa and Kasyapa Matanga, to undertake the dangerous journey across the Central Asian desert to Luoyang. Carrying Buddhist manuscripts, paintings, and ritual objects from India, they established the White Horse Temple, which became a center of the diffusion of Buddhist learning for many centuries. A stream of preachers and translators from Central Asia and India moved to China as Chinese monks continued their journey west.[12] The Indian monk Bodhiruci arrived in Luoyang in 508 and by the order of the emperor translated many texts, including the *Lotus Sutra* and the *Diamond Sutra,* which the Hungarian-born archaeologist Aurel Stein would find more than a millennium later. With the development of wood-block printing technology and paper many copies of the Chinese translation of the *Diamond Sutra* were printed. The copy found by Stein, dated to 868, is the oldest printed book on paper in the world.[13]

IN THE FOOTSTEPS OF THE BUDDHA

It's a hazy morning in China's ancient capital Xi'an, previously known as Chang'an. Bright green taxicabs, air-conditioned tourist buses, and lumbering trucks belching black smoke pass by a small park in a steady stream. The only visitor that morning to the park on the western edge of Xi'an, I wanted to see the spot where the Silk Road began. A fifteen-feet-high cement statue of a caravan ringed by a hedge forlornly marked the spot. Bearded traders and a monk in flowing robes sitting atop stone camels and other men on galloping horses were reminders that this road was a highway for traders, preachers, and soldiers. Amid the acrid plumes of exhaust left by trucks and buses rumbling down the dual carriageway, it was hard to imagine the dusty path that once led caravans from here to as far west as the Caspian Sea.

It was perhaps from here that at dusk in the autumn of 629, China's famous monk, scholar, and preacher Xuanzang sneaked out on a journey that would last sixteen years. For twelve years Xuanzang traveled through India, visiting holy Buddhist sites, studying at the famous Buddhist university in Nalanda, and debating and discussing with scholars. When in 643, he took leave of his patron and friend King Harsha, he was presented with elephants and a retinue of men and horses to carry nearly seven hundred Buddhist texts and a large number of images he had collected. In the course of the biggest information transfer of the epoch, one elephant drowned while crossing the Indus River but another, amazingly, carried on over the Hindu Kush until, chased by robbers, it fell into a ravine on the way to Kashgar.[14]

On a spring morning in 645, the news of Xuanzang's return from the land of the Buddha had spread, and streets overflowed with crowds eager to set their eyes on this amazing man who had defied the imperial ban on traveling to the west and had now returned from a distant land carrying unbelievable treasures of images of the Buddha and 657 volumes of sacred texts. The emperor Taizong, who had forbidden the travel, had a change of heart. Eager to meet the famous monk who had seen "traces not seen before, heard sacred words not heard before, witnessed spiritual prodigies exceeding those of nature," the emperor sent high officials to escort Xuanzang to Chang'an. A Chinese biographer described the monk's return: "The authorities, fearing that people may trade [tread] on one another, order them to stay still, burn incense, and scatter flowers where they are standing. Then the whole congregation witnesses a colored cloud in the sky that seems to float over the scriptures and the gold, silver, and sandal wood images as if it is welcoming the holy objects. It is indeed 'the most splendid event since the death of the Buddha.'"[15]

At Taizong's request, Xuanzang wrote a detailed record of his journey, describing the places, people, economic, educational, and social conditions, religious practices, manners, and customs of the lands he visited. He concluded his *Records of the Western Regions* with an observation surprising in its openness and acceptance of diversity: "I have set forth at length national scenery and ascertained territorial divisions. I have explained the qualities of national customs and climatic characteristics. Moral conduct is not constant and tastes vary; where matters cannot be thoroughly verified one cannot be dogmatic."[16]

Xuanzang is but one example from a multitude of preachers whose devotion and courage spread the Buddhist faith throughout Asia and eventually to other parts of the world. Ironically Buddhism, a religion of peace, was introduced to Japan by a Korean envoy visiting the Japanese court in 552 to seek military support against a foreign invader. It has since profoundly influenced Japanese society, art, and culture. Japan is now the home of some one hundred million Buddhists, and the Japanese are the most ardent promoters of the faith. As the Chinese scholar Tan Yun-Shan puts it, "Buddhism was born in India, enriched in China, and then scattered over the whole world."[17] Buddhist missionaries not only helped develop a global consciousness, they built connections that led to expansion of trade and a profound intermixing of culture that lent a commonality to an Asian identity.

Facing periodic opposition from the official Confucian hierarchy, Buddhist missionaries developed a vernacular language that bypassed formal court language to appeal to common folk. This was true throughout East Asia, where the need for creating Buddhist texts led to the creation of a written vernacular. This development was, of course, in accordance with the wishes of the Buddha, who once said, "You should speak in whatever language all the living beings can obtain enlightenment. For this reason it is called 'doing in accordance with the country.'"[18] Asian scholar Victor H. Mair writes that "aside from a handful of sinographically inspired scripts, nearly all of the written vernaculars east of the Pamirs to the Pacific Ocean were a direct result of the Buddhist missionary enterprise."[19]

TRADING ON SILK

Nothing perhaps is as closely associated with the spread of Buddhism as the great connector of two worlds: the Silk Road. In fact, the reputation of the road as the purveyor of China's silk to the world received a great boost thanks to the increasing number of pilgrims who made that hazardous journey carrying bolts of luxurious cloth to be donated to monasteries as acts of piety. Buddhism sustained the silk trade by contributing to the demand in India and Central Asia for Chinese weaves.[20] Beginning in the fourth century, Chinese silk exports boomed, as did the traffic of Indian missionaries to China and Chinese pilgrims to India. Buddhist paraphernalia such as incense, icons, and other religious materials became staple Indian exports.

Buddhist missionary connections with India encouraged diffusion of the Buddha's teachings and all theological discussion that followed. Texts written on palm leaves (the standard practice in ancient India) were translated into Chinese on paper, and soon they were printed and bound into books. Because the possession of holy texts was considered a meritorious act, demand grew for Buddhist books. In turn, the demand for paper led to refinements in the production process and brought down the cost of bookmaking. Ironically, the In-

dian practice of tying up individual palm leaves in thread seems to have inspired the Chinese to assemble printed paper into bound books, but Indians
learned papermaking and book production from Muslim rulers.

Tea drinking, known in China since the first century CE, also received new
impetus with the spread of Buddhism. In a remarkably similar vein to the
spread of coffee drinking by Islamic monks in Yemen (see Chapter 3), the habit
of tea drinking spread widely in China when monks began sipping tea to keep
themselves awake during their long hours of meditation. As China scholar John
Kieschnick notes, while monks began drinking tea in the early Tang period
(early seventh century) in areas where tea was already popular, the practice soon
spread to north and west China because monks were the most mobile segment
of the population. Other introductions by monks were the chair, from India,
and sugarcane, which allowed monks to sustain themselves after sunset. As participants in the transregional subculture of Buddhist monasticism, Kieschnick
says, Chinese monks were "more open to the habits, customs, foods, and furniture of India than, for instance, the Chinese literati, for whom Chineseness was
much more a central part of their identity."[21] The impact of Buddhism on the
prosperous Tang dynasty went beyond the expansion of the silk trade and tea
drinking. As Chinese scholar Xinru Liu notes,

> At a deeper level, as Buddhism shaped the eschatology of the Chinese people, from
> the rulers down to the people on the lowest rung in society—peasants, slaves, arti-
> sans, etc., their concern for a better afterlife, either for their loved ones or for them-
> selves, made them donate their wealth, in the form of the finest silk textiles and
> clothing to the Buddhist institutions and priests. The worship of Buddha's relics and
> the translation of relics from India to China best exemplifies how the T'ang Chinese
> made every effort to save themselves from damnation through material means, and
> how silks flowed into religious institutions, including those outside China, in spite
> of prohibitions imposed by a powerful government.[22]

Buddhism traveled to Japan from Korea, which received the faith from Tang
China. Missionaries also arrived on the island of Sumatra across the Indian
Ocean, and Buddhism spread widely in the Indonesian kingdom of Srivijaya.

At the beginning of the twenty-first century, Buddhism is present on every
continent. The emphasis has moved from pure devotionalism toward social reform and universalism as well as meditation. A member of a Vietnamese Buddhist association in Germany wishing to be initiated into monkhood now flies
to a monastery in Perth, Australia, to be ordained in the presence of monks who
have flown in from other parts of the world.[23] The current reincarnation of the
bodhisattva, the exiled Tibetan leader the Dalai Lama, now holds prayer ses-

sions all over the world attended by capacity crowds. The multitudes of nation-alities united in their devotion to the Buddha depicted in the cave paintings of Dunhuang is now a regular occurrence.

A CARPENTER IN NAZARETH

While the Kushan kings in what is now Afghanistan were busy building stupas in honor of the Buddha and saffron-clad missionaries were traveling along the Silk Road to preach his teachings, a new force emerged in Palestine that would eventually spread and win converts all over the world with its monotheism, morality, and assurance of eternal life with God.

When the young Jesus of Nazareth started preaching that "the Kingdom of God has arrived," the second era of proselytization began. Jesus—the son of a carpenter, a popular Jewish preacher who found God in every human being and was crucified for preaching monotheism, love, and compassion—launched a new faith that conquered the Mediterranean world before spreading to the four corners of the globe. His death on the cross only confirmed to his followers that he was the messiah prophesied in the Old Testament. His gospel, literally meaning good news, spread like wildfire, and despite persecution by the Roman Empire, the believers converted thousands who came to be known as Christians, the Messiah folk. Christ's life of doing good, his martyr-dom, and the story of his resurrection ignited passion among people in the Mediterranean world that eventually won over the Roman Empire. At the Council of Nicaea in 325, three hundred bishops from the far corners of the empire who gathered to decide on the divinity of Jesus themselves were living proof how far the faith had spread. Finally, with the conversion of the Roman emperor Constantine and Theodosius's proclamation of Christianity as the official religion of the empire in 380, the power of the state was harnessed to the missionary task.[24] Of the Christian bishops residing in major cities of the Roman Empire, the pope in Rome emerged as the preeminent authority over the western part of the expanding Christendom. In the words of one historian, the Roman Catholic Church has proved "the most impressive and durable non-governmental organization in the history of the world."[25]

Well before Rome took over the guardianship of Christianity and lent its power and authority to the expansion of the faith, Christianity had spread. India's ancient Syrian Christian community believes that the apostle Saint Thomas reached southern India around the year 52 and began to preach near today's Chennai. His preaching of the new religion provoked hostility and led to his murder in 68.[26] Historians, however, doubt that it was Saint Thomas who came to India. More likely, a Christian trader from Syria by the name of Thomas brought the religion to India. Whatever the truth, the first Christian church outside the Mediterranean world marked a significant step, proving that the new faith could win converts in a foreign culture steeped in old tradition. A missionary college was founded in Alexandria as early as the second century, another in Constantinople in the early fifth century. Saints Patrick, Augustine of Canterbury, and Boniface carried the gospel to Ireland, England, and Germany. Numerous others spread the faith throughout Europe.[27]

In the fourth century Frumentius evangelized in Ethiopia, and in the following century Nestorians from Persia carried their faith to China, although they met with limited success. Thanks to sustained missionary activities by monks, backed by the pope and the conversion of kings, Europe emerged as the home of the Christians. Soon, however, the rise of Islam united the Arabian Peninsula and North Africa and brought Spain under Islamic rule, effectively confining the Christian faith to Europe. Had the Muslim forces not been defeated by the Franks under Charles Martel in the battle of Poitiers in 732, all of Europe, too, could have become part of the Islamic Caliphate. It would take the rise of the Europeans' sea power and their fervent evangelism, forged by centuries of struggle with Islam and the Crusades, for Christianity to break out of its continental confinement. An early attempt was made in the thirteenth century by Pope Innocent IV, who sought to build an alliance with the emergent Mongol power in China and Central Asia. He sent friars as missionaries to "diligently search out all things that concerned the state of the Tartars" and to exhort them "to give over their bloody slaughter of mankind and to receive the Christian faith." Accordingly, papal emissary Giovanni da Pian del Carpini reached the court of the emperor at Karakorum in 1245 and returned confident that the emperor was about to become a Christian.[28] That proved to be a chimera. But missionaries continued to set out for China and in the process expanded the European horizon. Friar Odoric of Pordenone, an Italian monk, traveled through India and Malay, reaching China by sea. He returned to Europe by way of Central Asia, visiting Tibet in 1325—the first European to do so. Serious attempts at conversion in Asia had to wait another century, however. In the fifteenth century, the Portuguese and Spanish began to search for new trade routes to Asia, and the pope granted Portugal's Prince Henry the Navigator rights over all lands south of the Tropic of Cancer for trade and conversion.

MISSION GRAPES

In the religious fervor of the era, explorers and adventurers saw the discovery of new land rich in spice and gold as one way of spreading the faith. "Gold is most excellent," wrote Columbus. "Gold constitutes treasure, and anyone who has it can do whatever he likes in the world. With it he can succeed in bringing souls to Paradise."[29] To Columbus, the work of conversion was urgent. "Our Lord is hastening these things," he wrote. "The Gospel must now be proclaimed to so many lands in such a short time." Starting with his landing on the Caribbean island that he named San Salvador (Holy Savior), Columbus thought he was launched on that mission. At his initiative, twenty-four native Indians were kidnapped and brought to Spain to be translators in proclaiming the gospel. Only six survived to return to the New World.[30]

Missionary ambition aside, European colonial expansion was informed by the struggle with Islam since the period of the Crusades and, in the Iberian Peninsula, with the Cordoban caliphate. When Portuguese explorers landed on the African coast they erected *padraos,* limestone pillars with crosses, to indicate that their possession was imbued with religious symbolism.[31] Both Christianity and Portuguese sovereignty were advancing. And the Castilian monarchy in Spain that underwrote Columbus's journeys was interested in spices, of course, but also in winning converts to Christianity. In his letter to the monarchs announcing his discovery of the islands "in the Indies," Columbus reminded them that the express purpose of his voyage was to raise funds for the Spanish reconquest of the Holy Land. "I will be able to pay Your Highnesses for five thousand cavalry and fifty thousand foot soldiers for the war and conquest of Jerusalem, for which purpose this enterprise was undertaken."[32]

Another type of proselytization undertaken by the Spanish monarchy— forcible conversion of the Jews and deportation of some 150,000 who refused baptism—proved a landmark event for the Jewish diasporas, which had spread throughout the Middle East and Europe since the first century. As Karen Armstrong writes, "The Muslims of Spain had given Jews the best home they ever had in the Diaspora, so the annihilation of Spanish Jewry was mourned by Jews throughout the world as the greatest disaster to have fallen their people since the destruction of the Temple in CE 70." Driven from Spain, many Jews took refuge in Portugal, where they were required to undergo pro forma conversion but were valued for their linguistic and business skills. In sharp contrast to Portugal's dogmatic approach to religion, in Southeast Asia the "new Christians" of

Portugal were pragmatically used to help business interests in Africa, Brazil, and Asia and to attract Genoese and Catalan capital.[33]

Meanwhile, the papacy had become the cheerleader for conversion through the discovery of new lands. Two years after Columbus's voyage, the pope granted Spain the same rights as given earlier to Portugal on lands west of the 47 degrees West longitude, or eastern Brazil. It was the ordained responsibility of the monarchs of Portugal and Spain to convert the newly found peoples. The missionaries' zeal for conversion put the clergy at the cutting edge of the Spanish colonial advance in the New World, bringing in its wake European culture and lifestyle. Because communion could not be given without wine, missionaries soon started planting vineyards. In the 1770s Jesuit father Junípero Serra, who had set up a mission in San Diego, planted the first of the so-called Mission grapes (an offshoot of Sardinian vines brought to North America by the Conquistadors), thus introducing wine to California. In a similar religious fervor nearly a century earlier, about two hundred French Huguenot refugees established a wine industry in the Dutch colony of South Africa.

In 1542—some four decades after Vasco da Gama landed in India—the Jesuit missionary Francis Xavier reached the Portuguese enclave of Goa. He launched a new phase of evangelical efforts in Asia carried on by a succession of missionaries—from Roberto de Nobili, who read Sanskrit and dressed like a Hindu Brahman to be acceptable in India, to Matteo Ricci, whose deep scholarship and adoption of the manners of China's literati won him success in the Chinese capital, albeit for a brief time. Mounting opposition by traditionalists and the emperor's fear of harboring a community that owed its loyalty not to him but to the pope ended the evangelicals' hope of winning millions of Chinese to the fold by converting the emperor. In Japan, too, evangelizing efforts suffered a serious reversal when several Franciscan missionaries were executed in Nagasaki in 1596.

But the Portuguese mission in Macao found a way to use adversity to reinforce the missionary effort. Several paintings of the Franciscan martyrdom were produced in Macao and sent to Mexico and Spain. Catholic converts in Mexico paraded the streets carrying the images of Nagasaki martyrs on their shoulders as an act of devotion. As Serge Gruzinski observes in *Les quatre parties du monde,* this unprecedented episode of Christians in many continents celebrating the martyrdom of their own seemed to fulfill the Old Testament prophecy about the spread of the faith worldwide.[34] The missionary effort in Asia was unrelenting, despite the setbacks in Japan and Vietnam. After the Opium Wars of 1842 and 1858 forced China to open its ports to European trade, Western missionaries returned. Ironically, it was one of these Christian converts, Hong Xiuquan, who believed himself to be the younger son of Jesus sent to found the Heavenly Kingdom on earth. He launched a long and bloody rebellion under the banner of "Taiping Tianguo" (Heavenly Kingdom of Great Peace). Perhaps twenty million died in the rebellion before the Taiping were suppressed in 1864. Several decades later, in angry response to Western influences, a new group calling itself "The Fist of Righteous Harmony" (Europeans called them "Boxers") rose up in 1899–1900 and attacked all the symbols of foreign presence: embassies, traders, and missionaries. Some thirty thousand Chinese Christians and several hundred foreign missionaries were killed before the rebellion was quelled.

Despite the troubled relations Christian missionaries had with the Chinese and rather low number of converts (only about a hundred thousand by 1900), missionaries were pioneers in building cultural bridges.[35] In a bid to win converts in China by dazzling them with the wealth of Western culture, missionaries translated Western classics, set up libraries and a museum of natural history, and introduced the Chinese to Western science and philosophy. The missionaries also widely diffused works on Western governments and history, often through journal articles. As historian Jonathan Spence notes, "These works systematically placed China in a world context and made it possible for Chinese scholars to view their country's history in a new way."[36] It was through missionary initiative that Yung Wing, the first Chinese student to graduate from an American university, came to Yale in 1847. Later Yung would bring the first group of 120 Chinese students to the United States.

The missionaries also opened up China to the West by systematically translating all kinds of documents from Chinese to European languages. Missionary scholars laid the foundation of sinology, which would help the West fathom China's seemingly "inscrutable" political and social life. Thanks to their fluency in the language and deep knowledge about China, many missionaries and their children who had grown up in China later played key roles as academics and diplomats in reconnecting communist China to the Western world. During my early years in Hong Kong when access to China was limited, I, like many journalists and diplomats, used to consult Father Laszlo Ladany, a Hungarian-born Jesuit with an encyclopedic knowledge of China, who had fled China after the communist revolution. His *China News Analysis,* based on Chinese radio broadcasts and refugee reports, was a staple for all China-watchers.

Things were quite different in the new British colonies in America. Growing numbers of Quakers and Baptists considered the new lands to be the "wilderness" promised in the revelation to John the Baptist and began migrating there.

Britain's newly acquired colony in India also offered British missionaries virgin pasture. For the first time since the arrival of the purported apostle Thomas, spurring converts more than a thousand years earlier to build churches, new churches sprang up. In 1793 a cobbler-turned-Baptist missionary named William Carey arrived in India with a passion to preach, leading him to learn several Indian languages. While translating the New Testament, he became an eminent grammarian and lexicologist of many Indo-Aryan languages. He is credited with laying the foundation of modern Bengali and printing in Bengali script for the first time. Similar contributions have been made by Christian missionaries all over the world. As Yale professor of missions and world Christianity Lamin Sanneh writes, "Missionary translation was instrumental in the emergence of indigenous resistance to colonialism. Local Christians acquired from the vernacular translations confidence in the indigenous cause. While the colonial system represented a worldwide economic and military order, mission represented vindication for the vernacular."[37]

Vietnam offers an interesting example of the unintended consequences of the connections established by missionaries. In the mid-nineteenth century, the executions of several French missionaries by the Vietnamese emperor offered a pretext for French military intervention and the eventual installation of French rule in Indochina for more than a hundred years. One legacy of that rule was the creation of a Vietnamese national writing system (*quôc-ngu*), which until then had been written in Chinese characters. In order to win over people from traditional Confucian teaching and the use of Chinese characters to transcribe Vietnamese, the French missionary Alexandre de Rhodes produced the first Vietnamese catechism in romanized letters.[38] This unlinking of Vietnamese from Chinese would have a profound effect on the spread of literacy, development of printing, and loosening of Chinese influence on Vietnam, with long-term consequences for the country.

Christian missionaries played a pioneering role in training women physicians and nurses. A vast majority of nurses in India even today are Christian women, and not surprisingly nurses are commonly called "sister" as if they were nuns. In the Philippines, a former Spanish and American colony, missionary physicians built hospitals that required trained nurses. Today, skilled Filipina nurses are among the country's major manpower contributions to the world.

Conversions in Africa, where the northern part of the continent was already Islamic, often consisted of summary baptisms before slaves were sent off on their perilous journey to the New World. Despite traumatic mass baptisms, people of African descent and their progenies emerged as some of the most devout Christians in the Portuguese colonies—Brazil, Angola, and the Atlantic islands—where they supported the church with their alms and collectively celebrated Catholic holidays.[39] However, Protestant missionaries who began arriving in the latter half of the nineteenth century seemed to have a bigger impact in opening up Africa, for better or worse.

OPENING "GOD'S HIGHWAY" IN AFRICA

Scottish missionary David Livingstone's name is inextricably associated with Africa; he has been called "African Geography personified."[40] Yet his arrival in Africa was accidental. Born into a poor family in 1813, Livingstone started working in a cotton-ginning mill at age ten. Influenced by evangelicals, he prepared himself to become a missionary in China, but the outbreak of the Opium War forced a change of plans. A chance encounter with a famous Scottish missionary who had been working in Africa inspired him to leave for Africa instead. He had studied medicine along with Greek and theology in Glasgow to prepare himself for the task. Despite three hundred years of European contact with coastal Africa, the vast continent was unknown territory. Earlier contacts were to trade slaves and ivory for clothes, liquor, and industrial goods. Few missionaries, or for that matter any Europeans except slavers, had gone very far into the uncharted interior of the continent, which was covered with malarial forests, forbidding deserts, and roaring waters. Livingstone's search for suitable inhabited land to set up a missionary station lured him deeper and deeper into the interior. His missionary role proved a dismal failure—he converted just one African chief who, unable to endure the rigor of monogamy, eventually abandoned the faith—and Livingstone emerged as a full-time explorer.

Livingstone concluded that God's purpose for his life was to use his talents to explore and map the unknown continent and open up "God's Highway": the Zambezi River, which flowed from the west to east coast of Africa and could be the continent's highway to "Christianity, commerce, and civilization." Having grown up in a Britain transformed by the Industrial Revolution and Adam Smith, he believed that Christianity, along with legitimate free trade in Africa's rich produce, such as ivory and beeswax, would transform the continent and end the Arab slave trade.[41] His hopes of turning the Zambezi into an east-west highway failed with the discovery of a 355-foot-high waterfall. His eight-year long search for the source of the Nile, though, was a failure; that mystery eluded Livingstone, as it had eluded the Greek historian Herodotus in 460 BCE. But the thirty years he spent in Africa exploring—surviving a lion attack, fighting illness, and most often separated from his family—helped put Africa on the map and turned him into a British icon. Having "trod some 29,000 miles of African soil and laid open nearly one million square miles of new country," Livingstone earned the reputation of being the Man of Africa.[42] His illustrated *Missionary Travels* was an instant best-seller; some seventy thousand copies were sold, and it was translated into several languages. Although the camera had been invented, the technology for printing half-tone photographs was not yet available. As a result, the illustrations in Livingstone's books, which made them such a sensation, were British artists' often inaccurate impressions based on his accounts.[43] Yet for all their shortcomings, Livingstone and his books generated an enthusiasm and awareness of Africa in Europe. They even triggered the interest of former slaves in America, some of whom had adopted the contemporary white man's contempt for their homeland. The American missionary and former slave Booker T. Washington wrote in 1913, "The story of Livingstone's life brought to me as to many other colored people in this country, not only the first real knowledge of Africa and the African people but the first definite interest in them."[44]

Livingstone inspired hundreds of missionaries to travel to Africa. His role in bringing Africa—the continent from which humankind originated, although knowledge of that fact would emerge a hundred years later—to Western awareness won him the adulation of his contemporaries. But later he was accused of being a tool of imperialism because his explorations preceded the scramble for Africa's riches. After the discovery of the world's largest diamond and gold mines, Africa was carved into British, Portuguese, French, German, and Belgian colonies, a harsh colonialism that Livingstone would have been loath to see. A product of the heyday of British Empire and the age of discovery (Charles Darwin had returned from his journey around the globe four years before Livingstone left for Africa) he clearly held a paternalistic view of Africans. But as his biographer Andrew Ross points out, what Livingstone really wanted in the 1860s was not a colony but a missionary and commercial settlement that engaged constructively with African society. His extensive writings, personal journals, and private and public letters make it clear that he would have opposed the shameful scramble that followed the discovery of gold and diamond mines a few years after his death. A strong opponent of slavery—his eighteen-year-old son died fighting the American Civil War on the side of the Union army—Livingstone was a lifelong campaigner for abolition.

Livingstone left home to convert Africans to Christianity, but his experience in Africa led him to appreciate the broader trend that was under way, something that continues to play out even today.

> The tendency and spirit of the age are more and more toward the undertaking of industrial enterprises of such magnitude and skill as to require the capital of the world for their support and execution—as the Pacific Railroad, Suez Canal, Mont Cenis Tunnel, and railway in India, and Western Asia, Euphrates Railroad, etc. The extension and use of railroads, steamships, telegraphs, break down nationalities and bring peoples geographically remote into close connection commercially and politically. They make the world one, and capital, like water, tends to a common level.[45]

Since Livingstone penned those lines, the world has moved further on the way to becoming one. Capital has flowed like water wherever it could find profit, and the rich West has found many more resources and technological means to carry the message of Jesus, some missionaries with good intentions and others for taking advantage of the poor. Roman Catholic and Protestant missionary organizations in the United States and Europe have spent untold sums to proselytize in the poorer parts of the world.

The rise of international mail service and the printing of postcards for communication and collection gave Christian missionaries a new tool of proselytizing. The idea of displaying images of Franciscan martyrs that began in the seventeenth century flowered, since the postal service could deliver inspiring picture postcards depicting the God's work done by missionaries in the remotest parts of the world. Martha Smalley writes that visual images of the missionaries, the people they sought to reach, and their physical context could not help but arouse compassion and curiosity among the public and generate the financial support crucial to the missionary movement.[46] Whether the missionary postcards succeeded in "marketing" evangelism to converts or supporters, they certainly developed an awareness among Europeans and Americans about distant lands. However distorted an image the postcards presented of "native" societies, they reinforced the developing connections among continents.

The Utah-based Church of Jesus Christ of Latter-day Saints is a good example of the resources and devotion that continue the effort to make the world one. Every year the Missionary Training Center in Provo, Utah, trains thousands of young missionaries in multiple foreign languages before sending them off for the eighteen-month or two-year mission that is obligatory for all church members. Not surprisingly, many former Mormon missionaries find themselves employed in government agencies and businesses dealing with foreign issues—globalizers of today. Even the Central Intelligence Agency is believed to count a substantial number of Mormons in its ranks.

With the arrival of shortwave radio, Christian broadcasts reached all the corners of the world, and today's satellite television and Internet have expanded the missionary reach to an unprecedented level. For example the GOD Channel, the flagship channel of global Christian broadcaster GOD TV, is available on fifteen different satellites, reportedly reaching an audience of some 270 million people all over the world. A multitude of Internet-based Christian news networks and lists today constantly connect the faithful, spurring them to campaign and collective action. Christian networks played a role in alerting public opinion to massacres in Darfur and galvanizing other NGOs like Human Rights Watch into action. But as in the past, missionary activities have also brought hate, persecution, and suffering. One commentator has denounced the GOD channel for its "hour upon hour of hate-filled, rabble-rousing, homophobic bigotry, much of it featuring (and funded by) right-wing American evangelists."[47]

REVELATION IN THE DESERT

While Christian proselytizing led missionaries such as Alexandre de Rhodes, Matteo Ricci, and David Livingstone to learn foreign languages and produce translations of the Bible in many languages, Islam's global drive has been essentially monolingual. Translations of the Koran do exist, but a true Muslim can only learn the words of God in Arabic, the language in which he spoke to the Prophet Muhammad. Now Islamic TV channels and Internet sites offer Arabic-language courses so that the faithful all over the world can recite the words that Muhammad ibn Abdallah, a Meccan trader, heard in a dark night in Mecca in 610 CE. Muhammad, the trader who according to some accounts could neither read nor write, had a vision while on a spiritual retreat at Mount Hira outside the city. He was awakened by an angel and commanded to recite the words in praise of God: "Recite in the name of thy Sustainer, who has created man out of germ-cell! Recite—for thy Sustainer is the Most Bountiful. One who has taught [man] the use of the pen—taught what he did not know." Muhammad found himself uttering those words in beautiful Arabic. These were the first words of God in Arabic and the beginning of a scripture calling for a new community, or *umma*, based not on tribal loyalty but on faith. The revelations came to the Prophet line by line, verse by verse, during the next twenty-three years, and formed the Koran, or Recitation. He began by preaching submission to One God and living a moral life of brotherhood and justice to his tribe, the Quraysh. By the time the Prophet died in 632, nearly all the tribes of Arabia were united by this new religion known as Islam, meaning the act of total submission to the Creator. Within a hundred years under the Prophet's successors, the caliphs, Islam had conquered the large swath of territory from Armenia to Spain. Had the Battle of Tours at the gateway to France in 732 not ended in the Islamic army's defeat, Islam would have swept through Western Europe as well. In the late fourteenth century the conversion of some of the Mongols to Islam brought the ferocity of the horse-riding nomads to the task of spreading Islam. Another Turkish tribe inspired by the spirit of *ghaza,* or holy war, rose. Convinced that they were chosen to act as Allah's Sword "blazing forth the way of Islam from the East to the West," those holy warriors, led by Osman Bey (later called Ottoman), ended up building the biggest Islamic empire and restoring the caliphate.[48] The outcome of this and other Islamic conquests in Asia was the creation of a vast Islamic umma, united around one religion and culture. There were large-scale conversions of non-Arabs to Islam, and with the exception of southern Europe, non-Islamic populations within the caliphate were reduced to a small minority. In the Fertile Crescent, large numbers of Egyptians and North Africans adopted Arabic and abandoned their pre-Islamic languages. Islam and Arabic emerged as the core of a new civilization. So extensive was the Islamic empire and so intense was the interaction among the people living there that it foreshadowed today's globalization. Like the global society that is emerging today, as one scholar of Islam puts it, the Islamic oecumene "exhibited the subsistence, interaction, and engagement of the local and universal in the economic, political and cultural spheres. . . . It was a vast domain across which capital, commodities, ideas and people moved continuously."[49]

Christianity and Islam shared the same universalizing impulse founded on the idea that their faith should become the sole religion of humankind. But unlike Christianity, Islam is marked by the absence of any kind of priesthood or ecclesiastic organization charged with spreading the faith. Islamic scholars and preachers accompanied traders, but no missionary society or overseas mission was associated with the caliphate. Islam's spread in the first several hundred years came mainly through military conquest in the Mediterranean world and Central Asia. But Islam gained adherents in Africa and Southeast Asia through missionary activities of ordinary Muslims who found themselves among nonbelievers. As Thomas Arnold recounts in his classic study, Islam's first introduction to Eastern Europe was the work of an Islamic jurist who was taken prisoner in the Byzantine Empire.[50] More commonly, the traders carried the faith far and wide. The simplicity of the Islamic doctrine—"there is no god but God and Muhammad is his prophet"—and the ardor with which the faithful practiced it impressed others. Not only is the creed simple and devoid of theological complexities, the duties required of Muslims are simple, too: recital of the creed, observance of prayers five times a day, payment of legal alms, fasting during the month of Ramadan, and the pilgrimage to Mecca. As the famous fourteenth-century Moroccan traveler Ibn Battuta put it, Mecca emerged as "the annual congress of the Muslim world."[51] The trans-Saharan trade by camel caravan that had developed since the Roman times was the main avenue for the spread of Islam to West Africa. Yemeni and Omani traders traveling along the East African Swahili coast to buy ivory and slaves also won converts. By the beginning of the second millennium, many African kingdoms had embraced Islam, and Arabic had become the language of religion and learning. Mansa Musa, ruler of the vast Mali Empire, made a celebrated pilgrimage to Mecca in the fourteenth century.[52] While Arab traders carried the faith to Africa, Islam marched on in Asia—the longtime playground of traders from Arabia.

The spread of Islam in the Indian subcontinent began peacefully through traders (we have seen the rise of Mappila community in the Malabar Coast). But it became one of the most violent episodes in Islamic history. The Ghaznivid invasion of India, conceived of as a holy war against Hindu infidels, became an opportunity to loot gold and jewelry from the temples. After his capture of Delhi in 1000, Mahmud of Ghazni wrote: "I had come to Hindustan to war against infidels. I had triumphed over my adversaries, I had put to death some *lacs* [hundreds of thousands] of infidels and idolaters, and I had stained my proselytising sword with the blood of the enemies of faith."[53] For such a proselytizer there was obviously no conflict between converting the infidels and looting their gold.

Yet Mahmud of Ghazni, who spilled so much blood and consequently poisoned Hindu attitudes toward Muslims for generations to come—leading nine centuries later to bitter partition creating Islamic Pakistan—brought with him a remarkable scholar from Central Asia, Al-Biruni.[54] Al-Biruni's account of India, *Tahqiq-i-Hind,* produced after a ten-year sojourn, remains a gold mine for historians. Most important, it built a knowledge bridge between India and the Arab world. Al-Biruni learned Sanskrit in order to critique the idolatrous faith, but his translation of India's classics made them available to the wider world. His translation of Indian mathematical texts allowed the Arab mathematician Al-Khwarizmi to take Hindu numerals and the concept of the zero to the West. One historian calls Al-Biruni the "world's first orientalist," who made a "significant point about the culture of the Islamic world: that Muslims think thoughts that have nothing to do with Islam."[55] Seven hundred years of Islamic rule in India has left the world's second largest Muslim population in a Hindu-majority country, with attendant frictions and political division. But it has also created a rich fusion of culture embodied in the marble splendor of the Taj Mahal, music, painting, and literature.

HOLY WAR REACHES ASIA

Apart from the simplicity and egalitarian character of Islam, which attracted many in the hierarchical societies of Asia, the new faith was attractive for other temporal and practical reasons. Muslim traders reached Canton as early as the seventh or eighth century, where they built perhaps the first mosque outside the Middle East. But Islam did not gain a foothold in Southeast Asia until several centuries later, when the Arab traders' presence had grown. Use of lateen sails, the compass, and rising demand for Asian spices—the "spice-orgy" that began to affect Europeans after the Crusades—significantly boosted Arab trading with India and Southeast Asia's pepper kingdoms. Marco Polo reported in 1298 that "the people of Perlak [North Sumatra] used all to be idolaters, but owing to contact with Saracen merchants, who continually resort here in their ships, they have all been converted to the law of Mahomet."[56]

The growing colony of Muslims in Southeast Asian ports was strengthened by the rise of Islamic power in western India, from where Indian merchants set off for Southeast Asia for centuries. By 1500 Gujarati Muslim traders could be found in all the major ports of the Indian Ocean and Southeast Asia. They carried with them the influence of powerful Islamic potentates in India.[57] While Malays and Indonesians were attracted by the traders' devotion and their Holy Book, they were also impressed by their opulence and sophisticated lifestyle. Similar considerations led droves of Filipinos to embrace Islam. For many traders, the surest way to succeed in life was to join the Islamic brotherhood of traders. A sixteenth-century Spanish account explains that the Filipinos "believe that paradise and successful enterprises are reserved for those who submit to the religion of the Moros of Borney [Brunei], of which they make much account. . . . These are a richer people, because they are merchants, and with their slaves, cultivate the land."[58] Historian Anthony Reid points out that the mobile life that the trading profession offered called for a faith different from worshipping the spirits of ancestors, trees, and mountains: a faith based on an omnipresent god. "The trader who moved from place to place needed a faith of broader application. If he moved beyond his own island he needed acceptance and contacts in the trading cities. Islam provided both a faith and a social system for such traders."[59]

A dramatic example of the new power of Islam as an economic force occurred in 1409, when the Hindu king of Malacca, Parameswaram, and his entire court voluntarily embraced Islam. His example was followed by the Chinese ruler of the trading city of Palembang. Both cities became active promoters of Islam at home and abroad.[60] It was a sure way to ensure the continued prosperity of the most important trading posts in Southeast Asia. With the status of Gujarati and Arab traders on the rise in maritime Southeast Asia, larger and larger numbers of rural and urban people were converting to Islam, adopting its ways and identifying themselves with an international Islamic community. By the beginning of the seventeenth century, a sizable number of Turkish, Persian, and Arab merchants were based in Southeast Asia. An Islamic connection not only brought wealth and prestige but seemed to provide legitimacy. The ruler of the Java-based Mataram dynasty acquired the title of sultan by sending a delegation to Mecca.[61]

But the rise of a peaceful trade-based Islam was followed in the sixteenth century by the arrival of aggressive Christian powers who combined their craving for spice with evangelical zeal and enmity for Islam. Indiscriminate Portuguese attacks on Islamic shipping and their capture of the port city of Melaka introduced the spirit of the Crusades to Asia, projecting for the first time, as Anthony Reid notes, "the first of the world-power conflicts to bedevil its history. Local conflicts suddenly became crusades and holy wars, and rulers for the first time saw the conversion of their subjects as essential to their survival."[62] The Portuguese onslaught led dispossessed traders from Melaka to establish themselves in other trading centers, making these cities "self-consciously Muslim opponents of the infidel intruders."[63] The kingdom of Aceh on the tip of Sumatra earned its title "the verandah of Mecca" as the port and center where pilgrims and scholars awaited the journey aboard pepper ships to the Holy Land. In the new spirit of jihad introduced by the conflict, the ruler of Aceh wrote to the Ottoman sultan asking for help in fighting a holy war against the Portuguese. The opening of the pilgrimage routes to Muslims, he added, would enable him to gain innumerable riches in jewels, gold, and silver in the area currently exploited by the "infidels." Despite the Ottoman emperor's interest in the project, the support he sent had marginal effort in blunting the Portuguese power.

With the introduction of the crusading spirit in the region, Islamic states came to clash with the existing Hindu-Buddhist kingdoms. Small but determined Islamic armies, convinced that Allah was on their side and equipped with large Turkish cannons and other firearms, crushed the resistance. Vanquished rulers and their subjects accepted the faith of the victors. Yet that formal acceptance of Islam was layered atop the existing spirit worship and Hindu and Buddhist mythology and rituals. "The old culture," writes M. C. Ricklefs about Java, Indonesia's most populous island, where the towering Buddhist Borobudur monument still stands, "grew and lived on in a more-or-less Islamic garb. . . . Javanese Muslims probably had little doubt that their [Islamic] faith was true and correct."[64] This Indonesianized eclectic and tolerant Islam would soon collide with new Arab orthodoxy, fomenting civil war in the country. But Islam had already started influencing aspects of the region's culture.

The Muslim ban on the representation of living things in a realistic manner has led to the introduction of a whole new range of geometric designs and arabesque motifs while incorporating floral patterns from tropical Southeast Asia.[65] The same injunction against any form of art representing humans has led Indonesians to alter their traditional shadow puppets. The puppets representing characters of the Hindu classic *Ramayana* have been distorted into awkward shapes. The sultan of Mataram in Java even adopted Middle Eastern garb as an act of faith. The emulation spread to the traders. As shipping developed and more and more traders began making the hajj pilgrimage to Mecca, their attires changed, too. Merchants returned from the hajj dressed like their counterparts in Syria and Egypt.

ALL ROADS LEAD TO MECCA

Mecca's emergence as the center of the Islamic universe was reinforced and accelerated with the introduction of steamships and railways developed, ironically, by the Christian colonial powers. The opening of the Suez Canal in 1869 and the organization of regular hajj trips by Dutch and British shipping companies since the late nineteenth century have reinforced the pan-Islamic links.[66] Thanks to Dutch steamship service, the annual number of *hajis* from

Indonesia alone rose from around two thousand in the 1850s to seven thousand at the turn of the twentieth century. These annual gatherings of Muslims diffused the prevailing thinking heard in Saudi sermons and religious schools all over the world. In addition, the pilgrims often extended their sojourns in Mecca or Cairo for further religious studies.[67] This infusion of fresh ideas from the Arab world, especially the rising conservative thinking, soon produced some impact in Indonesia, which had emerged as the world's largest Islamic country.

The first instance of a violent political movement with long-distance inspiration occurred in 1803 when three Sumatran hajis returned from Mecca profoundly influenced by the orthodox Wahhabi movement. The founder of the school of thought, Muhammad ibn Abd al-Wahhab, called for a return to the unadulterated Muslim community established by Muhammad in Medina and the discarding of all rituals and customs acquired as Islam spread to other cultures. Any Muslims who refused to share this purist, exclusivist view, especially Shias and mystical Sufis, were put to the sword. Indonesia's eclectic Islam, with its overlay of Javanese mysticism, became the target of the returned Wahhabist converts. They soon launched a jihad against the Indonesian brand of Islam, which involved Sufi prayers to saints, the acceptance of a matriarchal society, and tolerance of drinking and gambling. The jihad in south Sumatra turned into a savage war. It was finally ended in 1838 with Dutch colonial intervention just as the original Wahhabist movement was brutally put down by the Egyptian army.[68]

But the Wahhabist school lived to fight another day. Protected by a powerful Arab tribal leader, Muhammad Ibn Saud, the founder of the current Saudi royal dynasty, the teaching survived until opportunity arose at the collapse of the Ottoman Empire. Backed by British arms, Ibn Saud's heir, Abd al-Aziz, took control of Arabia in 1932 and named it the Kingdom of Saudi Arabia. The story goes that Abd al-Wahhab wanted an oath from him "that you will perform jihad against the unbelievers [non-Wahhabi Muslims]. In return you will be leader of the Muslim community, and I will be leader in religious matters."[69]

He kept his promise by executing forty thousand men and establishing Wahhabism as the state religion.[70] The rise of orthodox faith in Saudi Arabia spurred many Indonesians into launching the Darul Islam movement (Arabic dar al-Islam, or "Islamic territory") to oppose the secular Indonesian Republic being set up by Indonesian nationalists like Mohammed Hatta and Sukarno. Darul Islam was crushed and its leaders were killed. But the Wahhabist-Salafi ideology that inspired Indonesian Muslims to try to capture power and install a state based on *sharia*, or Islamic law, lives on to this day.

Ever since Southeast Asians embraced Islam, they have slowly become part of the larger Islamic community linked by the bond of religious education in madrassas—Islamic universities—in Saudi Arabia and Egypt and, of course, the pilgrimage to Mecca. Since the Wahhabist-backed rise of the House of Saud in Saudi Arabia, the kingdom's ministry of religious affairs and the country's considerable oil-generated wealth have been devoted to the spread of the orthodox faith. Saudi funds have set up thousands of religious schools and mosques in many developing countries. Visiting a *pesantran*—an Islamic school—in Indonesia, I received a warm welcome, delivered in Arabic, because the teacher took me to be a visitor from the Holy Land. The school was teaching the students the language of the Holy Koran. Following the attacks of 11 September in the United States and the bombing of a nightclub in Bali by fundamentalist Islamists in 2002, the close connection between Wahhabist doctrine and al-Qaeda, a transnational terrorist organization dedicated to removing foreign influence in Muslim countries and restoring a Muslim caliphate, has come under international scrutiny.[71] The transformation of the region that began with the arrival of the faith from Arabia's desert five hundred years ago still plays out. Aceh, once called the "verandah of Mecca," has reemerged as a center of conservative Islam, enforcing sharia law with brutality. Since the 9/11 attacks, new trouble spots like Afghanistan and Pakistan have come into focus. The Saudi-supported madrassas, in addition to providing religious education to the young, have emerged as incubators of Islamic militancy, providing recruits for al-Qaeda terrorists. The al-Qaeda, says French expert on Islam Olivier Roy, dream of a virtual, universal umma, much as 1960s radicals dreamed of the "world proletariat" and "revolution": "They are a lost generation, unmoored from traditional societies and cultures, frustrated by a Western society that does not meet their expectations. And their vision of a global *umma* is both a mirror of and a form of revenge against the globalization that has made them what they are."[72]

The rise of modern travel and communication that has made the emergence of global terrorism possible has also reinforced the brotherhood of Islam. The obligation of a pilgrimage to Mecca at least once in one's lifetime has helped to create a strong global bond among Muslims. Mecca, the old entrepôt where for centuries the annual trade fair brought camel caravans and merchandise from afar, has been transformed into the world's most globalized holy site. In 2004 some 2.3 million Muslims from all over the world gathered in Mecca. Dressed in the same long, white, unstitched cotton robes, men and women of different colors and speaking different languages swirled around the Kaaba in a giant stream to partake of the divine, all differences dissolved.[73] Religious teachers from the Middle East and South Asia also travel to Europe, which boasts a large Muslim minority, to preach sermons during Friday prayers at European mosques.

While Mecca and the Saudi kingdom remain the world hub of the Islamic faith, modern technology has vastly expanded the scope of the preacher. Dozens of satellite television channels, including Saudi-based al-Arabiya, Qatar-based al-Jazeera, and the mouthpiece of Lebanon's Shiite Hezbollah, al-Manar, broadcast news and views that are accessible all over the world. The U.S.-based IslamiCity, set up in 1995, offers Arabic-language courses and claims to receive a million visitors a month who listen to the recitation of the Koran.[74] One popular Internet site, Islam Online, says its mission is "to create a unique, global Islamic site on the Internet that provides services to Muslims and non-Muslims in several languages. To become a reference for everything that deals with Islam, its sciences, civilization and nation."[75] In the autumn of 2005 the terrorist organization al-Qaeda launched its Internet-based news service, Sawt al-Khilafa, or Voice of the Caliphate. With a gun and a copy of the Koran on his desk, a newsreader dressed in a combat vest delivered to the faithful the news about the global jihad and sent its "best wishes to the Islamic nation."[76] It is not known how many people watched the broadcast, but it was a reminder of a new era of virtual proselytizing. The Prophet Muhammad's vision of an Islamic umma that transcends borders has come closer to realization than ever. While the bitter Shia-Sunni divide continues to trouble the faith, 1.6 billion Muslims all over the world are now connected by radio, television, and the Internet, and the number of converts continues to grow.

BOIL THERE, YOU OFFSPRING OF THE DEVIL!

The drive to find souls to convert has taken missionaries to distant countries and to continents that were discovered partly because of that missionary drive. That encounter between preachers and the indigenous peoples, we have seen, produced great suffering. As witnesses to this suffering, missionaries brought to the world tales of tragedy and great inhumanity. But they also raised for the first time, in concrete form, the question of what is a human being and what are his or her rights. The missionary concern and writing about human rights led to what can be called a globalization of values. That awareness about the rights of a fellow human being from a totally different culture and the search for common ethical principles and international social objectives have led to the rise of new "missionary" organizations such as Amnesty International and Human Rights Watch.

One of the earliest thinkers to draw attention to the issue was an extraordinary priest, Bartolomé de Las Casas, who traveled to the New World and returned from his forty-four-year sojourn with fundamental questions about human rights. He brought back to Spain the horror that was being perpetrated against the natives by Spanish Christians. In one of the gruesome passages in his publication *A Short Account of the Destruction of the Indies* (1542), he wrote:

> And the Christians, with their horses and swords and pikes began to carry out massacres and strange cruelties against them. They attacked the towns and spared neither the children nor the aged nor pregnant women nor women in childbed, not only stabbing them and dismembering them but cutting them to pieces as if dealing with sheep in the slaughterhouse. . . . They took infants from their mothers' breasts, snatching them by the legs and pitching them headfirst against the crags or snatched them by the arms and threw them into the rivers, roaring with laughter and saying as the babies fell into the water, "Boil there, you offspring of the devil!"

The book, dedicated to King Philip II, occasioned the first debate over human rights. Were the native Indians who practiced human sacrifice human? Did they have any rights? In a historic encounter, Las Casas debated leading theologian Juan Ginés de Sepúlveda, who held that Native Americans were "barbarous, simple, unlettered, and uneducated, brutes, totally incapable of learning anything but mechanical skills."[77] Las Casas answered the question about the humanity of the natives in the following words:

> For all the peoples of the world are human beings. And the definition of humans, collectively and severally, is one: that they are rational beings. All possess understanding and volition, being formed in the image and likeness of God; all have the natural capacity or faculties to understand and master the knowledge that they do not have—all take pleasure in goodness and all abhor evil. All men are alike in what concerns their creation. And no one is born enlightened. From this it follows that all of us must be guided and aided at first by those who were born before us. And the savage peoples of the earth may be compared to uncultivated soil that readily brings forth weeds and useless thorns, but has within itself such natural virtue that by labor and cultivation it may be made to yield sound and beneficial fruits. Thus all humankind is one.[78]

Las Casas persuaded the king to prohibit forcible conversion. Although the ban on forced conversion did not last and the realities of power and greed trumped the voices of morality, this debate would inspire future reformers.

David Livingstone, who started out on a mission of conversion, was the first European nonslaver to journey to the interior of Africa. His reports helped raise awareness of the horrors of the slave trade. He saw Arab traders leading slave caravans of up to a thousand slaves roped together with neck yokes or leg irons, hauling ivory or other heavy loads as they trudged through the jungle to the sea. Among the more memorable of his dispatches was Livingstone's eyewitness account of a massacre by slave traders in Nyangwe, Congo, that he chanced upon while searching for the source of the Nile. Having run out of paper, he wrote on any scrap he could find: "As I write I hear the loud wails on the left bank over those who are there slain, ignorant of their many friends who are now in the depths of the Lualaba. Oh, let Thy kingdom come!" Sending his account to Britain for publication, Livingstone said that if his writings should lead to the suppression of the terrible Ujijian slave trade, "I shall regard that as a greater matter by far than the discovery of all the Nile sources together."[79] Parliament did take up the issue, and in 1873, barely a month after Livingstone's death, England forced the sultan of Zanzibar to close the slave market by threatening naval blockades.

Livingstone's railing against the Boer regime in South Africa helped to turn British public opinion against the Boers' apartheid policy. He warned: "These white thieves will find imitators among the blacks; and though now the boers think a Caffre's blood as the same value as that of a baboon, the time may not be distant when their own will be counted as cheap. When that day arrives, we may be spared to say, the outbreak is neither "unjust nor unprovoked."[80]

Livingstone was following in a tradition of religious abolitionists in Britain. More than fifty years earlier William Wilberforce, an evangelist and member of Parliament, began a campaign against slavery in the United Kingdom. He introduced antislavery legislation in Parliament every year for eighteen years. In his famous first speech calling for the abolition of slave trade in 1789, Wilberforce appealed to traders' compassion: "I will not accuse the Liverpool merchants: I will allow them, nay, I will believe them to be men of humanity; and I will therefore believe, if it were not for the enormous magnitude and extent of the evil which distracts their attention from individual cases, and makes them think generally, and therefore less feelingly on the subject, they would never have persisted in the trade."[81]

In August 1833, a month after Wilberforce died, Parliament abolished slavery throughout the empire. His campaign did not, however, make much of a dent in slavery on America's plantations, where the practice continued for another thirty years. But the antislavery movement can be seen as the first transnational movement upholding the notion that all men are equal—a notion embodied in the U.S. Constitution and later in the Declaration of the Rights of Man during the French Revolution.

BETTER LIGHT A CANDLE THAN CURSE THE DARKNESS

In the 150 years following these developments, human rights remained a concept discussed by religious groups and intellectuals but devoid of practical meaning since governments continued to use violence against their citizens for reasons of state. The world had to wait until the global community was better connected by the media to respond to the calls for protecting human rights worldwide. It was perhaps no accident that the world's first nongovernmental organization to champion human rights emerged while the world was being drastically shrunk by the launch of the first communication satellites. The media coverage of world news, already facilitated by international telephone and telex, was getting a new boost. For the first time it was possible to be a missionary without leaving home.

A young British lawyer named Peter Benenson turned out to be just that—a missionary for human rights who did not need to leave home. Reading a newspaper on his way to work in London one spring morning in 1961, Benenson had an epiphany: it was possible to fight against injustice against fellow human beings without traveling where the victims lived. He was outraged at a report about two Portuguese students who had been arrested and sentenced to imprisonment for drinking a toast to liberty in a Lisbon restaurant. The action by Portugal's dictatorship under António de Oliveira Salazar was in character. But Benenson pondered about how to mobilize public opinion against such disregard for basic human rights. He would later write: "Open your newspaper—any day of the week—and you will find a report from somewhere in the world of someone being imprisoned, tortured or executed because his opinions or religion are unacceptable to his government. The newspaper reader feels a sickening sense of impotence. Yet if these feelings of disgust all over the world could be united into common action, something effective could be done."[82]

Benenson persuaded the editors of the *Observer* newspaper to publish a front-page appeal titled "The Forgotten Prisoners" in its Sunday supplement of 28 May. He knew that the pressure of public opinion a hundred years earlier had led to the emancipation of slaves. It was time to get public opinion mobilized to shame jailers in all countries who held political prisoners and prisoners of conscience or engaged in torture. Thanks to the internationalization of the media, his appeal was reprinted in newspapers around the world. Like-minded people from Britain, Belgium, France, Germany, Ireland, Switzerland, and the United States gathered in July to set up "a permanent international movement in defense of the freedom of opinion and religion."[83] Amnesty International, the first international NGO for human rights, was born. Its first office opened in London, and offices in West Germany, Holland, France, Italy, and Switzerland soon followed. Within a year a Prisoner of Conscience Fund was established to provide relief to prisoners and their families. Thanks to the media campaign, some 210 prisoners of conscience were adopted by seventy groups in seven countries. A candle surrounded by barbed wire was adopted as Amnesty International's logo. Benenson reminisced: "Once the concentration camps and the hell-holes of the world were in darkness. Now they are lit by the light of the Amnesty candle; the candle in barbed wire. When I first lit the Amnesty candle, I had in mind the old Chinese proverb: 'Better light a candle than curse the darkness.'"[84]

Benenson's conversion to a missionary role did not happen overnight. His concern about human suffering and justice began early. At sixteen, he launched his first campaign to raise support for Republican war orphans of the Spanish Civil War. Concerned about the fate of Jews in Hitler's Germany, he managed to raise funds from his Eton friends and their families to bring two young German Jews to Britain, perhaps saving their lives. As a young lawyer, he earned a reputation for his commitment to human rights. His experiences in Spain, Cyprus, Hungary, and South Africa confirmed for him the need to defend individuals against the power of the state and upholding the rule of law. It was his realization in 1961 that the world was sufficiently integrated and was ready for the launching of a transnational grass-roots campaign. When Amnesty International was awarded the Nobel Peace Prize in 1977, the organization accepted the award in the name of 168,000 individuals in 107 countries who were their active members and supporters. By 2005, the ranks of AI members and supporters had swollen to 1.8 million in more than 150 countries and territories.

HIGH-SPEED GLOBAL AWARENESS

Amnesty International has not only grown in size and influence, but its concerns have widened to cover human rights identified in the Universal Declaration of Human Rights. On 10 December 1948, the United Nations General Assembly adopted and proclaimed the Universal Declaration of Human Rights, announcing that everyone has the right to life, liberty, and security of person and that no one shall be subjected to arbitrary arrest, detention, or exile. Amnesty's secretary general, Irene Khan, originally from Bangladesh, laments the sorry state of human rights worldwide since the declaration was adopted. "Today," Khan wrote in AI's annual report in 2005, "the UN appears unable and unwilling to hold its member states to account. In the latest incident of paralysis, the UN Security Council has failed to muster the will to take effective action on Darfur. In this case it was held hostage to China's oil interests and Russia's trade in arms. The outcome is that poorly equipped African Union monitors stand by helplessly and bear witness to war crimes and crimes against humanity."[85] Amnesty International and the Coalition for an International Criminal Court organized pressure involving some two thousand international NGOs such as Human Rights Watch. Their joint efforts finally brought the Security Council to refer the Darfur situation to the ICC.

As Kenneth Roth, director of Human Rights Watch, explains, the ability to shame governments before their publics and peers is the most powerful tool that groups like his possess. And they do that through the press. Amnesty International, too, has only the weapon of publicity and the threat of publicity as its tool. By press, Roth means not just the steady stream of reports on human-rights violations his organization releases to newspapers and wire services but also the more powerful Internet, which allows detailed reports, images, and exchanges with visitors from all over the world. The Human Rights Watch Web site now offers reports in six languages, and its staff can speak about forty-five languages. The entire human rights movement rests on the simple belief that governments respond to public opinion. Governments also respond to pressure from other governments—not necessarily public opinion alone.[86] "When I think back to when I started doing human-rights work, which was over twenty years ago," says Roth, sitting in his office overlooking Manhattan, "human rights reporting was understood to be [that] you travel to a country, you spend a few weeks collecting information, you come back and write a report, you publish your report. It was all a very slow, very long term." It was only with the advent of the Internet that the human rights movement has taken off. "The Internet really did change things dramatically."[87]

Emperor Aśoka tried to promote Buddhism by engraving Buddha's teachings on rock faces. Xuanzang carried loads of Buddhist teachings on dozens of packhorses to China. Christian missionaries fanned out to the world, translated the Bible into many languages, and read the catechism with the converts. Islamic devotees have traveled thousands of miles to visit Mecca and attend madrassas. Now powerful radio and TV stations owned by Christian missionaries beam the teachings of Christ, and satellite channels owned by Islamic groups carry the message of jihad against infidels. The Internet has become the ubiquitous tool for all faiths and movements to spread their messages and win converts. Human rights groups and environmentalists all over the world are connected and are constantly striving to win over more people to their cause.

The Darfur vote at the Security Council succeeded, Dicker says, "through very intensive work, not only through creating public awareness about the atrocities in Darfur but building a sense of safety in numbers among governments that wanted to send the situation to the ICC but were afraid of U.S. retaliation."[88] He says it took a lot of work in Europe, Africa, and Latin America to develop a coalition of governments who were willing to stand up on principle and force the United States to back down at last. But, significant as this victory might be, human rights activists knew it was only the beginning of a new phase. Since the Security Council vote, bloodshed has continued. The African Union peacekeepers who were dispatched there to dissuade the Arab militia from continuing their genocidal attacks proved too weak for the post. Amid a worldwide campaign conducted by human rights NGOs, in November 2006 the Sudanese government agreed to accept twenty thousand mixed U.N.–African Union peacekeepers. There is a long road ahead to bring safety to Darfuris. As Irene Khan of Amnesty puts it, activists like her believe in the power of ordinary people to bring about extraordinary change. "We remain the eternal hope-mongers."[89]

Dicker is uncomfortable at being compared to a missionary, but he admits that people who become advocates for others have to be motivated by a sense of mission. It's not the most lucrative field, and it could mean long separations from family. For those engaged in on-the-ground reporting of abuses, this profession could even be dangerous. Some people come to the human rights movement for traditional religious reasons: they think it reflects the view that God created every individual and every individual is unique and special. But many people share a similar sentiment from a secular perspective. "Part of their personal morality, quite apart from whether they believe in God, is that there is something worth savoring or worth protecting and valuing," says Roth. "Our job is to provide that protection and help people. I guess there is an element of believing."[90]

Belief in an idea with universal application has tied the world together for more than two millennia. Global awareness has just become more instantaneous and its consequences, for better or worse, more immediate.

Chapter 5 World in Motion

Your Majesty will know best that what we should esteem and admire most is that we have discovered and made a course around the entire rotundity of the world—that going by the occident we have returned by the orient.
—Report to the Spanish monarch Charles I of Juan Sebastián Elcano, surviving captain of Ferdinand Magellan's Armada de Moluccas, 6 September 1522

On a calm June morning in 2004, the river Guadalquivir flowed gently past the flowering bushes and palms lining Seville's cemented embankments. I have come to sit by the silently flowing witness to the opening of the New World and beginning of a massive migration that forever changed the world. The Arabs who once ruled Spain called it *Wadi al-Kebir*, the great river. The sun had yet to burn off the morning mist, and the river that once upon a time teemed with boats was now covered in haze, dreaming of its past glory. There had been all manner of vessels, bearing silver and gold ingots from the New World, crates

---

Christopher Columbus reaches the New World. Etching from Washington Irving, *Columbus, His Life and Voyages* (New York: G. P. Putnam's Sons, 1914)

of fragrant cloves and cardamom from the Spice Islands coming in to unload and sailing away with barrels of famous Seville olive oil and wheat for foreign destinations. Tall-masted *nao* carrying emigrants unfurled their sails as they too went past the Torre del Oro (Tower of Gold) heading for the open ocean. Seville, once the capital of European exploration, had launched the first-ever voyage in search of a new route to Asia and then a journey around the globe, which in course of the sixteenth century sent nearly half a million Spaniards to the New World. This effort initiated a churning of the world's population that has not stopped since. One in five of the Spanish emigrants to the New World was from Seville.[1] It could be said that Seville gave birth to the modern era of globalization.

Standing on the riverbank almost five hundred years later, it was difficult for me to imagine the bright morning in August 1519, when Portuguese captain Ferdinand Magellan led massive black-painted sail ships under the Spanish flag of King Charles I to sea. The night before the crew had visited the church of Santa Maria de la Victoria to confess their sins and pray for a safe journey before waking up the next morning to fire a few salvoes of cannon, puncturing the morning calm with thundering noise and puffs of white smoke. A crowd had gathered on the banks of the river to watch the five vessels of the Armada de Moluccas begin their journey to the Atlantic Ocean, led by the ship *Trinidad.* The sailors knew only that they would be journeying to a faraway place—Spice Island—but most had no clue that their circuitous route would take them through the uncharted waters of South America in the hope of finding a new passage to the East via the West. Such a strait would indeed be discovered and named for the captain, but during their journey, the sailors' ships would also glide into a vast Pacific Ocean. Most of the crew would never return to Seville. Three years later, in September 1522, a lone ship, the *Victoria,* limped back to the quay of Guadalquivir, with only 18 of the original crew surviving the voyage. Dazed sailors in tattered clothes walked barefoot to the Santa Maria de la Victoria to thank God and repent the sins incurred during their travels around an unknown world. The somber return of that expedition was marked at the time only by the obligatory discharge of artillery, but we know now that it was a momentous event. For the first time since our human ancestors made it to the other side of the Pacific some twelve to fourteen thousand years earlier, progenies of their cousins in Europe had taken to the ocean and circled the earth in one lifetime. Human interconnectedness became global in the fullest geographic sense of the term.

Most humans are, as Saint Francis observed, *homines viatores,* perennial movers.[2] One could also add they are also the most *adventurous* of all creatures, "given to, or having many adventures, enterprising, daring," as defined by the *Oxford English Dictionary.* Humans have undertaken hazardous enterprises to learn about the unknown, escape hardship, or simply search for chances of personal advancement.

The history of our human ancestors' journey out of Africa is the best proof of that aspect of human nature. But the human journey did not stop with the beginning of sedentary agriculture. This chapter will show how adventurers—explorers, travelers, and migrants—have continued to cross borders, thus incessantly expanding connections among human communities. We have seen how the desire to find new and more hospitable areas to settle spurred the early migrations of agrarian populations throughout Central Asia and India. Migration has continued throughout history—at times forced by others and at other times undertaken spontaneously to seek new opportunities and better lives in a foreign land. Even refugees from war and persecution, who throughout history have been forced to make dangerous journeys to foreign lands, can be counted in this category as adventurers. Refugees have added to the trade diasporas that have grown since the time of Assyrian colonies in Anatolia.

The curiosity about what lay beyond the known border has led generations of explorers to undertake dangerous journeys and bring back knowledge that has connected wider and wider areas of the world. In the days when travel was extremely hazardous, the journey of exploration was often not just for the sake of new information. Even though the results of his voyage enriched human knowledge, Marco Polo's journey was a business trip in origin. Christopher Columbus, Vasco da Gama, and Ferdinand Magellan were official explorers seeking new pathways to fortune. Within three centuries their discoveries led to the biggest migration in human history. Even after every corner of the planet was "discovered," humans continued to travel. Yesterday's curious travelers who set out to find out what lay beyond the next mountain or ocean are today's tourists. Yesterday's fortune seekers and bonded immigrant laborers in a foreign land are today's immigrants, legal and illegal. Since the beginning of modern warfare with its mass casualties the number of refugees has swelled. As the means of transportation and conditions of travel have evolved, the movement of people across the globe has grown in volume with more people living in a country other than where they were born. In 2005 there were nearly two hundred million migrants in countries around the world. Even though most of the world's people have never crossed their home country's border, dispersal of their compatriots throughout the world has created a global village where the progenies of the ancestors who walked away from Africa are connected. As we will see in this chapter, the known world has been expanding through exploration and adventurous journeys, and the web of connections has been growing for a long, long time.

HANNO AND HIPPOPOTAMI

We read earlier of the expedition to the east coast of Africa sent by the Egyptian queen Hatshepsut in the third millennium BCE. One of the most tantalizing accounts of explorations of Africa's west coast comes from a report by a Carthaginian commander named Hanno. Around 500 BCE he set out in the Mediterranean to explore new places to set up colonies, and he ended up in the Atlantic. He apparently inscribed the account of his exploits in bronze in his hometown. A Greek traveler's copy of the inscription has survived to tell us the story. According to Hanno's report, the expedition passed through the Strait of Gibraltar and sailed along the Moroccan coast. With the help of friendly coastal Bedouins, the crew sailed further south until they crossed the mouth of a large river and reached a great gulf. The river with two mouths, Hanno wrote, was "deep and wide and infested with crocodiles and hippopotami." An island next to the gulf was the scene of the Mediterranean world's first encounter with primates. He reported seeing men and women "with hairy bodies"—most probably baboon or chimpanzee—and managed to bring back skins of these creatures to Carthage.

Since the fifteenth century, when the manuscript copy of Hanno's travel report was first discovered, historians have debated the accuracy of its descriptions.[3] Some surmise that the gulf that Hanno reached is the mouth of the Sherbro River in present-day Sierra Leone; others doubt whether he reached Central Africa. What is beyond doubt is that explorations like the one described by Hanno were undertaken from an early time.

Herodotus, the fifth-century BCE historian, recounts that sometime around 600 BCE, Phoenician sailors from present-day Lebanon and Syria circumnavigated Africa. He learned in Egypt that Necho, the pharaoh of Egypt, had sent out a naval expedition from the Red Sea and instructed it to return home by the way of the Strait of Gibraltar. The expedition spent three years sailing around the coast of Africa, halting in places for months to sow the soil and reap the harvest before moving on.

Herodotus wanted to maintain some skeptical distance from the account. "They reported things which others can believe if they want but I cannot," he

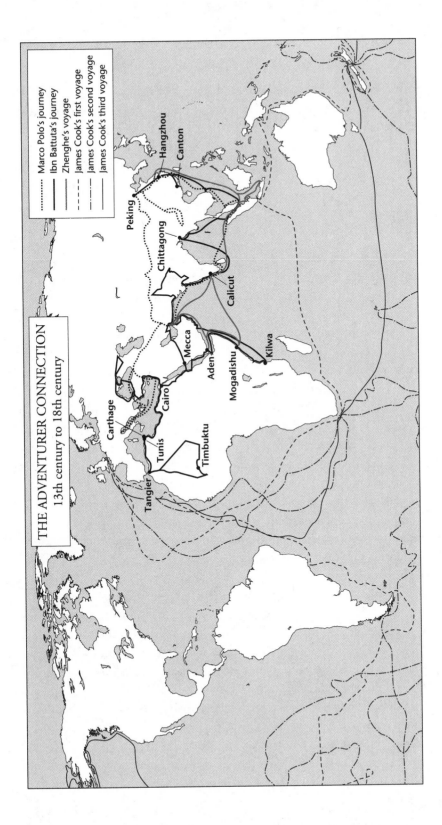

THE ADVENTURER CONNECTION
13th century to 18th century

Marco Polo's journey
Ibn Battuta's journey
Zhenghe's voyage
James Cook's first voyage
James Cook's second voyage
James Cook's third voyage

Hangzhou
Canton
Peking
Chittagong
Calicut
Mecca
Kilwa
Aden
Mogadishu
Cairo
Carthage
Tunis
Timbuktu
Tangier

wrote, "namely, that in sailing around Africa they had the sun on the right side"—meaning that they sailed north along Africa's west coast. Yet despite that skepticism, Herodotus seemed ready to accept their finding that "Libya, that is Africa, shows that it has sea all round except the part that borders on Asia." This apparently incredible story of circumnavigation of Africa, however, is not dismissed by modern historians, especially because of the intriguing reference to the sun. Had the brave sailors made it to a point beyond the tropics, their travels southwest or west could indeed have made the sun appear on their right side.[4]

Herodotus also tells of five young adventurers from North Africa who traveled across the desert to the southwest part of the continent for many months and found a great river that Herodotus thought was the Upper Nile. It was most probably the Niger.

Whether the account of the first circumnavigation of Africa was true or not, the continent of Africa remained an unexplored mystery. Herodotus, perhaps the world's first journalist-historian, himself traveled in search of the origin of the Nile and returned frustrated. Other Greeks advanced along the shores of the Black Sea and the Mediterranean and set up colonies. The Phoenicians also sailed and founded city-states in North Africa and the western Mediterranean. Only the Greek explorer Pytheas, in search of tin, seemed to have sailed around present-day Brittany before reaching the distinctly non-Mediterranean shores of England in 300 BCE. He wrote that after six days' sail further north, there is "neither sea nor air but a mixture like sea-lung . . . binds everything together," a reference perhaps to drifting ice or dense sea fog.[5] Arabs living on the Red Sea meanwhile sailed in their dhows—boats made of wood and animal hide—to explore the south along Africa's Swahili coast and to the east along the shores of Persia and the Indus Valley.

Official support was essential for explorations of new territory due to the expense and hazards of travel. With the exception of a few intrepid traders or missionaries, explorers normally ventured out with official protection and blessing. One of the first such recorded adventures took place in 510 BCE, when Darius the Great of Persia sent one of his officers, Scylax, to explore the Indus Valley. On reaching the Indus, Scylax followed it to the sea and sailed westward to the Persian Gulf and Red Sea. Two hundred years later, Alexander the Great's army would follow the Indus Valley route before returning home. Alexander left his admiral, Nearchus, in command of the expedition's naval forces to wait for the favorable monsoon before exploring the northern coast of the Persian Gulf. When Alexander's army took control of the island of Socotra at the mouth of the Red Sea, the soldiers were surprised to find an Indian settlement there. So-cotra's foreign population grew in the ensuing centuries. The first-century manual *Periplus of the Erythraean Sea* said the island had "foreigners, a mixture of Arabs and Indians and Greeks, who have emigrated to carry on trade there."[6] As with the "discovery" of the monsoon wind by Greco-Roman traders, the Indian Ocean trade grew. So did diasporas of Jewish, Arab, Persian, and Indian traders on both shores of the Indian Ocean.

BRINGING HOME A GIRAFFE

While the rising powers in the Mediterranean were sending scouts and explorers, similar moves were afoot in China and Central Asia. The emerging Chinese state in the Yellow River Valley began taking a keen interest in the region to their west because of the havoc wreaked by the Xiongnu nomads (later known as Mongols). Their depredations prompted the Chinese kingdoms to begin constructing the Great Wall. The Han emperor Wu wanted to explore the possibility of forging an opportunistic alliance with the Central Asian Yuezhi people against the Xiongnu, largely to halt the scourge of nomad raids. In 138 BCE, his envoy Zhang Qian, accompanied by more than a hundred men and a Xiongnu slave interpreter, journeyed west. They found no takers for an alliance, but Zhang Qian's thirteen-year journey through Central Asia brought the first detailed account of the geography, people, customs, and cultures of the thirty-six kingdoms that lay across the desert. This journey is the first known contact between the Chinese and the Greek colony of Bactria in modern-day Afghanistan. Zhang Qian piqued Chinese interest in the western region with his tales of a great kingdom of India ("kingdom of Shendu," derived from Sindhu, or Indus River) that lay southeast of Bactria. This first glimpse of India described the land as "hot and damp," where "the inhabitants ride elephants when they go into battle." As a Chinese historian recorded from Zhang Qian's account, the Chinese emperor learned of the existence of civilized states in the West, "rich in unusual products whose people cultivated the land and made their living in much the same way as the Chinese. All these states . . . were militarily weak and prized Han goods and wealth."[7] The envoy was also astonished to discover Chinese bamboo shoots and other products on sale in Bactria that had been brought by traders from southwest China via India. Even before the famed Silk Road came into being across the Central Asian mountains and deserts, a southwest Silk Road linking India with South China via Thailand and Burma had developed.[8]

China's interest in exploring the western region was short-lived, however. Two hundred years after Zhang Qian, another official, Gan Ying, appears to have curtailed an effort to reach Rome, turning back after reaching Mesopotamia. Parthian officials eager to maintain their monopoly of trade with Rome apparently dissuaded him from going further, warning that the journey to Rome could take several months or even years. Chinese records note that Gan Ying then headed back home, ensuring China's isolation from the Mediterranean world for more than a thousand years.[9] Until 1405, when the Ming emperor Yongle sent the eunuch admiral Zheng He to lead an exploratory armada, there was no known Chinese attempt to travel further west than India.

Unlike the Portuguese or Spanish armadas—dispatched to discover new ways to known but inaccessible resource-rich lands—Chinese motives in dispatching Zheng He's expeditions were a mix of reconnaissance and power display. As Ming dynasty historian Hok-Lam Chan notes, the emperor Yongle undertook seagoing expeditions "to display his power and wealth, to learn about the plans of Timur and other Mongols in western Asia, to extend the tributary system, to satisfy his vanity and greed for glory, and to make use of his eunuch staff."[10] The thirty-odd countries the fleet visited were all active in trade. The emperor ordered the building of a treasure fleet that would dazzle the barbarian countries.

Unlike the small, maneuverable Portuguese caravels, the Chinese ships were over four hundred feet long and 160 feet wide, with nine masts, twelve sails, and four decks, large enough to carry twenty-five hundred tons of cargo each and armed with dozens of small cannons. Between 1405 and 1433 the Chinese fleet sailed majestically through Southeast Asian waters and the Indian Ocean. It transported barbarian envoys willing to pay tribute to the Son of Heaven and brought home exotic products, from aphrodisiac rhinoceros horns to live giraffes. The explorers also succeeded in leaving some Chinese genes on African shores. Recently the Chinese government has identified some Sino-African descendants of shipwrecked sailors from Zheng He's expedition to Africa.[11] By the time Vasco da Gama's vessels appeared in the Indian Ocean in 1497, the Chinese presence was long gone.

Historian Philip Snow calls Zheng He the Chinese Columbus, but the resources he had at his disposal make the Genoese explorer look like an amateur: "Zheng He's voyage differed from Columbus's not only in scale but in kind. . . . Zheng He was not just financially sponsored, as Columbus was, by a sympathetic government: he and his captains, eunuchs of the palace, were the agents and chosen personal servants of their emperor."[12]

After seven expeditions the voyages abruptly ended. Palace officials, unenthusiastic about the forays to begin with, scrubbed them as a waste of resources and, according to some sources, destroyed the records of the voyages. Recent historians, however, have discounted that claim. Most of the records did survive and remain valuable evidence of China's widening geographic horizons in the fifteenth century.[13] Ma Huan, one of the four officials who accompanied Zheng He, was fluent in Persian and perhaps in Arabic and other Asian languages. He accompanied the admiral to Mecca, perhaps the first-ever Chinese to do the hajj. The account of the voyages Ma Huan left enormously widened China's knowledge of the Indian Ocean region.

TRAVELS OF A "MILLION"

European interest in the world outside came after a long period of relative quiescence when the rise of Islam had, in the words of Fernand Braudel, "emptied the sea of trade."[14] Despite flagging interest in the sea, the Middle Ages in Europe did not mark an end to travel. Medieval people did travel—mainly to earn money and glory or for pilgrimage.[15] With medical science in its infancy, visits to saints and holy places were often the preferred remedy for the sick.[16] Harvard historian Michael McCormick has searched the medieval archives and established the names of 669 persons—mostly diplomats, pilgrims, missionaries, and refugees—who traveled considerable distances of three hundred to six hundred miles between Western Europe and the Byzantine Empire.[17] Despite the unsettled conditions during the Crusades, though, Islamic travelers from Western Europe, like the famous Andalusian Arab Ibn Jubayr, journeyed to Mecca in 1183–84 and left a valuable account of the landscape he traversed.[18]

The almost two centuries of Crusades left a deep impact on European economy, politics, and culture. The rise of the Mongol Empire in the thirteenth century brought a revival of the Silk Road trade, which reemerged in its traditional role as a conveyor belt of trade and culture between Europe and China. Perhaps no one did more to bring the splendor of China to European consciousness than the Venetian trader Marco Polo. Europeans had visited China before Polo and after, but his *Travels* remains an all-time classic, a major building block in the rise of Western awareness about the mysterious Orient.

In late 1271, accompanied by his father and his uncle, both prosperous traders from Venice, seventeen-year-old Marco Polo set out on a voyage to China, carrying the pope's letter to Kublai Khan. The journey was meant to be a business trip with some religious duty thrown in. Like many European and

Arab traders who had preceded them, the Polos had no pretensions to being anything more than merchants seeking their fortune in a fabled land of silk, jade, and porcelain. But twenty-four years later the Polos returned with tales about the East that forever altered European perceptions of the world. Among the few books that Christopher Columbus took with him on the Santa Maria was a well-thumbed and commented copy of Marco Polo's *Description of the World*. Since there was no printing press then, what Columbus had procured was a precious hand-copied volume. From Polo's account, Columbus learned about the abundance of gold in Cipangu (vulgarized from Nippon or Japan), where roofs were reputedly made of gold instead of the slate used in Europe. The story of the golden roofs is just one of the fantastic tales that Marco Polo had dictated to a romance writer to produce the Description of the World. Many tales of strange creatures, bizarre practices, and exotic origins of spices along with many inconsistencies, omissions, and clear fabrications have raised doubts about the authenticity of Marco Polo's account. From the time he returned home and recounted stories of what he had seen, people were incredulous. Legend has it that because of his tall stories Marco Polo was nicknamed Marco, Il Millione—the teller of million lies. To convince the skeptics and naysayers the Polos would reach under their Oriental robes and pull out hidden jewels and precious stones bestowed on them by Kublai Khan.

HORSE TRADE OF A TRAVELER

The noted British Sinologist Frances Wood sums up the doubts about the authenticity of Polo's travels in her book *Did Marco Polo Go to China?* She notes that Polo's account fails to mention many special details that a visitor would normally note, from the Great Wall to chopsticks, tea, Chinese writing, and the practice of foot binding. Also, there is no mention of Polo in Chinese records, even though he is said to have served as a special emissary for Kublai Khan. The Chinese are normally meticulous record keepers.

Although Wood demonstrates the outright fabrications and questionable details in the book, she has not found evidence that Polo was in some other place than Cathay during his absence from Italy. She suggests that he never traveled beyond the Black Sea and that his *Travels* is based on family stories and printed secondary material from other authors. Others, however, argue that some of the incredible stories could have been added by his scribe, a romance writer familiar with the current style of travel writing. The fact that the existing 140 handwritten copies have materials that were clearly added by scribes or translators after Polo's time may also explain some inconsistencies. In any case, other detailed descriptions of things Chinese unknown in the West—from paper money, the Grand Canal, and the structure of a Mongol army to the imperial postal system—are evidence of authenticity. In what was the first information about an as-yet unknown stored solar energy or coal, Polo wrote about a fiery stone: "All over the country of Cathay there is a kind of stone existing in beds in the mountains which they dig out and burn like firewood. It is true that they have plenty of woods also but they do not burn it, because these stones burn better and cost less."[19] Three hundred years later Britain would launch the Industrial Revolution powered by those fiery stones from the mountains. Wood concludes that even though the book may not be an eyewitness account, it still contains useful and accurate details of China during the thirteenth century and, consequently, "remains a very rich source."[20]

Marco Polo's book gave Christopher Columbus the arguments to convince the Spanish court about the wealth of Asia. When Columbus arrived in the Caribbean, believing it to be near the fabled Cipangu with its gold-tiled roofs, he pressed deeper into the islands in search of gold. Polo's account also ignited scholars' interest in Chinese history, society, and politics, not to mention the greed it stoked among traders.[21] Translated in every language, Il Millione's travel book has inspired millions of tourists to set out for China. A country that was exotic and distant to the Western mind is now just another neighbor—rendering the world a much smaller place.

In 1466, decades before Vasco da Gama and Columbus took to the sea in search of "Christians and spices" in India, Russian trader Afanasii Nikitin set out from old Russian city of Tver (now Kalinin) on a voyage to India that he called a "journey beyond three seas." With support of Russian officials and the blessing of the local Orthodox bishop, Nikitin set off on the Volga before following the old caravan route to Persia. From the port of Hormuz he acquired one horse for selling in India, perhaps to pay for his trip. One horse may sound small, notes one historian, yet a pedigreed Arab stallion was certainly a prized article that at the time could have reaped him a good profit.[22] Nikitin's account gave Russian readers a firsthand account of a distant land that until then they had only a vague notion about. Throughout his six-year journey Nikitin, though an Orthodox Christian, was taken for a Muslim Persian trader. He had a largely trouble-free trip, staying in state-maintained hospices where slave girls offered their services to travelers.

A JEWISH MARCO POLO

During the Middle Ages in Europe, most travels were undertaken for pilgrimage. Religious fervor, we have seen, spurred Buddhist pilgrims to undertake long, perilous journeys to India and Southeast Asia. In the period following the Crusades, Jewish and Islamic travelers from the Mediterranean set out on voyages that considerably expanded the boundaries of the known world.

In 1160 a Spanish rabbi named Benjamin from the town of Tudela set out on a journey to visit the Holy Land. He has been called the Jewish Marco Polo, although his voyage was a century before the better-known Genoese set out on his famous journey. Benjamin's pilgrimage took a wide path through the Middle East and Central Asia, leading some to wonder if in addition to visiting fellow Jews and holy places he may also have been engaged in trading. He spent thirteen years on the road, traveling all the way to Samarkand via Jerusalem and Baghdad. He returned to Spain in 1173 via the Arabian Sea, the Red Sea, and Cairo. His travel account, *Voyages of Benjamin,* provided a vivid account of life in the Middle East during the era of the Crusades. His detailed report of the Jewish diaspora in different cities was and remains an invaluable source to map the connected world of the time. The city of Genoa, where Benjamin found only two Jews, did not endear itself to him, as can be seen from his harsh assessment of the rising commercial power: "The city is surrounded by a wall, and they have no king, but only judges, whom they themselves appoint at their will. Every man has a tower in his house, and when they are in disagreement they fight against one another on the tower-tops. They rule the sea, and construct vessels which are called galleys, and go to spoil and plunder throughout the Christian and Moslem seas, and the land of Greece as far as Sicily, and bring the spoil and booty of all these places to Genoa."[23]

His account of the Persian island town of Kish (near Hormuz) gives the picture of bustling commerce that marked the period: "It is a considerable market, being the place to which the Indian merchants and those of the Islands bring their commodities; while the traders of Iraq, Yemen and Pars import all sorts of silk and purple cloths, flax, cotton, hemp, mash [a type of pulse], wheat, barley, millet, rye and all other sorts of foodstuffs and pulses, which are objects of exchange; those from India import great quantities of spices and the inhabitants of the islands live by what they gain in their capacity as brokers for both parties. The island contains about 500 Jews."[24]

SEARCH FOR KNOWLEDGE, EVEN IN CHINA

Muslims from different parts of the world have long embarked on the pilgrimage to Mecca, as required of a pious Muslim. But Islam encouraged another kind of travel: the quest for new information. A famous hadith quotes the Prophet: "Search for knowledge, even in China." (China was a metaphor for domains outside Muslim territories.) In the Islamic literary tradition a distinctive genre has been Rihla, travel literature. Hundreds of Rihlas have been published, combining stories of adventures, accounts by sailors and traders, and reports of imaginary lands and people. The ninth-century stories of Sinbad the Sailor, which have enchanted readers all over the world, are a fictional take-off from Rihlas. Perhaps the first tourist in history, someone who undertook travel for its own sake, was an Islamic jurist from the Moroccan town of Tangiers named Ibn Battuta.

On a hot June day in 1325, twenty-two-year-old Ibn Battuta set out on a pilgrimage to Mecca that turned into the world's longest tourist trip of the epoch. When he left for hajj riding a donkey, he did not know that the journey would last thirty years and that he would return home only after traveling seventy-five thousand miles. It was the longest distance that one person could have traversed in a lifetime in the fourteenth century using every means available to him—foot, mule, horse, camel, ox-wagon, and boat. Battuta's travels were motivated by what in Arabic is called *baraka*—the desire to accumulate merit by visiting holy places and obtaining the blessings of saintly men. But his accounts make it clear that he was interested in many other things, including food and the opposite sex.

Battuta was no explorer, but curiosity about the world made him one of the world's first tourists, certainly the most famous. As he later explained, "[I] was swayed by an overmastering impulse within me and a desire long-cherished in my bosom to visit these illustrious sanctuaries. So I braced my resolution to quit all my dear ones, female and male, and forsook my home as birds forsake their nests." In his thirty years of travel he visited every Islamic country in the world, as well as the Mongol Empire from Central Asia to China. India's Islamic ruler, in whose court he served as a legal scholar, appointed him to go to China as his ambassador. The Chinese junks that were to take him to China sank in a storm in the Indian harbor, but he managed to reach China on another vessel.

Although he was impressed by certain aspects of Chinese civilization, his religious sensibilities were hurt by the outright rejection of Islam. In stark contrast with Marco Polo, he stayed indoors most of the time rather than be contaminated by what he considered odious Chinese social habits like eating pork. The Prophet Muhammad's admonition to seek knowledge in China clearly had its limits for Battuta. He wrote: "China was beautiful, but it did not please me. On the contrary, I was greatly troubled thinking about the way paganism dominated this country. Whenever I went out of my lodging, I saw many blameworthy things. That disturbed me so much that I stayed indoors most of the time and only went out when necessary." A rare pleasure for Battuta in China was to have run into a compatriot, a wealthy businessman at that. "He told me that he had about 50 white slaves and as many slave girls, and presented me with two of each, along with many other gifts."[25]

Battuta returned to Fez in 1349, but he was off again to visit Europe and North Africa, where he explored western Sudan "to the northernmost province of the Negroes." He reached the Niger, which he mistook to be the Nile. Like Hanno some two thousand years earlier, he was astonished by the huge hippopotami he saw in Africa and took them to be elephants. Curiously, though, Battuta had not thought of writing an account of his travels until the sultan of Morocco asked him to do so with the help of a scribe. Whether the amazing details that he provided or his lack of enthusiasm about exploration generally made his account suspect, Battuta's report languished until the early twentieth century, when it was discovered and translated into European languages. His description of the society and economy of many of the non-Islamic lands, especially those of the Mongol Empire, the most extensive land empire in the world, remains an invaluable resource. "No medieval traveller, eastern or western, who left a written account of his journeyings can compare with this," writes Dan Morgan. "The great western travellers in the Mongol Empire, such as William of Rubruck or Marco Polo, are not remotely in the same league."[26]

Religion continued to inspire individuals to set out for long journeys that reinforced connections. Jewish traveler David d'Beth Hillel was another such religiously inspired person whose voyage through Arabia, Kurdistan, Persia, and India produced valuable accounts of increasingly interconnected life in the early nineteenth century. Inspired by what one author calls "a vehement desire and anxiety for the search of his brethren, the forgotten 'Remnants of Israel' in far-off lands," Hillel traveled for eight years and left valuable information about social-economic conditions, linguistic and religious peculiarities, and the folklore and customs of the countries—a treasure trove for historians and anthropologists.[27] While religious devotion inspired trade, religion also emerged as a major obstruction to trade after the fall of Constantinople to Islam in 1453. The Ottoman Empire was a barrier, and the Atlantic Ocean was increasingly seen as a way to get around it. Merchants and financiers from Venice, Genoa, Florence, and Livorno were ready to back adventurers who would find another way to Asia for silk, spice, and diamonds. The city-states would also provide funds to sea captains like Christopher Columbus, Amerigo Vespucci, and John and Sebastian Cabot to apply the renewed interest in geography and search for new routes.

GOLD RUSH FOR THE NEW WORLD

Religious motivation also played its part. The devout monarch of Portugal Prince Henry the Navigator was eager to find a way to enlist the support of the mythical Christian kingdom of Prester John, believed to be in East Africa, against the rising power of Islam. He was equally anxious to find a way to the gold that had been trickling out of Africa.[28] He set up the first-ever maritime research and development laboratory, meticulously collecting information about oceans and coasts and innovating sailing technology. The result of the expeditions he financed bore fruit in 1444, when the first-ever human cargo from Guinea in Africa—two hundred miserable men, women, and children—was unloaded on European soil. Prince Henry was on the dock to claim his share of the slaves, the sale of which would improve his personal fortune. Daniel J. Boorstin notes how the arrival of the first human merchandise from Africa caused a change of attitude toward Prince Henry, who was earlier criticized for wasting public money on his frolics with exploration. Now a powerful motive for further exploration was added, as "everybody wanted a share of this promising Guinea trade."[29] Henry's successor, John II, carried on Henry's policy of sending explorations down the African coast with the goal of finding a direct route to the world of spice. Greed and fantasy drove explorations. Paolo Toscanelli, a Florentine cosmographer and astronomer, put before the Portuguese court a plan to reach eastern Asia by sailing directly westward from Europe. The most important destination, he advised, should be Cipangu, the name for Japan that Marco Polo used a century earlier. "This island [Cipangu]," he wrote, "is extraordinarily rich in gold, pearls, and precious stones; for, be it known, that the inhabitants make cloaks of gold with which to bedeck the temples and the palaces of their kings. . . . Certainly an attempt should be made to reach these islands." But above all it was necessary, he advised, to search for the 7,440 islands that Marco Polo described as not being under the dominion of the Great Khan and from which China was supplied with gold, costly woods, and every kind of spice.[30] The Portuguese, however, had already committed to the route toward India around Africa. The Atlantic route to Asia would be taken up by the Castilian monarch.

The race to the riches of Asia had heated up after the Portuguese navigator Bartolomeu Dias found the Cape of Good Hope in 1487. The prospect of making a fortune by discovering a direct route to Asia was a forerunner of many such competitions, resulting in various discoveries. Like hopeful entrepreneurs anxiously queuing for a meeting with investor "angels" in Silicon Valley five hundred years later, ambitious sailors, cartographers, and financiers flocked to the courts of Lisbon and Madrid in the hope of getting backing for their exploratory ventures—the prize for which was gold and glory.

With the financial backing of a Florentine banker, John II dispatched Pêro da Covilhã to investigate a northerly route to India—a route that Arab and Greek sailors had used for more than a thousand years but was unknown to the Europeans. In 1489, disguised as an Islamic trader, Covilhã managed to take an Arab dhow across the Indian Ocean to Calicut and witness a thriving trade in spices, fine cotton, and Arabian horses. On his return to Cairo he sent a detailed report of the origin of the spices and the existence of a sea route to the East. The ground was now ready for Vasco da Gama to round the Cape of Good Hope and make the historic voyage to Calicut.

A decade before da Gama, Columbus was a hopeful supplicant in Lisbon. His study of Ptolemy, Marco Polo, and others had convinced him that in a spherical world the Ocean Sea that separated Europe from Asia was navigable. He reasoned that by taking a southwesterly direction on the western ocean it would be possible to reach the golden-roofed island of Cipangu en route to the fabulous wealth of Cathay and India. Columbus, however, failed in 1484 to convince the Portuguese expert committee of the feasibility of his plan. Besides, Portuguese sailors were then tantalizingly close to the southern tip of Africa, which promised a surer route to Asia.

For the next seven years Columbus tried to win support for his project at the court of Castile (later Spain). He was on the point of giving up on Spain as well and heading for France when the summons came. Queen Isabella wished him to return to Santa Fe, where the sovereigns held court, and he was even given a mule to ride.[31] In addition to the prospects of securing gold and spices of the Orient, Isabella, fresh from the historic victory over Islamic Granada, saw a divine mission in sending Columbus to unknown parts of the world: to win new subjects and Christian converts. A devout Catholic, Columbus also saw the venture as a step toward meeting the Great Khan of Cathay to seek an alliance with him to recover Jerusalem from the Muslims.[32] In an agreement signed by representatives of the crown—the Capitulations of Santa Fe— Columbus was promised the honor that he craved. If successful, Columbus would receive the title Grand Admiral of the Ocean Sea. Columbus also would have the titles on any lands he might find and a tenth of "all and every kind of merchandise, whether pearls, precious stones, gold, silver, spices and other objects."[33] He was given royal letters of credence addressed to an assortment of rulers that he hoped to meet, including the Great Khan.

On the morning of 3 August 1492, Columbus's three vessels, Santa María, Niña, and Pinta, unfurled their sails and left the port of Palos. For all that the crown hoped to gain from the voyage the investment was modest: two million maravedís. For a royal wedding earlier the crown had spent thirty times more.[34] In the early hours of 12 October 1492, with a full moon lighting up the horizon, Juan Rodrigo Bermejo, a sailor on the lookout on Pinta, cried "Tierra, Tierra!" and fired a shot. After thirty-seven days of sailing during which the crew's hope of finding Asia was diminishing, the sailor had spotted the island that would be named San Salvador. When Columbus came ashore and knelt to pray, a crowd of natives wearing no clothes gathered to ogle the bearded men who had just landed from a vessel with wings. Fifty thousand years after humans left Africa and went their separate ways, cousins separated by two thousand generations had again found each other. It was a traumatic and bloody reunion. It also marked the beginning of the most ferocious and profoundly transformational integration of the world. Although Columbus died believing that he had reached India, the New World he had serendipitously found suddenly made the known world much bigger than before. By the beginning of the eighteenth century, close to a million Spaniards had migrated to Spain's new frontiers in the Americas, especially to New Spain, as Mexico was then called.

A VIOLENT END IN MACATAN

Similar encounters between Europe and Asia would take place six years later in the south Indian port of Calicut and on the Philippines island of Cebu. Guided by an Arab pilot picked up from Malindi in East Africa, the Portuguese fleet of Vasco da Gama crossed the Indian Ocean and cast anchor at Calicut on 20 May

1498. While Greek and Arab sailors had been plying the Indian Ocean for two millennia, da Gama became the first European to sail directly to India. Unlike in San Salvador, where Columbus's Arabic interpreter was of no help, the first scout off the boat in Calicut encountered Tunisian traders who spoke Castilian and Genoese. He could explain that the purpose of his voyage was finding Christians and gold.[35]

In less than a century, Portugal had built a spice monopoly. "The King of Portugal, Lord of Spices," the Municipal Council of Nuremberg complained, "has set . . . prices, just as he pleases, for pepper which, at any cost, no matter how dear, will not long go unsold to the Germans."[36] The lure of spice, gold, and slaves had turned the race to discover new sea routes into a scramble that threatened a tenuous harmony among the Christian powers of Europe. The pope had assumed the power to assign Catholic kings the right to govern the newly discovered lands and convert the natives, and he intervened to maintain peace between the first two in the race. In the Treaty of Tordesillas of 1494 Portugal and Spain agreed to a line of control proposed by the pope dividing the territories along a line down the middle of the Atlantic—twelve hundred nautical miles west of the Portuguese-controlled Cape Verde islands. Portugal would have the right to all newly discovered lands east of the line, and Spain would appropriate the western part. When Vasco da Gama left to find a direct route to India he had one less worry. There would be no challenge from the Spaniards. Years later the line would also allow Portugal to take possession of all of Africa, South and Southeast Asia, and newly discovered Brazil. However, the Treaty of Tordesillas could not yet address how the rights would fall on undiscovered lands on the other side of the globe. That problem soon reared its ugly head as Ferdinand Magellan's journey to the East via the West brought the two Iberian powers face to face in the Spice Islands of Southeast Asia.

Magellan's arrival in the Pacific also brought Europeans face to face with a people who had long before mastered the seas and colonized the island world—from the Pacific to Madagascar in the Indian Ocean. Unlike Columbus in the Caribbean, where he found the native "Indians" to be naive and docile, ready to be enslaved, Magellan's first encounter with the natives proved fatal. On landing on Cebu in the Philippines on 7 April 1521, Magellan was accorded great honor and pomp, and his men were entertained throughout the night by scantily clad women. But relations soured. The zealousness and cruelty with which he went about converting Filipinos to Christianity resulted in a violent backlash. Instead of returning to Seville as a hero who had circumnavigated the world, Magellan breathed his last where he made the historic land-

fall. The locals did not take kindly to a stranger imposing his god and his methods on them and brutally hacked the explorer to death on the beach of Maca-
tan. That violent end, however, did not snap the connection. In the ensuing
years, the Spanish quelled the locals' resistance with firepower, and the colony
in the Philippines emerged as a major link in the globe-girdling network of
commerce that developed. The early encounters of the Western "discoverers"
like Columbus, da Gama, and Magellan, however, foreshadowed the bitterness
of forced global integration to come in the next five centuries.

For the next two centuries other expeditions crisscrossed the oceans and established the European presence in the four corners of the world. Genoese
sailor John Cabot, sponsored by the English monarch, sailed west across the Atlantic and landed in Newfoundland. Cabot's search for a northwestern passage
to Asia would be pursued by a succession of English and French navigators. The
search for a northwest passage to the Pacific followed by the English, Dutch,
and the Nordic seamen would also open up vast stretches of land in northern
Europe and eventually lead to the discovery of the Bering Strait, the body of
water where the Beringia land bridge once had allowed our human ancestors to
cross over from Asia to North America. In 1577 two English seamen, Sir Francis
Drake and Thomas Cavendish, circumnavigated the world from west to east.
Once footholds had been secured in new lands, the royal courts and traders
sponsored further explorations to gather information for trade. South America
was mapped and occupied, and the colonization of North America began in
earnest. These commercially driven explorations slowly filled up the blanks in
the ancient maps, including the large part at the bottom of Ptolemy's map
marked "Terra Incognita." At the close of the eighteenth century Dutch navigator Abel Tasman, French navigator Louis-Antoine de Bougainville, British
captain James Cook, and navigators George Bass and Matthew Flinders,
among others, completed the connections between Europe, Australia, New
Zealand, and the Pacific. The names of the newly discovered lands bear the
memory of their discoverers. Australia was so named because it filled the pre-
supposition of the old European map of the existence of an unknown southern
territory: "Terra Australis Incognita." The Dutch who first found the island
that the native Maoris called Aotearoa, named it "Nieuw Zeeland" after the
Dutch province of Zeeland, and King Philip of Spain inspired the name of the
new Spanish colony in the Pacific, the Philippines.

French explorer Jean-François Galaup, comte de la Perouse, landed on
Easter Island on 9 April 1786. His crew stayed on the island for a matter of
hours, giving the inhabitants goats, sheep, and pigs and seeds of orange trees,

lemon trees, maize, and "every spices that might do well on their island."[37] The slow unveiling of the world that the settled human community had begun millennia earlier with tentative steps from the Fertile Crescent now reached full circle. With most of the inhabitable spaces on the earth now within view, the rush was now on for the humans to occupy and exploit as much of the territories as possible and link them with faster and bigger means of transportation. A new period of adventure began in which larger numbers of people left their ancestral homes for new lives in other countries.

TO GOVERN IS TO POPULATE

The world's biggest population movement since the transatlantic slave trade again followed the direction taken by Christopher Columbus. Historians estimate that at the peak of the Spanish rule in America perhaps 437,000 Spaniards and 100,000 Portuguese had immigrated to the respective colonies. "You must understand," a new arrival in Panama wrote to his son in Spain, "that those who want to better themselves cannot continue living where they were born." The way to better one's life was to go to Madrid, to get a license to emigrate, and then sell all one's possessions to raise money for the passage, travel to Seville, and secure a place on the boats that sailed in April and August.[38] The House of Trade in Seville was the place where prospective emigrants came to register. In the sixteenth century some fifty-six thousand registered despite the hazards of crossing the storm-swept Atlantic.

The arrival of steamships in the mid-nineteenth century removed a major constraint in the large-scale movement of populations across oceans. With regular steamship services between an overpopulated Europe and the vast expanse of the resource-rich, population-poor New World, the biggest migration in history began in the 1840s. As Kenneth Pomeranz and Steven Topik state, "With steam, the Atlantic and Pacific shrank to ponds and continents to small principalities. . . . The global supermarket began taking shape in the nineteenth century."[39] In the following seven decades some sixty million Europeans would leave their birthplace to settle abroad, some thirty-seven million of them in the United States and the remainder in South America. Migration to the United States reached an annual peak of over 2.1 million in 1913.[40]

The early-nineteenth-century migrants from Europe were mostly farmers and artisans who traveled in family groups to acquire land in the United States and settle down. Their motivation was not very different from that of the Anatolian farmers who migrated in all directions during the Neolithic era looking for settlements, carrying with them their wheat farming technology and their Proto-Indo-European languages. This time the farmers crossed the Atlantic on steamboats. As Europe industrialized, the composition of its emigrants also changed. Although the passport existed in England since the seventeenth century, it was designed to protect the traveler rather than erect barriers against those who did not own one. A British law in 1872 declared that "all foreigners have the unrestricted right of entrance into and residence in this country."[41]

The demand for labor shot up with the rise of capitalism and the development of industry and large-scale plantations, leading to the creation of large-scale interregional and international labor diasporas. The most often cited case is that of the Irish. The mills of Manchester drew more than a million Roman Catholic Irish workers, and as Friedrich Engels reported in 1844, some fifty thousand more kept arriving there each year, with their numbers bidding down the wages of English workers. On the other hand, famine and political struggle in Europe heightened people's suffering, making them more willing to abandon their homes in the hope of a better future. The Irish famine of 1846–50 drove more than four million to the United States.[42]

Large countries with small populations like Argentina not only granted land but financed the transportation and housing of immigrants in the mid-nineteenth century. Reflecting the view of the ruling elite in Argentina, the Argentinean thinker Juan Bautista Alberdi coined the phrase "To govern is to populate."[43] Brazil, too, tried to make up for the loss of slave labor by encouraging immigration and settlements through subsidies and special benefits.[44]

With the opening of Canada, Argentina, and Brazil to migration and the rise of industrial Japan the integration of the world economy that had begun with European colonies was accelerated. The millennia history of human migration was put on fast-forward.

SLAVES, COOLIES, AND SAHIBS

The most significant cross-border transfer of population was not that of Europeans seeking a better fortune but the forced migration of slaves to the colonies. What began as the transfer of the first human merchandise to Portugal in 1444 grew into a massive trade encompassing several continents. We have seen how the slave trade forced the migration of some twelve million Africans to the New World. With the British abolition of the slave trade in the 1830s, an end to the policy of populating the British colony of Australia with convicts, and the abolition of slavery in the United States in 1865, a new phase of migration began that witnessed the transfer of a new category of migrants—what David Northrup calls "unfree labor" from one part of the European colonial empire to another. It was a product of new complementarity. The New World and Australia's farms, plantations, and mines, starved of labor and facing rising wages, looked for new migrants. In the old world of China and India war, famine, and misery pushed the poor to escape their fate by voluntarily agreeing to be bonded labor in a foreign land. As Northrup argues, although this may be seen as a continuation of servitude of slave and penal labor migration—a "new system of slavery" at its worst—at its best it offered people a chance for a better life akin to that being sought by free emigrants from Europe at the same time.[45]

Major migrations of laborers and immigrants were also helped by emerging technologies of mass transportation and the shortening of distance with the opening of the Suez Canal in 1869. Already since the sixteenth century lower expenses per vessel and the use of larger vessels had brought about a sharp decline in the cost of a voyage.[46]

Populous China and India emerged as the major sources for this "unfree" migration. Historian Hugh R. Baker explains the new dynamics. At almost all times in Chinese history, population pressure resulted in a southward movement. During the mid-nineteenth century, in fact, that movement was exacerbated by people fleeing the fearsome destruction and bloodshed of the Taiping Rebellion and the Hakka-Punti Clan wars. To this push was added the pull of new colonies and job opportunities offered by plantations and mines in the New World and Australia. As Baker puts it:

> It did not matter that they [Chinese] were going to barbarian lands, what mattered was the sheer necessity of finding work and food. Chinese labour was kidnapped, seduced by tales of the undreamt of riches which could be found abroad, sold by the unscrupulous, signed up to cruelly unrewarding long contracts by rapacious merchants who cared only for profit and not for the misery and suffering they caused their hapless victims. It went to plant sugar in Cuba, to mine for gold in Australia and California, to hump cargo in Singapore, to man the coal-mines in South Africa, to dig phosphate in Nauru, to tap rubber and wash for tin in Malaya, to build the railways in America and Canada, to tan leather in India, and to be domestic servants and guano-shovellers in Peru.[47]

COFFIN SHIPS TO THE CARIBBEAN

A new type of shipping developed in order to carry this new category of Chinese "adventurers" who left home, whether coerced or tricked, to try their luck in the land of the "foreign devil." The vessels that would take them from China were known as coffin ships. Each of these crowded ships carried eight coffins on board in the anticipation of death during the long voyage of three to four months to the Caribbean. The first group of Chinese on board one such coffin ship arrived in Cuba in 1843.[48] Thirty years later Spanish-speaking Chinese from Cuba were brought into America's South to supplement the work of emancipated black slaves in the cotton and sugar plantations. An international network of Chinese and American "agents," planters, and bankers arose to facilitate the delivery of larger numbers of workers to California and New York, from where they would be taken to southern states.[49] At the peak of Chinese emigration, between 1842 and 1900, some four hundred thousand Chinese migrated to the United States, Australia, and Canada, another four hundred thousand went to the Caribbean and Latin America, and one and a half million migrated to British Malaya, Burma, the Philippines, and Indonesia.[50] Under a system of indentured contracts almost two million Asians went overseas in the nineteenth and early twentieth centuries. Between the 1830s and 1920s some 1.3 million Indian indentured and self-financed migrants moved to British, French, and Dutch colonial territories in the Indian Ocean and Caribbean Sea, Africa, and Fiji and to the colonizer nations Canada and the United States.[51]

Until the Chinese Exclusion Act of 1882—adopted by the U.S. Congress in response to domestic political opposition to the importation of Chinese laborers for railroad construction and other work in California and Oregon—the United States was the country most open to all immigrants. Additional restrictions on immigration from other countries came with the National Origins Act of 1924. But for European migrants World War I marked the end of the laissez-faire era of migration. Governments that had until then adopted an attitude of benign neglect began taking a more direct hand in regulating, sponsoring, or even forcing migration. British, Italian, and French governments followed Russian, Austrian, and German authorities in introducing immigration controls and regulations—practices that would become standard in the twentieth century. These were more sophisticated and stricter barriers against globalization than even those imposed by imperial China.

Before the doors started closing, migrations led to the emergence of a significant Indian diaspora in many of the former European colonies. In Mauritius people of Indian origin are the single largest ethnic group—some 70 percent. They make up significant percentages in other countries like Fiji (48 percent), Surinam (36 percent), Trinidad and Tobago (36 percent), and Guyana (30 percent). Following the ancient trade routes that linked India to the Mediterranean world, many Indians migrated to the oil-rich Middle East and now make up some 11 to 15 percent of the population of the United Arab Emirates.[52] In the twentieth century some fifty million people from Russia and Central Asia moved to Siberia and Manchuria in search of a better life.[53] Toward the end of colonial rule the total number of Indians outside India was estimated to have been in the neighborhood of 2.5 million, with one in six of them engaged in trading and finance.[54]

The closing of the American door in the early twentieth century was followed by similar restrictive policies in other countries, especially in Brazil, Argentina, and Australia. The door would open again after the massive dislocation of population in Europe during the two world wars.

JAMAICANS HIT LONDON

By the end of World War II, immigration and visa procedures were in place, but large-scale migration did resume and only the direction of population movement was reversed. Instead of Europeans and colonists leaving for the New World, people of color from the colonies were heading for the metropolitan countries in large numbers. The need for workers in war-devastated Europe provided the pull; the necessary push came from poverty in the colonies, war, and famine. People from one part of the British Empire could move easily to other parts. All that was needed was the will to travel and the cash to buy the passage. In 1948, the British steamship *Empire Windrush* left Jamaica for Britain carrying soldiers returning home after the war. Newspapers carried advertisements for tickets to London for £28.10 for passengers below deck. This was a chance not to be missed by the poor. They knew that postwar Britain needed workers, and some three hundred Jamaicans, descendants of African slaves who were originally brought there by the British, boarded the ship for the journey to the adopted mother country. The hostile reaction to these arrivals in white England set the tone for race relations for decades to come. Race riots and communal tension that mark the life of immigrants has not stopped the flow. Jamaicans have been joined by even larger numbers of Indians, Pakistanis, Bangladeshis, Africans, and Chinese, with minority populations making up about 8 percent of the British population totaling fifty-eight million in 2005.

The United States, which attracted the largest number of migrants during what historians call the first golden age of globalization in the nineteenth century, again emerged as one of the biggest draws for immigrants all over the world, especially from poorer neighboring countries to the south. Between 1990 and 2005 some fifteen million migrants entered the United States. In 2005, one in every five migrants in the world lived in America.

Between the graying population of Europe and the teeming populations of some of its former colonies, the Continent has become a major destination for migrants. Some fifty-six million of the world's two hundred million migrants are in Europe. In fact, migrants constitute 20 percent of the population in some forty-one of the world's largest countries.

History seems to have turned full circle. China and India, which once were driving forces behind precolonial globalization, have returned to the fore with surging economies and a fast-expanding diaspora. In 2005 an estimated thirty-five million Chinese were dispersed around the world, and some twenty million people of Indian origin lived outside their country.[55] Chinese are also emerging as the world's biggest tourists. World travel has skyrocketed in the past half-century; the number of international arrivals worldwide has grown from twenty-five million in 1950 to a whopping 806 million in 2005. In this period, Europe and America's share in international travel has dropped while that of Asia and the Pacific has shown the highest growth. Buoyed by economic expansion, some thirty-one million Chinese left for foreign tours in 2005. Chinese and international travel industry experts forecast that at least fifty million Chinese tourists will travel overseas annually by 2010, and one hundred million by 2020.[56] The country that beckoned generations of travelers and gave Marco Polo his fame will now be reversing the roles, with Chinese Marco Polos armed with cameras roaming the world on jet planes.

In another historical irony, a new out-of-Africa migration by thousands of destitute Africans is beginning to preoccupy Europe. At the beginning of the fifteenth century Portugal's Henry the Navigator launched his country on an expansionary path by conquering the Muslim port city of Ceuta. The riches found in that place and stories of what lay in the interior of Africa spurred Portugal to send expeditions south. Lately, Ceuta, now a Spanish enclave, shot into the news as the new corridor for African migration into Europe. Before dawn on 5 October 2005, more than five hundred young African migrants tried to storm the ten-foot-high fence that separates Morocco from the enclave. Some seventy migrants got through, and because they had no travel papers, Spain had no country to deport them back to. Since then waves of refugees have arrived in

Morocco from sub-Saharan Africa with the goal of making it to Europe. Thousands of Malians and Senegalese have boarded flimsy fishing boats to reach the Canary Islands with the same goal of entering Spain, and untold thousands have drowned. In the first five months of 2006 alone, some ten thousand landed in the Canary Islands, sparking an emergency in Europe. Meanwhile in Ceuta the authorities are planning to raise the wire fence by another ten feet.

Similar moves are being planned along the U.S.-Mexico border, which has been overwhelmed by waves of Mexican immigrants defying desert conditions and multiple barriers to enter the United States. The wire fences of Ceuta and the U.S.-Mexico border stand as a reminder of the forces that have shaped the world for the past six thousand years.

FAST-FORWARDING MIGRATION: SEVILLE TO SAIGON

Sitting on the bank of the placid Guadalquivir that June morning, I recalled another river thirty years earlier. The brown waters of the Saigon River flowed past French colonial era hotels, stucco office buildings, and docks and a cemented quay not unlike Guadalquivir's to empty into the South China Sea. In the last days of the Vietnam War, which I covered from Saigon, the river had emerged as virtually the only lifeline for a panic-stricken population facing a communist onslaught. Fears were high that revenge killings and massacres would follow the communist victory. Thousands of Vietnamese who had worked with the Americans and their families and millions of terror-stricken people had no place to flee. Although the U.S. forces had withdrawn two years earlier, it was still an American-backed war and the United States had the moral responsibility to protect its Vietnamese friends who now found themselves with their backs to the South China Sea and nowhere to flee.

In a massive airlift operation, giant U.S. Air Force transport planes had ferried out 57,300 Americans and Vietnamese officials and their dependents before the airport came under attack. On 29 April I watched thousands of desperate Vietnamese trying to squeeze on board hundreds of boats of all shapes and sizes that filled the Saigon harbor. Within a day another 7,800 American and other nationals were whisked from rooftops by helicopters of the U.S. Seventh Fleet. Airlifted evacuees even included 2,600 Vietnamese babies—supposedly orphans—who had been flown out days before the fall. On 30 April, as the victorious communist forces rumbled into Saigon in their Russian T-54 tanks, a huge flotilla under the U.S. Military Sealift Command was steaming out of Vietnamese ports carrying seventy-three thousand people headed for the American military bases in the Philippines and Guam.[57] I was struck by the coincidence of the world's largest one-time migration landing in places where Magellan had made his first landfall after crossing the Pacific. Then, thinking of that episode of recent history sitting by the Guadalquivir in Seville, I suddenly realized that what I had witnessed in Saigon was the latest twist in the scattering of people around the world that began right on the Guadalquivir's shores with Columbus and Magellan. The massive dispersal and mixing of the world population that has happened since the colonization of the Americas by the Europeans has continued. Nearly a million Chinese and tens of thousands of Indians had come to Vietnam, just as hundreds of thousands of Vietnamese had been taken by their French colonial masters to Cambodia, Laos, and distant French colonies. In 1975, in the latest twist, Vietnam generated the world's biggest one-shot migration. Nearly a quarter of the Spaniards and Portuguese who migrated to the New World in sailboats in a century were transferred halfway around the world in a few weeks. In the follow-on migration in the subsequent decade, the Vietnamese population in the United States swelled to 1.4 million. Before 30 April 1975, Vietnamese in the United States had numbered just fifteen thousand, about half of them war brides.

The dramatic exodus from Vietnam is only a modern example of a long-standing historical trend of people leaving their homes to escape persecution and danger. The exodus has swelled with the rise of modern warfare threatening vast numbers of people and the availability of bigger and faster transportation to move them. The danger to the civilians was even magnified for political reasons. "AT LEAST A MILLION VIETNAMESE WILL BE SLAUGHTERED" ran the banner headline in one of the last editions of the U.S. armed forces newspaper *Stars and Stripes* to reach Saigon before the fall.[58] Since Vietnam, media explosion has raised worldwide awareness of human suffering as well as of opportunities that exist elsewhere. The willingness of governments to resettle or shelter the unfortunate for political, humanitarian, or economic reasons (to take advantage of the exodus to solve their domestic labor shortages) meant the beginning of a new age of refugees at the start of the twentieth century. Some one and a half million Russians fled after the Bolshevik revolution, and more than a million Armenians took refuge in different countries of Europe to escape the Turkish genocide. All the twentieth-century conflicts from the Korean War to the Balkan wars generated more than four million refugees, who have changed the demographic maps of recipient countries. And the movements followed the golden age of migration, in the nineteenth century, when sixty million Europeans left for the United States and Australia and an estimated hundred million people in East and northeast Asia moved throughout the region. The effect of these churnings of population has been the emergence of a global crazy quilt. The largest Greek city outside Greece is Melbourne, Australia, and the biggest Cambodian and Vietnamese populations outside their home countries are now in Long Beach, California, and Lowell, Massachusetts. More Scots live outside Scotland than in its borders.

In many countries immigrants have become an integral part of life. Indian Gujaratis dominate the low-budget hotel business, Koreans specialize in grocery shops, and Chinese run restaurants. Algerians, Moroccans, and Tunisians dominate mom-and-pop groceries in their former metropolitan country France; migrants from South Asia run confectioners and newsagents in Britain; migrants of Turkish origin run bakeries and grocery stores in the Netherlands. Most strikingly, as a recent United Nations report notes, migration is changing as the labor market becomes global. A foreman from a company in Indiana moves to China to train workers in new production methods; a professor from Johannesburg, South Africa, chooses to live in Sydney, Australia, from where he commutes to a teaching post in Hong Kong, China; a nurse trained in Manila works in Dubai.

In a longue durée perspective of history, today's march of migrants is merely the continuation of a journey that began many millennia ago. The reasons for embarking on adventure, whether to explore or to migrate, have changed little since people like Hanno ventured out on a boat on the Mediterranean or Ibn Battuta rode a mule on the Sahara desert or a migrant from Seville boarded a galleon bound for New Spain. They have been looking ahead to new lands and new futures and leaving behind inhospitable climates, economic ruin or famine, or religious or political persecution. As we have seen, history has marked an unending procession of adventurers, explorers, migrants, and refugees who risked much of what they had in a bid to live a better life. In the process of their journeys, sojourns, and settlements they have tied the world closer together. With transportation becoming easier and cheaper and with the growing gap between poor and rich countries, the historical drive of migration is unstoppable. The curiosity to see the world beyond one's borders that drove humans for millennia has now gotten a new boost from advancements in transportation and communication technology. Antonio Pigafetta, a native of Vicenza, who joined Magellan's expedition in 1519 and survived to write the classic account of the voyage, explained how he ended up in the first ship to circumnavigate the world: "I was in Spain in the year 1519, and from books and conversations I learnt that there were wonderful things to see by traveling the ocean, so I determined to discover with my own eyes the truth of all that I have been told."[59] Today all one needs is a *Lonely Planet* guide and a travel agent. Easier still, one can get on the Internet to plan a trip to places that Pigafetta would have loved to see.

Chapter 6 The Imperial Weave

"Ministers in this country, where every part of the World affects us, in some way or another, should consider the *whole Globe.*"
—*Thomas Pelham, Duke of Newcastle and Prime Minister of Britain, 1760*

Monday, 30 June 1997, was the day the sun set on the British Empire in Asia, but in fact it had gone into hiding for the past twenty-four hours in Hong Kong. The sky would not let up—drizzling, then torrential downpour—without stop. The weather forecast predicted that low pressure over the South China Sea would make Britain's handover of Hong Kong's sovereignty to China a soggy affair. I had just come out of the studio after an interview with a French radio station, repeating for the umpteenth time, "No, I did not expect Chinese People's Liberation Army tanks to rumble through Hong Kong Central. No, I did not expect Chinese censors to take up positions at the office of the *Far Eastern Economic Review*," the publication that I edited at the time.

In this painting, *Robert Clive and Mir Jafar after the Battle of Plassey, 1757,* by Francis Hayman, c. 1760, the East India Company governor meets his Indian collaborator after their victory. © National Portrait Gallery, London

The transformation of Hong Kong from a freewheeling capitalist city to part of the socialist motherland China, I believed, would come slowly. But apprehension over the future had hung over Hong Kong like miasma, with the squall of the last evening of the British rule adding to the gloom. Standing at the pier of the Hong Kong harbor under a forest of glistening umbrellas, amid more than one pair of glistening eyes, I watched Hong Kong's last governor, Chris Patten, and Prince Charles board Queen Elizabeth's aging yacht *Britannia*. As the Royal Hong Kong Police Band's bagpipes struck up "Rule Britannia," the ship slipped from the dock and gently melted into the evening darkness. That low-key departure not only marked the end of 156 years of colonial rule of Hong Kong but brought down the curtain on the British Empire.

Hong Kong was born in one of the first wars of globalization. Varied elements from different corners of the globe—British traders, Indian opium, Chinese tea, and the New World's dwindling silver—came together to produce a maelstrom that led to the birth of Hong Kong. On 26 January 1841, a small British naval party—consisting mainly of Indian Sikh soldiers—took possession of a small fishing village on a rocky island at the mouth of China's Pearl River. Imperial China had ceded the island known as Hong Kong after losing a gun battle with the British, who insisted on enforcing their God-given right to trade Indian-grown opium freely for Chinese tea and silk. The Opium War of 1841—which resulted in the cession of Hong Kong by China—grew out of Britain's attempt to use opium to replace the dwindling and increasingly expensive silver that had flowed liberally since the Spanish conquistadors' occupation of Mexico and South America. Alarmed at the spread of opium addiction among the populace and the dwindling intake of silver bullion to the Chinese imperial coffers, China's rulers had tried to stop the British but failed.

Hong Kong, a rocky twenty-six-square-mile outcrop, once used to shelter fishermen and smugglers from storms, was eventually transformed into a glittering metropolis and a critical hub that helped draw East Asia into an ever growing financial and trade network. Its efficient air and seaports, multitude of hotels, emporia gorging with a cornucopia of goods from throughout the world, and truly global nature of its cuisine turned Hong Kong into a tourist Mecca that saw millions of visitors from all over the world pass through the last remnant of the British Empire. Hong Kong was thus a textbook illustration of *Webster's Dictionary*'s definition of globalization as "making [things] worldwide in scope or application."

In earlier chapters we have seen how the actions of traders, preachers, and adventurers spearheaded the reconnection and closer integration of settled communities that had come into existence some twelve thousand years earlier. The desire to live better, to convert others to one's belief, and to learn what lies beyond one's borders have been the prime motives bringing countries and people in contact, peacefully or violently. Warriors make up the fourth group of actors who have hastened the integration of the world—or, more precisely, the political organization called "empire," created by the force of arms. The Latin word *imperium,* or empire, grew out of *imperare,* to command. Many motives have driven the creation of empires: ambition to erect God's kingdom on earth, greed for wealth, visions of glory, and universalist political ideals. From the world's first empire created by Sargon of Akkad in the third millennium to the Islamic empire founded by the Prophet Muhammad, and from the Mongol ruler Genghis Khan to Spanish conquistador Francisco Pizarro, history is replete with warriors driven by such desires to invade distant lands and to bring vast numbers of people of different ethnic, religious, and linguistic groups under their control.

Imperial power built and secured long-distance trade routes and boosted commerce by providing currency and legal structures. In their urge to build empires, kings and sultans devoted state resources to explore beyond their borders, spending state funds to organize expeditions and to acquire scientific and technical knowledge necessary for long-distance travel. Empires worked like gene-mixers, intermixing the different genetic strains that marked geographically dispersed humans after their ancestors had left Africa. In the process, they brought about microbial and biological unity. Not only did empires extend legal systems to encompass a vast part of the earth, but they spread religion, promoted long-distance trading, and built worldwide transportation and communication networks, widely diffusing languages, flora, and fauna and bringing together knowledge and technology that would otherwise have been confined to separate corners of the world. In this chapter we will look at examples of how the warriors and the empires they built connected the world in myriad ways that none of them could ever imagine. Empires may seem a system of the past, but the notion of imperial domination still thrives. Not unlike the Pax Romana of the Romans, the Pax Americana dominates the world, linking the world ever tighter while provoking an anger that is as global as America's influence. Islamist extremists—still seething with rage at the humiliation suffered by Muslims since the collapse of the caliphate—plot terrorist attacks and dream of an empire establishing "Allah's sovereignty on earth."[1]

DREAMS OF UNIVERSAL EMPIRE

Whatever their motives, the empire builders—old and new—have never lacked philosophical and political justification for dominating other human beings. Plato justified the distinction between superior and inferior in linguistic terms. To him, Barbarians, or the non-Greek *barbaros* (all those who could not speak Greek and whose language sounded like people stuttering "bar bar") were less than fully human.[2] He deemed that barbarians were enemies by nature and that it was proper to wage war on them, even to the point of enslaving or extirpating them. Aristotle further developed the notion of enemies by nature and maintained that barbarians, especially those of Asia—meaning people living east of the Bosporus—were slaves by nature. He told his student, the young king of Macedon Alexander, that it was proper to treat barbarians as slaves.[3] But Alexander interpreted the good-evil difference not by race but by behavior, with the good as the true Greek and the bad the true barbarian. By subjugating the bad and uniting the good, he wished to achieve what has been the ideal of kingship: the creation of *homonoia,* or unity and concord, a union of hearts. As the great scholar of Hellenism Sir William Tarn put it, Alexander wanted to be "the harmonizer and reconciler of the world—that part of the world which his arm reached; he did have the intention of uniting the peoples of his empire in fellowship and concord and making them of one mind."[4] He wanted to be remembered not as a conqueror but, in Plutarch's words, "as one sent by the gods to be the conciliator and arbitrator of the universe."[5] In a bid to realize his dream of creating a universal empire of homonoia, Alexander the Great's army marched across West Asia and Asia Minor. After crushing the Persian Empire and pillaging and burning Persepolis, Alexander proceeded as far east as the Punjab plains of India, connecting for the first time the Mediterranean world with the Indian subcontinent. While Alexander and his troops marched on, thousands of soldiers and administrators were left behind to rule the annexed territories.

The Roman Empire that emerged from the small city-state in the Tiber River Valley and spread to what it believed to be the end of the oecumene, or inhabited world, developed other justifications to rule over people considered barbarous. The Romans developed an elaborate administrative system and a legal code to bring others under their control, and their actions were touted as acts of generosity, as spreading *civitas,* or civic society, the origin of civilization. "Roman imperialism came to be seen not as a form of oppression, as the seizure by one people of the lands, the goods, and the persons of others," Anthony Pag-

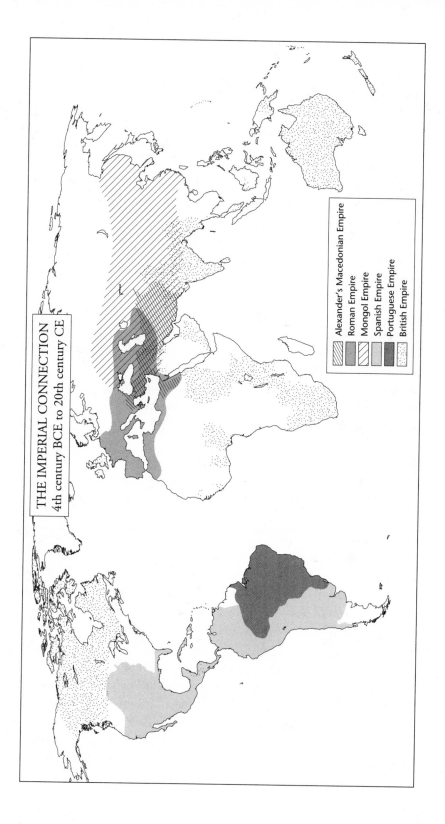

THE IMPERIAL CONNECTION
4th century BCE to 20th century CE

Alexander's Macedonian Empire
Roman Empire
Mongol Empire
Spanish Empire
Portuguese Empire
British Empire

den notes, "but as a form of beneficent rule that involved not conquest but patronage, and whose first purpose was the improvement of the lives of others."[6] In what could be seen as a precursor to the imperial British argument of the "white man's burden" and the French *mission civilisatrice,* Roman historian Cicero argued that even Africans, Spaniards, and Gauls, "savage and barbarous nations," were entitled to just government. Pagden quips that by extension this meant "if their own rulers were unable to provide it, then the Romans would be happy to do so for them."[7]

Often the dream of universal empire was simply the question of personal ambition for power and glory. From King Jayavarman VII of Cambodia, who proclaimed himself a universal emperor in the twelfth century, to the sixteenth-century Japanese warlord Toyotomi Hideyoshi, rulers were attracted to the idea of universal empire—even in a geographically limited universe. Hideyoshi saw himself as a universal monarch who would eventually "rule the whole human race from his residence in Peking or in India."[8] He invaded Korea twice in a failed bid to reach China, which presumably was the limit of his universe.

The classical Greco-Roman notion of political empire was updated after the American Revolution and the rise of the United States. The concept of empire as a civilizing mission was converted to Thomas Jefferson's "empire of liberty," and with the adoption of the Monroe Doctrine in 1823 it was presented as an anticolonial enterprise. Under President Theodore Roosevelt the doctrine was interpreted to give the United States a free hand in its Latin backyard. America's avowed mission to be a beacon of liberty in a broader world was challenged during the post–World War II period of Soviet military expansion. The notion of advancing liberty by extending American power abroad acquired greater urgency. America's responsibility, President Harry Truman admitted in 1947, was even greater than that which had faced "Darius I's Persia, Alexander's Greece, Hadrian's Rome [and] Victoria's Britain." The only way to "save the world from totalitarianism," he argued, was for "the whole world [to] adopt the American system," for "the American system" could survive only by becoming "a world system."[9]

Sixty years later that thesis still stands, and the collapse of the Soviet Empire has not weakened the rationale. Although the world's leading democracy may find the concept controversial, the United States—a central hub of the world economy, a far-flung military presence with more than seven hundred military installations worldwide and an immense political-cultural influence—has come to acquire the attributes of an empire. Writer Jonathan Schell would prefer to call the United States an imperial power without an empire. Whatever the name, American power, exercised in the name of promoting democracy and human rights, of securing global peace and ensuring freedom of the seas and skies, girds the globalized world. Whatever the United States chooses to do affects people and countries all over the world. The ubiquitous presence of American brand-name products—such as McDonald's, present in 120 countries—has led critics to call globalization nothing but Americanization.[10] Economic dominance aside, the global security concerns of the United States can be seen in the fact that the power-projection capability of the U.S. Air Force has a presence on six continents and American Special Forces have conducted thousands of training operations with some 170 countries.[11] The British writer and labor politician Harold Laski was prescient: "America bestrides the world like a colossus," he wrote in 1947. "Neither Rome at the height of its power nor Great Britain in the period of economic supremacy enjoyed an influence so direct, so profound, or so pervasive."[12] Laski's description of the American colossus has never been more true than today, but as we will see in this chapter, the dream of universal empire has an ancient pedigree and its integrating impact has been a long time coming.

The Aztecs and Incas had no universal pretensions; their empires were driven by their cosmology and faith in the spirits of the dead. Aztec cosmology dictated an unflagging effort to satisfy the sun god. If the sun was not nourished with the vigorous blood of warriors, he would grow too weak for his daily struggle against the forces of darkness, and the universe would be destroyed. So the Aztecs presented captives to the sun god in ritual ceremonies of human sacrifice.[13] The unrelenting quest for sacrificial victims brought many Central American tribes under Aztec power by the fifteenth century. The Incas' practice of worshipping their dead rulers required sizable amounts of land and labor for the maintenance of their mummies. This need forced the new emperor to conquer new territories and exploit their wealth and resources. "By creating unrelenting pressures for new agricultural lands, the cult of the royal mummies eventually drove [the Inca empire] Tawantinsuyu into disastrous military adventures."[14] An incredibly diverse collection of peoples were brought into the Inca domain—territory that would eventually fall in the hands of the Spanish conquistadors, aided partly by dissention within this heterogeneous empire.

Nearly a thousand years earlier, across the oceans a different empire was born to serve God. The empire founded by the Prophet Muhammad would be unlike any in the past. It would be God's empire, built not by a king but by millions of faithful led by a self-proclaimed messenger of God. Until the fateful night when the Prophet came down from the hill to proclaim the divine command of one god, the agency for spreading the Word was dispersed in many hands. There were priests to interpret gods' wishes and temporal rulers to carry them out. Islam eliminated not only the middleman but the distinction between religious and temporal power. The authority of God, as expressed in the Koran, was absolute, as was that of Muhammad as his Prophet. As the Koran states: "Say: O mankind, I am the Allah's Messenger to all of you. . . . There is no god but He. . . . Believe [then] in Allah and in his Messenger." This absolutist claim to universalism was matched by the brotherhood of the umma, or community, that the Prophet called for. Unlike religions such as Buddhism or Christianity, which found converts among temporal authorities who would propagate the faith, Islam was born as a state amid bitter strife among stateless Arab tribes. The Prophet enjoined that the umma be totally egalitarian: "O people, your Lord is one and your ancestor is [also] one. You are all descended from Adam and Adam was [born] of the earth." As members of the umma, Muslims have since been obligated to pay alms for the needy and refrain from fighting one another. Their duty is also to bring all humanity within the umma and fight "infidels" who resist.

SLAY THE IDOLATERS

Scholars have long debated whether an expansionist urge is inherent in Islam. Some passages in the Koran suggest only defensive warfare, such as "fight in the way of God with those who fight you, but aggress not: God loves not the aggressors." Others clearly call for proactive warfare: "Slay the idolaters wherever you find them, and take them, and confine them, and lie in wait for them at every place of ambush." In his last visit to Mecca in 632, the Prophet said that although all Muslims were brethren and should not fight one another, their mission as Muslims was "to fight people till they testify that there is no god but God and Muhammad is the messenger of God, and perform the prayer and pay the alms-tax."[15] Based on such conflicting statements, medieval Muslim scholars developed a doctrine of holy war, which Islam scholar Michael Cook says "endorsed the fundamental idea of aggressive warfare aimed at extending the dominion of Islam, but at the same time hedged it about with a variety of ifs and buts." Despite equivocation about applying the policy of holy war, the concept enjoys a central place of value in Islamic heritage, according to Cook. It "certainly made available to Muslims a moral charter for the continuing conquest of infidel lands. . . . In that sense, there clearly was something about Islam that lent itself to the creation of a global culture."[16]

Since the Prophet Muhammad forbade *razzias,* or traditional raids for cattle and property, against tribes who converted to Islam, local raiding parties had to look beyond traditional Arab lands. The Koran allowed believers to relieve infidels of their possessions, provided that the bounty was redistributed among the members of the expeditionary force. The other method of property acquisition was to collect tax from nonbelievers. In 630 Muhammad himself led an army of some thirty thousand soldiers toward the Byzantine frontier. After a five-hundred-mile journey up to the Gulf of Aqaba, he camped for twenty days and negotiated a peace agreement with the Christian prince of Aylah. In return for an oath of allegiance and an annual tribute, the *dhimm*i, or the people of the Book, like Christians, were placed under the umma's protection and granted freedom of worship. This practical arrangement for coexisting with other faiths emerged as a source of revenue for the Islamic empire as it expanded in the following centuries. Some scholars argue that the impulse to seek martyrdom in the cause of Allah and reach paradise may have attracted converts in the early years of Islam. "The immediate gratification of desires for the comforts and luxuries of the civilized regions of the Fertile Crescent was just as strong in the case of many."[17] Interestingly, the warfare of the first imperialist ruler, Sargon of Akkad, beyond his zone of direct political control was driven by a search for booty and tribute, not unlike that of Muhammad's some three thousand years later.

In 637, within five years of Muhammad's call to arms, an Arab army invaded Mesopotamia and won a famous victory at al-Qadisiyah, near modern Baghdad, bringing Islam to Persia. This victory has since inspired the faithful to make sacrifices for the glory of Islam. Even the secular dictator of Iraq Saddam Hussein alluded to the victory of al-Qadisiyah to cheer his troops when they were engaged in a protracted battle in the 1980s with Iran, modern Persia. Chalking up victory after victory in North Africa, the Arab army crossed the narrow Strait of Gibraltar and reached Europe. Its advance to the heart of the Continent was halted at last by the Frankish king Charles Martel at the Battle of Tours in 732. But the empire continued its march to the east and south. When the Mongols, who had earlier sacked the caliphate in Baghdad, converted to Islam, a vast part of the world from the Atlantic to the Pacific Ocean and most of sub-Saharan Africa came under Islamic rule, even though the Ottoman Empire was confined to the eastern Mediterranean and the Middle East. As we have seen in Chapter 2, Muslim traders spread the religion to Southeast Asia, which would eventually boast the largest Islamic nation on earth: Indonesia. Islam connected the globe and fused culture in a way that changed the world forever. Of course, the Islamic empire did not automatically mean expansion of the number of Muslims. Because Islam forbade taxing the faithful and the revenue of the empire had to be collected from the infidels, pragmatic Islamic rulers discouraged conversion to Islam. The logic of maintaining the temporal power by having a large tax base of nonbelievers often trumped over the urge to convert all humanity to Islam—the original mission laid down by the Prophet.[18]

The world's largest contiguous land-empire was not, however, built out of a desire to convert or liberate. It was, instead, accomplished by nomadic Mongols who had no religious mission other than to rule the world. Between 1190, when Genghis Khan began unifying the nomadic tribes of Mongolia, and 1258, when a grandson of Genghis sacked the Islamic caliphate in Baghdad, the Mongols overran the whole swath of territory from the coasts of southern Siberia to Hungary and Poland in the West and from the South China Sea to the Persian Gulf. Although the Mongols believed in one god, the Eternal Blue Sky, they were remarkably secular until they converted to Islam. The Mongol expansion was thus motivated by the need to move out of regular grazing areas for food and other necessities. Historians have advanced many theories to explain Mongol expansionism. Yale historian Valerie Hansen says one possible reason could be climatic: a steep and regular decline in the mean annual temperature in Mongolia between 1175 and 1260 resulted in less grass for the Mongol herds, prompting the Mongols to conquer new territories.[19] According to some, attacking and robbing neighbors became a strategy that unified the Mongol tribes that roamed the steppes of Central Asia.

As one scholar puts it, Genghis Khan "understood that the road to power went precisely through unification of the steppe nomads. Only having accomplished this would it be possible to conquer the settled civilizations. Simultaneously, however, he had to hold out the prospects of plunder to achieve the unification. The two could not be separated. Mongol society was a herder and hunter society, but it was also a predatory society."[20]

As the Prophet Muhammad had done with Arab tribes, the rising Mongol leader Genghis Khan forbade tribes from attacking each other and instead advocated unified raids against sedentary neighbors for food and other essentials and luxuries that nomadic life could not provide. Raiding well-entrenched powerful neighbors like China, Persia, or the Abbasid caliphate required large-scale organization. An empire not only offered internal peace among the various Mongol tribes but held out "an opportunity of enrichment at the expense of outside groups."[21] As they expanded their raids, capturing more booty and craftsmen, however, the Mongols needed more food and tools to put their captives to work. Like other conquerors before him, Genghis Khan came to view himself as anointed by heaven to bring the world under his control. A contemporary Armenian chronicle quotes Genghis Khan as saying that "it is the will of god that we take the earth and maintain order" to impose Mongol law and taxes. He added that the Mongols were obligated to "slay [their opponents] and destroy their place, so that the others who hear and see should fear and not act the same."[22]

THE LURE OF AFRICA

Religious fervor often combined with greed to drive imperial ambition. What was simply the desire to control minerals and timber in the time of Sargon's Akkadian empire evolved into greed for gold and other luxuries. Even Alexander the Great—who aspired to create a civilized universal empire—dispatched a fleet to conquer the island of Socotra in the Arabian Sea because it produced the most fragrant resin and aloe.[23] The Portuguese and Spanish empires were driven by greed for spices and gold, not just god and glory. For example, when Henry the Navigator attacked the Muslim port city of Ceuta on the North African shore, the unimaginable riches that he found, along with tales of mountains of gold being exchanged for Moroccan goods in the interior of Africa, inspired him to launch further expeditions into the continent.[24] Crusades against Islam and missions to convert pagans to Christianity also proved to be a lucrative business. Henry the Navigator's naval expeditions, launched in the early fifteenth century, culminated in Vasco da Gama's voyage to India around the Cape of Good Hope and to the founding of a Portuguese empire that would last four hundred years.

Within a hundred years of Prince Henry's seminal explorations in the Atlantic, the kingdom's far-flung empires in Asia and the Americas brought in three-fourths of all Portuguese government revenue.[25] Portugal itself became a coveted object for Spanish monarch Philip II, who was already the sovereign of an empire spanning Latin America and Southeast Asia. The creation of the Spanish Empire initiated by Columbus's serendipitous discovery of the New World was the outcome of the search for gold, spices, and souls to convert. A year after Columbus's voyage, the pope granted the Catholic monarchs of Castile, Ferdinand and Isabella, sovereignty over all non-Christian lands they might discover in the Atlantic, as well as the duty to evangelize all humans found there. The pope assumed the right of temporal authority over both Christians and believers in other faiths called "pagans."[26] Conquistadors like Hernán Cortés and Francisco Pizarro, who helped create the Spanish Empire in South America, were not only interested in the fame that came from their conquests but intent on enjoying the spoils of the New World. They positioned themselves as *encomenderos,* or patrons, to exploit, usually in brutal fashion, the labor of the Americas.[27]

The largest and longest-enduring empire—Britain's—also arose out of greed and envy. After Columbus returned from the New World with tales of unbelievable riches, the British crown, along with individual sailors and merchants, dreamed of gold and silver in a new continent. In March 1496, four years after Columbus's voyage, King Henry VII followed in the footsteps of the Castilian monarchs and sanctioned a journey by the Genoese navigator John Cabot, giving him and his sons "full and free authority, faculty and power to sail to all parts, regions and coasts of the eastern, western and northern sea . . . to conquer, occupy and possess, as our vassals and governors, lieutenants and deputies therein, acquiring for us the dominion, title and jurisdiction of the same towns, castles, cities, islands and main lands so discovered."[28] In succeeding times, however, as the Industrial Revolution transformed the British Empire and economic and political liberalism took hold, high-minded rationale replaced unabashed greed. As the English historian James Bryce argued in 1901, it seemed as if "a new sort of unity is being created among mankind." And while marching into Baghdad in 1908, General Frederick Stanley Maude declared: "Our armies do not come into your cities and lands as conquerors or enemies, but as liberators."[29] This was an eerie precursor of the pronouncements to come from the White House before the United States launched the invasion "Operation Iraqi Freedom" in March 2003.

The British venture in Iraq ended quickly, but what had begun centuries earlier with the innocent landings of adventurous traders carrying the British flag on the shores of Virginia and Surat, India, grew into a globe-spanning empire. I witnessed the sunset of that empire in Hong Kong almost exactly five hundred years later. In the intervening time, the British rationale for empire had evolved from the civilizing imperative of the "white man's burden" to the commercial arguments in favor of free trade, liberation from autocracy, and creation of a humane global community.

After the ancestors walked out of Africa, their descendants spread to the habitable parts of the earth and gradually changed their pigmentation and body shape. Humans demonstrated substantial diversity by the time sedentary agriculture developed. Interbreeding on a relatively small scale occurred through the diaspora of traders and missionary activities. Only with the rise of empires were large numbers of people of varied ethnicity, languages, and religious persuasions linked under a single authority. Empire thus emerged as history's most effective genetic blender, producing prolonged and extensive migrations. Some were voluntary; in others, the marginalized were forced, sometimes by poverty, sometimes by authority, to leave in search of a better and richer life. As Anthony Pagden has stated:

> All the way from Europe to the Americas, these migrations have inevitably destroyed societies that were once flourishing. They have also brought into being entire societies that did not exist before. And in time these have created new peoples. The inhabitants of modern Greece and the Balkans are not what they were under Alexander, neither are the modern Italians Romans, nor the black populations of the Americas much like the West African peoples from whom they are descended. The majority of the inhabitants of Spanish America are neither fully Europeans nor wholly Indian, but as Simon Bolivar said of them in 1810, "a sort of middle species between the legitimate owners of this land and the Spanish usurpers."[30]

A history of population movement since the rise of civilizations is beyond the scope of this book, but a cursory look at some examples shows the decisive role empires played in driving the growth of genetic and, consequently, social, economic, and cultural interconnections. Alexander the Great's empire in the fourth century BCE brought awareness of a wider world. Thousands of Greeks left home, married local women, and started new lives as soldiers and administrators in the distant corners of Alexander's empire, beginning a dynamic that produced far-reaching social and cultural effects. For all of Alexander's visions of a universal empire and brotherhood of man, his empire's legacy was, in the words of William Tarn, "a world empty of machines and full of slaves."[31] Non-Greeks turned into slaves, and even poorer Greeks were not exempt from bondage.

The Roman Empire brought even larger populations under its control— from the vales of Scotland to the shores of the Arabian Sea, a territory of about five million square miles and an estimated population of fifty-five million. As the empire grew, so did the machinery of its expansion. From a small standing army under an expansionist ruler, the entire free male population of the empire was turned into a conscript army irrespective of geographic origin. At a later stage of the empire, even some of the emperors themselves were descended from the conquered lands.[32]

SOWING MONGOL SEEDS

During the five centuries of its existence, the Roman Empire brought about a multidirectional intermixing of people, but later, the Islamic empire of the

Arabs took the genetic seeds in different directions. Intermarriage with the sub-jugated people who were converted to become *mawalis,* or clients, of the Arabs altered the genetic landscape of the Middle East. From Persia to Spain, Arab masters married the locals. In the process, the term *Arab* began its gradual tran-sition from the name for a bedouin nomad of the Arabian Peninsula to its pre-sent meaning of anyone whose culture and language are Arabic.[33] However, by the thirteenth century, the original bedouin Arabs were outnumbered by the other subjugated people and could no longer provide the army that the caliphate needed. The caliph started importing Central Asian slave boys—known as mamluks—from today's Turkmenistan and training them to be sol-diers. The same mamluks would one day take power themselves and rule part of the Islamic empire.

No empire, however, had as direct an effect on genetic blending by violence as did the Mongol Empire. "To have caused the dispersion of Turkic peoples to three corners of the earth—China, India and the Middle East—is thought by one historian to have been the principal outcome of the empire."[34] Genghis Khan has been quoted as saying that his supreme joy was "to cut my enemies to pieces, drive them before me, seize their possessions, witness the tears of those dear to them, and embrace their wives and daughters."[35] The mass murder of men and children and the large numbers of concubines amassed by Genghis and his successors have left their mark on the region's genetic landscape. The extent of their impact has been revealed in a remarkable study of population ge-netics in the areas that once formed part of the Mongol Empire. A team of sci-entists has found the Y chromosome that belonged to Genghis Khan in the DNA of 8 percent of the males of a large part of Asia. They estimate that the proportional percentage DNA inheritance would correspond to some sixteen million people all over the world.[36]

Forced migration also played a role. Because the nomadic Mongols knew nothing other than hunting and herding, they captured professionals and craft-workers of all types from the conquered territories. As historian Jack Weather-ford writes: "The Mongol armies rounded up translators, scribes, doctors, as-tronomers, and mathematicians to be parcelled out among the families in the same shares that they parcelled out musicians, cooks, goldsmiths, acrobats, and painters. The authorities divided these knowledge workers, together with all the other craftsmen, the animals, and other goods for transportation via a long caravan trek or sea journey to the various parts of the family."[37] For instance, Kublai Khan imported Persian translators and doctors, as well as some ten thousand Russian soldiers, to settle them on land north of present-day Beijing.

The Russians stayed as permanent residents for nearly a hundred years before they vanished from the official Chinese chronicles.[38]

CONQUER AND POPULATE

With the emergence of ocean-based European empires in the fifteenth and sixteenth centuries, there began the most far-reaching interbreeding in history. According to one estimate, every year in the sixteenth century between three and four thousand young men left Portugal bound for Portuguese India. By 1709, population levels in Portugal's northern provinces had fallen so drastically that King John V reiterated earlier orders requiring travelers to obtain passports before they departed. Meanwhile, the gold rush in Brazil saw the number of Portuguese settlers there leap from around two thousand a year in the late seventeenth century to five to six thousand annually between 1700 and 1720. To this influx was added a higher number of African slaves to work in the plantations and mines. In 1818, Brazil's population stood at about 3.8 million. Of these, only an estimated 250,000 were Indians. This means that over 93 percent of Brazil's population was the product of migration from Europe and Africa over the previous three centuries.[39]

Like the Mongols, the Spanish conquistadors killed male American Indians and took their women as concubines, an action that was attributable, in part, to the scant number of female voyagers accompanying them. Partial records kept in Seville suggest that less than 5 percent of people sailing to the New World were women. The consequent effects on the colonial population became a source of concern to the monarchy, and in 1514 King Ferdinand gave his approval for the intermarriage of Native Americans and Spaniards, saying that nothing "should impede marriage between Indians and Spaniards, and all should have complete liberty to marry whomever they please."[40]

The migration of other Europeans to the Spanish colonies was even more pronounced. As the population of Spain started to decline by the end of the sixteenth century, a law passed in 1590 in New Spain (present-day Mexico), allowed non-Spaniards—including Portuguese, Germans, Flemings, Italians, Greeks, and English—to settle. The result was the creation of a huge *mestizo,* or "mixed," population. The Spanish colony in the Philippines also heralded the arrival of Asians to the New World. Some six thousand "Orientals" were believed to have entered New Spain from Manila during each decade of the early seventeenth century.[41] Although reliable data are scarce, the import of African slaves into the Spanish Empire also visibly affected Latin American demography. In Lima in 1795, for instance, free blacks and slaves made up 45 percent of the city's population. As historian Henry Kamen has noted, "Though they had been brought in simply to work and serve, Africans transformed the society and economy of vast tracts of America, and firmly implanted their race and culture wherever they went."[42]

While the African presence among today's South American population is evident to casual observers, the deep impact of European migration is less so. A genetic study in Colombia offers a glimpse of the overwhelming preponderance of European male DNA in the Spanish colonies of South and Central America. That research showed that approximately 94 percent of the Y chromosomes—transmitted from the father—are European in origin. When viewed against a variety of Amerindian mtDNA—maternal DNA—found in Colombia, James D. Watson, one of the fathers of modern genetics, sees a clear explanation: "The invading Spaniards, who were men, took local women for their wives. The virtual absence of Amerindian Y chromosome types reveals the tragic story of colonial genocide: indigenous men were eliminated, while local women were sexually 'assimilated' by the conquistadors."[43]

The British trading diaspora of the seventeenth century morphed into the British Empire, and its legacy set the stage for today's multiethnic globalized world.[44] From the British landings in North America and the Caribbean to the development of the dominions of Australia, New Zealand, and Canada, the empire produced a steady flow of emigration from "the mother country" to the new territories, boosted by convicts from home and slaves from Africa. All through the nineteenth century, and continuing into the twentieth, especially after World War I, voluntary emigration was supported by state-funded inducements, including assisted passages and a ten-pound subsidy for travel and settlement in Canada. As a senior British official explained, "Empire migration" was designed to give "fuller opportunities for individual human beings" —meaning British citizens who could improve their life in the colonies.[45] Between the early 1600s and the 1950s, more than twenty million people left Britain to begin new lives in the colonies. As Niall Ferguson puts it, "The Britannic exodus changed the world. It turned whole continents white."[46] In the century before World War I, some fifty million Europeans emigrated, the vast majority of them, about forty-six million, leaving for the New World. The British Empire also contributed to diversifying the American continent. Between 1807 and 1882, British ships transported nearly 3.5 million Africans to the New World as slaves. That figure is more than three times the number of white migrants making the journey west over the same period. Only with decolonization did the color of colonial countries again begin to change.

Toward the beginning of the twentieth century, colonial empires began to see a reverse flow—of natives coming to the metropolitan countries in large numbers. In their West African colonies, the French converted former slaves into infantrymen known as *tirailleurs Sénégalais* to serve further colonial expansion. The region of Mali was one such conquest, which was later turned, in the memorable phrase of Lieutenant Colonel Charles Mangin, into a "reservoir of men." Mangin argued for using the tirailleurs to fight against the Germans in World War I, and as many as 160,000 West Africans did so.[47] After demobilization, a large number opted not to return to Africa, thus forming the core of France's African immigrant community. Along with North African Berbers who migrated to France after the loss of the French colony in the Maghreb, these immigrants, whose numbers would swell to five million by 2005, would prove to be an unintegrated, explosive component of French society.

At the end of World War II, the momentum of ex-colonial subjects returning to the metropole picked up, beginning with the celebrated case of the *Empire Windrush*. Reverse migration to the empires and prosperous former colonies like the United States would eventually emerge as one of the strongest currents of global population movements, laying ever-thickening webs of connection. Before the last British governor left Hong Kong, tens of thousands of former subjects fled the colony for safe havens in Britain, Canada, Australia, and the United States.

The U.S. global involvement in wars in foreign lands during the past century has had the effect of bringing migrants from those countries. The Vietnam War's legacy was more than a million Vietnamese, Cambodian, Lao, and Hmong settling in the United States. In an echo of the Roman Empire's granting of citizenships to elites in the Balkans, the Middle East, and North Africa to strengthen the armed forces in the second century, the Bush administration has expedited the naturalization of twenty thousand resident aliens in the U.S. Armed Forces.[48] Employing mercenaries in war is a longstanding practice, but today's closely integrated world has made it a global phenomenon. In recent years, Pentagon contractors have recruited some thirty-five thousand foreigners to serve the American forces in Iraq. The realization that a global village could be a lethal place came in 2005 to farming families in a remote place in Nepal. Some families, who may not have known where Iraq was until a few weeks earlier, woke up to the news that their children had been killed by insurgents in

Iraq. Those desperately poor young men were lured by manpower supply agencies to go to the Middle East to work as cooks and kitchen hands.[49]

THE WEB OF LANGUAGE

The relocation of peoples forced by empires brought in new languages, foods, dress, customs, and cultures, a skein that would grow into an interconnected world. In that sense, genetic diffusion that resulted from empires was like the first lines of text on the palimpsests of history that would be written over and over again in the ensuing centuries to create today's globalized world.

By promoting trade over vast areas, empires enriched local languages. For example, Malay is the traditional lingua franca of island Southeast Asia, but over time it has been overlaid with the expressions and vocabulary of the Arab or Indian principal traders. Portuguese and Dutch colonial rule introduced new vocabulary, but at the same time, pidgin or bazaar Malay spoken in different parts of the region was revitalized by the traders' expressions and vocabulary. Likewise, in East Africa, both the spread of Islam and the influence of European colonial powers enriched a similar bazaar language, Swahili.[50]

Of course, long before ambitious rulers began marching with their soldiers, people of Mesopotamia and the Indus Valley had begun exchanging goods, making use of elements of language common to them.[51] Koine, for instance, became the common speech among the elites and traders throughout the empire left behind by Alexander the Great.[52] Even after Latin became the official language of the Roman Empire, Greek remained the lingua franca. Latin, originally spoken by small groups of people in the lower Tiber River Valley, traveled with Roman political power, spreading from Italy to western and southern Europe and to the north shores of the Mediterranean and coastal regions of Africa. Later modern Romance languages grew out of the spoken Latin in territories under the Roman Empire.[53]

No language, however, spread as fast and over as vast a territory as Arabic. As the Prophet Muhammad and his successors carried Islam to Mesopotamia, Persia, and the North African Maghreb countries, the language of the Koran overwhelmed existing tongues—Kurdish, Berber, Aramaic, and Coptic.[54] By the beginning of the eighth century, Arabic had evolved into the official imperial language. As Michael Cook has noted: "A new elite culture was established, centered on the Islamic religion and the Arabic language; Arabic became the classical language of a civilization in the manner of classical Chinese or Latin, and everything that an educated elite might want to read became available in Arabic."[55] The language and culture of the Persians survived their conquest by the Arabs and their acceptance of the Islamic faith, but both were deeply transformed. By adopting Arabic script and extensively borrowing Arabic vocabulary, Persian Farsi emerged as a second great literary language and spread far afield, especially toward India and, much later, throughout the Ottoman Empire.[56] Although the Turks were not conquered by the Arabs, their conversion to Islam in the tenth century brought in significant Arabic vocabulary, and Turkish came to be written in the Arabic script.[57] Most important, the adoption of the Arabic language by all the conquered peoples—Iranians, Syrians, Greeks, Copts, Berbers, Jews, and Christians—opened up their stores of learning, art, science, history, and technology to scholars throughout the empire. The foundation was thus laid for the emergence of a dazzling Islamic civilization. Thanks to the Arabic translation of Greek classics, including Aristotle and Plato, a world intellectual heritage was preserved.

The Mongol conquerors, who lacked a written language, were transformed by their imperial experience. Despite its linguistic shortcomings, the Mongol Empire served as a diffuser of other languages. To rule such a vast empire, the Mongols needed administrators and clerks who spoke local languages. As Jack Weatherford notes, "After executing the soldiers, the Mongol officers sent clerks to divide the civilian population by profession. Professional people included anyone who could read and write in any language—clerks, doctors, astronomers, judges, soothsayers, engineers, teachers, imams, rabbis, or priests. The Mongols particularly needed merchants, cameleers, and people who spoke multiple languages, as well as craftsmen."[58]

European empires, starting with the Portuguese and Spanish and later the Dutch, French, and English, took the legacy of the Roman Empire across the oceans. Today nearly a third of the world population speaks European languages spread by colonial rule. After Mandarin Chinese and Hindi, English is the most widely spoken language in the world. Not surprisingly, the bulk of the speakers of this global lingua franca reside in the former British Empire. In his famous minute on education in India written in 2 February 1835, Lord Macaulay, a member of Britain's Supreme Council of India, wrote: "[English] is like[ly] to become the language of commerce throughout the seas of the East. It is the language of two great European communities which are raising, the one in south of Africa, the other in Australasia. . . . We must at present do our best to form a class who may be interpreters between us and the millions whom we govern; a class of persons, Indian in blood and colour, but English in taste, in opinions, in morals, and in intellect."[59]

A month later, on 7 March 1835, Governor-General William Bentinck issued an order supporting Macaulay's position. That historic decision to put the empire's resources to the teaching of English would have a far-reaching consequence in integrating the world. India became the largest English-speaking country in the world, and by the beginning of the twenty-first century, the nation's language was a principal source of attraction for the outsourcing of service jobs and foreign investment.

The differing impact of colonial education policies can be seen in the New World. Thanks to Britain's liberal education policy, at the time of America's war of independence there were nine universities for two and a half million people, and the thirteen colonies had an intellectual elite—the likes of John Adams, Benjamin Franklin, and Thomas Jefferson—who were thoroughly engaged with the world. But in the Spanish colonies, Brazil, and the Caribbean, where more than seventeen million people lived, there were just two universities, in Mexico City and Guadalajara, which concentrated on theology and law.

EMPIRE AS GOD'S TOOL

We have seen the inspiration that gods have given to create empires, but empires that were not expressly created for theological reasons nevertheless played a role in the diffusion of religion.

In the third century BCE, India's Mauryan emperor Aśoka became the first ruler in history to devote imperial authority to the spread of religious faith. By the time Aśoka was converted to Buddhism, founded three centuries earlier, he had already built a huge empire covering northern India. After Aśoka won the Battle of Kalinga, a monk converted him to the religion of nonviolence and compassion. The emperor not only set up rock inscriptions—akin to public billboards—laying down a Buddhist code of conduct, he also launched a campaign of religious conquest by dispatching missionaries all over the Indian subcontinent, as well as to Sri Lanka, Burma, and Hellenistic and Central Asian kingdoms.[60] Thanks to Aśoka's power and influence, missionaries gained access to the courts and the people and succeeded in converting many to Buddhism. One of the most successful of such missions was led by Aśoka's son, Mahinda, to Sri Lanka.[61] From there the religion later spread to Southeast Asia. Other rulers carried on Aśoka's missionary work, notably the Kushan ruler Kanishka (second century CE). Thanks to Kanishka's efforts, Afghanistan,

Bactria, eastern Iran, and Central Asia all became Buddhist and provided a pathway for the religion to reach China, which it did in the first century CE.[62]

The Roman emperor Constantine played a role, not unlike that of Aśoka, in promoting the diffusion of Christianity. After years of persecuting the Christians, Constantine converted in 312 to the faith propagated by Jesus, dramatically turning the religion's fortunes. Constantine diverted the massive state resources that had been lavished on pagan temples to Christianity, making it "the most-favored recipient of the near-limitless resources of imperial favor."[63] In 325 he and the pope convened a gathering of around three hundred bishops from all the corners of the empire. Clad in gold and sitting on a gold throne, Constantine presided over the first Council of Nicaea, marking the imperial launch of the church.[64] A historian summed up the result of Constantine's conversion: "A clergy recruited from the people and modestly sustained by member contributions suddenly gained immense power, status, and wealth as part of the imperial civil service."[65]

After the fall of Rome, the church had to revive its missionary spirit to dispatch monks to preach in non-Christian territories. An early success came in the late fifth century, when the great Frankish king Clovis converted to Christianity and immediately baptized three thousand of his armed followers. The Christianizing mission was carried out with zeal by Clovis's successors, so much so that Charlemagne was crowned Holy Roman Emperor by the pope in 800. Charlemagne took both his title and task seriously and sought the immediate conversion of all territories he conquered. As one historian notes, "Each victory was followed by forced mass baptisms, and thousands of captives who showed reluctance were beheaded."[66] Nearly 730 years later, in 1532, Spanish conquistadors subjugated native peoples in South America in the name of Christ. In one celebrated event, Francisco Pizarro killed two thousand Incas and took their emperor to protect Christian honor.[67] Violent conversion of native peoples continued, and despite a papal injunction against abusing natives, the Spaniards carried on destroying their temples and building churches in their stead. Backed by economic and military power, Portuguese and French colonial rulers, too, continued converting native peoples throughout their domains. Portugal claimed to have converted some 1.2 million people to Christianity from Mozambique to Japan.[68]

Even the British commercial empire took on religious duty as a Christian nation. As Niall Ferguson notes, "The English sense of empire envy only grew more acute after the Reformation, when proponents of war against Catholic Spain began to argue that England had a religious duty to build a Protestant empire to match the 'Popish' empires of the Spanish and Portuguese."[69] The British took care to place Christian evangelists in the highest positions of government in India, including at all levels of the army. With aid from London, missionaries ran almost half of all the subcontinent's schools.

The short-lived American colonial venture in Asia also promoted Christianity in the region. The U.S. seizure of the Philippines from the defeated Spaniards was justified as a civilizing mission thrust on the nation. As President William McKinley told Methodist clergymen: "There was nothing left for us to do but to take them all, and educate the Filipinos, and uplift and civilize and Christianize them, and by God's grace do the very best we could by them as our fellow-men for whom Christ also died."[70]

Beginning with the conquest of the Philippines until 1917, the United States tied the Atlantic to the Pacific through the purchase and military acquisition of territories, the forcible opening of markets (witness Commodore Matthew Perry's naval expedition to Japan in the 1850s), the setting up of naval bases, and the digging of the Panama Canal. Proselytizing, trade, and investment followed.

France's emperor Napoleon III sent an expeditionary force to Vietnam and eventually occupied the country, supposedly as retribution for Vietnam's persecution of Catholic missionaries.[71] Today Catholics constitute a significant minority in Vietnam and serve as an important institutional link with the world outside. A third of the world's population today is Christian, and the vast majority of Catholics among this group can be found in former Spanish, Portuguese, and French colonies.

But ironically, the European colonial empire that sought to win Christian converts unwittingly reinforced the sense of unity of the Islamic *umma*. The opening of the Suez Canal in 1869 and the introduction of regular shipping from India and Southeast Asia to Europe and the Mediterranean, for example, saw a dramatic rise in the number of Islamic pilgrims going for hajj in Mecca. A short-lived movement among Muslims in India to restore the caliphate in the early twentieth century was a reminder of the close linkage forged among Muslims dispersed over a wide territory. "Though separated from Turkey by thousands of miles, they were determined to fight Turkey's battle from India," a Pakistani historian proudly noted.[72]

The reach of the Ottoman Empire and the caliphate that was the House of Islam (Dar-al-Islam) and the subsequent rise of non-Islamic powers in the House of War (Dar-al-Harb) continue to haunt many. The sorry state of many of the successor Islamic states today has incited generations of Islamist radicals from the Egyptian Sayyid Qutb to the Saudi Osama bin Laden, all seeking to restore Islam to its pristine glory and power. A British-based Islamic group supports the establishment of a new caliphate, and terrorists who blew up trains in Spain were likewise intent on reclaiming the country for the caliphate. Bin Laden calls on Muslims the world over to "resist the current Zionist-Crusader campaign against the *umma,* or Islamic super-nation, since it threatens the entire umma, its religion, and its very existence."[73]

EMPIRE OF LAW

Along with language, religion, food, and customs, imperial powers brought their legal systems to their new territories. The practice of enacting legislation and then using the coercive power of the state to enforce laws was first systematized by the Roman Empire. Roman jurists assembled two reference works containing collections of past laws and the opinions of the great Roman jurists. The codes also contained elementary outlines of the law and a collection of the emperor Justinian's own new laws.

Roman law, modified by the Germanic tribe that succeeded to the Roman throne in the late fifth century, was eventually adopted by all of Europe, amplified by a legal category called the Law of Nations, which applied to both Romans and foreigners. Anthony Pagden notes that

> this concept was to have a prolonged and powerful impact on all subsequent European legal thinking. As the European powers reached outward into other areas of the globe, many of which the Romans had never ever imagined, it became the basis for what is now called "public international law," and it still governs all the actions, in theory if never consistently in practice, of the "international community." . . . The conqueror's right to possession lay merely in his success in battle. The Romans, however, introduced a complex distinction, which still governs the conduct of most modern conflicts, between "just" and "unjust" wars.[74]

The emerging global British Empire presented itself as a return to the lofty notions of the Roman Empire built on "a thought of a World-State, the universal law of nature, the brotherhood and the equality of men."[75] British customary law and the French Napoleonic code spread to the colonies in Africa and Asia, providing the basis for legal systems that have since emerged in the decolonized states.

The rule of the Islamic caliphate and the spread of Islam also introduced the Koran-based sharia and hadiths that now officially or unofficially govern the lives of some two billion people in the world. The struggle between the proponents of the national and secular civil law of European origin and the supporters of sharia has emerged as a major issue of global contention. The imperial legacy that initially brought large populations together under similar laws is now perceived as threatening to divide populations and pit communities against one another. The Nigerian government's threat to execute a Muslim woman for adultery under sharia in 2004 brought international condemnation and isolation of the nation, prompting authorities to reverse their ruling. But demands for the replacement of British customary law with sharia in many African and Asian countries continue to raise political tension.

Foreign policy, as well as the legal infrastructure that undergirds life and transactions in today's interconnected world, directed the development of new transportation routes by empires. The Roman Empire offered a huge boost to trading and communications by building roads and setting up a piracy-free transportation system that stretched from the Atlantic Ocean to Arabia. The Roman annexation of Egypt, and the subsequent campaign against Red Sea pirates, revived the ocean link between India and Southeast Asia. The trading often began with diplomatic missions to foreign capitals. In 25 BCE, an Indian king sent a mission to Rome that sailed from Barygaza, an ancient port near present-day Surat, and presumably transferred to caravans across Mesopotamia to make the journey to Rome in four years. The king's gifts included a strange assortment of men and animals: tigers, pheasants, snakes, tortoises, a monk, and an armless boy who could shoot arrows with his toes.[76]

The Islamic empire, founded by a spice merchant turned prophet, was particularly trade-friendly from the outset. "With the Arabs, Egyptians, and Persians newly unified under the common rule and ideology of Islam, the Persian Gulf and the Red Sea ceased to be rival routes but became two arms of the same sea as they had been in the age of Alexander."[77] In fact, the unity of the Islamic empire in the West and that of the trader-friendly Tang dynasty of China (618–907) produced a conjuncture that encouraged intercontinental trade. The transfer of the caliphate from Damascus to Baghdad moved the center of gravity eastward. As Peter Mansfield notes, Baghdad emerged as "the center of a vast and increasingly prosperous free-trade area in which most sections of the population had the opportunity to engage in vigorous commercial activity. Arab ships sailed to China, Sumatra, India and southwards along the east coast of Africa as far as Madagascar."[78]

Europe and the Mediterranean trade with China reached a peak under the Mongol Empire. The unification of the central Eurasian landmass by the Mongols in the thirteenth century, writes Janet L. Abu-Lughod, put the termini of Europe and China in direct contact with each other for the first time in a thousand years and opened up the northern route between China and the Black Sea.[79] Insecurity on the road, combined with the uncertainty of finding water and shelter along some of the most inhospitable terrain of Central Asia, limited Silk Road trade. Mongols—who produced only wool and meat and otherwise relied on merchandise from foreign countries—encouraged trade in every possible way, from setting up and maintaining shelters and wells to maintaining stations to provide transport animals. The Mongols even issued *gerege* or *paiza,* a tablet of gold or silver—what has been called a combined passport and credit card. It allowed the holder to travel throughout the Mongol Empire assured of protection, accommodation, and exemption from local taxes or duties.[80]

THE MONGOL GIFT OF TROUSERS
AND BOW STRING

It is ironic that the Mongol army emerged as a great champion of trade that intensified China's commercial links with Europe and prepared the terrain for the flowering of the Renaissance. Pax Mongolica exacted a terrible price in innocent lives but also contributed to an increasingly interconnected world. Although contemporaries experienced only devastation, misfortune, and terror, a French historian of the Mongols wrote that "later generations were able to enjoy the advantages bequeathed by the worldwide empire. To them came the fruits of the fertilizing contact between the great national cultures, which was perhaps the most outstanding requisite for extensive changes and the unanticipated impetus of Europe during the next few centuries."[81] Mongol traders introduced Chinese porcelain to Persia, from where they imported cobalt into China, thus allowing Chinese kilns to develop their famous blue-and-white porcelain. Chinese even took to calling the blue made from cobalt *Huihuiqing* or Muhammadan blue. From horsehair steppe bows to play the stringed instruments to trousers and new foods, the impact of Mongol contact with Europe was felt in every sphere of life. Europeans even picked up the Mongol exclamation "Hurray!" as a cry of bravado and encouragement.[82]

After the Mongol Empire fell apart and the Islamic Ottoman Empire took control of the Indian Ocean trade, seafaring in the Atlantic became imperative for the Europeans. As we noted earlier, Henry the Navigator of Portugal pioneered the development of new vessels and ocean routes. From his base in Sagres, he presided over an elaborate effort to develop technology that would allow safe long-distance travel. He designed light but sturdy four-masted ships, and his team developed navigational charts and maps that enabled Vasco da Gama to round the Cape of Good Hope and reach India in 1498, ushering in the age of European empires in Asia.

Empire building required not only military might to conquer others but the means to conquer distance. The roads that the Romans built, the routes that the Mongols developed for horse and camel journeys, and the pathways that the Incas built for controlling population and resources laid the basis for both future invasion and global trading.

Two of the three ships used by Columbus were caravels, or light ships, the likes of which were designed at Prince Henry's ocean-research station at Sagres. The technology spread, and in 1514, a ship built for King Henry VIII of England pioneered a design that allowed vessels to carry a row of cannons on each side. At a time when piracy was customary, the double-sided gunboat gave the English fleet the upper hand.[83]

With the Industrial Revolution and the rise of steam power, ocean liners and railway trains were mobilized for war and for peacetime commercial uses. The first railway that the British built in India, in 1853, linked Bombay to a suburb twenty-one miles away. The Indian railways eventually expanded into a robust twenty-four-thousand-mile network, allowing agricultural and mineral resources to be brought to ports and enabling the greater penetration of British manufactured products into the subcontinent.[84]

Empires not only developed trade routes and helped build reliable transportation to carry out commercial activity, they also provided the lubricant for transactions—namely, currencies that faraway countries and people would accept and honor. Alexander the Great started the trend by issuing international coinages. The Phoenicians in Egypt issued another currency, so by the third century BCE, the Mediterranean world was divided into two main currency spheres.[85] Roman and Byzantine gold and silver coins continued to be the legal tender for international trading for a long time until the Italian city-states of Florence, Venice, Genoa issued their own coins. Currencies minted by the Ottoman Empire dominated Levantine trade, but with less clout than coins issued by the Italian city-states.

Global trade reached unprecedented heights beginning in the sixteenth century, when the Portuguese and Spanish empires in South America began pumping huge quantities of silver bullion into the market. In the first half of the seventeenth century, Spanish coins became the effective international currency of Southeast Asia, prompting one Filipino official to comment that "the king of China could build a palace with the silver bars from Peru which have been carried to his country."[86]

The Spanish also promoted paper IOUs to replace precious metals as a means of immediate settlement of payments due. For instance, the Spanish government had difficulty financing its increasing military enterprises. To make payments to its troops, financiers, and suppliers, Spain began issuing "bills of credit," pieces of paper that kept the wheels of the empire turning. And as trade expanded, Spanish, British, and Dutch empires emerged as a vast emporia of world goods.[87]

CHINESE GUNPOWDER,
PERSIAN ENGINEERING

By the sheer necessity of traveling far to conquer other peoples and control vast spaces, empires often emerged as transmission belts for technology and their fusion. Genghis Khan, leader of a band of armed nomadic cattle herders, had more need than any other emperor to secure technology from others. He recruited his first engineers among the other nomadic tribes who had learned the Chinese technology of warfare using gunpowder—one of the earliest technologies for storing, transporting, and applying energy.[88] When Genghis took these men westward with him, he brought about a cross-stimulation of Chinese and Iranian engineering and technology, which almost certainly led to the eventual development of the cannon.[89] Chinese iron-smelting technology and gunpowder, combined with Persian and Arab engineering skill, gave the Mongols sophisticated weapons to defeat the powerful Song dynasty. Arnold Pacey, a technology historian, says that the siege engine used by the Mongols was of Arab design, with Chinese gunpowder that launched missiles and bombs much farther.[90] Not long after the victory in the thirteenth century, the same technology instigated a revolution in European warfare. As Alfred W. Crosby writes, "Europe took gunpowder to its bosom like a lover's bouquet."[91] Firearms assisted in the English conquest of Normandy and the Spanish Catholic victory against the Moors.[92] Eventually ship-deck cannons gave the Europeans a decisive edge in expanding their control to Asia and the New World.

Even during the twentieth century, with tanks and aircraft replacing horses, military planners in Britain and Germany continued to study Mongol strategy. During World War II, two of the leading exponents of mechanized combat, Field Marshal Erwin Rommel and General George S. Patton, were keen students of Mongol tactics.[93]

The bureaucratic-military power that allowed empires to promulgate and enforce laws also gave them the ability to introduce new crops and animals. Humans had long collected and traded animals and crops, but on a small scale, with limited impact on local agricultural development or animal husbandry. But imperial conquests and the expansion of administrative power led to a biological unification that Crosby has called "ecological imperialism." Imperial expansion broadened the horizon of biological knowledge. The Greek historian Aristobolus, who accompanied Alexander the Great's invasion of India in 327 BCE, may have been the first in the West to learn about rice: "a strange plant, standing in water and sown in beds . . . , [which] has many ears and yields a large produce."[94] Despite this discovery early on, rice did not reach the dinner tables of Europe until the Renaissance.[95]

The Song emperor Zhenzong (998–1022) learned about drought-resistant and quick-maturing rice from Champa, today's central Vietnam, and sent envoys to bring seeds back to China. This variety of rice had a marked impact on the food supply, spurring a dramatic population boom. Historian Jerry Bentley notes that the population of China almost doubled during the course of two centuries, from sixty million in the year 1000 to one hundred million a century later and 115 million by 1200.[96]

The Islamic empire also disseminated agricultural produce across the world. The eastern provinces of the Arab empire became the gateway for the entry of plants, medicines, and pharmacological knowledge to the western Mediterranean. As historian Andrew Watson has demonstrated, under the patronage of the Islamic rulers a great variety of major crops—cotton and sugarcane, as well as rice, hard wheat, sorghum, citrus fruits, the coconut, banana, artichoke, spinach, and eggplant—were diffused from the eastern margins of the empire in India all the way to Morocco and Spain. As Watson puts it, "Over this east-west route moved not only most of the new crops, the farming practices and the irrigation technology that were the main components of the agricultural revolution, but much else that was to shape the world of classical Islam: higher learning, industrial technology, fashions of dress, art forms, architecture, music, dance, culinary arts, etiquette, games and so forth. The end result of so much diffusion through this medium was at once to strengthen the unity, begun by the conquests, of this vast world and to set it apart from both its predecessors and its neighbors."[97]

The Mongol rulers were interested in crops like cotton that they themselves did not grow but could grow throughout their empire. Cotton was introduced to China during the tenth century but was promoted by the Mongols. The Mongol emperor created a Cotton Promotion Bureau in 1289 and dispersed representatives throughout the newly conquered Chinese provinces.[98] The Mongol empire also provided channels that allowed the mixing and comparison of Indian, Chinese, and Persian pharmacology, enabling each to enrich the others. The Mongols recognized that simply transporting medicinal herbs was not enough; the herbs had to be accompanied by detailed instructions for their use. The Mongol court imported Persian, Indian, and Arab doctors into China to run hospitals, and Kublai Khan founded a department for the study of Western medicine under the direction of a Christian scholar.[99]

KOREANS GET THEIR KIMCHI

Some imperial ventures into foreign lands unintentionally introduced new crops or species, perhaps the most important of which for Asia's taste buds was chili pepper from the New World, found by Columbus. The Aztec name for the piquant fruit, *chili,* which was believed to be a cousin of familiar peppercorn, was combined to call it "chili pepper." Asians are surprised to discover that the hot chili that defines their regional culinary identity arrived just 450 years ago, thanks to European adventureres and traders—that there would be no hot curry without Columbus. In the case of Koreans, the surprise can be even worse. Some modern Koreans, proud and nationalistic, might have difficulty acknowledging that they owe their fiery *kimchi*—fermented cabbage pickled in garlic and chilies—to the hated Japanese samurai Toyotomi Hideyoshi, who invaded Korea in the late sixteenth century. Chili pepper, originally introduced to Japan by Portuguese traders from the New World, was left behind in Korea by Japanese soldiers who had carried its seeds along with their food rations. Until the arrival of this red pepper, kimchi was bland garlic and cabbage. With an eye to the antiglobalization movement in South Korea spawned by the 1997 economic crisis, one writer commented: "It would not be the last time in the history of Korean food that globalization was associated with suffering, for the Japanese left behind not only red pepper in their 16th century incursions but widespread destruction as well."[100]

India's Mughal emperor Jahangir was curious about the new flora and fauna that the Portuguese galleons had brought to Goa from the New World and sent a representative to Goa every two weeks to look for novelties. Thus, pineapples were procured from a Portuguese ship, as immortalized by a court painter in Delhi, and thousands of "fruit of the European port," as the emperor would later proudly note, grew in the imperial gardens in Agra.[101]

The Portuguese domination of the seas, linking continents, made Portuguese vessels the principal carriers of plants and vegetables from one clime and soil to another. The huge price fetched by spices was a big incentive for the Portuguese to grow spices in lands under their own control. Legend has it that in 1498, when Vasco da Gama requested pepper stock for replanting, the ruler of Malabar, Zamorin, issued a calm response: "You can take our pepper, but you will never be able to take our rains." With the acquisition of Brazil, however, the Portuguese acquired enough sun and rain to make a go of it—and no longer had to request permission to transfer a pepper plant.[102]

Imperial Britain introduced one Amazon plant to the world and changed industrial history. The Native Americans called it *caoutchouc,* the same word as in French, and used it to make waterproof boots and bouncing balls. In 1755, King Joseph I of Portugal sent several pairs of his royal boots to Brazil to be coated with latex—the white secretion that natives tapped from trees.[103] The latex was carried back to Europe for experiments, and in the early nineteenth century, the rubber raincoat was born—named Mackintosh after the Scottish scientist Charles Mackintosh, who succeeded in making a waterproof fabric with rubber. Rubber soon became the substance on which the automobile revolution would run. With demand for rubber skyrocketing, the British Empire stepped in. In 1876, at the request of the government and of British citizens living in Brazil, Henry Alexander Wickham smuggled out seventy thousand rubber seeds. Botanists at the Royal Botanical Gardens at Kew successfully grew seedlings, which were then shipped to the British tropical colonies of Ceylon and Malaysia. As Henry Ford's assembly line for the Model-T revved up, a rush for "white gold" swept Malaysia, with large acres put under rubber plantations. By 1924, as the ten-millionth Ford hit the road, Malaya, as it was called then, was exporting more than two hundred thousand tons of rubber each year—accounting for more than half of global production. In the process, some 1.2 million Indian indentured workers were brought into the country, changing Malaysian demography forever. Today, 10 percent of the country's population is of Indian origin, many the descendants of the original rubber tappers.[104]

Under Spanish encouragement the Philippines was turned into the world's major coconut producer at the end of the nineteenth century. The Philippine coconut plantations got a further boost when the U.S. company Proctor and Gamble, hurting from a shortage of beef fat and tallow resulting from a series of blizzards and droughts, turned to the new American colony for a substitute. By 1930 nearly 13 percent of the country's arable land was turned into coconut plantations to meet the surging demand for coconut oil. Eventually, less expensive soybeans and cottonseed supplanted coconuts as sources for oil, and worldwide demand for coconut oil fell, leaving a third of Filipino peasants trapped in poverty.[105]

A VERITABLE NOAH'S ARK

The Spanish colonizers took their domesticated animals with them to the Americas, hoping to re-create the homes they had left behind. Horses, dogs, sheep, pigs, goats, cattle, and chickens were all new to the New World, but they quickly adapted. As Henry Kamen puts it, "Some vessels crossed the Atlantic as veritable arks of Noah."[106] American Indians took to horses as if they were made for each other. The Plains Indians culture of North America was transformed by the horse, and in South America, Argentina—with its vast grazing lands for cattle and sheep—eventually emerged as a major world supplier of beef and wool.

When Captain James Cook left for the Pacific on his first voyage in 1768, his explicit but confidential task was to cultivate diplomatic and trade relations with the natives and to pursue biological exchange: he was "to bring home Specimens of the Seeds of such Trees, Shrubs, Plants, Fruits, and Grains, peculiar to those Places, as you may be able to collect."[107] His right-hand man for the job was Joseph Banks, honorary director of the Royal Botanical Gardens at Kew. As one scholar has written, Banks was "the leading exponent of the 'gospel of plant interchange.'"[108]

Empires played a significant role in building up human knowledge about the world. It is hard to overestimate the role played by the Islamic caliphate in gathering, protecting, and diffusing knowledge. At the court of the early Abbasid caliphs in Baghdad, manuscripts from all over the world were collected and scholars were invited. Books from Greek, Persian, Sanskrit, and other languages were translated, and because many of the originals have since disappeared, the Arabic translations made in Baghdad often remain the only extant copies. The Umayyad rulers of Spain regularly sent agents to Baghdad, Damascus, and Cairo to attract scholars and buy rare books.[109] The European Renaissance would have been impossible without the rich libraries of Islamic Spain.

The gathering of knowledge continued hand in hand with the search for profitable plants and resources in European colonies. Plant and animal exchanges across continents—promoted by the Portuguese, Spanish, Dutch, and British empires—were followed by the establishment of various societies in European capitals, with specialties ranging from exploration and geography to botany and history. These institutions provided a justification for colonial expansion—the "civilizing mission"—and thickened the web of connections through knowledge. Adventurers of the past morphed into explorers and researchers in the employ of the colonial powers. No individual did more to establish the interconnected and interdependent nature of life than British naturalist Charles Darwin. The journey that he took as member of a British science team in 1831–36 aboard HMS *Beagle*'s expedition around the world brought him to the Galápagos Islands in the Pacific Ocean. His research and observation there and in many remote places led Darwin to his theory on evolution, set out in his seminal work *On the Origin of Species by Means of Natural Selection* (1859).

QUEEN VICTORIA'S GLOBAL CABLE

To send soldiers on horses, camels, and elephants to subjugate other peoples far away from home was both costly and difficult. But imperial rulers found out that they had an even more serious long-term problem: to conquer what historian Fernand Braudel has called "space, the enemy number one." To rule and maintain control over people across vast distances required an organized information network. Information had to be recorded on clay tablets, papyrus, parchment, and a variety of other media and dispatched with messengers. The Roman Empire, with its elaborate road network and horse carriages, developed the first information network. Under Roman occupation, the cattle-rich Anatolian city of Pergamum, with its tradition of parchment-making, emerged as the supplier par excellence of parchment to the world (the word is a vulgarization of the name Pergamum).[110] Parchment, made from animal skins, remained Europe's main medium of storing and transferring information before Europeans learned paper-making technology from the Chinese via the Arabs.

Information written on parchment or paper still had to be transmitted over physical distance. Alexander, Hannibal, and Caesar each developed an elaborate system of relays, by which messages were carried from one post to another by mounted messengers. The system was further developed in China's Tang dynasty and later in the Mongol Empire. In the days of Genghis Khan, a communication network consisting of rest stops and relay horse riders allowed messengers to travel a hundred miles a day for weeks on end.[111] The system was copied by the Egyptian Mamluk sultan, who had observed it in the Mongol domain, and from there it reached Latin Christendom and eventually the Habsburg Empire, where a full-blown postal service emerged.[112] Then, in the middle of the nineteenth century came the revolutionary telegraph. The first application of the telegraph in wartime was made by the British during the Crimean War in 1854. Four years later, undersea cables laid across the Atlantic allowed Queen Victoria to send the first telegraphic message to President James

Buchanan. It may have taken sixteen and a half hours to decode the message in Morse code, but its arrival was greeted by a huge celebration accompanied by fireworks, which inadvertently resulted in New York's City Hall burning down. By 1880, some 97,568 miles of cables had been laid across the world's oceans, linking Britain to its colonies in Asia, Canada, Africa, and Australia. Queen Victoria celebrated her Jubilee by sending something akin to a mass e-mail. As James Morris describes it: "On the morning of June 22, 1897, Queen Victoria of England went to the telegraph room at Buckingham palace. . . . It was a few minutes after eleven o'clock, she pressed an electric button; an impulse was transmitted to the Central Telegraph Office; in a matter of seconds her jubilee message was on its way to every corner of her Empire. The message simply said: 'Thank my beloved people. May God bless them.'"[113]

Almost like one billion Internet users today, who can walk to their home or office computers every morning to check e-mail, Queen Victoria could simply walk to the telegraph room in her palace basement and read the cables from the far corners of her empire. By the early twentieth century London had emerged as the capital of the industrial world, and the economist John Maynard Keynes could write these words, which sound familiar today: "The inhabitant of London could order by telephone, sipping his morning tea in bed, the various products of the whole earth in such quantity as he might see fit, and reasonably expect their early delivery upon his doorstep; he could at the same moment and by the same means adventure his wealth in the natural resources and new enterprises of any quarter of the world, and share, without exertion or even trouble, in their prospective fruits and advantages."[114]

Private entrepreneurs and companies played a key role in the development of the telegraph and telephone, but the imperial authorities' need for secure communication acted as a prime mover in developing what has been called "the world's system of electrical nerves."[115] The rise of the Internet, foreshadowed by the telegraph network, was itself initiated by the Pentagon, concerned about losing command and control in the event of a nuclear war.

It was perhaps fitting that the worldwide system of "electrical nerves" that the British Empire helped create would be used at the empire's final moment. As the royal yacht *Britannia* pulled out of Hong Kong harbor in the wee hours of 1 July 1997, Britain's last governor, Chris Patten, sent a terse cable from the ship: "I have relinquished the administration of this government. God Save the Queen."[116] As the *Britannia* melted into the darkness, the globally interconnected, multicultural world—that the British and others had done so much to create—continued to spin and pulsate, as if indifferent to the passing of empire.

Chapter 7 Slaves, Germs, and Trojan Horses

I saw a piece of land which is much like an island, though it is not one, on which there were six huts. It could be made into an island in two days, though I see no necessity to do so since these people are very unskilled in arms, as your Majesties will discover from seven whom I caused to be taken and brought aboard so that they may learn our language and return. However, should your Highnesses command it all the inhabitants could be taken away to Castile or held as slaves on the island, for with fifty men we could subjugate them all and make them do whatever we wish.
—*Christopher Columbus, letter to King Ferdinand and Queen Isabella of Castile after his first voyage to the New World, 1492*

It was an unbearably hot summer night at the English port of Dover. As the next day's papers would report, 18 June 2000 was the hottest day of the year. Five officers of HM Revenue and Customs at the Dover Eastern Docks Ferry Terminals waited for the midnight ferry from Zeebrugge to pull into the quay. Hours earlier, when the ferry

---

A nineteenth-century Arab slave raid in Africa. Illustration from H. Grattan Guinness, *The New World of Central Africa* (New York: Fleming B. Revell, 1890)

had left the Belgian port, they had received a faxed manifest of the trucks it had on board. Most of the truckers that plied this route were familiar, well-established companies hauling goods between the Continent and Britain. That night, one manifest caught the officers' attention.

The listed cargo of tomatoes was unremarkable, but the carrier—Van Der Spek Transportation—was not one that they had heard of before. Even more curious, the ferry charge was neither prepaid nor charged to a credit card. The truck driver, it seemed, had paid cash at the ferry counter at Zeebrugge. Such anomalies tend to raise suspicions about the contents of the cargo. Hidden among boxes of onions or fruit, customs officers often discovered undeclared crates of liquor or cartons of cigarettes—the usual high-value commodities smugglers try to sneak into England.

So when Van Der Spek's white Mercedes truck rolled down the gangplank to stop near the customs checkpoint, it was not waved through after a cursory look at its papers. While some officers went to talk with the driver, another went behind the refrigerated truck to open the steel doors and look inside. He noticed that the truck was oddly silent. There was no hum of a generator to keep the produce properly chilled. The only sounds were the snap and slide of the bolt on the door and the swoosh of suction as the officer loosed the door from its seal and swung it open. A rush of warm, putrid air immediately blasted his senses. In the dim light he saw overturned crates of tomatoes and the outlines of two human figures gasping for breath. Behind them, deeper in the shadows, half-naked bodies lay in heaps on the metal floor. The officer did not realize that he had chanced on one of the most gruesome discoveries of human trafficking in modern Europe. He shouted for his colleagues.

A forklift truck was brought in to help unload the crates of tomatoes that hid a shocking scene. "There were just piles and piles of bodies, it was absolutely sickening," one officer later told reporters. Fifty-four men and four women of "oriental" appearance found that night were later identified as illegal immigrants from China. Lured by the prospect of the good life in the West, they had paid traffickers thousands of dollars to embark on a long, tortuous—and ultimately fatal—journey across Russia and Eastern Europe. One of them was nineteen-year-old Chen Lin, who had regularly called his mother back in China throughout the harrowing voyage across the continents. In his final call home, he had told her that in a few days, he would be in Britain, where a cousin had already made it.[1]

Like thousands of slaves from Africa who perished during the journey across the Atlantic two centuries ago, Chen and his compatriots were the latest victims of one of the most noxious and tragic aspects of globalization: the international trading in human beings. In 1495, Christopher Columbus had organized the first-ever shipment of slaves to reach Europe. Despairing of finding any sizable quantity of gold in the New World, he organized an armed expedition to capture Indians from the island of Hispaniola. Exactly 505 years before the customs officers' shocking discovery in Dover, a vessel carrying 550 Native Americans left for Spain in February 1495. Favorable winds made the journey relatively swift by the standards of the day. But by the time the ship reached the island of Madeira, two hundred of the slaves had died of the cold.[2]

The transatlantic east-to-west slave trade received a boost in the seventeenth century with the arrival of large-hulled ships and the desire for cheap labor to exploit the virgin soil of the New World. For more than two centuries, African slaves were transported across the Atlantic in these specially constructed vessels that could pack up to 450 people sardine-like, shackled to the floor, in their large hulls.[3] During this dreaded month-long Middle Passage (which began with capture and forced march to Africa's Atlantic shores and ended with auction sales of slaves to new owners), as many as four in ten died of disease, thirst, or hunger. The bodies of the unfortunate were unceremoniously dumped overboard in the waters of what was known as the Ocean Sea.

THE EUROPEAN DREAM

For the fifty-four prospective Chinese workers headed for the "new world" of Britain, the metallic belly of a refrigeration truck became a suffocating coffin. Unlike in the previous era, however, they had not been kidnapped by slave traders to be sold in auctions for plantation owners. Slavery was abolished in most places by the late nineteenth century. Yet opportunistic middlemen found no shortage of hopeful and vulnerable would-be immigrants to prey on for profit. The emergence of inexpensive and faster mass travel in the 1970s had brought new opportunities for human traffickers to deliver cheap and often bonded laborers to employers in countries thousands of miles away. The clandestine nature of such operations meant that the comfort and speed of modern-day travel would be sacrificed for the sake of more furtive and dangerous journeys in the hidden compartments of ships and trucks.

Poverty and despair at home, combined with the dream of a better life in Europe, led the fifty-four Chinese to the door of modern-day slave traders. Instead of the land-owning masters in the New World, who bought slaves as chattel, many European and American businesses of the modern era turned to illegal

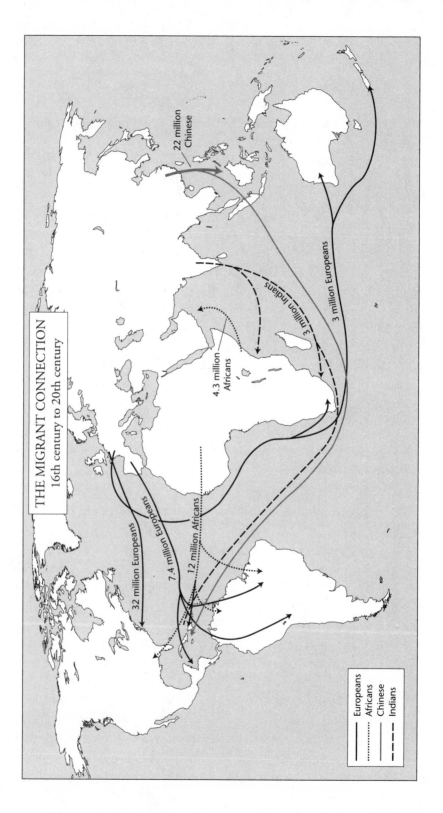

THE MIGRANT CONNECTION
16th century to 20th century

22 million
Chinese

3 million Europeans

3 million Indians

4.3 million
Africans

32 million Europeans

7.4 million Europeans

12 million Africans

Europeans
Africans
Chinese
Indians

immigrants to meet their need for low-cost labor. Instead of being kidnapped from their villages to be sold abroad (although that has also happened, as we will see later), the unfortunate Chinese immigrants had paid about thirty thousand dollars each to international human traffickers known as "snakeheads" for the covert voyage that ended in tragedy.

The Chinese formed, however, only a small part of the growing wave of illegal immigrants from all over the world flocking to Europe—from the former Yugoslavia, Afghanistan, Congo, Iran, Iraq, Romania, Sri Lanka, and the former Zaire. In 1999 alone, some seventy-one thousand persons illegally entered Britain and sought asylum. According to a CIA report, another forty-five to fifty thousand women and children were trafficked to the United States that same year out of the seven hundred thousand to two million women and children who were trafficked globally.[4] The number of immigrants trying to enter the United States illegally has continued to rise, as has the casualty rate. According to a *Wall Street Journal* report, since 2000, an average of about four hundred immigrants have died each year trying to enter the United States illegally across the Mexican border. That compares with about 240 people who died trying to cross the Berlin Wall during its twenty-eight-year existence.[5]

The same cocktail of economic disparity, power imbalance, and desire for profit that once drove the slave trade across continents is still the intoxicating elixir of the slave trade today. As Jesse Sage, a spokesman for the American Anti-Slavery Group, puts it, "Whether it is Bangladeshi toddlers trafficked into the United Arab Emirates or Chinese children smuggled into Los Angeles by snakehead criminal gangs, there is a lucrative trade in human beings. Our global economy creates demand for cheap goods and there is no cheaper labor than slave labor."[6] Maidservants and nannies are procured from poorer countries by the hundreds of thousands to work in households in rich countries—from the petrodollar-soaked Middle East to business-enriched metropolises in Asia. According to a World Bank estimate, migrant workers, including ill-treated and abused maidservants, sent home more than $150 billion in remittances in 2004 alone.[7] Those remittances have built homes, started businesses, sent children to school, and fueled a consumer economy in their home countries.

In the preceding chapters we have seen how the expanding economic connections among human communities, pushed by traders and propelled by consumer demand, have created an increasingly interdependent world. We also have seen the impact of imperial aggression in bringing far-flung communities under one ruler and producing today's interconnected world. Both these agents of globalization—traders and warriors—have in the same process brought suffering, upheaval, and heartaches. From the beginning of human connections through warfare or trade, slavery has been an important component. Winners took back captives as slaves, and traders profited by trafficking in humans across the borders. The fact is that the process of globalization has always had a dark side. As the tragedy at Dover demonstrated again, nothing has changed. In fact, with technology now speeding the process, the noxious effects of global interconnectedness may also spread and accelerate. The dark shadow falls not just on human trafficking. Both warfare and commerce have long transmitted pathogens, bringing catastrophic pandemics. That threat continues and speeds up as global trade and travel intensify. In this chapter we will see examples of how these negative consequences of globalization have evolved and how ever-faster communication and commerce have brought in their train new threats—hackers releasing destructive computer viruses, criminals stealing credit card numbers and personal information from personal computers hooked to cyberspace. The speed and ease that globalization has brought have come with a price tag.

THE OLDEST TRADE

Adam Smith saw slavery as an aberration. The Scottish economist lamented in 1776 how the beneficial new trade between Europe and the New World was spoiled by the rapacity of slave traders: "The commodities of Europe were almost all new to America, and many of those of America were new to Europe. A new set of exchanges, therefore, began to take place which had never been thought of before, and which naturally should have proved as advantageous to the new, as it certainly did to the old continent. The savage injustice of the Europeans rendered an event, which ought to have been beneficial to all, ruinous and destructive to several of those unfortunate countries."[8] The fact is, however, that although the scale and brutality of Atlantic slavery were unprecedented, slavery was, in the words of a Dutch historian, the "oldest trade" in the world. As David Christian has put it, the masters considered slaves as "living batteries, as human cattle." The importance of human beings as a source of energy helps explain why forced labor was so ubiquitous in the premodern world.[9] Many forms of slavery existed centuries before the word *slave* came into formal existence. People's insatiable search for wealth and drive for profit, combined with power imbalances between human communities, led to the growth of a system that reached its peak in the early nineteenth century and has since profoundly altered human civilization.

The word *slave* was coined in reference to the widespread enslavement of central European Slavs in the ninth century. This group constituted the main target or "resource" population for the Viking-Arab trade in the Middle Ages. Male and female "heathen" Slavs who had not yet been converted to Christianity were seen as objects, fair game for trading. From the beginning of history, war, famine, falling personal fortunes, and natural disasters have compelled people to leave their homes to find work elsewhere or accept bonded work to survive. In some cases, this has meant performing hard or dangerous tasks that could be assigned to slaves, whom Aristotle called "human instruments."[10]

Stripped of their humanity, such "working machines" were treated no better than draft animals to be bought and sold like other commodities in the marketplace. But unlike chattel, slaves brought their own races, languages, and cultures to venues far removed from their places of birth. Like migration, the slave trade brought face to face different branches of the human race that had dispersed since the ancestors left Africa more than fifty thousand years ago. The intermixing of people and their slaves (and, as we will see later, of migrants and settlers) over the millennia has transformed the size, shape, and color of the human community and its cultures. We have seen how Egyptians' first contact with Africans in the third millennium BCE led to the procurement of slaves for the pharaoh. Bartering human beings for other commodities began early in human history.

The first-century BCE historian Diodorus famously observed that Italian merchants could purchase a slave from Gaul in exchange for alcohol ("a crock of wine for a young slave boy"). Indigent parents sold their offspring to traders or handed them over to repay debts, and authorities sold convicted criminals. And of course, prisoners of war were the greatest source of able-bodied slaves. Cimon, an Athenian naval commander who fought against Persia in 468 BCE, sent twenty thousand prisoners to the slave market.[11] A primary occupation of these slaves was digging the earth with bare hands and stone tools for precious metals like silver. The ore played an important role in the rise of Athens. In the mid-first millennium BCE, silver mining in the Balkan-Aegean world employed tens of thousands of slaves and required a large-scale, well-organized slave trade. Slaves were also needed to fight as soldiers. Silver provided the means to fund wars like those Athens fought against Persia and Sparta, but the slaves themselves often were enlisted as soldiers to supplement the troops.

THE SLAVE: SOLDIER, LABORER, COMPANION

The anonymous author of the famous first-century CE account of ocean trade *Periplus of the Erythraen Sea* mentions slaves as routine merchandise in Roman trade. They were imported for manual labor as well as for entertainment such as singing and companionship. The Roman author Martial mocked Caelia, who, although Roman, consorted with various foreign men, presumably slaves: "Your Egyptian lover sails to you from Alexandria, the dark-skinned Indian one from the Red Sea." But slaves were traded from both sides of Indian Ocean shores. Ancient Indian literature offers evidence of the rich owning Western slaves who may have come from the Greco-Roman world.[12] Tribute sent to the Chinese imperial court by neighbors frequently included slave girls and performers such as acrobatic "twirling girls" from Central Asia.

The Slavic population of parts of central Europe furnished the largest number of humans for sale to the Romans. While the Roman aristocracy enjoyed the high life, for the common folk life was nasty, brutish, and short, especially in south-central Europe. With their high mortality rates and low life expectancies, societies with larger populations—historians call them "population reservoirs"—became natural targets for slavers. In addition to Slavs, Greeks, and Persians, the Germanic, Celtic, and Romance peoples inhabiting lands in the north of the Roman Empire and people from sub-Saharan Africa formed the main reservoirs for those who traded in human flesh.

As the Roman Empire demanded more and more slaves to work the plantations and serve the aristocracy, the kidnapping and trading of slaves grew apace. The Greek geographer and historian Strabo wrote that ten thousand slaves could be loaded and unloaded at the Delos docks in a single day. In order to prevent solidarity (early trade unions, perhaps) or unrest among the enslaved, slaves of diverse ethnic origins from different parts of Asia Minor and the Mediterranean were intentionally combined.[13] (Interestingly, nearly two millennia later the Portuguese slave traders followed a similar course of action in supplying African slaves to Brazil. The policy was "not to allow too many from one tribe to be collected in either the whole of Brazil or in any of its captaincies, so as to avoid possible ill consequences." Despite those precautions, one tribe from Sudan organized a series of revolts.)[14] As the Roman Empire extended from the Atlantic Ocean to the Euphrates in the first two centuries of the Christian era, the large foreign slave population in Rome turned it into "a world in miniature." Rome was the center of the slave trade, and its victims from all over the world brought with them the dress, speech, customs, and cultures of their native countries.[15] Over time, intermarriage among slaves, and between Romans and slaves of different races, produced a new mixture of people.

For the succeeding millennium, slavery remained a common feature of societies around the Mediterranean, all the while growing in scale. Although slavery for domestic production in Europe was gradually supplanted by serfdom in the eleventh century, mining and farming became more reliant on slave labor due to international trade and increasing demand.[16] In the ninth and tenth centuries, Viking and Russian traders took slaves from the eastern Slavic states to Moorish Spain and North Africa as domestic servants, soldiers, and mine workers. Slave trading was not confined to Europe and the Middle East. According to seventh-century Chinese sources, slaves were brought from Zenj (sub-Saharan Africa), and by 1119 the ownership of black slaves was a mark of wealth in Canton.[17] Slavic household slaves were a common sight in the Italian city-states as late as the fourteenth century, as were African slaves in sixteenth-century Spain and Portugal. Eric Wolf notes that much of the wealth of Venice came to depend on the trade in slaves. Although slaves could not be sold at public auctions in Venice after 1386, they continued to be sold by private contract through the sixteenth century.[18]

In the Middle East, slaves were often trained to perform as entertainers, craftworkers, and soldiers.[19] For the Abbasid caliphate of Baghdad, slaves were brought in from all over Europe, as well as sub-Saharan Africa. Female slaves, who were mostly from the Middle East or India, received a lot of attention, and their relative merits were the subject of comment in contemporary accounts. One report, almost like a product review, compared slaves of different origin and concluded: "The ideal female slave was of Berber origin, left her country at age nine, spent three years at al-Medina, three in Mecca, and then went to Iraq at sixteen to acquire some of that country's culture. When resold at twenty-five, she combined the coquettishness of al-Medina, the gentle manners of Mecca, and the culture of Iraq."[20]

As Arab traders ventured deeper and deeper south along the Indian Ocean coast and into West Africa, slaves from sub-Saharan Africa emerged as a major traded item. The Prophet Muhammad himself had slaves, and he authorized the owning of slaves in certain conditions. In Arabic the word for black, *abd*, became synonymous with slave. As early as the year 652, the Christian kingdom of Nubia (today's Ethiopia) signed a treaty with the Abbasid caliphate to supply the Abbasids three hundred slaves a year. The arrangement continued for six centuries.[21]

Some of the African slaves imported into the Abbasid empire (part of today's Iraq) were enrolled in the infantry, but more were put to work in large-scale production of sugar or in farm labor.[22] Landowners in ninth-century Basra brought in several thousand East African slaves to drain the salt marshes in what is now southern Iraq, hoping to turn the marsh into a breadbasket. The slaves' anger at their hard labor and minimal subsistence erupted into one of the earliest known black slave revolts, when Ali ibn Muhammad, a Persian who claimed descent from Ali, the fourth caliph, and Fatimah, Muhammad's daughter, won the support of slave work crews by promising them freedom and equality under his brand of Islam. For fourteen years, the African slaves, called the Zanj, joined by Africans in the caliphate's infantry, sacked Basra and kept the power of the caliphate at bay in parts of southern Iraq and eastern Persia. They were eventually crushed by the caliph's Egyptian-backed army.[23] Despite their eventual defeat, the Zanj nevertheless shook the honor of the caliphate by exacting terrible revenge. As one contemporary historian described it: "Ali's soldiers were so outrageous as to auction off publicly women from the lineage of al-Hassan and al-Hussein and al-'Abbas [meaning descendants of 'Ali ibn abi-Talib and the ruling Abbasids] as well as others from the lineage of Hashem, Qureish [the Prophet's lineage], and the rest of the Arabs. These women were sold as slaves for a mere one or three Dirhams, and were publicly advertised according to their proper lineage, each Zanji receiving ten, twenty, and thirty of them as concubines and to serve the Zanji women as maids."[24]

Military slavery came to play an important role in the Abbasid empire as the Abbasids grew concerned about recruits from the unreliable, independent-minded Arab tribal armies and began to enlist slaves—first blacks from Africa and later mostly horse-riding Turks from Central Asia. Although it is difficult to calculate the number of military slaves in the employ of the Arab empire over the centuries, one scholar estimates it to be into the tens of millions.[25] So deep-rooted was the practice of slavery in the Middle East that it persisted in Saudi Arabia into the 1960s.

THE SLAVE-SUGAR COMPLEX

When European Crusaders arrived on the eastern shores of the Mediterranean in the twelfth century, they found a delicious product—sugar—being grown in plantations with slave labor. Sugarcane originated in the Pacific islands before reaching India, which remained the source of that luxury for the Mediterranean world. Before then, Europe's craving for sweets was being met by sugar beets. The rise of Islam and intensified trade with the Arab world introduced sugarcane cultivation into the Levant. Italian colonies, especially Cyprus, became the principal sugar suppliers in Europe. Italian entrepreneurs in the eastern Mediterranean soon developed the so-called slave-sugar complex, an elaborate method of growing sugarcane and transforming it into sugar, made possible via the large-scale use of slaves. It became the earliest model of the system transplanted to the New World three centuries later. In this early capitalist model, land, capital, and labor were combined in a way that allowed profit to be maximized. Slaves, writes Barbara Solow, were not only "a new, improved factor of production, like a new kind of machine . . . [but] slave labor could be held as an asset in the portfolio of the slaver."[26]

Italy's experience in Crete, Cyprus, and later Sicily had shown how plantation slavery combined with exports could turn virgin lands into an enormous wealth-generating enterprise. When the Portuguese discovered the uninhabited Atlantic islands of Madeira in 1425, they followed in Italy's footsteps and introduced slave-sugar plantations. Slaves were raided or bought from the West African coast and harnessed to growing sugar to be sold in Europe. Other Europeans soon picked up the sugar-slavery model in use in Madeira, São Tomé, and the Canary Islands.

On his first voyage across the Atlantic, Columbus stopped in the Canary Islands for repair and had the opportunity to see firsthand how slave labor was being used in sugar plantations. Although he was disappointed not to find the spice or gold he had sought in Hispaniola, he did not miss the opportunity to appropriate free labor. As he wrote to the Spanish court: "I must add that this island [Hispaniola], as well as the others, belongs to your Highness as securely as the Kingdom of Castile. It only needs people to come and settle here, and to give orders to the inhabitants who will do whatever is asked of them. . . . The Indians have no weapons and are quite naked. They know nothing about the art of war and are so cowardly that a thousand of them would not stay to face three of our men. . . . they need only to be given order *to be made to work, to sow, or to do anything useful.*"[27]

Columbus was the first slaver to send a group of slaves from the New World back to Europe, but the direction of this traffic across the Atlantic quickly reversed. The pressing need for labor to develop the boundless resources offered by the New World had to be met from Africa, and thus did the transatlantic slave trade take off. Europeans came to realize that not only did slavery offer a highly profitable model for producing exportable commodities but trading in slaves was itself a lucrative business. The British learned that the Portuguese method of military raids to grab slaves could be costly; they sought instead the more profitable tactic of bartering with African chiefs to trade commodities for people.

In 1562–63, John Hawkins led England's first slaving voyage to Sierra Leone, returning with three vessels loaded with three hundred slaves and other goods.[28] Despite running the gauntlet of Spain's monopoly in the slave trade, he raised a hefty profit selling the slaves in Spain's Caribbean islands. News of his expedition displeased Queen Elizabeth, who denounced it as "detestable." But after realizing the scale of profits to be reaped through the slave trade, she had a change of heart and ended up investing in Hawkins's next slaving expedition. By carrying slaves from Portuguese Africa to Spanish America, Hawkins challenged the Iberian monopoly. Other slavers soon followed, and the path was laid for slavery-based commerce in the New World.

Supported by a steady stream of imported slaves, the Portuguese colony of Brazil eclipsed Madeira to emerge as the world's leading sugar producer. In 1513 the king of Portugal sent the pope a pompous gift—a life-size image of the pontiff surrounded by twelve cardinals and three hundred candles all made of sugar.[29] From 1575 to 1650 Brazil supplied most of Europe's sugar and imported significant quantities of manufactured goods and African slaves. Slaves were later employed to grow coffee plants introduced from French Guyana, where coffee had arrived after journeying across the world from Yemen to Sri Lanka and Indonesia, as we saw in Chapter 3. A seemingly inexhaustible supply of slave labor and endless plantations turned Brazil into the world's top coffee grower. The semitropical coastal lands of Peru and Mexico offered the Spaniards land to develop sugar plantations and vineyards. Rich silver mines— worked by slaves in northern Mexico and Bolivia—became a great source of wealth for Spain, as well as currency for international commerce. African slaves working in Brazil's diamond and gold mines added to the glitter of the Portuguese empire. The British, French, and Dutch made a fortune from sugar, coffee, and cocoa plantations in the Caribbean and from cotton and tobacco plantations in North America. The prosperity of European colonial powers and the rise of international trade that forged the creation of an interdependent world were based on the ruthless exploitation of African slaves—an estimated twelve million of whom were brought to the Americas in the eighteenth and nineteenth centuries.[30]

Rumblings against slavery in the New World first circulated among the Quakers in Philadelphia as early as 1688, and nearly a hundred years later English Quakers submitted the first important antislavery petition to Parliament. The growth of an evangelical-based, powerful philanthropic movement in England accompanied the rise of laissez-faire thinking and growing opposition to protectionism in the late eighteenth century to intensify opposition to slavery. The rise of the British Empire in India—with its vast population and resources—and the declining importance of the Caribbean also lent weight to the argument to abolish sugar-slavery. In 1807, Parliament passed the first antislavery act, prohibiting trade in African slaves. Ten years later, Britain and Spain signed a treaty in which Spain agreed to end the slave trade north of the equator immediately and south of the equator in 1820. The treaty gave British naval vessels the right to search for suspected slavers. Thanks to loopholes in the treaty, however, slave trade continued unabated until 1830, when another Anglo-Spanish treaty officially banned slavery in most of Central and South America.

In the United States, however, the emerging antislavery movement suffered a setback with Eli Whitney's invention of the cotton gin in 1793. Soaring demand for cotton from British mills, combined with the ease of cleaning cotton with Whitney's invention, made cotton king in America's South, making slavery integral to the southern way of life. It took the South's secession from the Union and a bloody civil war finally to end slavery. The expansion of coffee plantations in Brazil also kept slavery alive for fifty years past its official abolition by an act of Parliament in 1833 that emancipated slaves in the British West Indies. In 1800 there were about 1.5 million slaves in Brazil, 857,000 in the United States, 600,000 in British West Indies, 250,000 in Spanish America, and another 150,000 in other British colonies.[31]

Laws, however, have not ended what economic inequality between different parts of the world has maintained. The world's oldest trade is alive and well even today. The testimony of an escaped Brazilian slave in 2004 provided a glimpse of the dark world beneath the country's export success.[32] Brazil's government has admitted that even now, about fifty thousand people work in "conditions analogous to slavery," clearing the Amazon forest to make tropical hardwoods accessible to loggers, open land for cattle grazing, and clear farmland for soybeans. The resultant low-cost timber, beef, and soybean boost Brazilian exports and are marketed to consumers the world over by multinational corporations. The tragedy in Dover has been followed by incidents in other parts of the world, most notably in the United States, giving us an occasional glimpse of the tip of an iceberg that continues to float darkly under the current of globalization.[33]

BRIDGING ASIA AND THE NEW WORLD

Three centuries of unfettered slave trade profoundly changed our world, meshing it ever tighter—ethnically, economically, and culturally. The slave-sugar complex that arose in the Mediterranean and conquered the New World went on, as historian Robert Harms has shown, to create a vital link in the trading system that connected the continents, forming the backbone of global commerce. The slave trade amounted to "an essential bridge between Europe's New World trade and its Asia trade." In fact, in Africa a slave was known as a "piece," "uma peça d'India," in the old Portuguese expression, meaning the item of printed cotton for which he or she was exchanged.[34] French ships sailed to Africa carrying goods to be bartered for slaves. The slaves were then transported to France's New World colonies, where they were exchanged for sugar and other plantation products. Harms's study of a French slaving ship's travels offers a clear example:

> When the slave ship *Diligent* left France for the West African coast in 1731, over half its cargo consisted of cowry shells and various types of Indian textiles. The cowry shells, which served as the major currency along the West African coast, came from the Maldive Islands, near India. Company of the Indies ships returning from India and China would stop in the Maldive Islands and purchase cowry shells, which they used as packing material to cushion crates of porcelain and other goods much as we would use Styrofoam popcorn today. The cowries also served as ballast to keep the ship steady. Because the porcelain, tea, spices, and textiles of Asia were of higher value than the European trade goods that the ships brought from France, returning ships had a great deal of empty space in their holds that was filled with cowry shells. Once back in France, the cowries were removed and repacked in barrels to be shipped to West Africa.[35]

Historians are still trying to estimate the toll wrought upon Africa's population by the institution of slavery and the slave trade. Some one and a half million slaves were brought to the British Caribbean colonies between 1650 and 1800, but by the end of that period, diseases like dysentery, yellow fever, and malnutrition had decreased the Afro-Caribbean population to just over half a million.[36] Burgeoning international commerce came at a great human price.

We have seen how the emergence of larger-hulled and speedier sailing ships in the sixteenth century and steamships in the nineteenth century helped to break the weight barrier. Instead of light, expensive items like bolts of silk, bags of spice, and boxes of pearls and diamonds, ships could carry increasingly heavier goods. Slavery helped to change the scale of production by producing more goods to fill larger ships to satisfy growing consumer demand. Hundreds of thousands of slaves contributed to the expanding production of sugar, coffee, cocoa, and tobacco, and these one-time luxuries began to reach the masses. "By 1750 the poorest English farm laborer's wife took sugar in her tea."[37] Gone were the days when a king showed off by sending the pope a gift of sugar. Newly discovered cocoa so enchanted Queen Isabella of Spain that she drank chocolate all day, gradually staining her clothes with the drink's brown color. Even on the other side of the world, in Southeast Asia, King Rama III of Siam carried on a military campaign against neighboring Cambodia to bring back bonded labor to grow sugar. Thanks to the corvée labor, sugar had become Siam's most important export item by the first quarter of the nineteenth century.[38] As African slaves in America's South ramped up production and drove down the price of cotton, British textile manufacturing boomed, and the light cotton shirt was no longer a luxury limited to princes and peers.

Tens of thousands of African slaves toiling in the silver mines of Mexico and Peru produced the incredible amount of ingots that provided the lifeblood for world trade. Historians estimate that 130,000 to 150,000 tons of silver were extracted from the mines of Mexico and Peru between 1450 and 1800, before being shipped as bullion to Europe and to the outpost of the Spanish Empire in Asia, Manila.[39] From Manila silver bullion and minted coins circulated throughout the world to pay for the swelling volume of trade.

The slave trade, linked with other goods, tied the continents ever more closely. As Harms has noted, "The Asia trade supplied necessary trade goods for the slave ships, and the slave ships provided a steady market for the Asian products."[40] The slave trade encouraged brandy makers of Nantes and Bordeaux, but more important, the exchanges it brought about supported cloth industries in India and Hamburg, cowry diving in the Maldives, the firearms and pipe industries of Holland, and the iron industry in Sweden.[41]

The steady supply of slaves prolonged the lifespan of the colonial system, as the ready supply of labor could withstand the encroachment of new productivity-enhancing technologies, thus allowing a period of constant returns from colonial investment.[42] The wealth generated by the slavery-based plantation economy also provided a growing market for British industrial goods. As one historian has remarked, in the 1780s and 1790s "almost 60 percent of additional industrial output was exported."[43] By the nineteenth century the Atlantic slave trade had grown into a complex international trade involving East Indian textile manufacture, European metalworkers, African caravan traders, European shipping companies, and American planters.[44]

The intercontinental trading that developed primarily to trade slaves for sugar, cowries, rum, or tobacco expanded over time into other fields. And although the slave trade initially catered only to the needs of elites, soon it began providing commodities of mass consumption. As one scholar of the slave trade has noted, "In neither case did the majority of either people exhibit much knowledge of or interest in the tragic fate of those whose labors produced the goods thus consumed."[45] This is similar to today's consumers enjoying the "everyday good price" in retail outlets like Wal-Mart and Sears, which offer goods made by poor laborers in China and elsewhere working long hours in degrading conditions. Low prices have their cost! Even though consumers don't like the news they hear about working conditions abroad, buyers still flock to these stores. "Consumers are very schizophrenic," says Tristan Lecomte, chief executive and founder of Alter Eco, a French import company that assures decent prices to developing country producers. "On the one hand, they say that they want to be socially responsible, but then they all jump on the hard discounts."[46]

POWERING THE INDUSTRIAL REVOLUTION

The wealth generated by the slave trade contributed to the rise of some of the world's finest universities, including Harvard, Yale, and Brown. Slave traders in Providence, the home of Brown University, were involved in woolen and iron manufacturing, while Moses Brown, whose family founded the university, played a key role in developing the cotton textile industry. In 1790, Brown, then a leader of the antislavery movement, tapped English immigrant Samuel Slater (who bypassed Britain's prohibition on technology exports by memorizing machine designs) and offered him the capital to set up America's first cotton mill, in Pawtucket, just outside Providence.[47]

No power benefited more from slavery than Britain. Between 1662 and 1807 British ships carried approximately 3.4 million slaves from Africa to America, almost half of the total sent during this period.[48] At the height of the slave trade, Britain exported more slaves than any other nation. British industry prospered by selling its wares to the slave colonies, Britain's businesses racked up profits by selling slave-produced goods, and the country as a whole grew rich on the profits of African slavery. Before Britain turned against slavery in 1834, the Atlantic slave system had already laid the foundation for Britain's rise to global power.

Historians estimate that about a million slaves were taken to Asian destinations during the nineteenth century.[49] Asia, of course, had its own intraregional slave trade, in which people from weak and politically fragmented societies were forcibly subsumed into stronger and wealthier ones. The extent of slavery in Asian societies is evident in the fact that, before 1820, a majority of the continent's urban population had been recruited in a captive state through either war or trade.[50] This was an ironic contrast to Europe, where cities emerged on a feudal landscape with a guild-based production system, and city parameters provided sanctuary to serf escapees. Legally, if a serf could manage to live in a city for a year and a day, he became a free man. Hence the German saying, "Town air makes you free" (*Stadtluft macht frei*). By contrast, Southeast Asia's colonial towns became citadels of servitude. Selling slaves to the towns was so lucrative that a number of states rose and flourished based primarily on slave traffic by raiding expeditions on coastal settlements in island Southeast Asia. The region continued supplying slave labor to the rising industrial power, Japan, late into the twentieth century. Although deeply resistant to racial intermixing, the Japanese met their acute labor shortage during World War II by employing the forced labor of seven hundred thousand Asians between 1939 and 1945.[51]

One consequence of the international slave trade was the spread of slavery in Africa itself. Of the captured total, around one-third—or seven million— were brought into domestic slavery. Since exported slaves were overwhelmingly male, the sex ratio in west-central Africa was heavily tilted toward females. The resulting concentration of female slaves around courts led to the rise of polygyny—a form of polygamy in which one man has several wives at the same time.[52] Slavery became such an integral part of African life that "tribal leaders in Gambia, Congo, Dahomey, and other African nations that had prospered under the slave trade sent delegations to London and Paris to vigorously protest the abolition of slavery."[53] Not only did Africa lose its able-bodied population, which affected its population growth, but the warfare that ensued over the slave trade and the consequent social disruption also caused a decline in birth rates. The slave trade seriously affected and weakened African social, political, economic, and cultural institutions.

Another consequence of the slave trade was the introduction of new products in Africa, which had a lasting impact on the continent's cultural and culinary habits. On the Gold Coast (present-day Ghana) British slave traders introduced rum, cheese, beer, refined sugar, and leaf tobacco. Portuguese traders bartered slaves for sugar, brandy, tobacco, guns and gunpowder, manioc flour, and Asian and Portuguese fancy goods. As a result, African consumers became very knowledgeable about European products—a taste that far outlasted the slave trade.[54] The Portuguese also introduced the corn and manioc that became the two most important staples in the African diet, as well as sweet potato, pineapple, cashew, papaya, and dozens of other foods. Coffee plantations in Brazil sent coffee seeds back to São Tomé, from where it spread to the African mainland. Three hundred years of slave traffic left a distinctly Brazilian imprint on everyday life in West Africa, including diets, religion, popular festivals, and architecture.[55]

It was estimated that there were 1.5 million American Indians in Brazil when it was discovered by Europeans. Then 3.5 million African slaves were brought in. The impact of the African population on Brazil's demography is illustrated by the fact that, in the early 1960s, 1 percent of the population was American Indian, 11 percent of Brazilians were black, 26 percent were mixed, and the rest were of European extraction. The prominent Brazilian author Gilberto Freyre wrote that "every Brazilian, even if he is white-skinned or fair-haired, carried in his soul, and if not in his soul in his body—a shadow, or at least a spot of Negro blood."[56]

In every sphere of Brazilian life—food, clothing, religion, language, music, and folklore—centuries of slave trading have left an indelible imprint. From samba music to the *congadas* song and dance depicting the crowning of a Congolese king, from *acarajé* (a cake of baked beans in palm oil) and *caruru* (a stew of shrimp and okra) to *quibebe* (pumpkin pureé), life in Brazil is a daily reminder of the globalization that has shaped it.[57] The traditional religion brought from two major cradles of civilization, the Congo and the Gulf of Guinea, has influenced the African migrants' liturgical and visual presentation and often merged with rituals and practices of the ruling Christians. The most striking is Umbanda, considered by some to be the national religion of Brazil. As Nei Lopes explains, "Umbanda is a religion resulting from the assimilation of various elements, starting from Bantu ancestrism and the worship of the Fon-Yoruban Orishas. According to some of its scholars, Umbanda syncretizes with Hinduism, taking from it the laws of karma, evolution, and reincarnation; with Christianity, taking from it principally the rules of brotherhood and charity; and with the Native American religiosity."[58]

Similarly, Caribbean cuisine and its cultural forms—from Trinidadian calypso to Haitian vodoun—bear the hallmarks of centuries of interaction with African slaves. Creole, now spoken widely in the Caribbean, carries the imprint of years of slavery, when African languages combined with the language of French slave masters to produce a new language. The arrival of the Europeans in the New World brought more than slavery and its long-term socioeconomic consequences. It brought what some historians have called genocide—by microbial agents.

INVISIBLE DANGER FROM AFAR

On the early morning of 12 October 1492, strange-looking floating houses with masts appeared off an island in the Caribbean. Wide-eyed and naked natives gathered to watch. The pale, bearded sailors who emerged from the *Santa María, Niña,* and *Pinta* spoke an unknown tongue and wore strange coverings, but they seemed genuinely overjoyed to have found the rocky bay. That encounter between Europeans and American Indians reunited two human communities that had gone their separate ways on leaving Africa more than fifty thousand years earlier.

Neither the relieved Christopher Columbus and his sailors nor the curious natives could imagine what portent this encounter held for the future. Along with the unwashed and unshaven strangers in funny dress came invisible viruses and pathogens that would wreak havoc on the New World population. As Alfred W. Crosby, Jr., writes in his seminal book *The Columbian Exchange:* "When the isolation of the New World was broken, when Columbus brought the two halves of the planet together, the American Indian met for the first time his most hideous enemy; not the white man nor his black servant, but the invisible killers which these men brought in their blood and breath."[59]

Within a span of just seventy-odd years, eighty to a hundred million natives perished because of the disease brought by Europeans from across the seas: smallpox, influenza, diphtheria. "Like the rats of the medieval Black Death," Niall Ferguson comments, "the white men were the carriers of the fatal germ."[60] One of the things English pilgrims gave thanks for at Plymouth in 1621 was the fact that 90 percent of the indigenous peoples of New England had died of disease brought by previous visitors, having first—very considerately—tilled the land and buried stores of corn for the winter. As the governor of Carolina John Archdale stated in the 1690s, "The Hand of God [has been] eminently seen in thinning the *Indians,* to make room for the *English.*"[61]

The decimation of the American Indians was, however, just one episode in the long history of death and suffering that has accompanied human intercourse across the world. Along with humans, insects, cattle, and domesticated animals—all carrying viruses and pathogens—crossed borders and found new hosts. The global dissemination of disease was thus one of the earliest negative consequences of interconnectedness. It is not, however, the fact of human travel that lies behind the globalization of disease; early hunter-gatherers, who constantly moved around in search of food, appear to have been healthy. Because of their nomadic way of life, they did not live amid their waste, nor did they tend cattle or poultry. It was the rise of sedentary, agriculture-based communities that brought cattle, poultry, rodents, and insects living cheek by jowl with humans, providing vectors for the transmission of germs. As caravans and boats of traders began connecting dispersed human communities, they began inadvertently transporting, along with their goods, new pathogens: germs and germ-bearing rodents, mosquitoes, and fleas. Traded commodities like slaves carried communicable diseases that changed the recipient countries. Soldiers on expeditions carried germs to new lands and returned with new pathogens and infections ranging from the plague to influenza. With the advent of mass travel, even latter-day adventurers—tourists—have become vectors of pandemics. Thus at least three of the four agents of globalization—traders, warriors, and adventurers—were unwitting carriers of catastrophes.

Roman soldiers returning from the Parthian Wars in Mesopotamia in the second century brought with them the first documented case of an epidemic hitting the Mediterranean world of the Roman Empire. There is some debate whether it was a rat-borne plague or the first case of smallpox, but either way a terrible epidemic killed between a third and a half of those infected and triggered a decline in the Mediterranean population. The year 542 brought the first unmistakable case of bubonic plague, in which a rat-borne bacillus, *Y. pestis*, caused the swelling of lymph nodes into buboes and a fatal secondary lung infection. Called Justinius plague after the Roman emperor, the epidemic is believed to have originated in India and was brought to Egypt by rats adept in scurrying across the fastening lines that tied Arab trading ships to ports along the Red Sea. Colonies of fast-breeding rats and the fleas that fed on them spread the pestilence along the Mediterranean trade routes, all the way from Constantinople on the Bosporus to the Iberian Peninsula. The historian Procopius reported that at its peak, the plague killed ten thousand persons a day in Constantinople alone. Between 30 to 40 percent of the Roman Empire's population—estimated at sixteen to twenty-six million before the plague—perished in the pandemic.[62] A contemporary account put the loss graphically. The plague "depopulated towns, turned the country into desert and made the habitations of men to become the haunts of wild beasts."[63]

It is estimated that at least a quarter of the population in both the eastern and western halves of the Roman Empire perished. It was a record that was surpassed six centuries later by another plague pandemic, which came to be known as the Black Death (so named because of a mistranslation of the Latin expression *atra mors* as "black"—rather than "terrible"—death). Commonly the appellation is attributed to the discoloration of the skin and black buboes that occur on the second day after contracting the plague.[64]

HIGHWAY OF DEATH

In 1347 Italian merchant ships from the Crimean Black Sea port of Kaffa (today's Theodosia) arrived in Constantinople and in seaports along the coasts of the Mediterranean, bringing with them the plague bacillus. The plague then spread throughout Asia Minor, the Middle East, North Africa, and Europe. Traders crossing the rodent-infested Central Asian steppes offered themselves as unwilling carriers of the disease. As we have seen, the ancient Silk Road flourished under the Mongols' protection, but although the route was safe from bandits, it was not immune from germs passed to traders by rodents and fleas.

The Black Death, believed to have originated in China in an outbreak in 1331, reached the Crimea in 1345. By 1347 the plague had reached Constantinople, and soon Pisa and Genoa. Once the pestilence had reached the major ports in Europe it proceeded along overland routes to major cities, felling one after the other. The famous trading route that had once brought prosperity to European cities was transformed into a highway of death that traveled in the shape of furry black rats.

Historian Ole Benedictow concludes that about 60 percent of the population, or some fifty million of Europe's estimated eighty million, perished from the plague and related ailments.[65] Contemporary accounts describe mounds of rotting corpses that could not be collected, much less buried. In a city like Florence, with a population of one hundred thousand, some four hundred to a thousand people died every day. From 1347 until 1722 the plague returned to Europe periodically before dying out. For a period, trade almost came to a halt. If the word *globalization* had been known, one would have pronounced it dead

as well. Europe's falling population, however, set in motion economic and social trends and medical practices that proved a turning point in world history.
The devastation that followed helps to underline the interconnected nature of
the world that trade had already created. The death of half or more of the population meant a sharp rise in the per capita wealth among the survivors. Newly
wealthy from inheriting land, capital, and stocks of gold and silver, and exhila-
rated to be alive, Europeans went on a luxury buying binge that enriched Asian
suppliers of silk and spices and Arab and Venetian intermediaries. Their shopping spree also caused what one historian has called the "Great Bullion Famine
of the Fifteenth Century." This drastic shortage of coins led to an intensified
search for precious metals, and in 1516 "one of the greatest silver strikes in history" was made in the German town of Joachimsthal. The coins produced by
the town's mint were called *Joachimsthaler.* And the *thaler,* as it was later shortened, was the precursor to our word *dollar.*[66] But meanwhile, as we have seen,
the stranglehold of Venetian-Arab intermediaries on the spice trade led Europeans to intensify their search for alternate sea routes to Asia.[67] By promoting
the demand growth in Europe, the Black Death in many ways foreshadowed
another spurt toward formation of a consumer society that would arise from
the New World's supply boom.

More immediately, the labor shortage and its high cost led to a more rational
work organization, efficient production methods, and labor-saving devices.
Water-powered sawmills that had been developed in the early thirteenth century came into widespread use. The death of a large number of scribes sent the
price of copying manuscripts skyrocketing, pushing the need for some form of
automated copying. Paper-making, learned from the Chinese, had already led
to the production of cheap paper. Moveable type made of wood also was
known. In 1447 Johannes Gutenberg of Mainz, Germany, combined his skill in
metallurgy with printing technology to produce Europe's first moveable metal-
type printing press and launched a revolution.[68] The production of cheap consumer goods in Britain and Holland shifted the center of economic gravity
from the Mediterranean to the North—which would eventually pioneer modern shipbuilding and usher in the Industrial Revolution.

A catastrophe of such magnitude as the Black Death also revealed and drove
long-held prejudices against "outsiders" like Jews to a new height. The theory
that Jews and other "enemies of Christendom" caused these deaths by poisoning wells and other sources of drinking water led to a violent persecution of minorities in many parts of Europe. It was " a sort of medieval holocaust with extensive and indiscriminate murder of Jews, [hastening their] movement to

Eastern Europe, where their descendants were, to a large extent, annihilated in a new, and even more violent holocaust 600 years later."[69]

THE BIRTH OF QUARANTINE

The Black Death had far-reaching consequences on public health policy. The first known order to quarantine passengers was issued on 27 July 1377 by the Venetian colony of Ragusa (now Dubrovnik in Croatia) on the Dalmatian coast. The order for a thirty-day period of isolation for those coming from plague-stricken areas was later extended to forty days—hence the term *quarantine,* developed from Italian *quarantenaria.* "Thus stirred by the Black Death in the middle of the fourteenth century," writes George Rosen, "public officials in Italy, southern France, and the neighboring area created a system of sanitary control to combat contagious diseases, with observation stations, isolation hospitals, and disinfection procedures. This system was adopted and developed during the Renaissance and later periods and is still a part of public health practices today, although in a more rigorously defined form."[70]

But the quarantine system did not always work. In the spring of 1720 a Levantine boat carrying cases of human plague appeared in the port of Livorno. It was turned away there and at Marseille. But after a few months of wandering in the Mediterranean, including a stop at Tripoli, the boat returned to the French port of Toulon, where many passengers managed to bribe their way out of a token quarantine. Soon plague flared in Toulon and spread to Marseille, killing nearly half of its hundred thousand residents.[71] The disaster at Marseille led to stricter enforcement of quarantine and an effort to limit or eliminate the Middle Eastern cloth trade. The effort fitted well with the rising sea-borne textile trade between India and Europe.

As noted earlier, one of the greatest ravages of globalization—in the sense of the closer integration of human communities—was the transmission of diseases to American Indians in the New World, who had no immunity against the pathogens brought from Europe. In 1519 the Spanish conquistador Hernán Cortés succeeded in defeating the more numerous Aztecs with a small army because they were enfeebled by smallpox spread from an African slave accompanying Cortés. The Aztecs interpreted the selective pestilence as a demonstration of the superior power of the god the Spanish worshipped, says historian William McNeill. As a result, Cortés and his ragtag army were able easily to subjugate the Aztec empire of some twelve and a half million. From Mexico, smallpox spread to Guatemala and continued southward, reaching the Incan lands in present-day Peru around 1525. In 1563, Portuguese colonizers brought smallpox to Brazil, where it wiped out entire indigenous tribes.[72] Further north, there were probably about two million indigenous people in the territory of the modern United States in 1500. That number had fallen to 750,000 in 1700 before being further reduced to 325,000 by 1820.[73]

As the slave trade and conquest transmitted smallpox to new lands, its remedy also was passed on from one country to another. The practice of smallpox inoculation known as "buying the smallpox" or "variolation" is believed to have begun in India before 1000 BCE. It was spread to Tibet and then to China by monks at a Buddhist monastery in Sichuan province around the year 1000.[74] During the mid-seventeenth-century, merchant caravans brought the knowledge of variolation to Arabia, Persia, and North Africa, and it came to be practiced at the folk level throughout the Ottoman Empire. In the early eighteenth century Lady Mary Montagu, wife of the British ambassador to Constantinople and herself a survivor of smallpox, variolated her son and introduced the practice to Britain.[75]

Dr. Edward Jenner developed the technique of vaccination by inoculating people with pus from cowpox victims, which prevented the more serious smallpox infection. In his book describing the procedure in 1798, he coined the word *vaccine*, from the Latin word *vacca* for cow and named the process "vaccination." In 1881 the French microbiologist Louis Pasteur honored Jenner by expanding the use of the term *vaccination* to describe any inoculation that induced immunity against a communicable disease. More than any single medical invention, vaccination has since saved hundreds of millions of lives and transformed the world's demography. As J. N. Hays has noted: "One by one the perils of various infectious epidemic diseases seemed to fade away under the combined assault of enlightened public health and sanitation, the extension of the preventive principle of vaccination, and the curative powers of laboratory products, among which the antibiotics created the greatest sensation."[76]

Noted flu virologist Kennedy Shortridge believes that all flu pandemics that can be traced have always begun in China's Guangdong province, a densely populated region where people, pigs, ducks, and other fowl have long lived cheek by jowl. The Spanish flu of 1918 may also have begun as bird flu in Canton in 1888. During World War I, Chinese laborers traveled to camps in France to dig trenches for the Allies and may have carried the virus strain that set off the flu pandemic. Although the suspicion that the Spanish flu is a form of avian flu has now been confirmed by DNA analysis of the victims' remains, other specialists challenge the theory of its Chinese origin.[77]

SOLDIERS, STEAMBOATS, AND SPANISH FLU

Wherever the 1918 Flu Pandemic (or Spanish flu) originated, within a year of its emergence in Europe it had infected a fifth of the world's population, including 28 percent of the U.S. population. The estimated total of victims ranges from twenty million to forty million.[78] It was called Spanish flu because, as a non-aligned country during World War I, Spain did not censor news reports, and the spread of flu there became well known in the world.

In her book *Flu*, about the 1918 pandemic, Gina Kolata vividly describes its reach:

> The plague took off in September of that year, and when it was over, half a million Americans would be dead. The illness spread to the most remote parts of the globe. Some Eskimo villages were decimated, nearly eliminated from the face of the earth. Twenty percent of Western Samoans perished. . . . It came when the world was weary of war. It swept the globe in months, ending when the war did. It went away as mysteriously as it appeared. And when it was over, humanity had been struck by a disease that killed more people in a few months' time than any other illness in the history of the world.[79]

The 1918 flu was also the first truly global disease that spread as fast as the steamships and steam railways would carry people to the farthest corners of the world. Thousands of demobilized soldiers, who survived the most brutal war to date, returned home carrying the deadly infection that killed both them and their joyous family and friends. As most of the continents were by then connected by ocean liners and vast areas covered by railway networks, the flu spread out in every direction. Unlike the plague, which took three years to devastate populations from Central Asia to Europe, this flu did its damage across the world in a year and half.

Another pandemic caused by an avian flu virus, known as an H2N2 strain, which had killed between one and four million people worldwide in 1957–58, threatened to rear its head again in early 2005. This time the threat was posed not by the emergence of a newly mutated strain but by the accidental worldwide distribution of that old strain. In late 2004 a private company, Meridian Bio-science, Inc., of Cincinnati, sent a parcel of virus samples to nearly four thousand

laboratories and doctors' offices for testing as part of routine quality-control certification conducted by the College of American Pathologists. Unwittingly the
samples included the H2N2 virus, against which people today have no immunity. On discovery of the mistake six months later, an alarmed World Health Organization sent out an urgent advisory to destroy the dangerous samples.[80]

When the next flu pandemic SARS (severe acute respiratory syndrome)
arose in 2003, it spread from southern China to South Africa and to Australia
and Brazil in just six months. SARS originated in China's southern Guangdong
province, where some diners enjoyed a meal of wild civet and along with their
dinner ingested a newly mutated *Corona* virus (the cause of the common cold)
against which humans had no immunity. One of the Chinese diners, bearing
the highly contagious disease, went to Hong Kong and stayed in a hotel. One
of the world's major tourist and business hubs was soon transformed into a giant disseminator of the world's most infectious disease. Less than a month after
SARS claimed its first victim in Vietnam, the WHO issued a worldwide travel
advisory. With its flight information board silently flashing CANCELLED, Hong
Kong's cavernous Chek Lap Kok Airport looked desolate. Schools and businesses closed as frightened citizens in facemasks wondered if it was their turn.
In a bid to prevent the spread of SARS, Beijing sealed off three hospitals and ordered nearly eight thousand people who might have been exposed to stay
home. The Chinese capital's public schools, movie theaters, and discos were
shut down. In Singapore wet markets were closed and hospital visits blocked.
The most stringent quarantine procedures were set up at many of the world's
ports and airports, and scientists in thirteen labs in ten countries raced to identify the new killer in search of an antidote.

Compared to the 2.5 percent morbidity rate of the Spanish flu, SARS was
four times more virulent, killing 10 percent of its victims. Globally coordinated
quarantine and preventive measures contained the virus, but only after it had
caused 813 deaths in thirty countries, the vast majority in Hong Kong and
mainland China.[81] Had the WHO not issued its travel warning, and if not for
the advances in science and medical surveillance and the extraordinary worldwide cooperation of scientists to identify the virus, SARS could have spread
much further and faster than even the pandemic of 1918 did. Had the virus infected just 20 percent of China's population of 1.2 billion people, as many as
102 million would have died. Compared to the insignificant number of international travelers in 1918, by 2003 some 1.6 billion passengers took airplane
flights and a third of these crossed international borders, taking all manner of
viruses with them on their journeys. In a race against the fast-spreading virus,

scientists working in networked labs from Atlanta to Vancouver to Singapore stepped up their efforts to map the virus's genome, achieving this extraordinary feat within just one month. Thus, globalization not only gave viruses jet speed, but it accelerated the pace of countermeasures as well.

DISEASE WITHOUT BORDERS

At its annual meeting in May 2003, the WHO asserted that SARS is "the first severe infectious disease to emerge in the twenty-first century" and "poses a serious threat to global health security, the livelihood of populations, the functioning of health systems, and the stability and growth of economies." Crossing international borders on jet airplanes and challenging the global health system, the SARS virus has been called "the first post-Westphalian pathogen."[82] The Treaty of Westphalia of 1648 marked the formal emergence of an international order based on sovereign rights within fixed borders and included public health measures. Although the great powers in Europe began international legal rules and diplomatic processes to facilitate cooperation on infectious diseases in 1851, international cooperation did not intrude much on state sovereignty. But with its advisories against visiting certain countries and its aggressive inspection regime, the WHO created a new phenomenon: the first-ever globalized response to a global disease. Even a go-it-alone President George W. Bush admitted the need for international cooperation and transparency. The lesson of the SARS experience is clear, he said: "We all have a common interest in working together to stop outbreaks of deadly new viruses—so we can save the lives of people on both sides of the Pacific."[83]

The worry that another post-Westphalian virus—that would spread like wildfire across international borders—may be brewing in the genome cauldron makes scientists worry because they now know that the deadly flu of 1918 was in its origin an avian flu.[84] In 1997, another flu crossed the species barrier in southern China, after a boy became infected by a flu common among chickens and ducks and eventually died. Since then, the so-called jumping strain of avian flu has spread beyond Hong Kong and southern China to infect chicken and bird populations in Cambodia, Indonesia, Thailand, Vietnam, Malaysia, Korea, and Japan and, by the end of 2006, has infected ninety-three humans, of whom forty-two have died. The extraordinarily high morbidity rate of this avian flu—75 percent of those who caught the virus died (compared to less than 1 percent death in common human flu)—makes health officials shudder at the prospect of the avian flu's adapting itself for human-to-human transmission.[85] If SARS is any indicator, a transmuted virus of that type could spread across the world at the speed of a commercial jetliner and bring a catastrophe that would make the forty million flu deaths of 1918 look like a minor episode of early globalization.

The fact is that flu viruses mutate so fast that an antidote for one variety may be useless for another. In collaboration with the WHO's Global Influenza Program, scientists in some 120 laboratories around the world have been constantly peering through their electron microscopes at new samples to detect any transmutation that could indicate that the flu has gained the ability to transmit among humans. Once convinced of the threat, the WHO can issue a travel advisory that could ground thousands of passenger planes crisscrossing the world's skies and quarantine entire cities or countries. This is a capability that did not exist when Black Death or Spanish flu ravaged the planet.

There is, however, no such international system of protection against another type of danger that lurks in the cyberspace.

VIRUS HUNTERS

It's late evening. The glow of the setting sun fades and stars begin twinkling over the Pacific Ocean. But the lights are burning on the second floor of the glass-lined building of the Symantec Corporation. Banks of tall servers in glass-enclosed safe rooms glow eerily with blinking red LED lights in the software company's laboratory in Santa Monica, California. In an adjoining room, behind high partitioned cubicles young men and women in tee-shirts and blue jeans peer intently into their screens. They come from different parts of the world and speak different languages, but they have one common goal in that quiet laboratory. They are trying to find the "signatures" of and antidotes to the newest viruses that the quietly blinking servers in the safe room have prescreened and spit out to them to fight. These young guardians of the Internet in Santa Monica and in other labs in different time zones are not fundamentally different from scientists in medical labs all over the world working with WHO. The scientists watch out for mutated flu viruses while the computer engineers scan the Web for deadly pathogens in cyberspace. The pathogens deliberately created by humans stalk nearly a billion computers worldwide, threatening the new highways of globalization. These malicious programs infect your computer, delete and alter your files, steal your data, and take over your machine to perform pernicious acts. To call the programs viruses is to give the natural ones a bad name. Invisible to the naked eye, biological viruses are simply doing the same basic jobs—survival and proliferation—that all life-forms struggle to do. The efforts of the Spanish flu virus and SARS to survive and proliferate by taking over hosts have been deadly to humans and other animals, but these natural viruses are not driven by malice or greed. Computer viruses function with greater intent; with each new technological innovation, some of our fellow human beings search for a way to exploit the innovation in order to steal, profit at another's expense, or simply hurt anonymous others out of sheer malice. The deliberate corruption of communications is by no means a twenty-first century phenomenon unique to the Internet. Some of the first uses of the telegraph, for example, were to make illegal bets on horse races and to defraud unsuspecting citizens remitting money by cable. The use of computers has brought no exception to this tale of human malevolency.

There was, however, one major difference with other technologies; most technology historians agree that in the case of computers, life imitated art. In his novel *When HARLIE Was One* (1972), science fiction author David Gerrold came up with the idea of writing a rogue program and called it a virus.[86] More than a decade later, Fred Cohen, a bright graduate student at the University of Southern California, wrote as part of his class work the first program to replicate itself and self-propagate. His professor, impressed with its similarity to the biological phenomenon, suggested he call the program a "computer virus." Cohen proceeded to write his thesis on his invention and devoted his life to studying the new manmade viruses.[87] Computer lore has it that it was the Farooq Alvi brothers of Lahore, Pakistan, Amjad and Basit, who created the first worldwide virus program in 1986. Any time someone copied a software floppy disk from their computer store, a virus called Brain would place a copy of itself on the hard disk and issue a patent warning.[88]

Just as a virus in the natural world needs a host from which to extract sustenance in order to proliferate, the computer virus, too, needs a host. Before computers were connected by the Internet, the floppy disk was the vector for viruses traveling from computer to computer. Like the Pakistani virus Brain, most early computer viruses were pranks and show-offs. As the use of computers soared and the Internet created pathways, more virulent virus strains—called "malware"—proliferated. From playing a tune or displaying a funny message the viruses evolved to do nasty things like erasing your precious data and stealing your password and credit card information. New forms of malware appeared—from self-replicating viruses to worms that would install themselves in a computer and send out e-mail, to the Trojan horse, which, like the famous wooden horse of Troy that hid soldiers in its belly, pretended to do something benign but surreptitiously carried a malicious payload. A Trojan horse like Zelu, for instance, pretended to be a program that would fix the "millennium bug" but instead chewed up data from the hard drive.[89]

LOVE BITES

It was a typical summer day in 2000, when the cool interior of an office was more inviting than the color and smell of life in Hong Kong. But I was soon to find out that the cool and quiet of my office in Causeway Bay could not keep out the invasion of something unpleasant from a faraway place. I had returned from lunch and switched on the computer to check my e-mail. I had clicked on a few messages to read. Suddenly my inbox came to life with a message from someone I had no clue about. The intriguing missive with the subject line ILOVEYOU began a torrent. Within minutes, dozens of e-mails bearing the same enticing subject line were cascading down my monitor's screen. I immediately knew it was a virus attack and began block deleting the messages that were rapidly filling up the screen. Soon the tech support manager, Vincent, poked his head through my office door, warned, "Don't open any ILOVEYOU message!" and scurried off. But the damage was done. Some of my curious colleagues had clicked on the attachment and had given the not-so-loving e-mail access to their Outlook address books. Within minutes, hundreds of messages bearing the same profession of love had been squirted out of their computers headed for many destinations, ricocheting to computers thousands of miles apart. The virus had also begun carrying out its programmed task on the infected computers—destroying masses of data, image, and music files on the hard disk. As I learned later, it was a virus that didn't spare any user of e-mail. Singapore's powerful senior minister Lee Kuan Yew, who had only recently begun to use a computer to write his memoir, found an e-mail proclaiming love. He did not know the sender, but as he explained to me with an embarrassed laugh, "I was curious. Who would send me such a message?"[90] His computer was soon knocked out. His geek son, then Deputy Prime Minister Lee Hsien-Loong, who had coaxed him to embrace the computer, came over to disinfect the machine. Thousand of miles away, in Britain, the Parliament's computer system had to be shut down because curious members of Parliament had opened their e-mail and inadvertently sent out many more such infected missives. Throughout the day of 4 May 2000 the Love Bug tracked the path of the sun around the globe, erasing files and knocking out computer systems from Asia to Europe to the Americas. Investigators later traced the mayhem to twenty-four-year-old Onel de Guzman, a disgruntled Filipino hacker in Manila. "I hate to go to school," he wrote in a note with the malicious code, which was uploaded on one Internet server and sent out on its merry path of destruction.[91] In the course of its romp across cyberspace the Love Bug infected an estimated ten million computers worldwide, including terminals at the White House, the U.S. Congress, and the Pentagon, as well as at the British and Danish parliaments and at hundreds of European and American companies, causing, according to one estimate, economic damage worth ten billion dollars.[92]

The virus Code Red, launched in July 2001, was one of the first viruses that did not need any user interaction, no clicking on anything. It exploited a security hole in the computer's operating system and propagated itself from one computer to another through the Internet. It could infect your machine while you were sleeping. It took three weeks for a virus writer to exploit that security hole, Javier Santoyo of Symantec says, but "today that three week period has been reduced to 24 hours or less."[93] In less than fourteen hours on 19 July, the Code Red worm infected 359,104 computers and servers all over the world. You can watch an animated depiction of the fast-spreading worm on the Internet.[94]

WATCHING FOR A ZERO-DAY VIRUS

In retrospect, despite the depredations of the Love Bug, it was almost an innocent prank. At the beginning, it was a matter of prestige for people who wrote virus programs. They could do something others could not. Now it is more and more motivated by profit. As the speed of the Internet has accelerated from dial-up connection to cable and DSL (digital subscriber line), so has the maliciousness of the Web-borne bugs. There are spyware programs that quietly reside in your computer and monitor what sites you visit or what you type. There are adware programs that constantly spam you with ads for cheap drugs and cheap hotels. Many computer users unknowingly have machines that have been taken over by a rogue program and turned into members of the army of slave computers that are constantly bombarding others with spam. There also are "phishing" programs that try to steal your bank and credit card information or your Social Security number. By being vigilant I had dodged the ILOVEYOU attack. But by 2004 the Internet had gotten much more troublesome and dangerous. I had been annoyed by the pop-up ads whenever I visited a Web site, but one winter morning in 2004 I could not even switch on my computer without cascading pop-up ads filling up my screen. The more I tried closing them the more popped up, covering up my monitor like college bulletin boards pasted over with notice after notice. But these were no notices for a lecture or a dance performance. These were advertisements for cheap Viagra and lottery tickets and cheap air tickets. The spyware that caused this nuisance had exploited loopholes in the Microsoft Web browser and secretly entered my hard disk to wait the right stimuli to do their job. The result was wasted hours and frustration when I felt like picking up the damn thing and hurling it out the window. Thank you very much, globalization! How I missed my Olivetti typewriter.

In the end, I upgraded my computer's operating system and installed a whole slew of anti-spyware and anti-virus software to reclaim my computer. I was still luckier than many others whose computers had been seized by worms that deleted their files and stole their personal data without their ever suspecting anything amiss. Others have fallen for the bait used by "phishing" scammers who warn you about a security breach in your electronic banking and urge you to reactivate your closed account by providing them all your personal information.

You may have never heard of Cornell graduate student Robert Morris, Jr., Ching Ing-hau, a sergeant in the Taiwanese army, David Smith of New Jersey, Jan de Wit of the Netherlands, or for that matter a German teenager named Sven Jaschan, but their malicious creations have directly or indirectly affected computer users' life worldwide. Morris created the so-called Morris Worm, which spread within days to about six thousand mainframes. The disgruntled Taiwanese army man's creation, the Chernobyl virus, erased an infected computer's hard drive. David Smith's Melissa virus in 1999 clogged up the mailbox, as did Jan de Wit's virus, named for Russian tennis star Anna Kournikova. From his home computer in the small town of Waffensen, German hacker Jaschan launched viruses that launched so-called denial of service attacks, which involved flooding target Web sites with data, causing them to crash. In the past twenty-five years some fifty-six thousand computer viruses and worms and Trojan horses have been released on the Internet, generating enough bumps and grind on the path of globalization.[95] And they keep coming as the virus fighters sharpen their weapons.

You are unlikely to have met Yana Liu, the earnest young woman with large plastic-framed glasses and an easy smile who sits in front of two monitors in her cubicle at Symantec. A native of Chengdu, the capital of China's Sichuan province, she graduated from the University of Electronic Science and Technology of China before joining the antivirus software company's army of engineers. Hundreds like her work for such leading vendors as Symantec, Sophos, McAfee, and Trend Micro. Each engineer can take from seven to thirty hours to find an antidote to the latest strain of malware.[96] They monitor the pattern of continuous attacks on clients' servers around the world, looking for what is known as a "zero-day virus." Once a virus is launched, it circles the world along the same path as the sun. In the morning, people wake up, open their Internet mailbox to check their messages, and innocently click on an attachment or open an e-mail, thus triggering the proliferation of the malicious virus. Often the virus is sent out to everyone in the address book on the computer, thus multiplying the virus at an accelerating rate. The task of engineers like Liu is to identify and decode the virus so that it does not have a chance to proliferate another day. The malicious software has to be killed before the sun goes down and the "zero-day virus" lives another day to infect millions more.

A CRIMINAL BAZAAR

The viruses that send out millions of spam messages or delete all the data on your hard drive are still relatively harmless compared to the hard-core criminal activity that has become the hallmark of the Internet. In 2004 *Business Week* magazine reported on a rare success scored by law enforcement against the cybercriminals who seem to operate with impunity in the Internet-connected world. The Federal Bureau of Investigation busted the aptly named cybercrime gang ShadowCrew after it had stolen nearly two million credit card numbers, accessed data from more than eighteen million e-mail accounts, and gathered identity data for thousands of people, including counterfeit British passports and U.S. driver's licenses. The FBI said that the gang, set up by a part-time student in Arizona and a New Jersey mortgage broker, ran the criminal equivalent of eBay in which they sold credit card numbers to four thousand members located throughout the world—from Bulgaria to Sweden. As one FBI official summed up the operation: "It was a criminal bazaar."[97]

ShadowCrew was only one of thousands of criminal gangs that prowl the Web. In January 2004 a new virus called MyDoom attacked the Web, installing Trojan horse software in unsuspecting computers. The malware later opened a secret door to the computer for MyDoom's author to steal credit numbers and banking information from any hard drive. By the time it was detected and stopped, MyDoom is reported to have caused $4.8 billion in damage. Another computer crime gang called HangUp, operating from Archangel, Russia, created a worm called Scob that pounced on visitors to certain sites to plant a program in their computer that spied on their keystrokes to copy and send thousands of passwords and credit card numbers to a server in Russia. As a biological virus takes over a host cell to proliferate, cybercriminals also seem to be on the lookout for countries that have weak cybercrime laws, poor enforcement, or official corruption. Thanks to the ease of operating in the high-speed Internet world, they can be located in one country and operate from servers in another country. Globalization has created a borderless world that allows me to order an iPod and have it delivered from across the ocean in a couple of days. Criminals can steal millions of credit card numbers to order much more expensive things in much shorter time. Banks and credit card companies that have been victimized do not want to admit their losses for fear of bad publicity. But according to a U.S. research firm, the total damage in 2004 from cybercrime was at least $17.5 billion, a record figure—and 30 percent higher than 2003.

Globalization, like slavery, arouses great passion. Yet Madge Dresser, a lecturer at the University of West England, has not stopped at denouncing nineteenth-century globalization as responsible for human misery. The "slave trade," she said, "initiated globalization." In fact Dresser sees globalization as synonymous with slavery. "[Slavery] . . . epitomizes a most exploitative form of globalization, which has since resurfaced in new forms," she has written.[98] She is only partly right. As we have seen, globalization as a growing trend of connecting human societies and making them interdependent has been part of our history. The slave trade certainly played a major role in intensifying globalization, but the broad trend has meant much more than the enslavement of people. Globalization is not a morality play on a world scale. It is not the story of a ceaseless battle between the forces of good and evil. It is a never-ending saga in which the striving for a better life and greater security by millions of individuals manifests itself in the search for profit, for a livelihood, for knowledge, for inner peace, for protection for oneself, one's dear ones, and one's community. Humans' striving and searching have constantly led them to cross borders, both geographic and mental. The result of this unremitting process has been triumph for some and unbelievable misery and suffering for others. Slaves and slavers, the afflicted and the healers, the jobless and the new recruits—all have provided the warp and woof of the ever-changing texture of life and thereby created the world we know today.

The intensifying pace of human intercourse, trade, and communications has given wings to diseases and opened virtual doors to criminals and miscreants to take advantage of today's easy and fast communications. The communicable diseases that left their places of origin on trade caravans and ships and brought disasters now have new means to expand their reach and increase their speed. We have seen how the ceaseless search for knowledge and understanding of our physical world by scientists and engineers over centuries has brought us the microchip and the technology to connect with others at the speed of light. It would be ahistorical to think that the effect of this speed will always be for the good.

Chapter 8 Globalization:

From Buzzword to Curse

> Globalization—a focal point of hostile passions and sometimes violent protests—has become a phenomenon doomed to unending controversy. Advocates cite its virtues and its inevitability. Opponents proclaim its supposed vices and vincibility. Central to many of the protests against it is a trilogy of discontents about the idea of capitalism, the process of globalization, and the behavior of corporations. And all three of these discontents have become interlinked in the minds of many protesters. Globalization's enemies see it as the worldwide extension of capitalism, with multinational corporations as its far-ranging B-52s.
> —*Jagdish N. Bhagwati, writing in* Foreign Affairs *in 2002*

The clunky five-syllable *globalization* was perhaps the world's most contested word at the end of the last century and promises to remain controversial in the decade ahead. Why did a word that has been in our vocabulary for more than forty years become such a polarizing term, drawing tens of thousands of demonstrators onto the streets and inducing thousands of writers to produce millions of words debating

---

The German geographer Martin Behaim and his globe

its meaning? Is globalization "dangerous," as many editorialists proclaim, or was it responsible for lifting millions out of wrenching poverty, as the World Bank claims? Before addressing these questions, which I will attempt in the next chapter, it is useful to trace the evolution of the concept of globalization. As we have seen in the preceding chapters, globalization in the sense of a growing interconnectedness and interdependence of the world is an ancient historical process. Yet the single word that defines the process has been slow to emerge. As a survey of newspapers, magazines, and government reports shows, the meaning of the term itself has undergone considerable changes as the pace of globalization has quickened and its scope enlarged. Rising criticism of the consequences of globalization has come to define the process. Judging by the number of times the word has been used, globalization in both its positive and negative connotations has taken a back seat, and two of the more operational aspects of economic integration that appear to affect the middle class in the developed world have come to the front burner: outsourcing or offshoring.

Frustrating the discussion, the much touted word *globalization* means all things to all people. In their book *Globalization: A Short History*, German historians Jürgen Osterhammel and Niels P. Petersson take a shot at journalists for trying to sound profound by using the word *globalization*. The term, they say, is in danger of becoming just another word generously used in the art of terminological name-dropping. Yet they recognize that the popularity of the term may be due to its ability to fulfill a legitimate need: to give us a name for the times in which we live.[1] The times we live in surely have shaped the way we perceive the term. To trace how the word has evolved in the public perception, I consulted the electronic database Factiva. A combined product of the archives of Reuters news agency and Dow Jones News Retrieval system, the electronic archive of some eight thousand newspapers, magazines, and reports worldwide is as good a source as any for the job.[2] In Factiva's archives, the term *globalization* (with an "s") first appears in 1979 in an administrative document of the European Economic Community, obscure like a tiny dot of light in the night sky. The frequency with which the term reappeared accelerated progressively over the late 1980s, becoming increasingly more visible, like a comet approaching the earth. From a mere two in 1981, the number of items mentioning globalization had grown to 57,235 by 2001. Usage of the word then dropped through 2003. Its use climbed again to 49,722 in 2005 before sliding in 2006, reaching 43,448 that October.

The flurry of sightings of this contested word may thus be subsiding, but the intense focus on the subject has illuminated public understanding of the phenomenon. There is a quiet but growing acceptance of the fact that for all its al-

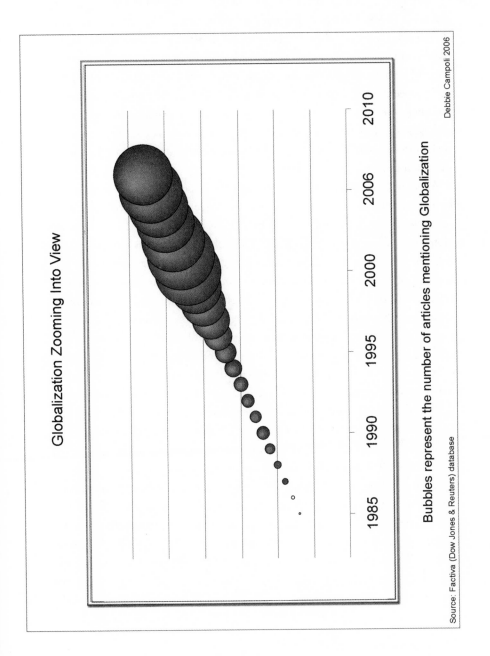

Globalization Zooming Into View

Bubbles represent the number of articles mentioning Globalization

Source: Factiva (Dow Jones & Reuters) database

Debbie Campoli 2006

leged evil consequences, the trend of an increasing integration and interdependence of the world that globalization signifies is here to stay. Erstwhile critics of globalization now say they are not opposed to it; they are simply calling for "alter-globalization," or an alternative approach to managing the irreversible trend of globalization. Their new slogan, now heard at demonstrations outside WTO meetings or Group of Eight summits of developed country leaders, is "another world is possible." The new buzzwords that have come to replace globalization in public discourse are specific consequences of the same trend, such as "outsourcing" of jobs and "offshoring" of manufacturing facilities from the developed to the developing world.

As we will see in this chapter, although the discussion of globalization has been essentially ahistoric, the evolution of the word itself is directly linked to recent socioeconomic and cultural history. In countless articles mentioning globalization over the past four decades, the phenomenon has been seen as the result of expanding trade, investments, and deliberate policies of governments and corporations rather than as a continuum or the accumulated outcome of millennia of different human urges. A brief survey of the last four decades of the twentieth century—the period during which the word *globalization* has evolved and come to occupy the center stage of public debate—will help to situate the idea behind the word in its proper historical context.

We have seen how the knowledge about the known world has grown through trade, warfare, the spread of religion, and exploration. The notion that we live on a round planet had to arise before one could imagine globalization or, as *Webster's Dictionary* defined it in 1961, "making worldwide in scope or application." The first terrestrial globe as a product of human imagination existed in the early fifteenth century, and the credit for creating the earliest surviving terrestrial globe goes to a Nuremberg geographer named Martin Behaim, who built it in 1492. It was certainly no accident that in the same year Christopher Columbus set out for the East by going west and ushered in hemispheric integration. Although Columbus is not believed to have seen Behaim's globe before his historic journey, the globe clearly shows why Columbus took the Atlantic route to the spice country. Behaim's globe marked the squarish territory across the Atlantic as China and India.

SPUTNIK AND AMNESTY INTERNATIONAL

Although *globalization*'s first appearance in *Webster's* in 1961 did not address the issue of time and space compression, it is fair to assume that the reality of a shrinking world set the scene for coining the term. In many ways technological change had reinforced the notion of one world. On the morning of 4 October 1957, a Russian rocket blasted off the launchpad at the Baikonur Cosmodrome to launch the world's first artificial satellite. *Sputnik* circled the earth every ninety-six minutes, emitting a radio signal that could be heard from everywhere on the globe under its flight path. The era of global communication was born, dramatically shrinking the world. In 1964, for the first time in Olympic history thrilling images of triumphs and failures at the Tokyo Olympics were transmitted live all over the globe. Five years later television viewers around the world could watch the same image of the earth seen by the crew of the moon-bound *Apollo 11* craft speeding through outer space. The photo of the earth rising over the moon—the Earthrise—taken by the *Apollo 11* crew in 1969 has since become the iconic image of the planet we call home. In 1961, the year *globalization* entered the dictionary, the postwar world's first nongovernmental organization to care about the planet was set up: the World Wildlife Fund. It was also the year that a Catholic lawyer and a Quaker founded the world's first human rights organization, Amnesty International.

Although clearly related to the growing integration of the world, those events were not then linked with globalization. As we will see, the word began to be used as a bureaucratic and later business buzzword in the 1970s and 1980s, and its currency expanded with the visibly growing economic integration of the world. Both the frequency with which the term *globalization* was used and its changing meaning are directly related to economic and political changes in the world. Although the globalization of manufacturing and sale of products developed slowly until the mid-1980s, the process got a significant boost with the rise of electronic banking and the Big Bang financial reform in Britain of 1986. The growing liberalization of capital markets promoted by the International Monetary Fund (IMF), the successful conclusion of the GATT (General Agreement on Tariffs and Trade) round, and the signing of NAFTA (North American Free Trade Agreement) combined to intensify global integration to an unprecedented level. The number of stories about globalization—and especially positive ones—reached a new high between 1995 and 1997. Concerns about the negative consequences of untrammeled market-led expansion—synonymous with globalization—began growing in the mid-1990s, snowballed in the years following the Asian financial crisis of 1997, and finally exploded into anger at the WTO summit in Seattle in 1999. By 2001, when the number of articles mentioning globalization reached a record high, they were no longer focused on defining the new phenomenon or discussing how it was promoting growth. A large proportion of the press articles reported a backlash against the perceived evil of globalization or described the antiglobalization movement. Globalization thus reached the widest public consciousness just at the time when the buzzword turned into a curse. As a British observer shrewdly noted, "It was the anti-globalization movement that really put globalization on the map." The word has existed since the 1960s, he wrote, "but the protests against this allegedly new process, which its opponents condemn as a way of ordering people's lives, brought globalization out of the financial and academic worlds and into everyday current affairs jargon."[3]

GLOBALIZATION = PROTECTIONISM

Judging by its occurrence in the electronic database in the first two decades of its existence, the term *globalization* was rarely used—and then only in a figurative sense, to mean an aggregate number, rather than in an all-encompassing geographic sense. Yet it did not take long for the word to provoke controversy. In 1977 bureaucrats in European Economic Community introduced their so-called globalization scheme of imposing tariffs on the textile exports of poor countries. A globalization of tariffs was necessary, they argued, in order to be equitable. In reality this was a device to restrict textile imports from major suppliers like Hong Kong and South Korea, and the plan provoked strong opposition.[4]

Use of the word in a similar vein continued for a number of years. The British newspaper the *Guardian* reported in 1981 that "the developing countries wish to do away with the idea of globalization, by which Third World exports are aggregated for the purpose of imposing import controls." A *Wall Street Journal* report in the same year said: "Exporters are most fearful that any new MFA [Multi-fiber Agreement] pact would include a 'globalization' clause, which would allow importers to set overall quotas for imports from all sources. In effect, such a clause, the exporters say, would allow discrimination against strong competitors such as Hong Kong, Taiwan and South Korea."[5]

The first major switch in the meaning of *globalization* came in the early 1980s when, thanks to the GATT negotiations, trade barriers started falling and manufacturing industries of the developed countries began moving to low-wage countries. With the greater ease of connecting with different parts of the world, the term *globalization* was increasingly used in its original Webster's sense of making things "worldwide in scope and application."

The revolution in transport and communication that began in the 1970s opened the door wide for the large-scale transport of goods and people and the rapid transfer of information. The five-hundred-seat Boeing Jumbo Jet was rolled into service in 1970. The containerization of cargo had grown during the Vietnam War and, by seamlessly transferring cargo from ship to truck and train, had sharply lowered freight costs. The medium of exchange—the currency used for international trading—also underwent a dramatic change. With the end of the gold standard and the floating of the U.S. dollar in 1971, trading in currency became a major part of world business. The development of an electronic money transfer and stock trading system, combined with financial market reform, opened up a whole new area of global commerce. Money converted into electronic zeroes and ones could circle the globe in a flash. Thanks to the opening of new markets in reforming developing economies and growth in developed countries, opportunities arose for spreading that digitized cash. The early 1980s thus marked the development of general theories about globalization and attempts at the conceptualization of a process that had crept into business practice in the 1970s. In a seminal article entitled "The Globalization of Markets" and published in the *Harvard Business Review* in May 1983, Ted Levitt advanced a thesis that caught fire: "The world's needs and desires have been irrevocably homogenized. This makes the multinational corporation obsolete and the global corporation absolute." According to Levitt, homogenization was possible because, unlike multinational companies, which adjusted their products and practices for different countries at high costs, global corporations operated as though the entire world were a single market. They sold the same products in the same way everywhere, at relatively low costs. "Only companies that adopt a global approach to markets will achieve long-term success," Levitt predicted.[6]

Levitt's essay and later his book of the same title started a scramble among the world's multinational companies to go global, in their actual operations as well as in the images they projected. One of Levitt's most famous disciples was Maurice Saatchi of the advertising giant Saatchi and Saatchi. He set about establishing his firm as a global operation that would market new global brands with global advertising campaigns. The firm's ad campaign for British Airways, "the world's favorite airline," showed a sci-fi–like scene of Manhattan Island landing in London's Heathrow Airport. Another Saatchi and Saatchi global ad campaign in the same period sought to turn a Danish lager into a global brand. It featured a truck bearing the distinctive Carlsberg beer logo in different world settings with the slogan "Carlsberg: Probably the best beer in the world."

Levitt's essay also provided the occasion, in a *Financial Times* article in July

1984, for the first headline to use the word *globalization.* Levitt's work was followed in 1985 by business guru Kenichi Ohmae's *Triad Power.* The Japanese head of McKinsey and Company elaborated on the main factors behind the growing globalization of industries and products and laid down the business strategy for the age of globalization.[7]

Business publications noted that a globalization strategy allowed a company to overcome the limitation of a small home market by developing larger markets abroad through advertisements. Executives in different parts of industry felt it was essential to globalize whatever business they were in because everything, including taste, was being globalized.[8] The word also came to be associated with taking production offshore to low-cost countries and thus resisting union demands for wage hikes. Ford Motor Company's chairman Philip Caldwell observed in 1984 that "the globalization of the auto industry, marked by increased competition from countries with substantially lower labor and materials costs, is forcing automakers here to reconsider product investment strategies."[9] The deindustrialization and job loss that this strategy brought to automobile towns like Flint, Michigan, offered material for a biting documentary by Michael Moore, *Roger and Me,* in 1989. It railed against the selfish corporate policy of General Motors Corporation that left thirty thousand workers in Flint in the lurch by relocating its operation to Mexico. It may have been one of the first antiglobalization films, even though globalization as business jargon had not yet entered the lexicon of contestation.

INTERNATIONAL TRADE IS THE PAST, GLOBALIZATION IS THE FUTURE

Newspapers at the time remarked, in wide-eyed wonder, on this new phenomenon that had begun to change the North American industrial landscape. A Canadian newspaper reported: "Industry rumors have it that Ford's next small car could come from Mazda Motor Corp. of Japan, in which Ford has a 25 per cent interest. GM has equity in several Asian auto makers. All of this, analysts say, points to a 'globalization' of the automobile industry."[10] A decade later, supply-chain management and the practice of assembling product parts produced in different corners of the world had become so widespread that the American Apparel Manufacturers Association (AAMA) even came up with a campaign theme: MADE ON THE PLANET EARTH. The association announced that in order to compete against low-cost, foreign apparel producers, it would develop worldwide sourcing as well as exporting. Explaining the strategy Norman Fryman, the incoming chairman of AAMA, said: "The point is that it doesn't make a difference where you are making the goods, so long as you can get the right products at the right price at the right time."[11] A newspaper supplement produced on the occasion proclaimed: "International Trade Is the Past. Globalization Is the Future."

It was, however, not fancy apparel produced from multiple sources but a bright orange plastic container of liquid detergent that became the unlikely embodiment of a globalized product. In the winter of 1983 Proctor and Gamble's multinational team developed a liquid detergent for simultaneous release in the United States and Japan, calling it Liquid Tide in the United States and Bonus 2000 in Japan. As a company official explained, by thinking about a new product on a global basis from the start it was saving years of development for other markets. According to the *Financial Times,* the orange plastic container of detergent represented one of Proctor and Gamble's "first steps on the road to what is becoming known as 'globalization,' the development, production and sale of products on a near-global basis."[12] The globalization craze soon extended to other sectors of the economy. "This time the word is 'globalization' and refers to a growing trend by airlines to stop thinking in terms of national boundaries," noted a Canadian newspaper in 1988. "Today, carriers are linking together in international partnerships as never before, and the trend seems likely to accelerate."[13]

The wave of deregulation launched by the conservative governments of Ronald Reagan and Margaret Thatcher in the 1980s, propelled by technological advances that allowed fast flow of information and funds, laid the groundwork for what was hailed as the "globalization of financial markets."[14] By the end of 1985, the world's major stock markets were working around the clock. Newspapers noted that "most major U.K. and European share offerings are now made up of portions to be sold outside of their domestic market and for investors this global view has created new opportunities."[15] In the twenty-four-hour trading environment set up earlier by the first American electronic stock market, the National Association of Securities Dealers Automated Quotations (NASDAQ) rose to prominence in 1985. It linked its network to the London exchange. Globalization of financial markets became a reality.[16]

The so-called Big Bang financial reform of 1986 in Britain that opened up the country's financial market also brought a dramatic change in the financial world. By allowing foreign financial institutions and brokerage firms to operate in Britain, the Thatcher government created an opening for capital flow across national borders that would soon create a global capital market. "Though the concept of globalization has swiftly become a hot cliché, it is not an empty one," a finance writer commented on the eve of Big Bang reform. "No one is questioning the assertion that London's autumnal reforms will transform the world's securities markets."[17] He said that "the ultimate rationale for globalization" was that the efficient use of capital requires free access to the world's best rates of return while artificial boundaries and regulations distort the flow of capital and hinder the development of national economies. Globalization now had a new definition given by bankers. "'Globalization' is a short-hand term for the various forces transforming capital markets and the financial services industry on a world-wide basis."[18]

American Banker magazine, which among others gave a great deal of attention to this new phenomenon, analyzed the forces behind globalization as increasing international mobility of capital across national boundaries, reflected in a shift of American jobs overseas as companies sought to lower their costs; technology, in the form of computer communications; and so-called financial engineering or new techniques for raising funds like interest rate and currency swaps.[19] Globalization was now seen as an inescapable trend. *American Banker* defined "globalization" as the world-girdling reach of today's lending, deposit-taking, and capital-raising functions. It noted that between 1985 and 1987 alone, the annual volume of international bank lending grew an astonishing 62 percent—to $5.2 trillion from $3.2 trillion.[20] The chairman of the Federal Reserve Bank of New York put it bluntly: "Whether we like it or not, the globalization of financial markets and institutions is a reality. Since that reality has been brought about importantly by technology and innovation, it cannot be reversed in any material way by regulation or legislation."[21] His observation about the irreversible reality of globalization seemed to have been borne out by the way financial market shrugged off the crash of 1987 and moved on.

BLACK MONDAY

With Wall Street's Black Monday panic of 19 October 1987 rippling through the high-technology trading rooms around the world, the danger of twenty-four-hour trading in a globalized market hit home. But it was also clear that there was no retreat from the core forces such as advances in communications and computer technology and deregulation of financial markets that had contributed to the crisis. "The crash has not stopped firms from proceeding with their globalization programs," a finance industry leader was quoted as saying. "But we will see a more cautious, rational approach to expansion now."[22]

While the strengthening of global capital markets served as the engine of globalization, the upgrading of the developed world's computing and communications infrastructure and the resultant fall in cost led to a massive increase in cross-border information flows. That in turn speeded up investment flow and the expansion of markets worldwide. Louis Uchitelle, writing in the *New York Times* in 1989, summed up the buoyant mood of companies taking part in a globalized market:

> Globalization is emerging as corporate America's strategy of choice for the 1990s, one heralded in an early 1989 issue of the Harvard Business Review as a main road to industrial prowess. In the name of globalization, U.S. companies' overseas spending on plants and equipment has revived for the first time in a decade. Executives increasingly speak as if the United States were no longer home port. "The United States does not have an automatic call on our resources," said Cyrill Siewert, chief financial officer at Colgate-Palmolive Co. of New York, which then sold more toothpaste, soaps and other toiletries outside the United States than inside.[23]

That sense of the inevitable was echoed by Cynthia Barnum and Natasha Walniansky writing in *Management Review:*

> Whether we like it or not, whether we understand it or not, it's happening all around us, 24 hours a day. Ideas, takeover plans and business are traveling east, west, north and south by telephone, fax and overnight mail, while goods, services and capital are circling the globe by airplane, ship and electronic transfer. These billions of crisscrossing transactions make up the process we call globalization, the vastly accelerated rate of business interaction that characterizes life on this planet as we head into the 21st century.

Barnum and Walniansky also questioned the validity of thinking in strictly national terms. American jobs are being sent offshore and foreign investment is coming to America. "What can we do about it?" they asked and answered, "Buy American? But what if that 'American' GTE product happens to be manufactured in Taiwan?"[24] In December 1993 a retail business publication even pronounced: "Globalization is the single most important issue confronting retail industry executives now and into the 21st century."[25] As companies saw it, globalization was not just a trend, it was a goal to be achieved, almost a survival strategy for the new world. The first time newspapers described some companies as about to "go global" was in 1983. By 1988 the phrase "go global" was used fifty-two times. It shot up to 236 the next year and steadily grew to a peak in

2000, when some 2,600 articles used the term. However, by 2002 it was no longer *the* favored term to describe a company's strategy in public. The number of articles using the term sharply dropped in 2002 to 1,833 items. More about that decline later.

By 1995 globalization had come to mean a production system involving a borderless world. As one writer wrote, "Time was that a car was designed, built in its entirety, and marketed from Detroit. Now, the design centre for the American (and Japanese) car industry is California. Assembly is done in lower-wage, lower-skill states such as Tennessee or Alabama. The thousands of parts that go into the car may come from Malaysia, Mexico, or Mississauga, Ontario. This same globalization trend has hit almost every other industry."[26]

GO-GO GLOBALIZATION

There was palpable excitement—and some worry—among companies about going global. To globalize became the corporate mantra. Newspaper and industry publications in the early 1990s were filled with news about companies busy setting up their globalization strategies. Conferences and seminars were held to learn the globalization business strategy and how to take advantage of this new method to boost profit. There was panic among many companies who were bewildered by this rush to go global and worried about losing out to the competition. The globalization craze infected other entities, too. The South Korean government and its state-backed business conglomerates—the *chaebols*—launched a globalization campaign as a means of getting ahead.

A breathless *Fortune* magazine report on globalization of retail industry in 1995 said, "Mega-merchants like Wal-Mart and Carrefour are building monster stores worldwide at a breakneck rate. The planet isn't big enough for all of them." This massive deployment of new stores, the report said, threatened to collapse the price umbrella that once sheltered global retailers when they moved into virgin territory. So a race was on by merchants to transform their store names into global brands, much like Coke and Pepsi.[27]

The World Bank came in with its own imprimatur. "Globalization drives growth," the World Bank proclaimed in a report, *Global Economic Prospects and the Developing Countries, 1995.* "The integration of developing countries in the global economy and the increased openness of their markets provides a major, perhaps the most important, opportunity to raise incomes in both developing and industrial countries in the long term."[28]

In late March 1997, barely three months before the globalized world of Asia faced the biggest crash of the post–World War II years, the *Wall Street Journal's* normally cautious reporter G. Pascal Zachary waxed ecstatic about a new golden age brought about by globalization: "Economists are saying that the global economy is showing signs of entering an extraordinary period of long-term growth." Globalization in the form of a vast expansion of economic freedom and property rights, coupled with reductions in the scope of government and an explosion in trade and private investment, was said to have "produced a world growth rate in the past three years nearly double that of the prior two decades." Barring a major war or environmental catastrophe, Harvard economist Jeffrey Sachs was quoted as saying, "Economic growth will raise the living standards of more people in more parts of the world than at any prior time in history." Perhaps understandably, Domingo Cavallo, the architect of Argentina's dramatic economic restructuring in the 1990s, was euphoric. "We've entered a golden age that will last for decades," he said. Even United Nations Secretary General Kofi Annan, not usually given to hyperbole about business, thought the world entering "a new golden age." In his view, soaring private investment and technical advances would enable poorer nations "to leapfrog what others had to go through to develop."[29]

A survey of the database of articles relating to globalization reveals a time lag between the spread of globalization and its consequences and media awareness about it. The trend of globalization of capital markets, investment, and trade reached its high point in 1995–96, but public awareness of the trend did not spread much until about four years later, when a wider section of people felt its impact. Cross-border capital flows—minus foreign direct investment—rose to $1.2 trillion in 1996 from $536 billion four years earlier. Foreign investment, which had averaged $26.2 billion between 1986 and 1990, rose nearly ten times to more than $250 billion in 1996.[30] Yet the number of articles in the press mentioning the phenomenon grew slowly. President Bill Clinton, who spearheaded the effort to sign the NAFTA accord and emerged as the most ardent champion of globalization, though, was aware of the opposition it would encounter.

Addressing the World Bank and International Monetary Fund meeting in October 1995, President Clinton noted the immense force of integration and disintegration released by globalization and urged caution in managing its consequences. "It is the most intensive period of economic change since the industrial revolution," he said, noting the enormous advantages for those who can embrace and succeed in the new global economy. "But," he cautioned, "these forces have also made all our societies more vulnerable to disturbances that once may have seemed distant but which now directly affect the jobs and liveli-hoods in every nation in the world, from the richest to the poorest." Clinton concluded with the observation that "interdependence among nations has grown so deep that literally it is now meaningless to speak of a sharp dividing line between foreign and domestic policy."[31]

Clinton found out how accurate the observation was two years later when his fast-track authority for WTO was blocked in Congress. In 1999 he had to abandon the WTO summit in Seattle in the face of massive demonstrations against the trade body and globalization.

GLOBALIZATION'S "BAMBOO EFFECT"

Although the "downside" of globalization was first mentioned in a newspaper article in 1989, *downside* became more commonplace in association with glob-alization in the late 1990s and peaked in 2000. An often-mentioned downside of globalization was the job loss suffered in developed countries when compa-nies moved their operations offshore to low-wage economies. The impact of offshoring was being felt not only in the United States but in Japan as well. The unprecedented rise in the value of the yen resulting from the Plaza Accord of 22 September 1985, in which agreement was reached on devaluing the U.S. dollar in relation to the Japanese yen and the Deutschemark, forced major Japanese exporters to move their production offshore. This process of the globalization of Japanese industry came to be known colloquially as the "bamboo effect." In-dustrial operations in Japan were hollowed out like bamboo stalks, leaving only the shells of head offices on Japanese soil. Although workers were absorbed, in keeping with Japanese practice, globalization raised, for the first time, the fear of unemployment and shorter working hours in Japan.[32]

The sharply rising number of headlines kept the importance of globalization in public view, but the tone was increasingly negative as the number of articles about the antiglobalization sentiment skyrocketed. Even in the year after the Asian Crisis of 1997, which turned globalization from a miracle to a menace, only sixty-seven articles mentioned antiglobalization sentiment. But as the domino-like impact of the Asian Crisis rippled through the world from Brazil to Russia and began taking its toll in developed nations, the phrases "backlash against globalization" and "antiglobalization" entered public discourse and became increasingly associated with the phenomenon that had so far been seen as the driver for growth and prosperity. Newspaper articles mentioning an antiglobalization mood rose to 292 in 2000 and then shot up to nearly nine thousand items by 2003.

In fact, three years before the Seattle fiasco, two of the high priests of globalization, the president of the World Economic Forum in Davos, Klaus Schwab, and its secretary, Claude Smadja, had warned: "A mounting backlash against its effects, especially in the industrial democracies, is threatening a very disruptive impact on economic activity and social stability in many countries. . . . The mood in these democracies is one of helplessness and anxiety."[33] This was a highly significant acknowledgment coming from the leaders of a forum closely associated with corporate-led globalization. The World Economic Forum, a club for business executives and government officials that had been assembling in the Swiss ski resort of Davos since 1971, had emerged in the late 1990s as a champion of globalization, and the discussion at the annual meeting of the World Economic Forum had served as a weathervane for the world business climate.

That feared backlash came soon as globalization hit a massive road bump on the morning of 2 July 1997. A devaluation of the Thai baht triggered a currency stampede by edgy investors that soon blew into a full-fledged crisis in Asia. Billions of dollars invested in Asia evaporated as loans were recalled by panicky foreign banks and investors, factories were shut down, debt-ridden assets were auctioned off, and tens of thousands took to the streets to protest. Within months several governments in the region fell. Critics of globalization now compared the movement to a big casino where the big boys played for big stakes and little people lost their shirts. Economic globalization was seen as the root cause of the turmoil. From a business buzzword, *globalization* soon turned into a cussword. It was the source of all evil. Globalization meant exploitation by the multinationals, ravaging of the natural resources, slaughter of dolphins and sea turtles caught in the net of globalized fishing, pollution of the earth, destruction of developing countries' cultures and traditions, McDonaldization of eating habits, and rape of the sovereignty of weaker nations by the powerful working through the WTO.

The aftermath of the Asian Crisis made it clear that the growing interdependence that had pulled many nations out of poverty could just as easily push them back into misery.[34] With the world economy increasingly integrated, the malfunctioning of even a small part, like Russia, could have global repercussions. Kofi Annan compared the globalized world to a small boat. "[We cannot] afford to ignore the condition of our fellow passengers on this little boat," he said. "If they are sick, all of us risk infection. And if they are angry, all of us can easily get hurt." India's influential newspaper the *Hindu* headlined an article "Globalisation Fraught with Danger." A Canadian newspaper editorial opined, "Globalization seems to have us in its jaws."[35]

In his State of the Union address in January 1999, President Clinton implicitly admitted that globalization had run into trouble: "I think trade has divided us and divided Americans outside this chamber for too long. Somehow we have to find a common ground. . . . We have got to put a human face on the global economy." With a gesture toward his critics on the left he embraced a new International Labor Organization initiative "to raise labor standards around the world" and pledged to work for a treaty "to ban abusive child labor everywhere in the world." He also promised trade rules that would promote "the dignity of work and the rights of workers" and "protect the environment."[36]

Sensing the mounting anger against the supposed ill effects of globalization, a succession of world leaders including Kofi Annan, who only months earlier predicted a "golden age," issued warnings. Annan called for giving "a human face" to globalization. Speaking at the annual meeting of the World Economic Forum in Davos, Yashwant Sinha, finance minister of India, said governments crucially needed to balance liberal markets with social concerns. "The process of globalisation must be seen as a process of democratisation . . . [otherwise] those people who are marginalised will be a threat to globalisation." Sinha warned that for those disenfranchised by the process, "globalization will remain a 13-letter dirty word."[37]

THE WTO KILLS, KILL THE WTO

It was indeed a dirty word. Globalization's formal fall from grace came a few months later in Seattle, when fifty thousand antiglobalization demonstrators shut down the first summit of the World Trade Organization. The year 1999 marked the emergence of a globalized antiglobalization movement, and the word *globalization* entered the lexicon as a cussword that opponents felt must be contested by all means. Some protesters threw confetti and chanted, "The WTO kills; kill the WTO."[38] The frustrated head of the World Trade Organization, New Zealander Mike Moore, lashed out at his opponents in Seattle: "For some, the attacks on economic openness are part of a broader assault on internationalism—on foreigners, immigration, a more pluralistic and integrated world. Anti-globalization becomes the latest chapter in the age-old call to separatism, tribalism and racism."[39]

Moore's was a rather lone voice in 1999 when passion—and the media focus—was on the antiglobalization movement. The public became aware of the globalization phenomenon largely because of the protests. Antiglobalization sentiments helped define several heroes who had emerged in different continents to give voice to the disparate opposition that challenged the free market and an IMF-led world economic order. Canadian Maude Barlow emerged as a global leader of the antiglobalization movement, opposing every aspect of economic deregulation. In France a mustachioed, pipe-smoking sheep farmer named Jose Bové shot to fame by leading a campaign against the fast-food chain McDonald's as a symbol of American trade "hegemony" and economic globalization. American anti-WTO activist leader Laurie Wallach became a familiar face in Seattle. Images of protesters battling police and breaking down Starbucks storefronts were on the front pages of newspapers. Starbucks was a symbol of business globalization, accused of exploiting poor coffee farmers in the developing world to make big bucks.

In the two years that followed the Seattle protests, the term *globalization* appeared in tens of thousands of articles. Not only was it a more visible phenomenon, it was no longer an abstract word. It was jargon used by business gurus and consultants, a catchall for everything that was wrong with the world. My electrician in New Haven knew globalization as a bad thing that destroyed the rain forest.

The transformation of globalization into a dirty word that began in the late 1990s grew apace in the months following Seattle. Argentina, which had followed the IMF recommendations to some extent, found itself in dire economic straits with its currency crumbling and millions thrown out of jobs. The World Bank, which had earlier listed Argentina as a success story in its report on globalization, quickly removed the reference when the crisis happened.[40] Russians, already struggling since the collapse of the Soviet empire, were reduced to penury in the crisis after 1997. Thailand, which had earned plaudits from the IMF for its management of the economy, was looking at massive bankruptcy and layoffs. Indonesia's crumbling economy was on its knees, surviving on the IMF dole. The long-time critics of globalization had a field day. India's leading environmentalist activist, Vandana Shiva, said, "Globalisation can best be described as economic totalitarianism—a totalitarianism that is leading to another frightening extreme in the form of fundamentalism."[41]

While the free market and export-led model associated with globalization had been humbled by the end of the 1990s, Ted Levitt's theory about the globalization of markets also had ended its triumphant run. Localization became the new mantra. Owners of global brands who had enjoyed forays into new virgin markets now worried about local competition and a resurgence of local rather than global tastes. The concept of globalization of markets was ready for a revision.

In his State of the Union address on 27 January 2000, President Clinton reaffirmed his belief that globalization is "the central reality of our time" but added that "globalization is about more than economics." Unchastened by Seattle, he said, "Our purpose must be to bring together the world around freedom and democracy and peace, and to oppose those who would tear it apart." Three years later, President Clinton admitted to me in an interview that a lot of people are angry about globalization because "the system is not working for about half the people on earth." He argued that since there cannot be a global economic system without building a global social system, "we need to have more labor and environmental provisions in the trade agreements."[42]

GLOBALIZATION IS HERE TO STAY

By the end of the 1990s, most global brand owners were switching chief executives as their share prices plummeted in response to slowing growth rates. In March 2000, in a signed article in the *Financial Times*, Douglas Daft, Coca-Cola's new chief executive, offered a glimpse of the new thinking. Coca-Cola, Daft wrote, had traditionally been a "multi-local" company, but as globalization had gathered pace, it had centralized its decision-making processes and standardized its practices. The current phase of globalization required "nimbleness, speed, transparency and local sensitivity." The next big evolutionary step of "going global," Daft wrote, now has to be "going local." Contrary to the fear expressed by globalization's critics that it would homogenize products with cultural contents, it led to a broadening of choices available to consumers.[43] This *Financial Times* column was symbolic of changes in the appreciation of globalization that had come from many quarters. As a Manila newspaper put it: "Globalization is a much-abused word. . . . Infantile leftists equate it with imperialism. Politicians use it to appear intelligent. They rabble-rouse against it to appear populist. From Seattle to Manila, globalization is the word that everybody loves to kick around." The writer concluded, "It's ok to be afraid of globalization. It's ok even to hate it. But whether we like it or not, globalization is here to stay."[44]

One U.S. economist, Robert Litan, acknowledged the problem globalization faced from a skeptical American public and said in 2000 that "more must be done to address Americans' continuing anxieties about globalization and, indeed, economic change more broadly. . . . We should embrace the opportunities that globalization affords, ease the anxieties it generates, and reform and strengthen the international economic institutions created to promote both global economic stability and growth."[45]

The World Bank published a study of globalization, acknowledging problems that it has caused but delicately pointing out: "it may not be surprising (though it is not very helpful) that 'globalization' is sometimes used in a much broader economic sense, as another name for capitalism or the market economy. When used in this sense the concerns expressed are really about key features of the market economy, such as production by privately-owned and profit-motivated corporations, frequent reshuffling of resources according to changes in supply and demand, and unpredictable and rapid technological change."[46]

Having won a great victory in Seattle, the opponents of globalization began searching for an alternative program. Their opportunity came with the first meeting of the World Social Forum. The WSF was the brainchild of a group of NGOs that wished to challenge the orthodoxy represented by the Davos-based World Economic Forum. The first meeting of the WSF was in January 2001 in Porto Alegre, Brazil. Their official motto: "Another world is possible." Canadian author Naomi Klein, who has been a leading opponent of corporate globalization, wrote:

> After a year and a half of protests against the World Trade Organization, the World Bank and the International Monetary Fund, the World Social Forum was billed as an opportunity for this emerging movement to stop screaming about what it is against and start articulating what it is for. If Seattle was, for many people, the coming-out party of a resistance movement, then, according to Soren Ambrose, policy analyst with 50 Years Is Enough, "Porto Alegre is the coming-out party for the existence of serious thinking about alternatives."[47]

THE SHOCK OF 9/11

The need to devise serious alternatives to the current globalization process gained urgency from the terrorist attack of 9/11 on the United States. The carnage in New York and Washington raised ever more urgently the questions about the viability of an increasingly open world. Already critics viewed globalization as an Americanization of the world through cultural domination. Terrorism was now added to the growing list of negative effects of what passed for globalization. The 9/11 attack provided the latest evidence that growing interconnectedness not only allowed the exploitation of illegal migrants but opened the doors to terrorists and criminals as well. The terrorists plotted their attack on the Internet and via cell phones, and they bought their tickets online. Globalization was also seen to be at fault for causing the anger that fuelled the terrorists' assault. Regular protesters were put on the defensive, however, by the fact that the 9/11 attack was seen by many as the most violent form of antiglobalization protest. The leading French antiglobalization group Attac issued a strong condemnation of the 9/11 attacks. In the midst of shock and anger, the planned antiglobalization protests during the World Bank–IMF annual meeting in Washington were canceled. Even in Seattle a few weeks later, a demonstration to mark the second anniversary of their successful demonstration drew about two hundred protesters, compared with more than a thousand the previous year. In the chastened mood after the 9/11 attacks, Congress gave President George W. Bush the fast-track authority to negotiate a global trade agreement that they had earlier denied President Clinton. A WTO summit meeting that had been scuttled in Seattle was held in Doha, Qatar. In a chastened mood about growing danger to globalization, the meeting participants agreed to launch a new round of global trade talks designed to reduce poverty through trade called the "Doha Development Round."

Not surprisingly, the number of newspaper articles about antiglobalization sentiments or movements dropped from the all-time high of 8,718 in 2001 to 6,021 the next year and steadily downward to 1,695 in 2005. However, preoccupation with the antiglobalization mood remained much higher than interest in globalization as a whole. Mentions of globalization in 2004 dropped to 24,516, to rise only slightly in 2005 to 26,627. The number of both articles mentioning globalization and headlined articles has been gradually dropping ever since 2005. This falling reference to globalization in newspapers is not because the novelty of globalization has diminished. Globalization is still mentioned often and as a fact of life, but gone are the excitement and passion of the late 1990s in describing the phenomenon.

FROM ANTI- TO ALTER-GLOBALIZATION

With the passage of time, the antiglobalization movement staged a comeback more outside than within the United States. When the World Economic Forum moved its annual meeting from Davos to New York in early 2002, protesters greeted the participants. But given the tight security arrangements and concern about terrorist attacks in the aftermath of 9/11, the protests were more restrained. The venue of large antiglobalization protests had shifted to Porto Alegre when the World Social Forum held its first meeting there in January 2001.[48] In 2003 the WSF meeting moved to Mumbai, India. There, participants cheered lustily for a new adherent to their movement, Nobel laureate and former World Bank official Joseph Stiglitz. Author of *Globalization and Its Discontents,* Stiglitz excoriated the IMF for imposing a fundamentalist dogma on developing nations with disastrous consequences.

The ministerial meetings of the WTO, first in Doha and then in Cancún, offered further opportunities for antiglobalization groups to gather and protest various ills they blamed on neoliberal policies. Thousands of demonstrators who gathered in Cancún for the WTO ministerial meeting in October 2003 danced with joy after the participants failed to reach agreement on the issue of the removal of Western farm subsidies. A group of developing nations, backed by the demonstrators, banded together to reject an American and European proposal to make limited cuts in farm subsidies. For the protesters it was the beginning of "another world" that they wanted to create—a world in which poorer nations would control their destinies and resist exploitation by the rich.

Perhaps in part out of a concern not to appear as negative about globalization at a time when al-Qaeda terrorists were also attempting to torpedo globalization, and in part out of the need to shed their nihilistic image, the antiglobalization critics adopted a more constructive approach. The habitual critics who gathered at various rallies to denounce globalization—from environmentalists and labor groups to human rights and trade protesters—joined their voices to call for "another globalization." The protesters began implicitly admitting that globalization was not just an insidious plot of corporations or a destructive policy pursued by governments. It was a trend that could not be wished away by antiglobalization slogans.

For a variety of reasons, public opinion in Europe was more accepting of a greater integration of the world than was U.S. public opinion. At the end of 2003 a public opinion poll conducted by Flash Eurobaromètre found that 63 percent of Europeans favored development of globalization and that more than half saw an advantage to themselves with the intensification of globalization. Some 62 percent polled believed that the process of globalization could be controlled and effectively regulated. Nearly 80 percent believed that antiglobalization movements raised valid questions, but more than half found that they were lacking in concrete solutions.[49]

The switch to a new approach in protesters' opposition to globalization was evident during the annual meeting of the WEF in Davos in January 2004. For years, this annual gathering at the trendy Swiss ski resort has given protesters an occasion to demonstrate against globalization and assorted ills of the capitalist system. At this meeting, the protesters said that they still opposed "an exploitative neo-liberal world order in which environmental and social concerns are trampled in the interests of profit and shareholder value," but they now opted for a different tactic. They acknowledged that the increasing integration of the world meant that globalization was irreversible. Instead of pursuing their Quixotic tilting at the globalization windmill, they now pressed for "alter-globalization," or alternative forms of the process they could not stop (the word "alter-globalization" first appeared in a French essay in 2001).[50] "We are not against globalization, we just want another type of globalization that protects the rights of workers and the environment," said Swiss activist Matthias Herfeldt.[51] The alter-globalization campaign now focused on lobbying companies and governments on specific issues, such as negotiating a WTO agreement that would ensure access to medicines for people in developing countries and pressuring the fashion and clothes industry to give up exploitative labor practices. Instead of defying the police and protesting against the WEF, activists organized an alternative conference in Davos called Public Eye on Davos to challenge the WEF and its stated mission of improving the state of the world. The protesters of yesteryear drew quiet satisfaction that as the promoters of alter-globalization they were invited to the table of the "masters of the world" when the Group of Eight industrialized nations met in Evian, France, in early 2003.[52] At the Saint Petersburg summit of the G8 industrial nations in the summer of 2006, Russian President Vladimir Putin even held a summit meeting with the NGOs who favor alter-globalization.

THE THREAT OF OUTSOURCING

The catchall term *globalization* retreated somewhat in 2003–4, ceding the ground to one of the more controversial aspects of the process: outsourcing. The term was first used in 1981 when the chairman of General Motors, Roger B. Smith, said that GM was looking increasingly to outside suppliers as a means of lowering its labor costs and predicted that the practice, known as "outsourcing," would become more common throughout the automobile industry.[53] In 2004 it was not just the automobile industry but the entire service economy that seemed vulnerable to job loss through outsourcing. As the U.S. economy continued its jobless recovery and a presidential election battle gathered steam, the outsourcing of software, back office, and call-center jobs became the hot-button issue for editorial writers and politicians. Globalization was too vague a word for political campaigning, but outsourcing of jobs was an issue everybody understood. Newspaper articles explained the political calculation behind the Democratic Party presidential candidate Senator John Kerry's embrace of outsourcing as a major campaign issue.

At the Democratic Party's electoral primary held in New Hampshire, job loss was a serious issue. From July 2000 to June 2003, New Hampshire lost twenty-one thousand, or nearly 20 percent, of its manufacturing jobs, according to the National Association of Manufacturers. The other states important for Electoral College votes in the 2004 election—California, Illinois, Michigan, Ohio, and Pennsylvania—all saw manufacturing jobs fall by from 15 percent to 18 percent in this period. The next five biggest manufacturing states—Georgia, Indiana, New York, North Carolina, and Wisconsin—also lost from 13 percent to 20 percent of their manufacturing jobs. Nor surprisingly, with the election approaching in November, articles using the word *outsourcing* rose sharply to 60,622 in 2003.

The number of articles with "globalization" or "globalisation" in the text dropped sharply after 2001—from 51,641 to 43,545 in 2004, when the outsourcing issue was rising. In contrast, the number of articles with "outsourcing" in the text rose from 53,259 in 2002 to 96,387 in 2004. Although a small number of jobs had been shipped out because of the outsourcing of service jobs, the novelty of this development was deeply disturbing. In this trend, it was not the usual low-skilled blue-collar workers who were being laid off but highly skilled programmers, engineers, and radiologists who were losing jobs to equally skilled but low-paid foreigners. The clunky and abstract word *globalization* was now less menacing than *outsourcing*—a more urgent and immediate threat to America's white-collar workers. Yet once the heat of the electoral battle dissipated, the number of articles with "outsourcing" in the text dropped sharply to 79,863 in 2005 and has since dropped even more. Since the economy was picking up and the number of jobs lost to outsourcing appeared to be small, outsourcing as a stand-in for globalization also seemed to be losing steam. There also seems to be a fresh look at the impact of globalization on the U.S. economy. Economists from the Federal Reserve Bank chairman on down have noted that recently the globalization of capital markets, combined with a glut of savings outside the United States, has kept U.S. long-term rates low and steady.

Forty years after it made its entrance in the dictionary, *globalization,* the buzzword-turned-cussword of the 1990s, seems to be losing its punch in the public's perception. Although the process of increasing integration and interdependence that the word has always meant continues unabated, "globalization" is invoked less and less frequently to explain prosperity or blame misery. After dominating the public discourse for a decade, it is settling into a quieter existence as the description of a long-term trend rather than a catchall for expressing the anger and frustration generated by untrammeled economic intercourse. The concern and anger instead is now directed more and more at the visible impact of globalization: the offshoring of manufacturing and outsourcing of many business processes to foreign nations.

In a *New York Times* commentary in August 2006, "Why 'Outsourcing' May Lose Its Power as a Scare Word," one columnist argued that the projected job loss of about 280,000 a year was a drop in the bucket for a labor force that amounted to 135 million in July. But not everybody is sure that outsourcing would not grow and come to grab the headlines in another political season. "As the technology improves, and as the quality and experience of offshore work forces improves, the capacity to deliver services electronically will rise," economist Alan Blinder said in the column. Over the long term, far more than the 2 percent of all service workers that has been predicted may be in danger of having their jobs outsourced overseas. "We shouldn't be deluded that this has subsided as an issue," Blinder said.[54]

In 2006 globalization still loomed as a dark cloud over the horizon of American workers, though it did not occasion as many news stories or commentaries as in 2004 or even 2005. Editorial comments and op-eds still reflect gnawing anxiety over globalization but with less stridency and anger. Without directly linking American wage stagnation to the impact of globalization, Treasury Secretary Hank Paulson acknowledged in August 2006 that "unfortunately the clear benefits of trade—such as stronger economic growth, more jobs, and a higher standard of living for Americans—are broader, sometimes take longer to manifest themselves and are less visible than some of the immediate dislocations which are linked to trade."[55]

From bureaucratic jargon to business buzzword, from a tool for miracle growth to an evil plot, and finally from an incitement to protest to a call for an alternative model, alter-globalization, the term *globalization* has evolved, as has the reality of a complex, inextricably connected world that it is invoked to describe. A better way to understand the reality of our interconnected and interdependent world is perhaps not to get embroiled in the semantics of globalization but to examine the forces that drive this interconnection and the historical trajectory it has followed.

Chapter 9 Who's Afraid of Globalization?

[Globalization] is a process that has been going almost throughout recorded history and that has conferred huge benefits. Globalization involves change, so it is often feared, even by those who end up gaining from it. And some do lose in the short run when things change. But globalization is like breathing: It is a not a process one can or should try to stop; of course, if there are obvious ways of breathing easier and better one should certainly do so.
—*Anne O. Krueger, First Deputy Managing Director, International Monetary Fund, 2002*

Globalisation, a word invented to convey the false hope of an integrated, inclusive world, has in reality meant the opposite: the rejection and exclusion of hundreds of millions who contribute little or nothing to production and consumption and are thereby considered useless by 21st-century capitalism.
—*Susan George, Khaleej Times, 2004*

Wednesday, 10 September 2003, seemed to be a typical summer day in Cancún, the popular resort island off Mexico's Yucatán Peninsula.

Anti-WTO protesters confront police in Cancún, Mexico, September 2003. Photo: infernalnoise.com

The turquoise water of the Caribbean shimmered under the midday sun. Along the ten-mile stretch of white sand and gentle waves, thousands of tourists splashed in the warm water and basked lizardlike on the sand. Only the silhouettes of two Mexican navy gunboats on the horizon served as a reminder that it was not an ordinary day in Cancún.

The reason for the presence of those gunboats became apparent as one moved closer to the palatial convention center on the sandy northern tip of the S-shaped island. The ministers of the 149-member World Trade Organization had gathered to discuss issues that affect hundreds of millions of people. Illustrating the impact of the WTO's deliberations on the world, thousands of antiglobalization protesters had also gathered in Cancún in what has become part of the WTO meeting routine. Ever since rioting demonstrators scuttled the WTO summit in Seattle in 1999, every major gathering of global institutions—from the World Bank and International Monetary Fund to the Group of Eight—has had to deal with antiglobalization demonstrators.

Crowd-control fences of steel and wire had been erected at both entrances to the island and around the convention center. Mexican police were determined to avoid another fiasco like Seattle or the bad press brought by the death of a demonstrator in Genoa during the G8 meeting in 2001. Rows of helmeted police with batons and pepper spray stood behind the fence to keep out unauthorized visitors. Perhaps no group assembled in Cancún was more unwelcome than Via Campesina, a farmers' organization that claimed one hundred million members worldwide. Founded in 1993, the group of small farmers and agricultural workers was organized to fight for what its members called "food sovereignty," agrarian reform, and credit and against external debt. The most aggressive members were the Korean farmers who combined their years of experience in public demonstration and martial arts discipline with imaginative protest props. The Korean contingent also had one of the most committed leaders in a middle-aged farmer named Lee Kyung-hae. A stocky man with a broad, friendly face and an easy smile, Lee had set up an experimental farm in South Korea's North Jeolla province. In the 1970s, he had taught students from agricultural colleges about scientific farming and methods for gaining greater crop yields. But his farming life had been a disappointment. Unable to earn enough from his crops, he later lost his land to creditors. He attributed the hardships of Korean farmers to the opening of South Korea's agricultural market to the world and the resultant fall in prices. As the world's twelfth largest trading nation and supplier of world's industrial goods from giant container ships and cars to televisions and cell phones, South Korea had been forced to lower its barriers to agricultural imports. Korean industrialists raked in profits and urban workers made a good living, but farmers—who formed one-tenth of the population in the late twentieth century—were hurting. As the WTO's agricultural exporters exerted steady pressure on Korea's government to remove its import quotas and farm subsidies and lower the 100 percent tariff barriers that shielded Korean growers, the farmers faced ruin. Many farmers, unable to repay their debts, attempted suicide by swallowing insecticide. Lee visited one such farmer's home and wrote: "I could do nothing but listen to the howling of his wife. If you were me, how would you feel?" He showed how he felt in 2002, when he traveled to Geneva, where WTO members deliberated on agricultural trade. Carrying a placard that read, "The WTO Kills Farmers," Lee waged a monthlong hunger strike while camped outside the Centre William Rappard—for the thirtieth time in his life.

A year later, Lee left home again to join forces with the thousands of protesters gathered in Cancún to demonstrate against the WTO. On the morning of 10 September, they had set out from a downtown park heading toward the convention center, where they encountered a steel fence to block their advance. In an unintended irony, the fence was set up just below the billboards that welcomed visitors to the resort city. As the midday sun beat down on them, amid the beating of drums and clanging of cymbals, and cries of "Death to WTO," a group of Korean farmers charged the fence carrying a paper coffin marked WTO. After setting an American flag on fire, hundreds of demonstrators hurled themselves against the steel fence, destroying parts of the barricade. Police rushed in with hoses to douse the flames. Lee, wearing a checkered yellow shirt and a beach hat with a red bandana, climbed to the top of the fence. He tossed out leaflets to the crowd and raised his fist to shout once again, "Death to WTO!" As the crowd chanted and the cameras of the international news media rolled, he suddenly pulled out an old Swiss Army knife and plunged it swiftly into his heart. With a grim determination born of despair, he drove the knife deeper with both hands. As the stunned demonstrators screamed, a bleeding Lee collapsed from his perch. Paramedics rushed him to the hospital, but to no avail. Lee Kyung-hae was pronounced dead in Cancún on 10 September 2003.

Lee's suicide, which made him the first high-profile martyr of the antiglobalization struggle, was a premeditated act. Before leaving for Cancún, he had apparently visited his wife's grave and mowed the grass around it, as if to prepare the ground for his own. In the leaflet he handed out before his death he wrote: "I am 56 years old, a farmer from South Korea who has strived to solve our problems with the great hope in the ways to organize farmers' unions. But I have mostly failed, as many other farm leaders elsewhere have failed. I am crying out my words to you, that have for so long boiled in my body: . . . Take agriculture out of the WTO system."[1]

Slogans like "Take agriculture off the WTO table" and "Restore food sovereignty" have emerged as battle cries in antiglobalization demonstrations, just as the black-framed photo of Lee Kyung-hae has become an obligatory icon of solidarity with the international antiglobalization struggle. Antiglobalization activists like French farmer Jose Bové combine the struggle for food sovereignty with opposition to *malbouffe* (the pejorative term meaning "bad food" was coined in 1981 by Stella and Joël de Rosnay in their book *La malbouffe* to describe unhealthy fast food), exemplified by McDonald's and genetically modified produce. Of course, such opposition is not limited to the world's farmers. The ranks of those who routinely demonstrate in protest of all international meetings—WTO, World Bank, IMF, and G8 summits—have been swelled by discontented parties from every walk of life. In the eye of the protesters and critics, globalization is a curse. They see globalization, as Thai Buddhist critic Sulak Sivaraksa puts it, as "a new demonic religion." "Since globalisation is under the control of the big corporations," Sulak writes, "the media is used to direct us blindly toward the monoculture of more and more technology, of the McWorld of fast food, junk food and the cola and jeans syndrome."[2] In their eyes, globalization has wrought every imaginable ill: increased poverty and inequality, the ruthless exploitation of natural resources, the spread of crime and disease, global terrorism, and ecological catastrophe.

Judging by the depth of their opposition to what passes for globalization, critics clearly do not see the phenomenon as a long-term historical process propelled by multiple forces. They view globalization as deliberate policy choice of groups of people or institutions. Media and academic reports on the myriad ills of globalization sometimes identify a neoliberal political philosophy and its handmaidens, the International Monetary Fund, World Bank, and the World Trade Organization, as the forces behind globalization. At other times globalization is portrayed as shorthand for capitalism or free-market policies. An examination of all the civic organizations that join their voices to condemn globalization could throw light on what bothers them about the growing interconnectedness of the world, but there are too many to list. A cursory look would show their disparate origins and at times competing agendas against globalization: They include anarchists, anticapitalists (socialists and communists), opponents of genetically modified products, environmentalists, antinuclear campaigners, indigenous rights advocates, labor unions, pro- and antimigration lobbies, and anti-sweatshop organizations. They include groups that are antiwar, pro-biodiversity, pro-cultural autonomy, and just plain anti-American. The most important and serious challenge to globalization comes from working-class and white-collar workers in developed countries who fear the loss of their jobs due to competition from low-wage countries. Other factors driving antiglobalization sentiment, although seldom aired in public demonstrations, are people's fear of losing their ethnic or cultural identity under the tide of immigration and anger at the hegemonic culture of a dominant and rich West that will erase or corrupt other cultures.

Environmentalists criticize the export of pollution from rich to poor countries and bemoan the ecological disasters produced in part by globalized trade and tourism. Yet others who accept that trade is a primary driver of economic prosperity still ask, "Has globalization gone too far?"[3] Critics on the left blame neoliberal capitalist globalization for producing inequality and injustice and demand an alternative they call "alter-globalization."[4] The label "antiglobalization" has become a shorthand. Their criticism is against the negative outcomes of the accelerated process of interconnectedness. These problems were there before modern transportation, communication, and highly mobile capitalism made its effect ubiquitous or even before the word *globalization* appeared in our vocabulary.

Throughout history, increasing integration has provoked resistance from those who were subjected to foreign domination or suffered from the arrival of alien goods or unfamiliar ideas. The resistance of those exposed to the key actors of globalization—traders, preachers, adventurers, warriors, and migrants—has come in many forms, ranging from armed opposition to the closure of borders to the imposition of tariffs and trade barriers. Two of history's principal globalizers—Ferdinand Magellan and Captain James Cook—met their deaths at the hands of the natives with whom they attempted connections.[5] What makes the impact of today's globalization appear so different is that it is highly visible. In our media-connected world the visibility of the losers' sorry plight and the winners' riches adds a new dynamic to an old story. Opposition to the violent and inhuman aspects of interconnection has come not only from those forcibly globalized but from within the ranks of the globalizers. Periodically throughout history, voices of conscience and moral rectitude such as those of Bartolomé de Las Casas or William Wilberforce have risen to condemn the suffering inflicted on fellow humans in foreign lands in the name of God, racial superiority, or the proclaimed right to free trade. Thanks to an ever-thickening communication network, critics across the planet today are as closely connected as the globalizing corporations and institutions they denounce. Unlike in the past, when opposition to the evil consequences of globalization was almost invariably local, today's critics are often the most globalized or globally aware of world citizens. Thus it is not just the marginalized poor, increasingly aware how the rich other half lives in faraway lands, but conscientious members of societies and countries that benefit from globalization who now clamor to rectify the inequities and injustice that have always been part of global interconnectedness.

The most important difference, however, lies in the development of a new analytical tool used in today's antiglobalization discourse. Unlike opposition to aspects of globalization over the past two millennia of human history, the objection today is not just to specific negative consequences of interconnectedness but to the very ideology and philosophy associated with the perceived globalizers—big business and its backers. In denouncing greedy corporations driving today's globalization, critics are consciously or unconsciously informed by the critique Karl Marx formulated in the early years of rising capitalism. The following passage from Marx and Friedrich Engels's *Communist Manifesto,* published in 1848, is worth quoting because, although written with clinical detachment, the *Manifesto* may be the first modern critique of globalization: "The need of a constantly expanding market for its products chases the bourgeoisie over the entire surface of the globe. . . . In place of the old wants, satisfied by the production of the country, we find new wants, requiring for their satisfaction the products of distant lands and climes. In place of the old local and national seclusion and self-sufficiency, we have intercourse in every direction, *universal inter-dependence* of nations."[6]

Marx saw this rise of "universal inter-dependence" as the result of the capitalist drive for profit—in his words, the "enormous werewolfish hunger for surplus labour."[7] However much modern critics find fault with profit-hungry capitalism, with the collapse of socialism they have lost an alternative model, finding it harder to argue against capitalism. In this void "globalization" has become a handy substitute term for an exploitative capitalism without necessarily espousing a discredited socialist system.

TROUBLES FROM TRADE

Leaving aside ideological arguments, at its core, criticism of globalization is aimed at the "other"—namely, foreign actions and foreign goods, ideas, and institutions. From the dawn of history, the most important foreign agents in a country were traders from another land and preachers of other faiths. Until the advent of large-scale ocean shipping, though, trade and travel were limited. Empires, Roman, Ottoman, Chinese, and others, nevertheless all tried to constrain the impact of interconnectedness. The first law promulgated by the Romans dealt with duties to be imposed on imports. Not only were tariffs a major source of government revenue but some imports were always disfavored. The Chinese attempt to prohibit trade in opium, which the British insisted on exporting to China to pay for silk and tea, sparked the Opium Wars of the mid-nineteenth century. Reliance on the export of agricultural commodities, imposed by colonial powers, thrust farmers and workers in developing countries through incessant cycles of boom and bust—not so different from what happens in today's globalized economy.[8] A classic example was in Dutch-ruled Indonesia in the early eighteenth century. A collapse in coffee and sugar prices led Dutch planters in Indonesia to lay off thousands of workers, many of them immigrant Chinese. When these laborers got wind of the Dutch plan to deport them to China, a riot erupted, and some ten thousand "Chinamen" died in what has since been called the "Batavian fury."[9] Anger at Dutch exploitation coincided with the arrival of Arabian-inspired Wahhabist Islam, leading to the Java War (1825–30)—another early salvo in the antiglobalization struggle.[10] Two decades later in India, indebted peasants forced by the East India Company to grow low-priced indigo rose up in another instance of antiglobalization resistance that came to be known by the color of the miserable crop they produced—the Blue Mutiny.[11] In an earlier chapter we saw how the "bones of Indian weavers [were] bleaching the plains of India" because of British textile competition. Industrializing countries, too, were not immune from the effect of global trade as they fought battles over tariff barriers. While the interests of Britain's fledgling industry led Parliament in 1846 to repeal the Corn Laws, which had barred grain imports, continental Europe raised tariff barriers to protect its farmers against the American grain invasion. But global trade posed a different challenge to the countries that exported shiploads of grain. In order to protect its fledgling domestic industries, the United States, beginning in the early years of independence, imposed tariffs on imports of cheap foreign industrial goods such as British textiles.[12]

ALL FALL DOWN

It was during this period that migrants, whom I have grouped with adventurers as key actors in the promotion of globalization, spawned controversy and opposition not unlike the current anti-immigrant sentiments in the United States. The protectionist policies adopted in the first decades of the twentieth century by the United States and other New World countries ultimately spelled the end of what has been called the golden era of globalization. The open-door migration policy adopted by the United States in the later part of the nineteenth century also ended. Concern about growing income inequality in the United States that resulted from the arrival of low-wage labor—reasons not unlike those being advanced by proponents of tighter immigration policies in the United States in 2006—brought about the reversal. The result of the closed door proved more pernicious than the legislators had bargained for. As Kevin O'Rourke and Jeffrey Williamson, who have studied this period, note, "The rising inequality in the rich countries ceased exactly when labor migration was choked off by quotas, global capital markets collapsed, and the international community retreated behind high trade barriers."[13]

Australia, another major destination for international migration, also adopted a policy that has been called "the Great White Wall" to keep "yellow" races out.[14] The White Australia Policy, which ended only in the second half of the twentieth century, was dictated not by any concerns about political or military intervention by imperial China but rather by Australians' fear of being swamped by a culturally different race of "inferior" immigrants ready to work for extremely low wages and undercut local laborers—concerns that are familiar in today's Western Europe and the United States.

The choking off of migration was accompanied by another blow to globalization—the gradual strangulation of trade. During the presidential campaign of 1929, Herbert Hoover promised American farmers relief from collapsing prices by introducing tough tariff legislation. Before the bill was passed, however, jitters and uncertainty about what the massive Smoot-Hawley bill might do precipitated the stock market collapse of 24 October 1929. A chain of linkages running through the globally integrated financial market brought about a domino effect throughout the world, turning a one-day stock-market setback into the Great Depression. The final nail in the coffin of globalization in that era was hammered in by the passage in June 1930 of the protectionist Smoot-Hawley bill. In the Senate alone anxious members piled on 1,253 amendments, and the result was a tax bill with twenty-one thousand tariff positions. As Harold James writes in *The End of Globalization*, "The domestic and international tensions that followed destroyed the mechanisms and institutions that had kept the world together. The reaction against the international economy put an end to globalization."[15]

Of course, globalization never ended, but actions in 1930 sounded the screeching of brakes and brought the process of global interconnectedness to a crawl. Thanks to the Smoot-Hawley tariffs, U.S. imports, which totaled $4.4 billion in 1929, dropped by more than $1.3 billion within a year.[16]

During the toughest years of the Great Depression from 1929 to 1933, world trade shrank by more than half.[17] The cross-border lending and investment that had greased the wheels of the world economy dried up. Global commerce took further knocks during the conflagration of World War II, when self-reliance and rationing became the norm in much of the world. As historian Niall Ferguson notes, "No one made more political capital out of the failure of globalisation than Hitler." The economic turmoil, political disillusionment, and quest for national identity that the depression generated laid the groundwork for the rise of Nazism. The question Hitler asked voters during his barnstorming election campaign of July 1932 resonates eerily in much of today's antiglobalization anger in developed countries. "There's so much internationalism, so much world conscience, so many international contracts; there's the League of Nations, the Disarmament Conference, Moscow, the Second International, the Third International—and what did all that produce for Germany?" As Ferguson responds, "What they all produced in the end was, of course, Hitler himself."[18] This is a lesson worth remembering as politicians rail against immigrants and cultural "others" with a view to achieving power.

FLYING COWS AND BIG MACS

If the WTO today is synonymous with globalization, its predecessor, the General Agreement on Tariffs and Trade (GATT), played that role until 1995. The organization helped to bring down the tariff walls erected before World War II. Set up by the United Nations, the GATT concluded nearly a dozen multilateral trade agreements, giving global trade a huge boost. In the past sixty years world trade has grown from ten billion dollars to twelve trillion dollars. Exports, which accounted for only 5 percent of the two-hundred-billion-dollar world economy in 1950, now represent 60 percent of a sixty-trillion-dollar economy. However, the wealth created by this phenomenal growth in trade was distributed in a lopsided way because of the way trade rules worked. According to the WTO, the total trade of all nations in 2004 was almost nineteen trillion dollars, but just $133 billion, or less than 1 percent, was accounted for by the fifty least developed countries.[19] While the removal of tariff barriers helped developed nations step up their manufactured exports quickly, poor countries, which relied on textiles, leather goods, fisheries, and farming, were held back by tariff walls and subsidies. The WTO adoped three framework agreements dealing with trade in goods, services, and intellectual property rights but excluded two of the most sensitive issues, agriculture and textiles, from the general agreement on trade.[20] Setting them aside turned out to be merely postponing the battle. The sensitivity of the textile trade labor unions of the rich countries was shown in 2005. According to an agreement, the Multi-Fiber Arrangement (MFA) that had protected the textile industry of developed countries was abolished in January 2005. Freed from constraints, low-cost producer China flooded the market, triggering protests from the American textile lobby. The American Manufacturing Trade Action Coalition claimed that nineteen factories have closed and some twenty-six thousand jobs have been eliminated since the end of the Multi-Fiber Arrangement.[21] Fearful of unleashing a protectionist backlash, American and European officials turned to a safeguard clause in the WTO provisions to reimpose production restrictions on the Chinese. The critics of globalization got a reprieve, but only for four years.

Farm trade, although it makes up barely 10 percent of world trade, touches sensitive nerves in the developing world. It involves food and the livelihoods of the vast majority of people in the least developed countries (LDCs), which incidentally make up more than 20 percent of the WTO's membership. The Korean farmers who have battled police outside WTO meetings from Cancún to Hong Kong remind one of farmers' fears for their livelihood in the face of competition from big multinationals. Farmers in South Korea, Brazil, India, Kenya, and other African countries have resisted opening up their economies further to developed countries unless unfair subsidies, antidumping regulations, and other nontariff barriers by rich countries are removed. One calculation shows that the three hundred billion dollars that rich countries lavish on farm subsidies would be enough to fly every cow in the industrial countries of the OECD (Organization for Economic Co-operation and Development) around the world first class every year, with plenty of money to spare.[22]

Aside from flying cows first class, the subsidy policy of developed nations amounts to the world trade equivalent of sending a beefy sumo wrestler to battle a scrawny and malnourished competitor. Traveling in Senegal in the fall of 2005, I saw huge chicken farms abandoned and hundreds of unemployed youth milling about in the streets. The chicken farms that had once provided employment had been shut down after heavily subsidized European poultry products were dumped in Senegal, making it impossible for local suppliers to sell their more expensive poultry. The most scandalous example of rich country protectionism has been the story of cotton. Not surprisingly, it is frequently invoked by critics as evidence of the rigged trading rules that typify globalization. Farmers from such countries as Benin, Burkina Faso, Cameroon, Chad, and Mali, who rely on cotton farming, have no prayer of selling their produce in world markets, where massive American and European Union cotton subsidies ($230 for every acre of American cotton farmland) have lowered prices to a level below their own production costs.[23] According to one estimate, in the three years between 1999 and 2001, eight African cotton-growing countries lost $330 million in export earnings—a huge amount for some of the poorest nations in the world.[24] Compare this with the $3.9 billion subsidy that America's twenty-five thousand cotton farmers received in 2001–2.[25] The European Union meanwhile pays Greek farmers a billion dollars a year to grow cotton. If such subsidies were dismantled, the price of world cotton would perhaps rise by 15 percent or more, allowing thousands of African farmers to make a living.[26]

What also riles critics of globalization is the apparent hypocrisy of developed countries' promoting free trade and much-ballyhooed economic aid to the poor. For instance, in 2002 the rich industrial nations of the OECD gave fifty-eight billion dollars in aid to developing countries but provided $318 billion—or 5.5 times that amount—in subsidies to their own farmers.[27] The fact is that the annual loss to developing nations as a group from agricultural tariffs and subsidies in rich countries is estimated at forty-five billion dollars, and their annual loss from trade barriers on textiles and clothing is estimated at twenty-four billion dollars. The foreign aid that rich countries offer to poor nations is far less than the toll that their protectionism exacts. Whether these inequities could be ended was put to the test in a make-or-break WTO meeting in Geneva in July 2006. The Doha Round of the WTO, which met three months after the 9/11 attacks had jolted the world to attention to the accumulated anger, pledged to harness trade to the development of poor nations.

But the Geneva meeting collapsed when the United States and European Union blamed each other for not making enough concessions on removing subsidies and the developing countries refused to accept steep cuts in manufacturing tariffs until Western farming subsidies and tariffs were substantially reduced. Some antiglobalization activists greeted the failure in Geneva as a victory for poor countries because their poor citizens would not be swamped by the rich nations. But Director General of the WTO Pascal Lamy accurately summed up the failure as "a blow to the development prospects of the three quarters of WTO members whose economies are poorer or weaker than [rich countries]."[28] With the WTO multilateral trade agreement process damaged, poor countries would now have to seek bilateral deals with rich countries in which they would have little bargaining power.

Although the farm trade issue concerns mostly the poor countries, which see the unfairness of globalization in rich country subsidies and tariffs, it has produced contention in rich countries as well. At the root lies European concern over food safety from chemical use and bioengineering in the American farm business. Prominent among protesters in Seattle was a mustachioed farmer from France who had shot to fame a few months earlier. The trouble started in 1998 when the WTO ruled in favor of America's right to export hormone-fed beef, which the Europeans had banned. Critics immediately accused the WTO's dispute-resolution body as being biased toward the United States. However, although the members of the settlement panel are WTO appointees, they nevertheless have to be approved by member states on both sides of the Atlantic.

When the European Union refused to lift its ban on American beef (which the United States viewed as simple protectionism disguised as health concerns), the WTO allowed the United States to impose retaliatory tariffs on European products. One item hit with a heavy customs duty was Roquefort cheese from Normandy. Incensed by the loss of business implied by the elevated customs charge, the antiglobalization activist and Roquefort cheese grower Jose Bové organized fellow sheep farmers to protest with an assault on one of the most visible manifestations of American cultural (and culinary) imperialism. The group drove tractors to the construction site of a new McDonald's and ransacked it. Bové was jailed for twenty days, and almost overnight an international antiglobalization star was born. Bové, who resembles the irreverent French comic book hero Astérix, traveled to Seattle in 1999 as part of the French delegation to lead the protest against the commercialization of food crops promoted by the WTO. Food, in the view of his group, is too vital a part of life to be trusted to the vagaries of world trade. In Seattle, he led a demonstration in which some ski-masked protesters trashed a McDonald's. As Bové explained, his was a movement for small farmers against industrial farming brought about by globalization. For them, McDonald's was a symbol of globalization, implying the standardization of food through industrial farming. If this was allowed to go on, he said, there would no longer be a need for farmers. "For us," he declared, McDonald's "is a symbol of what WTO and the big companies want to do with the world."[29] Ironically, for all of Bové's fulminations against McDonald's "malbouffe," the fast-food chain counts its French operations among its most profitable in 120 countries. As the employer of some thirty-five thousand workers, in 2006 McDonald's was also one of France's biggest foreign employers.

McDonald's may have been unaffected by Bové, but his other campaign against so-called Frankenfood brought into the limelight the growing international opposition to GMO (genetically modified organisms) crops promoted by the United States. Antiglobalization groups charged that GMO crops developed by profit-hungry multinationals like Monsanto and Cargill not only would make farmers in developing countries perpetually dependent on these big firms for their seeds but would also have unforeseen health consequences for consumers. The WTO's refusal to ban GMO food was seen as evidence of the organization's collusion with big business. The arguments that scientific studies had not yet detected any adverse consequences from eating GMO food or that biotechnology held the promise of abundant and nutritious food for the world's galloping population cut no ice with demonstrators from Larzac to Bombay. In 2003, under the glare of television cameras, Bové led supporters to trash an experimental French field planted with genetically modified corn and rice crops. On parole from prison for that act of vandalism, Bové could not travel to Cancún to protest the WTO meeting. Instead, he addressed a rally of a quarter-million people in Larzac, urging farmers to take to the streets and scuttle the meeting.[30]

Although the WTO meeting of 2003 ended in failure, it failed because of the stubborn opposition of developing countries to Western farm subsidies rather than because of street protests. Ironically, the developing nations opposed subsidies of the very type that Bové and his farmer friends supported. The subsidies that cushion French sheep farmers and American cotton growers from competition also hurt American cattle ranchers and African cotton growers. The globalization of agriculture produces winners and losers, divided not just across the globe but inside the same country. Take the example of South Korean rice farmers, in defense of whom the unfortunate Lee Kyung-hae committed suicide in Cancún. South Korean rice farmers would surely suffer with the phased opening of their country's market. But a greater number of South Korean consumers would benefit from the variety of products and low prices that would result. One good example is the ordinary banana, now imported in massive quantities from the Philippines and South America. In the 1960s, when the Korean market was closed, bananas were such luxury items that student rebels who toppled the dictatorship of Syngman Rhee were scandalized to find bananas in the refrigerator of Vice President Lee Ki-Poon when they raided his home. Demonstrators came out of Lee's home holding aloft a bunch of bananas as evidence of corruption and unearned wealth! South Korea's prosperity today is based on its export machine, which in 2005 churned out $170 billion worth of semiconductors, ships, cars, electronics, and other industrial goods. Seoul's cab drivers, who once were farmers, now clamor for cheaper rice that could come with the opening of the rice market to foreign growers.

The opening of the rice market would help not just giant American rice growers but also poorer and more efficient rice producers from Thailand and Vietnam. In fact, the same WTO that Lee charged with killing Korean farmers—and that led him to kill himself—has brought new life to poor rice farmers of Thailand and Vietnam, and their subsequent success has made their countries two of the world's leading rice exporters. Traveling through the Mekong Delta in the winter of 2005, I saw bustling markets, new homes, shiny new motorbikes, and a forest of television antennas. Farmers now can afford to send their children to school and enjoy a living that would have been unimaginable a few years ago. Oxfam, the British NGO and frequent critic of WTO, titled its report on WTO and the rice trade *Kicking Down the Door* but acknowledged that for Thailand and Vietnam, "more open markets among importing developing countries would further boost their rice sectors and raise incomes for their rice farmers. South–South trade clearly has an important and growing role to play, and there may be collective benefits from further tariff reductions between developing countries."[31]

Given the gulf of differences that exists among poor countries, sauce for the gander is not often sauce for the goose. When the WTO ruled against the EU policy of subsidizing sugar and bananas, which kept prices high in domestic markets, African, Caribbean, and Pacific states were the unhappiest about the removal of subsidies, for they had enjoyed special rights from their former colonial masters to export bananas and sugar to the EU on favorable terms. The removal of subsidies exposed them to competition with more efficient producers in the developed and developing worlds.[32]

LONG-DISTANCE POLLUTION

Antiglobalization activists charge that multinational companies not only overexploit resources and damage the livelihoods of the poor in their drive to maximize profit at all costs but also wreak havoc on the global environment by moving operations to countries where environmental regulations are weak or nonexistent. A World Bank study in 2003, however, found little evidence that companies chose to invest in such countries to shirk the pollution-abatement costs in rich countries. Instead, the most important factor in determining the amount of investment was the size of the local market.[33] It has also been found that, within a given industry, foreign-operated plants tended to pollute less than their local peers.

The WTO, and by extension globalization, also stands accused of destroying the global environment. Expanding trade driven by globalization has brought about increased fishing, destruction of forestland, and the spread of polluting industries to the developing world. In a report in November 2005 the U.N. Food and Agricultural Organization reported that each year about eighteen million acres of the world's forests—an area the size of Panama or Sierra Leone—are lost due to deforestation. Serious critics of globalization acknowledge that deforestation cannot be laid at the door of globalization alone, as my electrician in New Haven believed. But they rightly point out that globalization does clearly serve as both a conduit and an accelerator for many of the forces that have been causing the loss of forest cover worldwide. It is obvious that by encouraging trade, globalization encourages consumption, which leads to more logging worldwide. The failure of governance at both local and global levels to promote conservation and reforestation clearly carries equal responsibility for deforestation.

China is a case in point. A major beneficiary of globalization as the world's factory, it has been turning increasingly to other countries to meet its burgeoning demand for food. That is good news for Brazilian farmers who want to cash in on the growing Chinese demand for soybeans: the environmental organization Greenpeace estimates that more than two and a half million acres of tropical forest have been cleared in recent years to plant soybeans.[34] Brazil can also ramp up its export of soybeans, which are in high demand as feed for Europe's subsidized cattle.[35] Greenpeace claims that there is "a 7,000 km chain that starts with the clearing of virgin forest by farmers and leads directly to chicken nuggets being sold in British and European fast food restaurants" and labels the British import of soy animal feed from Brazil as tantamount to "forest crime."[36]

China's blazing economic growth and the cheap products it has supplied to the world have other costs, too. Its accelerated burning of coal and its use of chemicals to fuel its export machine have been polluting not only China's air and water but the world environment as well. A study conducted in 2004 found that chemicals like mercury, spewed by factories in China, had been dispersed by the jet stream to locations thousands of miles away. A researcher traced a plume of dirty air from Asia to New England, where analysis of collected samples revealed that chemicals in them had originated in China.[37]

THEATER OF THE ABSURD

International protesters, though, rarely take on developing countries like China for the ills of globalization, focusing their attention instead on multilateral organizations. One of the many criticisms of the WTO, indeed against the United Nations, the European Union, and all supranational organizations, is that they—like much of what passes for globalization—are woefully undemocratic. Trade negotiation sessions take place behind closed doors without any representation of affected communities but with a strong behind-the-scenes role by multinational corporations. Developed country critics standing for weaker nations have charged that the WTO has become a handmaiden of the United States and Europe, and especially of the powerful agribusiness, pharmaceutical, and financial services lobbies in these countries. Important deals, as one critic says, are hammered out in negotiations attended by the trade ministers of a few dozen powerful nations, while those of poor countries wait in the bar outside for news.[38]

Defenders of the WTO respond, of course, that negotiations do take place among representatives of member countries because it is an organization of sovereign states and their representatives prefer to negotiate out of public view. But depending on the nature of each government, the signatory countries have to face their affected groups and NGOs to defend the agreements they signed onto. In that sense, the WTO is indeed as democratic—but no more so—as its members are. The charge of the body's inherently undemocratic nature holds more water when one sees the reality. Theoretically, all members are equal, but—as in other international organizations—in reality the rules are dictated by the countries with the largest markets. Before joining the WTO, every country has to sign a bilateral trade agreement with the United States and the other major partners that it would engage in trade. China, which has emerged as the world's second largest trading nation, had to cool its heels outside the WTO until Washington granted it most-favored nation status in 1999. Vietnam's hope of joining the WTO was continually pushed back as American negotiators pressed for concessions, until finally it met all demands and was admitted as the body's 150th member on 8 November 2006. Vietnam had benefited much from globalization and gritted its teeth to cross the last hurdle to enter the WTO.

The grim determination of Vietnam, once a hero of the anti-imperialist struggle, to join the WTO stands in sharp contrast to the scorn with which the traditional left views the organization. For the left, the WTO is not just a club for multinational corporations but the doorway to a global sweatshop. To the dismay of the left, the once-revolutionary Vietnam was determined in the 1990s to open that door. Following its victory in 1975, Vietnam, then a self-proclaimed "outpost of socialism," attempted to stamp out capitalism and expel capitalists who were largely ethnic Chinese. Within three years the drive to build semi-autarkic socialism brought Vietnam to the precipice of disaster. Throughout the 1970s I sadly watched the steady decline as the country sank into poverty. Finally aid cut-off by the tottering Soviet empire and food riots forced Vietnam to embrace a market economy and open its doors to the world. Economic reforms launched since the mid-1980s and increasing integration with the global economy have turned Vietnam into the latest Asian economic tiger, growing at 8.4 percent in 2006. The proportion of people living on a dollar a day shrank from 51 percent to 8 percent in 1990.[39]

However, Vietnam was far from the protesters' minds. Many American labor unions and human rights groups that had gathered in Seattle to oppose globalization argued that the WTO promoted a race to the bottom, in which business exploited poor-nation workers in sweatshop conditions and denied them basic workers' rights. Sharing these concerns, the Clinton administration tried to introduce the issue of labor standards in trade discussions in Seattle. The move proved to be the last straw for a summit meeting already rocked by violent demonstrations. To the developing countries, this patronizing Western concern for the plight of workers was hypocritical, a blatant introduction of non-tariff barriers under the facade of human and labor rights. After all, they argued, in the early stage of economic development, countries were expected to participate in global trade by leveraging their main comparative advantage—low wages.

Despite their common distaste for capitalism, antiglobalization activists from developing countries, however, had a different approach from their Western counterparts on the key issue of labor rights. One Indian participant described the Seattle protest as a "theater of the absurd"—a clever neoimperialist manipulation by the rich nations of the North to protect their industries under the guise of instituting labor, human rights, or environmental standards on poor countries. He sarcastically noted that the demonstrators in Seattle included American "steelworkers unions (who had been demanding protection, quotas and anti-dumping investigations to keep out steel from the poorer countries), [and] textiles and clothing unions using the plea of 'child labor' to shut out imports from the developing world."[40]

Another aspect of the WTO that angers antiglobalization critics is its strong defense of intellectual property rights, often to the detriment of weak and poor countries. This old issue of globalization has pitted the holders of exclusive products or technology against the rest who don't have them. From Chinese silkworm eggs to coffee beans, from rubber seeds to textile machine design, intellectual property rights (IPR) have long been a bone of contention. With the massive research and development investment by high-technology and pharmaceutical corporations, the stakes have become much higher and the resultant battles more acute. Since poorer countries cannot finance the research needed to produce intellectual property—from microchips to medicine—enormous sums of money will flow from the developing world to the developed countries to compensate them for access to the fruits of research. Joseph Stiglitz, chief economist of the World Bank, says that the WTO has "strengthened 'intellectual property' in ways that make it more difficult for developing countries to have access to 'intellectual property.' It is not a level playing field."[41] Antiglobalization critics in India have campaigned against Western demands for patent protection because that would deprive the country's poor of the benefits of cheap generic drugs. Before India signed on to the WTO rule, Indian pharmaceutical companies had reverse-engineered the process, providing medicines to its citizens at affordable prices. But IPR is a double-edged weapon. For a country counting on innovation, patent protection is essential. Not surprisingly, now that it stands at the cusp of major gains from its own innovations, India has quietly dropped its objections and signed on to the WTO rules on intellectual property rights.

Even more than WTO, the institution that has drawn the most intense criticism from antiglobalization protesters is the International Monetary Fund. The IMF has long been considered to be the high priest of neoliberal economic policy—the so-called Washington Consensus that prescribes, among other things, free trade, capital market liberalization, secure property rights, deregulation, and the transfer of assets from the public to the private sectors.[42] In the fall of 2001, the "50 Years Is Enough" network, a coalition of environmentalists, development economists, missionaries, and others seeking a fundamental reform of the World Bank and the International Monetary Fund, issued a call that sums up the sentiment of the leftwing antiglobalization movement: "The IMF and the World Bank are the primary architects of neo-liberal globalization. . . . It is imperative that supporters of global economic justice send a clear message: the movement for global justice continues to grow, and will not stand for continuing efforts by these institutions and the G-7 governments to structure the world for the benefit of corporations and the wealthy and to deny basic justice to the majority of the world's people."[43]

Even moderate critics who do not want to abolish the IMF have complained that an organization that was created to prevent future Great Depressions and to be the lender of last resort had become "a champion of market supremacy in all situations, echoing the voice of Wall Street and the United States Treasury Department, more interested in getting wealthy creditors repaid than in serving the poor."[44] Critics like Stiglitz have held the IMF responsible for designing policies that helped international lenders, but hit workers and domestic firms hard. Stiglitz identifies globalization with IMF policies, comparing the IMF's dispensing of disastrous advice to poor countries to high-altitude bombing. IMF economists, he writes, "make themselves comfortable in five-star hotels in the capitals" in developing countries, and "from one's luxury hotel, one can callously impose policies about which one would think twice if one knew the people whose lives one was destroying."[45]

PINK SLIPS AND WAL-MART

While the policy issues involving the IMF and the World Bank have preoccupied intellectuals, the effects of trade on employment have been the most enduring and contentious aspects of globalization affecting the public and the mass media. The concerns about global policy and sweatshop labor that moved demonstrators in Seattle appeared to recede into the background in early 2004 as the direct consequences of globalization on the U.S. and Western labor market and economy in general came into sharper focus.

As America's trade deficit headed toward a record $750 billion in 2006 and the Western economy in general witnesses jobless growth, the anxiety about globalization has grown.[46] In 2004 Democratic presidential candidate Senator John Kerry made the outsourcing of American jobs a main plank of his campaign and helped to raise public awareness about the issue. However, Nobel Prize–winning economist and free-trade advocate Paul A. Samuelson's entry into the foray elevated the issue to a higher policy level. He caused a stir in 2004 when he seemed to side with critics who question the benefits of globalization. Writing in the *Journal of Economic Perspectives,* he reiterated his long-held view that trade is a substitute for massive immigration. He claimed that since U.S. labor has lost its old monopoly on American advanced know-how and capital, free trade could indeed lower the share of wages in the U.S. gross domestic product and increase overall inequality. Samuelson pointed to the drastic change in mean U.S. incomes and in inequalities among different classes and suggested that this may be the consequence of unfettered trade, including in services. He stated that the outsourcing of jobs to foreign countries is tantamount to importing labor from those countries into the United States, with the similar consequence of depressing wages. A low-wage country that is rapidly improving its technology, like India or China, he argued, has the potential to change the terms of trade with America and reduce U.S. per capita income. The ability to import consumer items at low cost was a poor consolation to the jobless. He quipped, "Being able to purchase groceries 20 percent cheaper at Wal-Mart does not necessarily make up for the wage losses."[47]

While much ink has been spilled in the media on the negative impact of trade in services, and especially the outsourcing of white-collar jobs, statistical support has been harder to get. In 1984, the U.S. Bureau of Labor Statistics began to count "worker displacement," which was estimated to have risen to at least thirty million full-time workers by 2004. However, it was impossible to ascertain how many of those jobs were displaced because of trade. Yet the absence of hard numbers does not prevent those who have lost jobs from blaming cheap imports and globalization. Especially disturbing is the realization that what was supposed to be the "creative destruction" of capitalist progress—a phrase immortalized by economist Joseph Schumpeter—was in reality terminating many more jobs than it was creating. People who accepted without question the unpleasant but unavoidable reality of a capitalist economy—that layoffs are a necessary part of renewal—have been waking up to the fact that jobs that leave their shores rarely return. The argument that countries benefiting from this "creative destruction" have also emerged as major importers of Western products does not cut much ice with the public. The fact that China, India, or other developing countries import a large number of Boeing and Airbus aircrafts and machineries or buy more Motorola cell phones does not produce tangible gains for the average citizen. Economists examining long-range data find that the globalization of the American economy has helped to freeze or lower middle-class incomes, further widening the gap between the very rich and the middle class.

Whether as a result of global sourcing and marketing or smart management of supply chain logistics and efficient use of technology, corporate earnings in the United States have been rising. Meanwhile wages have stagnated. After-tax corporate profit in the United States grew from $292 billion in 1990 to $900 billion in 2004.[48] With the relatively weak labor market, companies were able to keep their gains rather than share them with workers. Thus while incomes at the bottom of the ladder stagnated, critics point out, America's rich were enjoying the fruits of globalization.

World Bank economist Branko Milanovic ascribes the souring on globalization in the United States to some basic economic facts—such as whereas the median U.S. wage has not risen in real terms over the past twenty-five years, real wages of the top 1 percent of earners have more than doubled. "The richest 1 percent of Americans today," he says, "controls almost 20 percent of total U.S. income, a proportion higher than at any time since the Roaring Twenties."[49] Most of the workers laid off from industrial jobs have ended up in the service sector—in jobs as truck drivers or security guards—earning less than they did before. The income divide has widened between the rich and the highly educated, who are able to take advantage of the globalized economy, and those in the middle classes and the unskilled, who cannot.

INVASION OF THE JOB SNATCHERS

In Don Siegel's movie *Invasion of the Body Snatchers* (1956), a town doctor discovered that aliens from outer space were replacing the population of his community. By the turn of the twenty-first century, a similar science-fiction phenomenon was becoming a reality in workplaces across America. In such instances, the "job snatcher" was invisible, sitting in a nondescript cubicle thousands of miles away and delivering his or her assigned task from a computer at the end of a high-speed fiber-optic line. An encounter with one such invisible worker spooked Matt, a Yale undergraduate who had a summer job in a multinational firm's New York office. Matt had called the tech support department to resolve a computer glitch. Someone from Bangalore answered the call and asked him to hand over the control of his PC. Mesmerized, Matt watched the cursor race across the screen, opening and closing windows, as an unseen hand typed gobbledygook on the screen before the system returned to normal. His problem was fixed remotely by someone sitting thousands of miles away and who probably earned one-tenth of what a techie sitting in New York would have earned. As Andrew Grove, the former CEO of Intel Corporation, put it, "From a technical and productivity standpoint, the engineer sitting 6,000 miles away might as well be in the next cubicle and on the local area network."[50] It is not just the spooky, invisible worker moving the cursor on your computer screen but the voice with the unfamiliar accent on the other end of the line answering your queries about mortgage payments or helping to track your lost luggage. These daily encounters are reminiscent of the aliens in the movie who take over the work of your neighbors, the people you thought you knew. Unlike in the movies, most Americans and Europeans speaking to Indian operators in Gurgaon, outside of Delhi, or Japanese callers contacting call-center operators in China's industrial town of Dalian, have become used to hearing an assortment of accents on the help line. However, the deeper implications of the process known in industry jargon as business process outsourcing (BPO) are emerging as a major concern in the West. It means that the so-called job snatchers are moving up the food chain. They are no longer threatening just blue-collar jobs and operators at call centers but inexorably, if slowly, the better-paid white-collar employees with political clout.

Like many other developments in world economy, the outsourcing of service jobs evolved innocuously. Credit card companies and banks hauled their records to low-wage countries for data entry or reconciliation. But the shipping of such back-office work really took off literally with a millennial convergence. At the turn of the millennium, corporations the world over were seized by the so-called Y2K crisis. Fearing that old software codes—which allowed for only two digits to record the year—would read the year 2000 as 1900 and would cause massive data loss and system crashes, corporations scrambled for help. In a fortuitous turn of history, India, the country that invented the zero, was now ready to help solve the world's problem with zeroes with its thousands of software engineers. By then India's nascent information technology (IT) industry, with its large pool of engineers and the beginnings of high-speed Internet connection and enabled by economic reform, had come into its own. Just as the Portuguese, Dutch, and British traders arriving in India in the seventeenth century found a huge source of wealth in the country's ancient textile industry and in its large pool of skilled workers, American and European captains of industry on the cusp of the twenty-first century found in India a pot of gold.[51] General Electric CEO Jack Welch, who had ruthlessly cut costs to increase the shareholder value, visited India in 1989 and found "a developing country with developed intellectual capability." Translation: a country of high skills with low wages. In 1997, Gecis (GE Capital International Services) was launched, ushering India into large-scale service outsourcing.[52]

Alex Taylor, head of British Telecom's technical services, visited India and wondered, "What should we keep onshore? Because they can do everything there now."[53] And Indian executives shared that thinking. "Almost everything that is done can be done by us faster, cheaper and better," says Nandan Nilekani, CEO of India's leading software company, Infosys.[54] British Telecom decided to outsource the entire life cycle of its IT process to India.

As corporations engaged in a race to cut costs and ramp up profitability, Taylor's question was being asked by many top executives in the West, sending shivers down the spines of their workers and ripples of joy among millions of India's new graduates. In a seemingly endless litany, all the world's major corporations announced that they were laying off people at home and hiring lower-cost workers elsewhere. Alarmed American labor leaders complained that globalization meant the ability to "move capital thousands of miles with the click of a mouse and send jobs halfway around the world in the time it takes numbers to travel along fiber-optic cable."[55] Some, like General Motors, cut costs by outsourcing their entire IT process to IBM and Hewlett-Packard, which in turn sent the work offshore.[56] Adding insult to injury, the workers being laid off were often asked to spend the last weeks of their employment training the very foreign workers who would replace them.[57]

Customer care services, call centers, and medical transcription services were just the beginning. The possibility of IT-enabled service outsourcing has grown with every passing day—from managing the physical hardware and corporate computer networks to maintaining and developing business software and doing legal paperwork, tax preparation, research, analysis, and work-flow modeling. What started as wage-arbitrage or simple cost cutting by sending some low-end jobs overseas has grown into a massive system overhaul to turn a company into an efficient global operation, integrating expertise and efficiencies on a global scale. In an article in early 2006, *BusinessWeek* described what such transformations typically entail: "Genpact, Accenture, IBM Services, or another big outsourcing specialist dispatches teams to meticulously dissect the workflow of an entire human resources, finance, or info tech department. The team then helps build a new IT platform, redesigns all processes, and administers programs, acting as a virtual subsidiary. The contractor then disperses work among global networks of staff ranging from the U.S. to Asia to Eastern Europe."[58]

LOW WAGE, HIGH BANDWIDTH

The monsoon winds and tri-masted sailboats that had enabled European traders to carry shiploads of Indian textiles to market were now replaced by the electronic highways of fiber-optic cables, carrying very different products: voice, text, data, and brainwave. As Thomas L. Friedman explains in *The World*

Is Flat, a convergence of factors—from the emergence of common software platforms like Microsoft Windows and a Netscape Web browser that allowed across-the-board cooperation, new technologies of PDA (personal digital assistant) and Voice over Internet Protocol (VoIP) as well as the dot-com bust in the United States—suddenly produced a glut of bandwidth[59] that helped create the conditions for the outsourcing boom to India.[60] In the decade that followed, GE and scores of other companies rushed to India to tap this newfound resource. By 2006, more than a million Indians participated in a round-the-clock operation, performing a variety of customer relations and back-office jobs for American and European companies.

Leftist intellectuals quickly denounced the call-center workers as "cyber-coolies of our global age," but Indians were ready to seize the opportunity that the electronic superhighway had brought to their door.[61] It was the same in other countries with high-speed network connections and educated populations. From Ireland to Lithuania, and from Senegal to the Philippines, graduate workers could now find work with foreign companies without leaving home. On a visit to the Infosys campus in Bangalore in 2004, I saw dozens of young men and women in a large glass-paneled hall sitting at computer terminals doing maintenance work on their foreign clients' servers located in Europe and the United States. Similarly, at a call center in a Dakar suburb, I watched hundreds of young Senegalese sitting with earphones telling customers in France (Senegal's former colonial master) how to get their washing machines to work or how to install their e-mail software. Ready to work at a fraction of the wages that their counterparts in developed countries would earn, these workers and their IT-aided services had suddenly expanded the pool of workers that foreign companies could tap, thus turning networked countries into the world's back office.

A NATION OF FAT CATS AND HAIRDRESSERS

Quietly, noticed only by the trade press, a massive restructuring of business was under way that could only make the specter of globalization loom larger. A study by the McKinsey Global Institute in 2005 predicted that from software to infotech, from banking to insurance and pharmaceuticals to engineering and accounting, between 13 and 50 percent of jobs could be sent offshore.[62] Princeton economist Alan S. Blinder, writing in *Foreign Affairs,* makes an even bleaker forecast. He writes that the total number of current U.S. service-sector jobs susceptible to offshoring in the electronic future is roughly two to three times the total number of current manufacturing jobs (which is about fourteen million). Although little service-sector offshoring has happened to date, "it may eventually amount to a third Industrial Revolution, and industrial revolutions have a way of transforming societies."[63] Job churning is a regular feature of the American employment market, but what worries some economists is that most of the new jobs are in domestic services and low-paying work. The British white-collar science and engineering union Amicus warned that, unless action was taken to stem the tide of outsourcing, the United Kingdom could be left as a nation of "fat cats and hairdressers, with nothing in between."[64]

Many American and European corporations have been resorting to outsourcing, further weakening the already tenuous territorial loyalty of global corporations. With giant multinationals making 60 to 80 percent of their sales abroad, executives are loyal to their global customers rather than to a single country or its people. Dell, the world's largest computer maker, earned 43 percent of its revenues from non-U.S. sales. It was no surprise that Dell hired six times more people for its foreign operations than it did in the United States. A study conducted in 2002 found that fifty of the world's largest multinational companies had 55 percent of their employees and 59 percent of their sales outside of their "home" countries.[65] Thanks to globalization and the opening of new markets, a British banker was quoted as saying, "It's increasingly difficult to argue that companies themselves are attached to a country."[66]

The sheer size of the new white-collar labor force competing in the world's job market is causing anxiety about the effects of globalization. Corporate leaders like Intel CEO Craig Barrett have raised the alarm. "If you look at India, China and Russia," he told a newspaper interviewer, "they all have strong education heritages. Even if you discount 90 percent of the people there as uneducated farmers, you still end up with about 300 million people who are educated. That's bigger than the U.S. work force."[67] The numbers do look staggering unless one considers other little-known and less-understood facts that severely limit the possibility of large-scale offshoring of jobs. For instance, India produces four hundred thousand engineers every year, but given the poor quality of education in general, only a quarter of them are considered employable.[68] An even smaller percentage are of world-class capability or have the linguistic ability to work for foreign companies. Studies have shown that, the media alarm not withstanding, the number of American or European jobs that have been shipped abroad represent a small fraction of the total jobs lost. Preliminary U.S. data for the first quarter of 2004 showed that 1.9 percent of total layoffs were attributable to "overseas relocation."[69] Although the trend of companies outsourcing some functions to save money has grown, a large proportion of the work has merely been diverted to other companies in the same nation and is likely to be so in the future. An example of such in-country outsourcing is General Motors, which spun out the production of many components to Delphi Corporation and sources significant parts of its cars from independent U.S. suppliers. Surveys show that most outsourced jobs will stay in-country not because of any policy barrier but simply for company-specific reasons, including operational issues, hostile management attitudes to offshoring, and unprofitable scale of production. Findings by the management consulting firm McKinsey that every dollar spent on offshoring to India leads to $1.12–$1.14 in benefits back home in the United States show the fallacy of viewing the phenomenon purely in terms of labor.[70] Looking beyond the hyped prediction by Forrester Research that 3.3 million American jobs will be outsourced over fifteen years, one can see that on annual terms this would affect less than 0.2 percent of employed Americans.[71] Facts and figures, however, do not matter because the issue is more one of psychology than one of economics. More important, as political economist David Rothkopf has put it, most jobs are not lost to outsourcing to India or China—most lost jobs are "outsourced to the past."[72] They are eliminated because a new technology comes along, not because a foreigner grabs the job. For instance, many offices have eliminated receptionists, installing voicemail instead, and airlines have replaced ticketing clerks with electronic tickets booked online. This trend is as true in Europe and the United States as it is in Japan and South Korea. In Korea, militant trade unions regularly confront big business and vote for populist politicians. In the West, politicians play on middle-class fears and make job loss a hot-button issue for their political gain. Since the people affected by outsourcing of service jobs are mostly white-collar workers with political clout, their grievances get a wider hearing. As Princeton economist Alan Blinder has cautioned, unlike the voiceless blue-collar workers who have so far borne the brunt of offshoring, "the new cadres of displaced workers, especially those who are drawn from the upper educational reaches, will be neither as passive nor as quiet."[73]

SPECTER OF THE POLISH PLUMBER

Of course, the fear of globalization does not stem only from outsourcing. A more visceral fear is provoked by rising migration from the poorer periphery of the rich West. New waves of out-of-Africa migration have been arriving on European shores, raising alarm about lost jobs and changing national identity.

The presence of some thirteen million illegal immigrants in the United States has emerged as a highly divisive and contentious issue. Economist Milanovic notes the irony that "while the fear of job loss is driven by fast economic growth of the two giants [China and India], the fear of immigration is, ironically, caused by the slow economic growth of the rest of the developing world."[73] Those from Africa and Asia who are trying to reach Europe or those who cross from Mexico into the United States come from countries that have been unable to hop onto the globalization train. He points out that in 1980 Mexico's real per-capita income (adjusted for the differential price level between Mexico and the United States) was a third of that in the United States. Today the ratio is almost four and a half to one. The poor Africans who land daily on the beaches of the Spanish Canary Islands or the Italian island of Lampedusa in the Mediterranean come from countries that have seen little economic growth in fifty years.

European workers with strong labor union traditions have resisted the kind of job loss that has become commonplace in the United States. However, their demands for lifetime job security and benefits have meant that companies are making their new investments abroad rather than accepting long-term wage burdens at home. One consequence has been high levels of unemployment across the Continent. On the other hand, flat growth rates and the graying of Europe's population have placed an increasingly heavy burden of retirement benefits and healthcare costs onto governments. Against strong protest, the government of Chancellor Gerhard Schröder cut German pension benefits and limited employment security and paid for it by losing the 2005 election.

Not surprisingly, such reductions in social security, the high unemployment rate, and a growing income gap in Europe have been laid at the door of globalization. France, one of the strongest critics of globalization in Europe, offers an interesting example of the paradox produced by global integration. In order to promote growth France offers attractive terms to foreign investors, yet President Jacques Chirac makes populist statements expressing public sympathy with critics of globalization. France has been Europe's third biggest recipient of foreign direct investment, which reached fifty billion dollars in 2005 and accounted for 42 percent of gross domestic product. French businesses' ability to offshore their productions and outsource services (like the call center in Dakar) has not only brought them rising profit but has also given companies leverage to hold down wages at home with the unstated threat: Accept our terms, or else we will move to India or Poland.[74] Fat years of economic growth and strong unions have created a two-tier society—an "insider" class of workers with high wages and benefits and a growing class of underemployed or unemployed "outsiders." Since the expansion of the European Union to include former Soviet bloc countries, the specter of the "Polish plumber" and other immigrants taking advantage of EU labor laws and coming to Western Europe has haunted not only the French but sections of the British public. Anti-immigrant sentiment has risen all over Europe, especially in Germany and France. Unemployed young immigrants in French urban ghettos, as well as the children of the comfortable middle classes, have rioted in recent years.

The French government's attempt to introduce labor market reforms triggered the middle-class youth revolt in the spring of 2006. Ironically, the proposed employment reforms could have encouraged the hiring of more young people. Instead, the plans had to be scrapped in the face of violent riots. France, like some of the other industrial countries, seems caught in its own contradictions. It has on one hand benefited from globalization as its successful global companies have brought wealth and its encouragement of foreign investment have integrated it to the world, but its social policy and its populist approach have protected the population from the inevitable competitive pressures. The country's economy benefits from globalization, but the citizens fear the uncertainty and competition. "What does globalization mean to you?" a poll asked French youth between the ages of twenty and twenty-five in 2005. Forty-eight percent answered, "Fear," and only 27 percent said, "Hope."[75] French author Patrick Artus spelled out the fear in his book *Délocalisations: aurons-nous encore des emplois demain?* (Offshoring: will we still have jobs tomorrow?), published in 2005.

As the twentieth century ended, the most feared term in American industry circles was "China price." The fact that Chinese workers were ready to work for wages thirty times less than the American average raised the specter of plummeting U.S. wages and the mass transfer of manufacturing jobs to the world's factory, China. By 2006, even supporters of globalization in the West worried that Chinese and Indian gains from globalization might have been, in the words of Morgan Stanley's economist Stephen Roach, "translated into powerful headwinds for wages and labor income generation in the developed world. With economic recoveries in the high-wage industrial world becoming increasingly jobless, or wageless, or both."[76] In what seemed to be a growing chorus of concerned voices, economist Joseph Stiglitz warned about the dangers of outsourcing jobs. "American and rich-country engineers and computer specialists will either have to accept a wage cut or be forced into unemployment or to seek other employment—almost surely at lower wages."[77] Stiglitz's prognosis got support from an unlikely quarter. Introducing the organization's outlook for

2006, a senior IMF official acknowledged that foreign competition has constrained wage increases in industries most open to global competition and even lowered the sensitivity of wages to productivity increases. While noting that this does not mean that globalization necessarily lowers wages, because it also spurs productivity, he conceded that "the effect of globalization on wages will become an increasingly debated issue, especially as the share of labor income in total output of developed countries continues to fall."[78]

WINNERS AND LOSERS IN FULL VIEW

Developments in the early years of the second millennium have managed to put a new twist on an old debate: Does globalization help or hurt the poor? Since the late 1990s, especially since the antiglobalization riots in Seattle, opponents and supporters of globalization have argued about the merits and dangers of the greater economic integration between developed and developing countries.

On the basis of household survey data collected by different agencies, in the early 1990s, the World Bank estimated that the percentage of the developing nation population earning less than a dollar a day (at 1993 prices) had fallen. World Bank economist David Dollar argued that "the fast-growing economies in the world in this era of globalization are developing countries that are aggressively integrating with the world economy."[79] According to the bank's study, poverty had declined sharply in poor and populous countries of Asia such as China, India, Indonesia, and Vietnam. Between 1981 and 2001, the percentage of rural people living on less than a dollar a day decreased from 79 to 27 percent in China, from 63 to 42 percent in India, and from 55 to 11 percent in Indonesia. Thanks to globalization, China has achieved unprecedented prosperity within the space of a generation. The number of China's rural population living on less than a dollar a day dropped dramatically from 250 million in 1978 to ninety million in 2003. But critics question whether the credit for poverty alleviation should not go to domestic policy initiatives like agrarian reforms in China or the green revolution in India rather than to the opening of the global market. They also challenge the happy picture of poverty reduction by pointing to the growing income gaps within China and other globalizing countries.

The antiglobalization critics maintain that global integration leads to growing inequality within countries, with no benefits for the poor. However, the data supporting this claim are ambiguous at best. The Gini coefficient, a commonly used measure of inequality (0 signifies perfect equality, 1.00 represents complete inequality), certainly shows a growing gap in China since that country embraced globalization. In 1983, China's Gini index showed only moderate inequality of 0.28. But after two decades of economic reforms and closer integration with the world, China's income gap in 2003 had widened to 0.45—more unequal even than the capitalist United States, which had a Gini coefficient of 0.41.[80] In another fast-globalizing country, India, the consumption gap has grown only marginally to 0.33, although by another measure, the Gini index for asset distribution inequality in 2002 was 0.63 in rural India and 0.66 in urban India. This is considerably higher than the corresponding figures for China, which were 0.39 and 0.47, respectively.[81] One also has to note that the total number of extreme poor (those living on less than a dollar a day measured at purchasing power parity) was increasing throughout history up to about 1980. Since 1980, that number has declined by two hundred million, while the world population has increased by 1.8 billion. The progress is heartening, but 1.6 billion people still live in poverty.

The globalization and poverty discussion has also led economists to take a fresh look at the old debate on whether trade increases all-round prosperity or has the effect of widening economic gaps. A study of ninety-two countries over four decades done by World Bank economists David Dollar and Aart Kraay in 2000 concluded that although trade is good for growth, it is neutral as to income distribution—that is, the effects across all income groups are the same.[82] On the other hand, World Bank economists M. Lundberg and L. Squire surveyed a sample of thirty-eight countries between 1965 and 1992 to conclude that greater openness to trade has helped the upper strata of society to raise their income while lowering the incomes of the poorest 40 percent of the population. The costs of adjusting to greater openness, they write, are borne *exclusively* by the poor because they are far more vulnerable to shifts in international prices than are their wealthier compatriots.[83]

What should one conclude? Branko Milanovic of the World Bank has used new and more elaborate data of household income of ninety-five countries in his survey of 2003 and comes closer to analysts Lundberg and Squire's conclusion. "We find rather robust evidence that at a very low income level, it is the rich who benefit from openness." As income levels rise in middle-income countries, the relative income of the poor and the middle classes rises compared to the top 20 percent. "It seems," he concludes, "that openness makes income distribution worse before making it better."[84] Overall, findings suggest that increased trade tends to result in greater inequality as the income of the poorest rises more slowly. Segments of the population and parts of the country better equipped to benefit from global connections often surge ahead, leaving the less fortunate further behind than before. Although the case for trade as an engine of growth for the poorest of the poor is not irretrievably damaged, trade must raise average incomes before it can also lift the real incomes of the poor.

DUBIOUS PROGRESS IN LATIN AMERICA
AND AFRICA

Growing trade and the movement of capital, which represented globalization in the last decades of the twentieth century, have brought dubious progress in Africa and Latin America. In fact many in Latin America and Africa tend to view globalization as nothing but an attempt at recolonization by the West. In the 1990s, the proglobalization policy pursued by Latin American countries produced anemic rates of 1 percent per capita growth. As economist Nancy Birdsall wryly notes, the limited gains from global integration went to "a privileged few who had a university education or a good sense of timing in shifting their assets abroad."[85] Africa, the mother of historical globalization and one of the continents most open to trade, has emerged as the poster child for failed globalization. Although reforms undertaken in the 1990s brought investments in some countries, and some nations, such as Mauritius, have experienced galloping growth, two-thirds of the continent is sunk in poverty. Between 1981 and 2001, the proportion of Africans living below the international poverty line of a dollar a day increased from 42 to 47 percent. But just as China's and India's success cannot be attributed exclusively to globalization, neither can Africa's decline be laid at its door. A host of historical reasons and bad governance combined with unfortunate geography and climatic disasters and disease have brought sub-Saharan Africa to a state of dismal poverty. Coastal African countries that could have attracted footloose investment in the 1980s missed the boat because of bad governance and lack of infrastructure. Instead investors flocked to Asia. As Berkeley economist Pranab Bardhan puts it, "Globalization is not the main cause of developing countries' problems, contrary to the claim of critics of globalization—just as globalization is often not the main solution to these problems, contrary to the claim of overenthusiastic free traders."[86]

In fact, the poor themselves have answered the old debate on whether globalization is good or bad for the poor. Contrary to the antiglobalization activists who gather at international meetings to speak on their behalf and to cheer at the failure of the WTO, most of the poor would like to be a part of globalization. A trend that was spotted early in a global survey conducted in 2003 by the Pew Research Center for the People and the Press has now become abundantly clear: globalization is viewed much more favorably in low-income countries than in rich ones. The survey showed that although most people worldwide viewed growing global trade and business ties as good for their country, only 28 percent of people in the United States and Western Europe thought that such integration was "very good." Looked at it from other side, a significant minority (27 percent of households) in rich countries thought that "globalization has a bad effect on my country," compared to negligible numbers of households supporting that view in developing Asia (9 percent) or Sub-Saharan Africa (10 percent). "Beyond their common desire for democracy and free markets, people in emerging nations also generally acknowledge and accept globalization," the survey concluded. Three-quarters or more of those interviewed in almost every country thought children needed to learn English to succeed in the world today.[87] To the poor, globalization means opening to the world, access to the goods and services they aspire to and see on their television screens.

A survey of 23,500 consumers online in forty-two markets in Europe, North America, Asia Pacific, Latin America, South Africa, and the Middle East conducted by A. C. Nielsen in 2005 offered an interesting glimpse of the newly emerging middle class in the developing world benefiting from globalization. For Indians (78 percent) globalization means better job opportunities that help them to shape their careers better, followed by Filipinos (73 percent), and Chinese (71 percent). Over half of Latin Americans (57 percent) and consumers in Asia Pacific (53 percent) believe that more global business in their markets brings greater job opportunities and better working lives.[88]

The poor's positive view about globalization should not come as a surprise. The growing interconnectedness of the world through trade and travel has not brought equality, but clearly it has promoted economic growth. Since 1985, the *share* of the world's population living in poverty has declined, although the absolute *number* of people living in poverty has risen by one hundred million to 1.6 billion.[89] Unlike in the past, those left out in today's globalization cannot be ignored. Thanks to the global spread of television, even the poorest know how the rich in the West, and even their own elites, live. Their eagerness to join the globalized world and their frustration at their failure to achieve it poses a danger to social stability in many countries. As we have seen, the process of globalization has always produced winners and losers, and winners have usually succeeded in laying down the rules of interconnection. The current wave of antiglobalization sentiment in the West is seen as yet another example of the powerful seeking to change the rules of the game when the score is not in their favor. Having preached the virtues of free trade—ever since the days of Opium

Wars—the West suddenly appears worried now that millions of Chinese, Indians, and Vietnamese want to join in the global trading system. The growing concern in the West about a rising China and India and the impact on their economy is seen by many in the developing world as overblown fear about countries that are still desperately poor. According to the World Bank's calculations, of the 2.3 billion people who live in these two countries, nearly 1.5 billion earn less than two dollars a day.[90] These and millions of people in the developing world are aware of what they are being deprived of by being shut out of the world market and the chasm that separates them from the beneficiaries of globalization. The plight of the losers in today's globalization, too, is in full view of the world. The complex mix of hopes, desires, and fears that have driven people throughout history is still at work at an ever higher level. The high-speed connections that bind the world today make it impossible, even dangerous, for the winners to ignore the losers as they could in the era of sailboats and camel caravans. From a historical perspective it is clear that this process that has grown over the millennia and created the present globalized world cannot be reversed. It can be slowed down by raising barriers, but those barriers are only temporary hurdles to the march of global interconnection. Yet the problems that high-speed globalization has created and the growing sense of injustice and inequality it has engendered cannot be ignored. Protesters like the Korean farmer Lee Kyung-hae in Cancún may not be numerous, but millions in the developing countries who are silently seething at being left out of the connected world or at being given just the crumbs can be ignored only at great risk to world stability. The fact remains that those who benefit from globalization, whether in developing countries or the rich West, do not take to the streets to celebrate globalization. Boeing workers have not demonstrated in favor of globalization because China and India have placed big orders for Jumbo Jets, nor for that matter do happy customers march in parades to cheer the lowering of prices in the shopping aisles of Wal-Mart. But the standard of living people generally enjoy in the West is intimately linked to growing connections with the developing world and rising opportunities they offer their citizens to improve their lives. Thanks to the possibility of harnessing the vast pool of human resources and creativity that today's interconnected world presents, it would be a grave mistake for the rich industrial nations suddenly to try to block the process because it is politically convenient. The early-twentieth-century wars and recessions offer stark lessons about the consequences of forcibly disconnecting the human community because of the inability to find easy solutions to the inevitable problems that result from growing integration of the world.

Chapter 10 The Road Ahead

Who has ever known hard times
when one has money to spend?
Who with money has ever encountered
hindrance to pleasure?
Is it not right that enjoying this world
makes one oblivious of the other?
— *Seventeenth-century Hispanic poet Bernardo de Balbuena*

Early November 2006. I was on Korean Air's nonstop flight KE82 from New York to Seoul, a journey to honor an old commitment. But I welcomed this fourteen-hour flight as a respite from the intensity of wrapping up this manuscript, which has been with me for five years. I hoped to use the time to rest, to reflect on all I have learned about how our life has been shaped over the millennia, and perhaps sketch out some thoughts about the future.

The flight proved even more interesting. After a lunch of *bulbibi—*

Illegal immigrants are rounded up at the U.S.-Mexico border, 1997. Photo: Jeffrey D. Scott, The Alicia Patterson Foundation a traditional Korean dish of rice, vegetables, and shredded beef smothered in sesame oil and red chili paste, I dozed off for a few hours. I remembered that sesame oil was the first vegetable oil that Indians learned to extract from seeds some three thousand years ago, turning it into a major export item to the Roman Empire. My red chili paste came in a tube, an industrial version of the Mexican plant that Portuguese and Spanish traders had introduced to Asia in the sixteenth century. The wines offered with lunch came from Chile and California. The Boeing 747-400 that carried me across an ocean was the realization of humanity's dream of flight made possible by countless experiments and audacious attempts over the millennia. Many of this jet's components came from different parts of the world before being assembled in Boeing's plant in Everett, Washington. I fell asleep wondering where the rice served at lunch came from—from Korea, Texas, Vietnam, or Thailand. When I awoke in the darkened cabin, suffused in spots with the eerie glow of flat-screen television screens, I had the sensation of being somewhere in outer space. As I opened my window shade to peer at the world below, a flood of sunlight nearly blinded me. When my eyes adjusted, I saw the contours of Alaska receding across the hazy blue of the Pacific. I marveled at the thought that some twelve thousand years ago, our human ancestors had trudged over this desolate landscape, crossing the ice over Beringia, which has since vanished under rising water, separating Asia from America. I pulled down the window shade and turned on my notebook computer.

As the computer loaded the Windows operating system, I noticed a number of green bars light up in the system tray. A bubble message informed me that a wireless internet connection was available. Intrigued, I clicked to find that my computer was picking up the signal from a wireless service offered by Boeing's Connexion. To my delight, the service was free—a gift to passengers before the Wi-Fi service went out of business in January. I quickly logged onto my e-mail and sent a message to members of my family, dispersed thousands of miles away on other continents and in different time zones. As I sat back, read, and replied to messages, the enormity of the communications revolution that I described earlier sank in. Here I was, cruising high over the Pacific at 550 miles an hour, and from my humble Dell Latitude notebook, I was accessing information stored on Yale University's servers in New Haven. The darkened cabin I was sharing with hundreds of fellow passengers was a virtual office. As a journalist who left home to discover the world, I fall into the category of adventurers who have contributed to shrinking the world. That afternoon I continued in that role of connecting locations by sending out e-mails to various points on earth from Korean Airlines flight KE82.

After checking my e-mail, I clicked on Google News, which aggregates news headlines from all over the world as they appear on different Web sites. Judging by the headlines I read, the world below was a troubled place. Reading about happenings on the planet's surface while aloft at an altitude where I could see the earth's curvature, I had the strange sensation of being an outside observer, perhaps a less acute version of how the *Apollo* astronauts felt as they watched the earth's orb hanging in the pitch black of outer space. This awareness of being physically distant and yet intimately connected with the blue sphere below was similar to the feeling one has while reading a history of an ancient civilization.

I wondered about the distances that humans have traveled in the process of reconnecting with other communities through trade, religion, migration, and imperial control. Tiny clay tablets listing the inventories of merchandise once carried by the Assyrian trader Pusu-ken have been replaced by BlackBerry electronic tablets. Container ships and cargo planes have replaced the donkey and caravan. Today's legion of preachers includes televangelists airing the Gospel on satellite television and online NGO activists alerting the world about human-rights abuses and environmental degradation. Yesterday's handful of adventurers are today's millions of tourists who, like me, are aloft on passenger jets guided by global positioning "stars" rather than those aboard sailing ships following a celestial reckoning. The tools of imperial power have evolved from bows and arrows to tanks, globe-spanning missiles, and unmanned Predator drones that fire missiles at targets in Afghanistan at the press of a button by an "aviator" sitting at an air force base in Nevada. The world is smaller than ever, yet the news headlines reminded me how far apart human communities have become by taking or being forced into different paths for development.

MILLIONS LIFTED FROM POVERTY

As the coastlines of Siberia and China came into view, I reflected on how global connections have transformed the continent I was descending onto. Over a vast swath of Asia, rice paddies have within the space of a generation been transformed into bustling urban metropolises, replete with gleaming skyscrapers and bustling malls. Opinions may differ on how much globalization has reduced poverty in the more integrated parts of developing countries like China and India, but the speed of that amelioration would have been impossible without the flow of goods, capital, and technology. Nearly a third of China's 1.3 billion people have been lifted out of poverty, and in India a smaller but still significant proportion have moved up to the ranks of the middle class. China has become the world's fourth-largest economy and third-largest trading nation. India's growing global connections have enabled it to leverage its comparative advantage in software and English to corner half the world's outsourced service jobs. In the longer perspective of history, China and India—which in 1700 accounted for 22.3 percent and 24.4 percent, respectively, of the world's gross domestic product—have begun climbing back to their preeminent position after two and half centuries of decline. This is a remarkable turnaround brought about in no small measure by economic reform and global trade, technology and investment transfer.[1]

But the news headlines I skimmed also spoke of an angry and anxious world, concerned about the consequences of global interconnectedness. In developing countries, poverty is growing, while in the developed world, growing economic inequality, unemployment, and fears about job security are fueling demand for trade protections and more restrictive immigration policies. Meanwhile, rapid economic growth, especially in China, has led to a worsening of environmental conditions, and climate change has emerged as more an immediate concern than a distant threat.

Some of the concerns most often articulated about globalization stem from the income inequality between rich and poor countries and within countries open to the winds of global trade. The interconnectedness that we call globalization has bypassed a huge swath of territory from Africa, the Balkans, the Caucasus, and Central and Southwest Asia to South Asia and parts of Southeast Asia as well as parts of the Caribbean. Poorer countries' share of world trade has fallen over the past twenty years.

More than a billion people still live on less than a dollar a day, and most are likely never to have made a phone call or to have traveled beyond their place of birth. Lacking such basic infrastructure as drinking water, primary education, health services, roads, electricity, and ports, nearly two billion people are the forgotten and invisible denizens of a world I could not access from my plane. Yet it is this population that presents both a moral and a practical challenge to the developed world. Malnourished and disease-ridden children in Africa and Asia—whose numbers have grown with failing agriculture, stunted in part by the pressure of rich countries' farm subsidies—stare at the glittering West in silent rebuke. To the policymakers of rich countries, they are simply sources of insecurity—from illegal immigration to drug smuggling and crime—and vectors of disease. A Pentagon strategist calls this region the "non-integrating gap," from which new and unconventional security challenges are likely to emerge.

The U.S. Defense Department has quietly dispatched dozens of special advisers to hold thousands of exercises in more than a hundred nations to preempt and prepare for such threats.[2] But the dangers posed by this glaring socioeconomic disparity are more fundamental and long-term. An inability to use the enormous human potential that this left-out population represents would not only limit the markets for goods and services that developed and rapidly growing countries generate but would result in stagnant economies and failed states that can only become source of increasing numbers of illegal immigrants and recruits for crime and terrorism.

In a great historical irony, the adventurers and migrants who have since the dawn of history been the principal actors of globalization are now seen as major threats to the stability of a globalized world. In 2005, the United Nations estimated that the number of international migrants stood at around two hundred million. If they all lived in one territory, they would equal the population of the world's fifth most populous country, Brazil. And that number is poised to rise. Immigration laws have been tightening against a rising tide of poor migrants, and the planned erection of a seven-hundred-mile-long fence along the U.S.-Mexican border could become a symbol of anti-immigrant sentiment across the Western world.

Though remittances from immigrants have brought in valuable revenue, from the point of view of the less developed countries, large-scale emigration has not been all positive. In a countertrend, most developed countries, even immigration-resistant Japan, have also been drawing up legislation to encourage immigration by foreign doctors, engineers, programmers, and MBAs from the developing world. The exodus of educated personnel often condemns the poor countries to stagnation and decline, decimating, for example, the health services of some countries in sub-Saharan Africa. While health services in the United Kingdom are staffed by African and Asian health workers, only one in twelve doctors trained since Zambian independence is still practicing in that nation. And it is estimated that there are more Malawian doctors practicing medicine in the northern English city of Manchester than in all of Malawi, with its population of thirteen million.[3]

The migration crisis is in effect a global jobs crisis resulting from economic failure in countries in the "non-integrating gap." Some 185 million people all over the world were unemployed in 2004, and half the world's 2.8 billion workers earn less than two dollars a day, according to the International Labour Organization. With the per capita GDP of high-income countries growing at a rate of sixty-six times that of low-income countries, the lure of better-paid jobs has become stronger than ever. Tens of thousands of people from the hopeless economies of sub-Saharan Africa make desperate attempts to enter Europe. In 2006 some thirty thousand Africans reached the Spanish-controlled Canary Islands, and the motivation of many immigrants was summed up in a commonly heard phrase in Senegal: "Barcelone ou barxax," Barcelona or death. The newest poster child of failed states is Somalia, where in 2007 foreign intervention removed the Islamists from power only to create a possible new incubator of terrorism.

Across the ocean, thousands of Central American farmers trek through Mexican deserts at night, trying to reach the bright lights of the United States. Unable to compete with cheaper imported grain, many Mexican farmers have abandoned rural life for a hazardous journey north as illegal immigrants. The influx of Mexican immigrants to the United States, in particular, proved to be an explosive issue in an election year. With the proposed trade agreement between Colombia and the United States in peril after the Democrats' congressional victories in 2006, there were fears that without legitimate export growth in Colombia, narco-trafficking and illegal migration might reemerge as the only viable option.

"Globalization" has equally become a dirty word in Latin America, the continent described as "the most inequitable on the planet."[4] The failure of the World Trade Organization's Doha Round in the face both of American and European obstinacy about trade-distorting farm subsidies and of developing countries' resistance to opening their markets further was bad news for poor farmers in Africa, Asia, and Latin America. Talk of providing aid instead of market access sounds like hollow rhetoric when the world's richer countries spend three hundred billion dollars a year in agricultural subsidies, more than six times the amount they dole out on overseas aid. The subsidies depress world prices for such agricultural commodities as cotton, peanuts, and poultry and make it harder for farmers in developing nations to make a living.

UNSHACKLED CAPITAL, UNEMPLOYED LABOR

Migration apart, the economic consequences of greater integration with the world have stoked fear of globalization among the middle class in developed countries, which have long built their prosperity through international trade and investment. Electronic transactions and eased banking regulations have given financiers mobility across borders, but not always to the benefit of ordinary citizens. Even those whose jobs have been spared so far live in fear that their skills will become outmoded in a fast-changing world.

As unshackled capital roams in search of cheaper labor or better skills, workers in the United States are feeling increasingly vulnerable, as are their European counterparts. Unemployment in the European Union has remained at a stubborn 8 percent, while U.S. jobless rates hover around 5 percent. In the past three decades, thousands of American jobs have been lost to automation and offshoring. There are fears that new technologies and globalized labor markets may now threaten some of the remaining mid-level jobs. Western factories shut down because the widgets they once produced can be made by a factory in China or the Czech Republic for a few cents less per unit. Massive Chinese exports to the United States, responsible for eliminating American factory jobs, are most often American-designed products manufactured in China. The offshoring of production has boosted company earnings and provided cheap goods at Wal-Mart, but these gains have been concentrated in the pockets of CEOs and diffused among millions of consumers, doing nothing for the pain of laid-off workers. There is a gnawing concern that, given the nearly unlimited supply of low-cost workers abroad, jobs that are now leaving the West may never return. The theory of creative destruction, in which a continuous rise in productivity leads to the demise of old industries but also gives rise to new ones, may not be working this time around. Jobs are eliminated, but new ones at equal or higher pay do not materialize. The classic solution to the job loss problem—education and retraining—may not work in the new global economy, not when high skills are available at the end of a high-speed Internet connection for a tenth of the salary demanded in the United States or Europe.

The worry is not simply about current job loss, it is about the future more broadly. Even when jobs are retained at lower wages, they often come at the cost of cutbacks in health and retirement benefits, pushing workers down the poverty ladder over time. In a candid speech in November 2006, Janet L. Yellen, president of the Federal Reserve Bank of San Francisco, said that the American government should give workers buffeted by powerful economic forces a fair shot at retooling and finding new careers by offering retraining. Even though the cost to the federal government of strengthening the safety net would be high, she argued that to protect free trade, the United States should give workers unemployment and disability insurance, raise the minimum wage, and boost the social security protection of workers affected by globalization. Anger is also growing in Western Europe. Although strong social security systems prevent European companies from following the American example of mass layoffs, Continental firms have succeeded in holding down wages by dangling the Damocles Sword of outsourcing over their workers. Ironically, not only low-level employees but highly paid company executives now worry about being overtaken by rivals who could appear from nowhere with a killer product or a new source of equally skilled but lower-paid workers. Individual workers must be ever ready to learn new skills and start new careers if they wish to remain competitive. Stagnant job growth and rising social costs have spurred economic nationalism in many Western nations. Worse, governments seem bereft of ideas about how to deal with the job losses engendered by an enlarged global labor market. In the summer of 2006, U.S. Treasury Secretary Henry Paulson admitted that for certain issues, the government had no immediate answers and went on to say, "We will see major upheavals. Throughout history there have been upheavals. Just think of the Industrial Revolution in the nineteenth century. I only hope that we will manage them better this time around."[5]

Across the pond, his counterpart Chancellor of the Exchequer Gordon Brown issued a stark warning about "retreating back into the kind of beggar-thy-neighbor, heads-in-the-sand protectionism that set nation against nation in the 1930s." Brown expressed dismay that "ironically, even globalization's beneficiaries—the millions who are seeing cuts in consumer goods prices, lower inflation and lower interest rates, and higher economic growth and employment—are acting as if they are victims." Even winners were thinking like losers and were being influenced by the losers and by the popular focus on manufacturing job losses, service jobs lost to offshoring, and jobs lost to newcomers to communities.[6]

PARTY TIME FOR THE RICH

Brown did not address another reason for the public's pessimism about globalization—namely, the issue of growing income inequality in the United States and in globalizing countries in general. A Federal Reserve survey in 2004 found that the top 1 percent of American families held more wealth than the bottom 90 percent of other families combined. Corporations reaping the benefits of globalization have generously compensated their CEOs while leaving workers' wages stagnant. The Federal Reserve noted that the typical American chief executive in 2004 got a compensation package 170 times greater than that of the average American worker; in Britain it was twenty-two times greater, and in Japan, eleven times greater. Federal Reserve Bank of San Francisco President Yellen warned that "there are signs that rising inequality is intensifying resistance to globalization, impairing social cohesion, and could, ultimately, undermine American democracy." She admitted that technological changes and globalization had begun to affect educated mid-level workers, who "are seeing erosion of their job security relative to their less-educated counterparts."[7] Antiglobalization sentiment was reflected in the midterm congressional elections of November 2006 as Democratic Party candidates responded to widespread anger over job losses and uncertainty with a protectionist platform that swept the polls in the Midwest industrial belt. In election-day exit polls, 40 percent of voters said that they expected the next generation of Americans to have a lower standard of living as compared to 30 percent who said that they expected life to improve. Industry leaders took note of the pessimism. Even when U.S. exports are booming, "the message that globalization is a good thing has fallen flat and no longer resonates," confessed Bill Reinsch, president of the National Foreign Trade Council. He said, "Not enough people believe it anymore."[8]

The failure of many European governments to deal with the inevitable dislocation caused by technology and trade in their countries has led to protectionist demands from workers. Short-term political maneuvering and populist concerns have prevented governments from taking the hard decisions necessary to sustain openness. In the gathering gloom over the future of free trade after the Doha Round's failure, WTO Director General Pascal Lamy reminded world leaders of protectionism's terrible cost. After the Smoot-Hawley Act of 1930, U.S. unemployment rose from 9 percent to 25 percent in 1933. Exports fell by 60 percent; imports fell by two-thirds. "The aggressive use of sanctions," he recalled, "gave rise to the economic nationalism that was among the factors leading to World War II."[9]

Inequality has grown even more sharply in developing countries that have tried to integrate with the global economy: the gap between rural and urban areas has widened; urban sectors and the middle class, hooked into the world's transportation and communication networks, have benefited from the global connection, whereas the uneducated rural poor have fallen sharply behind. According to one estimate, less than 0.5 percent of Chinese households now own over 60 percent of the nation's personal wealth.[10] Meanwhile, the 150 million-odd migrant workers building China's gleaming cities and the millions more in antiquated rural factories live in Dickensian squalor. In India, the prosperity brought about by globalization has also dramatically widened the economic divide between rich and poor.

History is replete with examples of growing foreign connections and new technologies producing some winners and many losers. There have been many backlashes against the effects of global connection. The biggest difference between interconnections then and globalization now lies in information. In to-day's hyperconnected world, that backlash could rise and proliferate faster than in the past. The speed with which television news and Internet blogging re-ported the projected sale of companies to foreigners in early 2006, sparking economic nationalism in Europe and the United States and forcing govern-ments into taking swift action against their better judgment, was an indicator of the perils of fast-paced globalization. In the developing world, too, the com-munications revolution has increased social pressures. Big city lights no longer wink from afar. Viewers can see their allure on the small screens in their homes, whether in village shacks, urban slums, or the farthest rural outposts. Today the have-nots know only too well how the haves live. The problems are revealed much faster than any wise policy to solve them can be conceived or imple-mented.

The instantaneous transmission of news and images has turned the thor-oughly connected and even marginally connected citizens of the world into spectators and consumers of ideas and information. Images of natural disasters and human suffering elicit instinctive human sympathy and support in the wake of a tsunami or an earthquake. Televised Olympics and World Cup soccer championships reach a billion people, bringing diverse populations closer. Yet social, cultural, and political discourse aired freely over satellite television and the Internet also bewilders and alienates people, reinforcing prejudices.

The technological advances that have enhanced the human community's ability to tackle global problems have also empowered disaffected individuals to strike and cause harm, as has been demonstrated so devastatingly in New York, Washington, Madrid, London, Mumbai, and Bali. In early November 2006, Eliza Manningham-Buller, head of Britain's MI5, warned about the looming threat posed by some sixteen hundred British Muslims who have been plotting to carry out terrorist attacks in coordination with al-Qaeda leaders in Pakistan and Afghanistan. Among their tools is the technology that brings one instantaneous news during a flight. Manningham-Buller noted the sophisti-cated "propaganda machine" of terrorists who posted Internet video footage of insurgent attacks in Iraq within thirty minutes, along with audio translation into different languages, facilitating the dissemination of their particular views to a global audience. "And, chillingly," she noted, "we see the results here. Young teenagers being groomed to be suicide bombers."[11]

Just as sports channels or television drama serials attract fans worldwide, the airwaves offer the opportunity of a free exchange of hatred. In subjugating time and distance, globalization has wrought a clash of centuries. People still living in the eighteenth-century stages of economic development have been brought face to face with their long-separated cousins living in the twenty-first century. Instead of promoting dialogue and understanding, these jarring encounters have often provoked violent antipathy and xenophobia.

THE DARK CLOUDS OF A PANDEMIC

International contacts have brought not only undesirable cultural attitudes but nasty pathogens. In the past—whether during the Black Death in fourteenth-century Europe or the flu pandemic of 1918—the progress of the pathogen was constrained by the volume and velocity of transportation. Today's shrinking world and high speed of travel have brought unprecedented challenges. As I write these words, the world is bracing for the possibility of another pandemic from Asia if the avian flu that lurks in the region mutates into a form transmittable among humans.

The dark cloud of the SARS epidemic of 2003 displayed a silver lining, however. It showed that our closely integrated world, which allowed the rapid transmission of infection, could also be mobilized to halt that infection in its tracks. Even before achieving the rapid-response capabilities that twenty-first-century technology now permit, the World Health Organization by 1977 managed to contain and eliminate the epidemic of smallpox that killed, during the first three quarters of the twentieth centuries, about twice as many human beings as World Wars I and II, the Holocaust, and the Stalinist and Maoist purges combined. As the director of the World Health Organization at the time put it, the elimination of smallpox was a "triumph of management, not of medicine"—or the success of governance.[12]

Repeating that triumph in the currently heightened climate of national rights would not be easy. In 2003, the WTO with strong backing from developed nations as well as affected regional countries like Hong Kong and Singapore succeeded in overcoming the foot-dragging by others. After all, the SARS crisis did demonstrate the world community's vulnerability to threats emerging from any far corner of the planet and underlined the critical importance of governmental transparency in safeguarding global health. The Chinese government's initial refusal to disclose information about SARS, in order to safeguard the nation's economic growth, had given the virus a chance to spread beyond its initial borders.

The threat of global warming, which has been a matter of increasing concern (the in-flight entertainment on board my plane included Al Gore's foreboding documentary *An Inconvenient Truth*), was claiming front-page attention in newspapers with the issuance of a 575-page report by the British government. Global warming has the potential, the report prepared by economist Nicholas Stern said, to shrink the global economy by 20 percent and to cause economic and social disruption on a par with World Wars I and II and the Great Depression.[13] The connection between carbon-emitting economic growth and increasing trade and industrialization brought by globalization is unmistakable. As world trade grows and millions of factories join the global supply chain, and as mines are exploited and timber is felled to meet rising consumer demands, increased pollution is often the price. Pollution hits the originating country first, contaminating its soil and water, but soon it is absorbed in the atmosphere, where it becomes a global problem—poisoning the air and bringing acid rain to other parts of the world.

The millions of migrants who might be forced out of their homes because of flooding caused by global warming are still in the realm of speculation. Unlike the SARS crisis, damage to the environment has not had the mobilizing effect of a threatened pandemic. Surprisingly, despite the availability of energy-efficient technologies and know-how, little use is made of them and the world seems paralyzed about how to face the threat of global warming. The world's top emitter of greenhouse gases, the United States, has refused to sign the Kyoto Protocol, and the nations that have signed it have been inconsistent with its implementation, making only perfunctory attempts to grapple with the challenge of global warming. Although full implementation of the Kyoto Protocol would have had a marginal effect on greenhouse-gas emissions, even that limited gain has not been achieved. In the sixteen years since the Kyoto negotiations started, atmospheric concentrations of greenhouse gases that cause global warming have risen steadily, and experts believe they will go on rising even as the Kyoto Protocol is implemented.

Yet there is dramatic evidence that with the commitment of nations and effective global governance, it is possible to avert dangerous trends. Thanks to concerted action taken in combating ozone depletion through the Montreal Protocol, the ozone hole has shrunk and the threat of an epidemic of skin cancer in the southern hemisphere has receded. There are even signs that as a result of economic growth, urbanization, and enlightened public policies born of global awareness, a large and growing number of nations is reversing the long-standing trend toward destruction of their forests.

A host of technical agencies working under the auspices of the United Nations have created global standards that keep international telecommunication, trade, aviation, and shipping running smoothly. Common standards allow for a seamless operation of trade and financial transactions. But applying these standards has been the hard part, brushing against the states' sovereign rights and the interests of their political and financial elites. Despite developed nations' commitment to promote equity through the principles of free trade in the Doha Round, the talks have collapsed. They have also failed to help the poor, unconnected countries with the wherewithal to participate in the globalized economy. Even the developing countries that have enthusiastically embraced globalization have not always tried to build global connections with the consent and understanding of their citizenry. The absence of democracy in many globalizing countries has allowed the elites to adopt a high-handed approach. Because of the lack of accountability in one-party states like China and Vietnam, globalization has come with massive corruption and inequity, undermining the benefits of global connection and in the long run affecting the sustainability of their policy of openness. By contrast, globalization by a democratically elected government, as the experience of India has shown, runs the risk of going stop and start, and even reversing. The slow and uneven redistribution that capitalist economic growth inevitably generates can turn impatient citizens against openness, but in the long run democracy is a surer guarantee for a sustainable system of interdependence.

Yet life in every country today is so inextricably intertwined with the rest of the world that failure to appreciate this interdependence and its long-term effects could risk the world's drifting toward a major crisis. The international system is clearly suffering from a shortage of institutional capacity to address the issues we face. The current ineffective state of the United Nations in tackling some of the major humanitarian disasters illustrates the dilemma. Blaming the United Nations as such makes little sense, however. The root cause is rather the unwillingness—or inability—of key actors on the global scene and their constituencies to empower the United Nations to a level that corresponds with today's and tomorrow's global realities and possibilities. A multitude of nongovernmental organizations worldwide, the new preachers, have performed valuable services in addressing many problems raised by interconnectedness. But nothing can replace the power of sovereign governments working in concert to tackle global challenges.

To suggest that governments need to be proactive in sustaining an interdependent world that seems to be spinning out of control is not to undercut this book's thesis that globalization is a process propelled by many actors in pursuit of their own interests. Although no one is in charge of globalization, history shows that political power can channel or obstruct the multitude of currents that feed globalization, leading to a change in course.

THE TROUBLED LEGACY OF EMPIRES

Governments acting in isolation, disregarding global interests, have been a major problem. As we move further into the twenty-first century, the global connections forged by history's warriors have emerged as globalization's most problematic legacy. The world's sole superpower, the United States, which many view as the new Rome, has enormous, near-imperial power without an obvious empire. It is engaged in mortal combat with shadowy extremists who do not have a state but who are grimly determined to advance the cause of a long-defunct Islamic empire. The vast majority of Muslims share neither the extremists' dream of reviving a new virtual caliphate nor their zealotry in battling the "Crusaders and infidels." Yet the sense of hurt and injustice felt by the members of the Islamic umma, who perceive the American war on terror as a disguised war on Islam, is destabilizing for a connected world. Even if they may not be sympathetic to Islam, a vast majority of the world's population shares the Muslim world's antipathy toward a unilateralist American foreign policy. The initial world sympathy for the United States following the 9/11 attacks—when students in Tehran lit candles in memory of the victims and the acerbic French daily *Le Monde* declared, "We are all Americans"—has dissipated among the daily images of devastation, carnage, and torture following the American-led invasion of Iraq. In thousands of years of history, the world has seen worse violence and suffering of the innocent, but never before have those tragedies played out on television and computer screens in billions of homes. As noted earlier, information today is more fragile than when news traveled at the speed of the messenger. In 1453, it took forty days for the pope to learn of Constantinople's fall to the Turks; in 2001 the Twin Towers of the World Trade Center fell in real time, on live television, as the world watched on in horror. Within a month, American B-52s were raining bombs on Afghanistan and the Taliban regime was overthown. The attacks of 9/11 and succession of terrorist bombings that followed showed how economic integration has democratized access to the technology of destruction, rendered borders meaningless, and turned the word "globalization" into a threatening curse full of foreboding.

So, is globalization in danger of being derailed? The complacent argument that the world is too tightly intertwined by myriad ties to fall apart inevitably recalls British author Norman Angell's famous prediction on the eve of World

War I about the "economic impossibility" of just such a conflict. History is replete with examples of passion trumping faith in economic pragmatism and rationality. The future will always bring surprises, but a reading of history does not suggest that globalization—the integration that has grown over time—could ever be terminated. The complex process of interconnectedness that has gathered momentum over the course of millennia cannot be halted, nor can its myriad threads be neatly unwound. Major disruptive events—from the collapse of the Roman Empire and the Black Death to the collapse of trade and migration in the interwar years of the twentieth century—have temporarily halted the process and slowed the interconnections. It is possible that we could be headed toward such a breach as you read these words.

Such disruptions have always caused enormous suffering, but the crucial difference today is that the global economy is so integrated that the stakes are much higher for everyone. In fact, seen from the glittering metropolises of Asia, from the semiconductor labs in Taiwan and South Korea, from the world's busiest container port in Singapore, from Vietnam's Mekong Delta or India's once-sleepy towns now buzzing with shops and Internet cafés, or even the resurgent Irish business district of Dublin, the suggestion that globalization is in trouble would be incomprehensible. For the first time in history, hundreds of millions of people have seen their lives transformed and found hope that their children would live better than their parents did. The optimism of millions in Asia and in the rising economies of Ireland, former Soviet-bloc Europe, Africa, and Latin America and the desire of ordinary citizens to grab the opportunities afforded by an open economy is as much a fact of the globalized world as are the anxiety of American and European middle classes and the grinding poverty and despair of those left out of the equation. The question is, will anxiety and fear prevail over optimism and lead the world back to another dark period of isolation?

Economic integration, and with it cultural globalization, has far outpaced our global mindset, which is still rooted in nationalist terms. We benefit from all that the world has to offer, but we think only in narrow terms of protecting the land and people within our national borders—the borders that have been established only in the modern era. The barbed wire, chain-link fences, security forces, and immigration and customs agents that separate us from the rest of the world—all originating from the same village in a land that we called Duniya—cannot change the fact that we are bound together through the invisible filament of history. When our ancestors dipped their toes into the Red Sea to begin a millennial journey, they knew the world only as far as their eyes could see. Now not only can we look at the bigger picture, but we know how we have reached where we are and where we may be headed. We are in a position to know that the sum of human desires, aspirations, and fears that have woven our fates together can neither be disentangled nor reeled back. But neither are we capable of accurately gauging how this elemental mix will shape our planet's future. Still, compared to the past, when thickening global connectedness brought surprises, we are better equipped to look over the horizon at both the dangers and the opportunities. We now possess global institutions and tens of thousands of civil-society organizations to avoid setbacks to the process of global integration and fully realize the potential for a brighter future for those so far outside the globalized world. There is no alternative to rising above our tribal interests: over the centuries to come, our destinies will remain inextricably bound together. Calls to shut down globalization are pointless, because nobody is in charge, but together, we can attempt to nudge our rapidly integrating world toward a more harmonious course—because we are all connected.

Chronology

	Traders	Preachers	Warriors	Adventurers
50,000–28,000 BCE				Ancestors walk out of Africa; ancestors reach India; ancestors reach Malaysia; ancestors reach Australia; ancestors reach China, Korea; ancestors reach Europe
12,000 BCE				Ancestors reach Chile
8th millennium BCE	Traders travel to Çatal Höyük to buy obsidian for use as scythes			Indo-European migrants search for land
6th millennium BCE	Clay tablets and cuneiform script are used to count goods			
4th millennium BCE	Pusu-Ken, Assyrian trader, travels to Anatolia for profit; trade develops between India and Mesopotamia			Horse is domesticated in Ukraine
3rd millennium BCE	Phoenician traders establish wide network from western Mediterranean to Egypt		Sargon establishes empire of Akkad; Akkadian becomes lingua franca in empire and periphery	Egyptian queen Hatshepsut sends trading expedition to Africa
1st millennium BCE	Greek traders set up trading colonies in eastern Mediterranean			

Century				
7th century BCE	Necho sails around Africa		Buddha attains bodhi and urges disciples to go on preaching mission	Athenian gold coinage becomes common tender
6th century BCE	Hanno goes past Gibraltar to West African coast; Persian king Darius sends Scylax to explore Indus region			Camel use expands with invention of new type of saddle
5th century BCE	Herodotus seeks source of Nile			
4th century BCE	Pytheas travels to Britain in search of tin; Xenophon travels through Turkey to south-central Europe	Alexander the Great creates first transcontinental empire; Indo-Greek agreement allows inter-marriage; Greek (Koine) becomes lingua franca of much of the known world		
3rd century BCE		Indian emperor Aśoka promotes Buddhism	Buddhist council dispatches missionaries	Silk Road trade connects China with Mediterranean; Greek and Phoenician coins create two main currency spheres in Mediterranean
2nd century BCE		Han envoy Zhang Qian travels to Scythia		
1st century BCE		Indian king sends mission to Rome	Buddhism reaches China	Indian king sends trade mission to Rome; fake Italian wine is exported to India

	Traders	Preachers	Warriors	Adventurers
1st century CE	Discovery of monsoon wind, reported by Greek sailor, boosts Indian Ocean trade	Jesus says: "Go then, and make disciples of all nations"; Christianity reaches India	Han emperor Wu Di sends envoy to Persia	
2nd century CE	Roman spice trade with India booms	Stream of Buddhist missionaries arrives in China; Christian missionary college is founded in Alexandria	Kushan ruler of today's Afghanistan promotes Buddhism in Central Asia	
4th century CE	Spreading Buddhist faith promotes silk trade in Central Asia	Council of Nicaea appoints bishops in Christendom; Frumentius evangelizes in Ethiopia	Roman emperor Constantine embraces Christianity	
5th century CE	Roman and Byzantine gold and silver coins become international legal tenders	Frankish king Clovis converts to Christianity; missionaries fan out to western Europe; missionary college is founded in Constantinople	Roman law, adopted in Europe, forms basis of many legal systems; Latin becomes lingua franca of Roman Empire	
6th century CE		Korean envoy introduces Buddhism to Japan; Nestorian monks carry Christianity to China	Roman emperor Justinian introduces tariffs for imported items; Tang dynasty settles in Chang'an, eastern terminus of Silk Road	

7th century CE	Tang dynasty imports Central Asian horses and exports silk; cotton from India is introduced to Iraq and Middle East		Xuanzang returns to China from India with Buddhist texts, leading to beginning of book printing; Muhammad leads Muslim army to conquer infidel lands	Arab Muslim army invades Mesopotamia; Islam comes to Persia
8th century CE	Chinese coins and products reach East Africa; Canton hosts large diaspora of Asian, Arab, and European traders		Caliph Monsoor builds new capital in Baghdad; Arab armies capture Spain from North Africa and are halted at Battle of Tours	Charlemagne is anointed Holy Roman Emperor by pope; with Islamic empire, Arabic replaces vernacular languages; Greek classics are translated into Arabic; al-Fazari translates Brahmagupta's work on zero
9th century CE	Baghdad becomes terminus for trades from East and West; Persian port of Siraf is major entrepôt for trade between India, China, and Africa		Pretender to caliph's family leads to uprisings of black slaves (Zanj) in Iraq	al-Khwarizmi, whose name inspired *algorithm*, writes *Al-Jabr wa-al-Muqabilah* using "Hindu" numerals
11th century CE	Supply-chain production involving African ivory and Indian artisans rises	Buyids (Persians) invade Baghdad and seize power from caliph	Song emperor introduces new Champa rice; Turkish Seljuks capture Baghdad; Mahmoud of Ghazni captures Delhi; caliphate imports slave boys from Central Asia to be soldiers	Al-Biruni's account of India in Arabic opens door to West; Leif Eriksson sails to Vinland

	Traders	Preachers	Warriors	Adventurers
12th century CE	African slaves are sold in China	Rabbi Benjamin of Tudela, Spain, visits eastern	Genghis Khan begins his conquest	Andalusian traveler Ibn Jubayr visits Mecca; al-Khwarizmi's work on algebra is translated into Latin
13th century CE	Genoa receives Chinese merchandise via Arab traders; Mongols introduce travel pass cum credit card; invention of rudder and compass boosts year-round trade with Europe; Cairo-based Jewish traders run manufacturing and commercial operations in India	Christian crusaders sack Constantinople; papal emissary visits Mongol court seeking alliance against Islam; Southeast Asian traders embrace Islam; coffee drinking is popularized by devout Muslims in Middle East	Genghis Khan creates Mongol Empire; Islamic warriors conquer India; slave soldiers take power in Egypt and Syria as Mamluks; holy warriors in Turkey found Ottoman Empire	Marco Polo returns to Venice after trip through Asia
14th century CE	Large-scale cotton production begins in China	Malian ruler Mansa Musa makes hajj to Mecca; Friar Odoric of Pordenone, Italy, visits Tibet		Ibn Battuta sets out on travels, covering 75,000 miles
15th century CE	Russian trader Afanasii Nikitin travels to India; Port of Melaka rises as Venice of Southeast Asia; financial instruments such as the bill of exchange promote trade in Europe	Melaka, led by its ruler, embraces Islam; Christopher Columbus hopes gold found in East will enable Christian recovery of Jerusalem; Catholic Spain expels 150,000 Jews	Chinese navigator Zheng He explores Indian Ocean; Portuguese bring back first African slaves; Ottoman Turks capture Constantinople; Treaty of Tordesillas divides world between Spain and Portugal	Christopher Columbus lands in the Caribbean; Vasco da Gama arrives in India

16th century CE	Gujarati Muslim traders spread in Southeast Asia; Chinese porcelain shops open in Lisbon; Dutch-built fluyts speed long-distance trade	Jesuit missionary Francis Xavier lands in Goa; Pope Clement VIII gives blessing to coffee; Spanish missionary Las Casas condemns violent conversions and upholds human rights; sultan of Aceh seeks Ottoman protection and adopts Turkish flag	Pizarro conquers Peru and begins forced conversion of natives; Portuguese convert 1.2 million to Christianity in Asia; Japanese invader Hideyoshi introduces chili to Korea; failed Turkish siege of Vienna introduces coffee to Central Europe	Spanish king authorizes marriage with native Indians; Magellan's ship circumnavigates the globe; Francis Drake and Thomas Cavendish circumnavigate the globe; King Henry VIII launches large cannon-bearing boats
17th century CE	English and Dutch East India companies emerge as first multinational companies; New World silver bullion produces boom in European trade with Asia; first European coffeehouse opens in Oxford; French and Dutch trade Indian textile for spices in Southeast Asia and slaves in Africa	Imams persuade Ottoman emperor Murad IV to shut down coffeehouses in Istanbul	Ottoman ambassador to France Suleyman Aga becomes envoy extraordinaire of coffee	Portuguese rush to Brazil begins; Portuguese emigrate to Asia; British migration to American colonies begins
18th century CE	Dutch introduce coffee in Java; French take coffee to Caribbean; gold is mined in Africa; Brazil pays for Portuguese imports of Asian luxuries; British workers demonstrate against imported Indian textile; Eli Whitney's invention of cotton gin revolutionizes American cotton trade	Jesuit missionary creates national language by romanizing Vietnamese; Protestant school in New Haven secures funds from a former British governor in India to start Yale University in 1701	Englishman William Congreve learns rocketry from India's Tipu sultan (knowledge originated with Mongols and Persians)	Asians from Spanish-controlled Philippines migrate to Mexico in large numbers; Captain Cook claims Australia for Britain; Jean-François Galaup lands in Easter Island

	Traders	Preachers	Warriors	Adventurers
19th century CE	Commodore Perry opens Japan to trade; stock news, delivered by homing pigeon of Reuters, is upgraded with introduction of telegraph; invention of stock ticker; transatlantic cable for stock quotes is built; invention of steamship reduces shipping costs; British smuggle rubber seeds from Brazil; first refrigerated ship is introduced; petroleum is discovered, ushering in another transportation revolution	Dutch shipping brings many Muslims to Mecca for hajj; China undergoes Taiping and Boxer rebellions; missionary David Livingstone's account of Africa opens it to West; religious war in Java; British missionary-led campaign bans slave trade; American missionaries in China send first Chinese student to U.S., to Yale University	British launch English teaching program in India; British begin building railway in India; French-built Suez Canal opens; French create Senegalese shooter force; France conquers Vietnam to protect Catholics; Queen Victoria sends telegraphic message to empire; U.S. takes over Philippines; British invaders capture Baghdad	Charles Darwin leaves on voyage of exploration and later produces seminal work on evolution; British archaeologists decode cuneiform script; Jewish traveler David d'Beth Hillel visits Arabia and India; with steamships, largest migration in history begins; Chinese and Indian bonded laborers migrate to Caribbean and North America; U.S. Congress passes Chinese Exclusion Act in 1882
1900–1960	Malaysian rubber helps build tires for Ford Model T; Diner's Card is launched; AT&T installs transatlantic telephone; first container ship is launched	Kingdom of Saudi Arabia, born with Wahhabist support, rises to spread Islam; Universal Declaration of Human Rights is adopted in 1948; Wahhabist-inspired Darul Islam movement challenges Indonesia's national government; Mormon Missionary Training Center is founded in Utah	Panama Canal opens; French import 160,000 Senegalese shooters to fight Germany in World War I	Hungarian-born archaeologist Aurel Stein discovers ancient Buddhist texts in Dunhuang; first Caribbean migrants land in Britain; U.S. migrations peak at 2.1 million annually; precursor of World Tourism Organization is founded in 1925; international travel arrivals reach 25 million in 1950

1961–1969	1970–1979	1980–1989	1990–1999
Globalization enters *Webster's Dictionary*; fax machine is invented by Xerox; ASCII code is introduced for transferring data by computer	Boeing 747 is launched; Federal Express is founded; UPC bar code is introduced; Apple Computer launches PC revolution; Multi-Fiber Arrangement promotes distribution of textile production to developing countries	Transatlantic fiber-optic cable is laid; Indian software company Infosys begins bodyshopping	Chicago Stock Exchange introduces 24-hour trading; eBay, world's online marketplace, is launched; global online payment company PayPal is introduced
Peter Benenson founds Amnesty International; World Wildlife Foundation is created	Helsinki Watch begins to monitor human rights; environmental organization Greenpeace is founded		Many Islamic countries face demand for adoption of sharia; Christian group launches GOD TV; 172 countries attend Rio Earth Summit; treaty to ban land mines is signed because of NGO campaign; Islamist Taliban movement takes power in Afghanistan; Osama bin Laden calls for jihad against West; antiglobalization movements disrupt WTO's Seattle summit
Vietnam War leads to wider U.S. presence in Asia	Sino-Vietnam war and Khmer Rouge revolution generate millions of refugees	Russian invasion of Afghanistan stokes Islamic resistance and eventual rise of Taliban	Soviet Union collapses, freeing up East European satellites and promoting globalization; British colonial empire in Asia ends as Hong Kong is handed over to China
	1.4 million Vietnamese arrive in U.S.; Boeing 747 helps international travel; international arrivals reach 165 million		Tim Berners-Lee invents hypertext protocol, preparing launch of World Wide Web International travel arrivals reach 441 million in 1990

	Traders	Preachers	Warriors	Adventurers
2000–2007	Apple Computer launches iPod; Indian and Singaporean companies buy massive fiber-optic lines at fire-sale prices from bankrupt companies; call center is established in Senegal	Osama bin Laden-trained terrorists take jihad to U.S. on 11 September 2001; al-Qaeda launches Voice of the Caliphate Internet radio in 2005	Pentagon recruits 35,000 foreigners to serve in Iraq	U.S. expedites naturalization of 20,000 immigrants for Iraq War; tens of thousands of Africans attempt to migrate to Europe illegally; international travel arrivals reach 806 million

Acknowledgments

Globalization produced this book. It is the result of my wanderings around the world, visiting places that are or have been nodes for global connection, talking to countless people who have been involved in the process, and absorbing the ideas of others through their writings. It is impossible to fully acknowledge the debt I owe to all those who have helped me to understand, research, and write about this much-contested yet all-pervasive phenomenon of our existence.

My longtime friends Strobe Talbott, president of the Brookings Institution, and his wife, Brooke, have been instrumental in the writing of this book. The idea that we needed to come to grips with the phenomenon of globalization germinated during months of intense discussions with Strobe in 1991, when he was pitching the idea of a new monthly magazine, *Globe,* to his then employers at Time-Warner. The publisher nixed the idea, however, and shortly thereafter, Strobe joined the Clinton administration and I moved to the Hong Kong head office of the *Far Eastern Economic Review,* my magazine of twenty years. But my appetite had been whetted, and my desire to explore the issue further continued to grow. The opportunity to delve back into the topic came in 1999 when, as editor of the *Far Eastern Economic Review,* I began to plan a series of special millennium issues.

Delving into Asian history of the previous millennia and gaining the insights of some of the world's most brilliant thinkers immersed me even deeper into the project. So when Strobe, fresh out of government in 2001, invited me to join him in founding the Yale Center for the Study of Globalization, my answer was easy. Yale, with its incredible faculty and formidable academic resources, and the presence of many friends, was an inviting place for me to focus my energy on exploring globalization and seriously launch the book project. Although the Talbotts have since moved back to Washington, Strobe and Brooke have remained enthusiastic and steadfast supporters of the book, as well as an integral part of our extended family. Strobe has read many drafts of the manuscript and offered me both his time and his valuable advice. Readers may decide how well I have succeeded in this project, but the impetus for this wonderful journey came from Strobe, and so I thank him for setting me on this adventure.

Ernesto Zedillo, who took over from Strobe as director of the Yale Center for the Study of Globalization, has been unstinting in his support and has offered sharp insights into the world of trade and commerce. My colleague Haynie Wheeler has loyally read every draft and offered valuable suggestions. I am especially grateful to my colleague Susan Froetschel, whose meticulous reading of the manuscript and the proof has helped me avoid many embarrassments. Anthony Spire helped me with research, and Debbie Campoli produced some of the illustrations that appear in the book. Sarah Alexander, Abraham Koogler, Matthew Lee, and Amy Suntoke, student volunteers at *YaleGlobal* magazine, have helped in finding material and checking facts. Alain and Michèle Archambault, Paul de Bakker, David Goodman, Carol Honsa, Valerie Hansen, and Preminder Singh have read parts of the manuscript and have offered valuable suggestions.

Over the years, as I researched the book, so many friends and colleagues have helped me crystallize ideas and have suggested sources that it would be impossible to name them all. A few, however, stand out: Borje Ljunggren has been a friend for two decades and across three continents. He is a fellow observer of the world, and he carefully read the first draft and offered numerous suggestions to make the book more solidly grounded and accessible. Derek Shearer's exuberant enthusiasm for the book throughout has been a great morale booster. Bo Ekman took the time to read some chapters and has been an enthusiastic supporter of the project. He and the Tallberg Forum gave me a unique opportunity to test out my thesis on globalization among some of the world's leading thinkers on the subject. I would also like to acknowledge support and encouragement from Paresh Chattopadhyay, L. Gordon Crovitz, David Dapice, David Dollar, Staci Ford, Paul Freedman, Banning Garrett, Rajeshwari Ghose, Riaz Hassan, Masato Iso, Shim Jae Hoon, Seth Lipsky, Jonathan Lizee, Kishore Mahbubani, Bruce Mazlish, Rakesh Mohan, Deane Neubauer, Clyde Prestowitz, Jordan Ryan, Ramamurti Shankar, Gordon Slethaug, Martha Smalley, Tomoda Seki, Francesca Trivellato, Oyungerel Tsedevdamba, and Minky Warden. On my first trip to Africa, Dr. Abdoul Aziz Kasse was an amazing guide—patient, generous, and a fountain of knowledge.

The eminent historian Romila Thapar and sociologist Immanuel Wallerstein have been generous guides. Thapar has shown me how deep the roots of globalization are, while Wallerstein offered many insights into its development in the modern period. Continuing discussions with Thomas L. Friedman over the years have been an intellectual joy and a constant source of new perspectives on globalization. Kenneth Roth and Richard Dicker of Human Rights Watch have spent precious time explaining their work. Corporate leaders in globalizing industries, including N. R. Narayana Murthy of Infosys, Michael Ducker of Federal Express, and Javier Santoyo of Symantec, have aided my understanding of modern commerce by generously spending their time in explaining just how their respective systems operated.

I am indebted to my editor at the *Far Eastern Economic Review*, the late Derek Davies, for opening the door to a vast region and to my professors at Calcutta's Presidency College and Jadavpur University—Dilip Kumar Biswas, Ashin Das Gupta, Amalesh Tripathi, Sipra Sarkar—who whetted my appetite for a lifetime of studying the world. My supervisor at the University of Paris, François Joyaux, opened the window to international politics and taught me how to analyze complex global issues.

I am grateful to John Donatich, director of Yale University Press, his former colleague Larisa Heimert, now with Basic Books, and Tina Weiner, marketing director, for their warm support of the book. My thanks to my editor Michael O'Malley for his enthusiastic support and critical comments and to Alex Larson for keeping order in the chaos that book production involves. Finally, I was fortunate to find in Laura Jones Dooley an extraordinary editor, erudite, patient, and ever enthusiastic, in short an author's dream.

In a way, this book has been in the making over a thirty-five-year journey since leaving home. My partner on this journey has always been my wife, Geetanjali. The book is the outcome of countless debates and discussions over world events and visits to places and people we have encountered together. She has been the first, and often most severe, critic and editor of the various drafts. Our sons, Amit and Ateesh, have also read and edited countless drafts, and their thoughtful critiques have helped sharpen the book's focus. They have always been ready with love to lift the flagging spirit. My brother Pulak, himself an author and a publisher, has painstakingly read through the manuscript, corrected errors, and offered valuable suggestions for stylistic improvement. My computer whiz niece Amrita kept me abreast of developments in the digital world. My families in Calcutta, Bangalore, and Delhi have been a bedrock of support and encouragement. *Bound Together* has truly been a family enterprise.

Notes

INTRODUCTION

1. Branko Milanovic, "Can We Discern the Effect of Globalization on Income Distribution? Evidence from Household Surveys" (Washington, DC: World Bank, Development Research Group, 22 September 2003).
2. Roland Robertson, *Globalization: Social Theory and Global Culture* (London: Granta Books, 1991), 8.

CHAPTER 1: THE AFRICAN BEGINNING

Epigraph: Quoted at http://www.pbs.org/empires/egypt/special/virtual_library/hatshepsut_punt.html.
1. Nicholas Wade, *Before the Dawn: Recovering the Lost History of Our Ancestors* (New York: Penguin Press, 2006), 75, 81.
2. Charles Darwin, *The Descent of Man,* reprint ed. (New York: Penguin Classics, 2004), chap. 6.
3. Matt Ridley, *Genome: The Autobiography of a Species in 23 Chapters* (New York: HarperCollins, 2000), 49.
4. The estimated dates of human colonization are based on mtDNA data; James D. Watson, *DNA: The Secret of Life* (New York: Alfred A. Knopf, 2003), 246.
5. Richard Klein and Blake Edgar, *The Dawn of Human Culture* (New York: J. Wiley, 2002).

•

6. Wade, *Before the Dawn,* 58.

7. Steve Olson, *Mapping Human History: Genes, Race, and Our Common Human Origins* (New York: Houghton Mifflin, 2003), 206.

8. Rebecca L. Cann, Mark Stoneking, and Allan C. Wilson, "Mitochondrial DNA and Human Evolution," *Nature* 325 (1 January 1987): 31–36.

9. Watson, *DNA,* 233–39.

10. Olson, *Mapping Human History,* 26.

11. Rebecca L. Cann, "DNA and Human Origins," *Annual Review of Anthropology* 17 (1988): 127–43, at 127.

12. A. Underhill et al., "The Phylogeography of Y Chromosome Binary Haplotypes and the Origins of Modern Human Populations," *Annals of Human Genetics* 65 (2001): 43–62.

13. Russell Thomson et al., "Recent Common Ancestry of Human Y Chromosomes: Evidence from DNA Sequence Data," *Proceedings of the National Academy of Sciences of the United States* 97 (20 June 2000): 7360–65.

14. Xinzhi Wu, "On the Origin of Modern Humans in China," *Quaternary International* 117 (2004): 131–40.

15. Robert Lee Hotz, "Chinese Roots Lie in Africa, Research Says," *Los Angeles Times,* 29 September 1998.

16. Yuehai Ke et al., "African Origin of Modern Humans in East Asia: A Tale of 12,000 Y Chromosomes," *Science* 292 (11 May 2001): 1151–53; see also Li Jin and Bing Su, "Natives or Immigrants: Modern Human Origin in East Asia," *Nature Reviews: Genetics* 1 (November 2000): 126–33.

17. Peter Forster and Shuichi Matsumura, "Did Early Humans Go North or South?" *Science* 308 (13 May 2005): 965–66.

18. Nicholas Kristof, "Is Race Real?" *New York Times,* 11 July 2003, and personal communication with author.

19. Kumarasamy Thangara et al., "Reconstructing the Origin of Andaman Islanders," *Science* 308 (13 May 2005): 996.

20. Vincent Macaulay et al., "Single, Rapid Coastal Settlement of Asia Revealed by Analysis of Complete Mitochondrial Genomes," *Science* 308 (13 May 2005): 1034–36.

21. Ibid., 69.

22. Robert C. Walter et al., "Early Human Occupation of the Red Sea Coast of Eritrea during the Last Interglacial," *Nature* 405 (4 May 2000): 65–69.

23. Stephen Oppenheimer, *The Real Eve: Modern Man's Journey Out of Africa* (New York: Carroll and Graf, 2003), 80; Walter et al., "Early Human Occupation of the Red Sea Coast of Eritrea," 65–69.

24. Spencer Wells, *The Journey of Man: A Genetic Odyssey* (London: Penguin, 2002), 104. This section heavily relies on Wells and the analysis of my own genome done by Genographic Project, which he heads; ibid., 78.

25. Wade, *Before the Dawn,* 81.

26. Alan J. Redd et al., "Gene Flow from the Indian Subcontinent to Australia: Evidence from the Y Chromosome," *Current Biology* 12 (16 April 2002): 676.

27. Paul Plotz, quoted in Elia T. Ben-Ari, "Molecular Biographies: Anthropological Geneti-

cists Are Using the Genome to Decode Human History," *BioScience* 49, no. 2 (1999): 98–103.

28. Spencer Wells, quoted in ibid., 104.

29. Cengiz Cinnioğlu et al., "Excavating Y-Chromosome Haplotype Strata in Anatolia," *Human Genetics* 114 (2004): 134.

30. Susanta Roychoudhury et al., "Fundamental Genomic Unity of Ethnic India Is Revealed by Analysis of Mitochondrial DNA," *Current Science* 79 (10 November 2000): 1182–91; Toomas Kivisild et al., "An Indian Ancestry: A Key for Understanding Human Diversity in Europe and Beyond," in Colin Renfrew and Katie Boyle, eds., *Archaeogenetics: DNA and the Population Prehistory of Europe* (Cambridge: McDonald Institute for Archaeological Research, 2000).

31. Wells, *Journey of Man*, 117.

32. Wei Deng et al., "Evolution and Migration History of the Chinese Population Inferred from Chinese Y-Chromosome Evidence," *Journal of Human Genetics* 49 (July 2004): 339–48.

33. Olson, *Mapping Human History*, 131; Ke et al., "African Origin of Modern Humans in East Asia."

34. Ke et al., "African Origin of Modern Humans in East Asia."

35. Wells, *Journey of Man*, 121.

36. Olson, *Mapping Human History*, 131.

37. Jin and Su, "Natives or Immigrants."

38. Michael F. Hammer et al., "Dual Origins of the Japanese: Common Ground for Hunter-Gatherer and Farmer Y Chromosomes," *Journal of Human Genetics* (Tokyo) 51 (2006): 47–58.

39. Svante Pääbo, "The Mosaic That Is Our Genome," *Nature* 421 (23 January 2003): 409–12. In November 2006 scientists were reported to have found new genetic evidence suggesting that modern humans and Neanderthals interbred, at least on rare occasions. The legacy of that interbreeding is now found in a gene that is present among 70 percent of the world's population. John Noble Wilford, "Neanderthals in Gene Pool, Study Suggests," *New York Times*, 9 November 2006.

40. Watson, *DNA*, 245; Charles Pasternak, *Quest: The Essence of Humanity* (Chichester: Wiley, 2003), 97.

41. Paul Mellars, "A New Radiocarbon Revolution and the Dispersal of Modern Humans in Eurasia," *Nature* 439 (23 February 2006): 931–35.

42. Diego Hurtado de Mendoza and Ricardo Braginski, "Y Chromosomes Point to Native American Adam," *Science* 283 (5 March 1999): 1439–40.

43. Olson, *Mapping Human History*, 207.

44. A. Gibbons, "Geneticists Trace the DNA Trail of the First Americans," *Science* 259 (15 January 1993): 312–13.

45. Olson, *Mapping Human History*, 205.

46. David Christian, *Maps of Time: An Introduction to Big History* (Berkeley: University of California Press, 2004), 212.

47. Carles Vilà et al., "Widespread Origins of Domestic Horse Lineages," *Science* 291 (19 January 2001), 474–77.

48. Francis S. Collins, "What We Do and Don't Know About 'Race,' 'Ethnicity,' Genetics and Health at the Dawn of the Genome Era," *Nature Genetics Supplement* 36 (November 2004): S13–S15.

49. Luigi Luca Cavalli-Sforza, *Genes, Peoples, and Languages,* trans. Mark Seielstad (Berkeley: University of California Press, 2001), 11.

50. Ian J. Jackson, "Pigmentary Diversity: Identifying the Genes Causing Human Diversity," *European Journal of Human Genetics* 14 (24 May 2006), 978–80.

51. Wade, *Before the Dawn*, 16.

52. Watson, *DNA*, 254.

53. Ibid., 255.

54. Olson, *Mapping Human History*, 133.

55. Luigi Luca Cavalli-Sforza and Francesco Cavalli-Sforza, *The Great Human Diasporas: A History of Diversity and Evolution,* trans. Serah Thorne (Reading, MA: Addison-Wesley, 1995), 124, emphasis in original.

56. Ben-Ari, "Molecular Biographies," 103.

57. Olson, *Mapping Human History*, 99.

58. Ofer Bar-Yosef quoted in John Noble Wilford, "In West Bank, a First Hint of Agriculture: Figs," *New York Times*, 2 June 2006.

59. J. M. J. DeWet, "Grasses and the Culture History of Man," *Annals of the Missouri Botanical Garden* 68 (1981): 87–104.

60. Dennis Normile, "Archaeology: Yangtze Seen as Earliest Rice Site," *Science* 275 (17 January 1997): 309–10.

61. Mordechai E. Kislev, Anat Hartmann, and Ofer Bar-Yosef, "Early Domesticated Fig in the Jordan Valley," *Science* 312 (2 June 2006): 1372–74.

62. Not surprisingly, five of the biblical seven species derive from fruit trees: olive oil, wine, dry raisins, dates, and figs.

63. Daniel Zohary and Pinhas Spiegel-Roy, "Beginnings of Fruit Growing in the Old World," *Science* 187 (31 January 1975): 318–27.

64. Romana Unger-Hamilton, "The Epi-Palaeolithic Southern Levant and the Origins of Cultivation," *Current Anthropology* 30 (February 1989): 88–103.

65. David W. Anthony, "Migration in Archeology: The Baby and the Bathwater," *American Anthropologist* 92 (1990): 895–914.

66. Ibid., 898.

67. Michael Balter, "Search for the Indo-Europeans," *Science* 303 (27 February 2004): 1323.

68. For a summary of the debate between two schools, see Guido Barbujani and Andrea Pilastro, "Genetic Evidence on Origin and Dispersal of Human Populations Speaking Languages of the Nostratic Macrofamily," *Proceedings of the National Academy of Sciences* 90 (May 1993): 4670–73.

69. David W. Anthony, "The 'Kurgan Culture,' Indo-European Origins, and the Domestication of the Horse: A Reconsideration," *Current Anthropology* 27 (August–October 1986): 291–313.

70. David Anthony, Dimitri Y. Telegin, and Dorcas Brown, "The Origin of Horseback Riding," *Scientific American* (December 1991): 44–48.

71. Steven Mithen, *After the Ice: A Global Human History, 20,000–5000 BC* (Cambridge, MA: Harvard University Press, 2004), 67.

72. Robert P. Clark, *The Global Imperative: An Interpretive History of the Spread of Humankind* (Boulder, CO: Westview, 1997), 46.

73. Ian Hodder, "This Old House," *Natural History,* June 2006.

74. Joan Oates, "Trade and Power in the Fifth and Fourth Millennia BC: New Evidence from Northern Mesopotamia," *World Archaeology* 24, no. 3 (1993): 403–22.

75. Rita Smith Kipp and Edward M. Schortman, "The Political Impact of Trade in Chiefdoms," *American Anthropologist* 91 (1989): 370–85.

76. G. A. Wainwright, "Early Foreign Trade in East Africa," *Man* 47 (November 1947): 143–48.

77. Philip D. Curtin, *Cross-Cultural Trade in World History* (Cambridge: Cambridge University Press, 1984).

78. Christian, *Maps of Time,* 248.

79. Saul N. Vitkus, "Sargon Unseated," *Biblical Archaeologist,* September 1976, 114–17.

80. Fernand Braudel, *Memory and the Mediterranean,* trans. Sian Reynolds (New York: Alfred A. Knopf, 2001), 60.

81. Christopher Edens, "Dynamics of Trade in the Ancient Mesopotamian 'World System,'" *American Anthropologist* 94 (1992): 131.

82. Cited in ibid., 132.

83. Charles O. Hucker, *China's Imperial Past: An Introduction to Chinese History and Culture* (Stanford, CA: Stanford University Press, 1975), 126.

84. R. H. Pfeiffer, "Hammurabi Code: Critical Notes," *American Journal of Semitic Languages and Literatures* (1920): 310–15.

85. "Business in Babylon," *Bulletin of the Business Historical Society* 12 (1938): 25–27.

86. Cited by Christian, *Maps of Time,* 317.

87. Robert N. Bellah, "Religious Evolution" (lecture, University of Chicago, 16 October 1963).

CHAPTER 2: FROM CAMEL COMMERCE TO E-COMMERCE

Epigraph: E. Backhouse and J. O. P. Bland, *Annals and Memoirs of the Court of Peking* (Boston: Houghton Mifflin, 1914), 322–31.

1. The United Nations defines a Multinational Enterprise, or MNE, as "an enterprise that engages in foreign direct investment and owns or controls value-adding activities in more than one country."

2. As calculated by Cécile Michel, *Correspondance des marchands de kanish* (Paris: Éditions du Cerf, 2001), 173.

3. Ibid., 434.

4. Ibid., 296.

5. Louis Lawrence Orlin, *Assyrian Colonies in Cappadocia* (The Hague: Mouton, 1970), 53.

6. Mogens Trolle Larsen, *Old Assyrian Caravan Procedures* (Istanbul: Nederlands Historisch-Archaeologisch Institut in het Nabije Oosten, 1967), 83.

7. Richard W. Bulliet, *The Camel and the Wheel* (Cambridge, MA: Harvard University Press, 1975), 56.

8. William H. McNeill, "The Eccentricity of Wheels, or Eurasian Transportation in Historical Perspective," *American Historical Review* 92 (1987): 1111–26.

9. One million bolts of silk were paid for one hundred thousand horses. In the mid-eighth century, the most prosperous days of the Tang dynasty, the government collected 7.4 million bolts of plain silk as revenue. Xinru Liu, *Silk and Religion: An Exploration of Material Life and the Thought of People, AD 600–1200* (Delhi: Oxford University Press, 1996), 183.

10. David Christian, "Silk Roads or Steppe Roads? The Silk Roads in World History," *Journal of World History* 11, no. 1 (2000): 1–26; Tansen Sen, *Buddhism, Diplomacy, and Trade: The Realignment of Sino-Indian Relations, 600–1400* (Honolulu: Association of Asian Studies and University of Hawai'i Press, 2003), 118, 197–215.

11. Morris Rossabi, "'Decline' of the Central Asian Caravan Trade," in James D. Tracy, ed., *The Rise of Merchant Empires: Long Distance Trade in the Early Modern World, 1350–1750* (Cambridge: Cambridge University Press, 1990), 352.

12. Chinese paper technicians sent by the Chinese to set up a paper factory in Samarkand were captured by the Arabs in 751 CE. They introduced papermaking technology to Europe. James Burke, *Connections* (Boston: Little, Brown, 1978), 100. The story of the Chinese prisoner has since been discredited, but there is no question that papermaking technology from China was diffused to Europe through Islamic control of Central Asia. See Jonathan M. Bloom, *Paper before Print: The History and Impact of Paper in the Islamic World* (New Haven and London: Yale University Press, 2001), 62–65.

13. Rossabi, "'Decline' of the Central Asian Caravan Trade," 358.

14. Philip D. Curtin, *Cross-Cultural Trade in World History* (Cambridge: Cambridge University Press, 1984), 39.

15. Valerie Hansen, *The Open Empire: A History of China to 1600* (New York: W.W. Norton, 2000), 205.

16. Shereen Ratnagar, *Trading Encounters: From the Euphrates to the Indus in the Bronze Age,* 2nd ed. (New Delhi: Oxford University Press, 2004), 129–33.

17. Bridget and Raymond Allchin, *The Birth of Indian Civilization: India and Pakistan before 500 B.C.* (Baltimore: Penguin, 1968), 271–72.

18. Shereen Ratnagar, *Understanding Harappa: Civilization in the Greater Indus Valley* (New Delhi: Tulika, 2001), 10, 53.

19. Rondo Cameron, *A Concise Economic History of the World: From Paleolithic Times to the Present* (New York: Oxford University Press, 1997), 35.

20. Romila Thapar, *Early India: From the Origins to A.D. 1300* (London: Penguin, London, 2003), 178.

21. Quoted in Jay S. Fein and Pamela L. Stephens, eds., *Monsoons* (New York: Wiley, 1987), 143.

22. Pliny's comment that it took forty days to reach the Malabar Coast is considered a mistake. With the Southeast Monsoon pushing the sail, modern researchers say, it would have taken twenty days to make the journey from Bab el Mandeb to the Malabar Coast. Lionel Casson, "Rome's Trade with the East: The Sea Voyage to Africa and India," *Transactions of the American Philological Association* 110 (1980): 33.

23. Felipe Fernández-Armesto, *Civilizations* (London: Pan Books, 2001), 462.

24. Cited by Lionel Casson, "Rome's Trade with the East: The Sea Voyage to Africa and India," *Transactions of the American Philological Association* 110 (1980): 21–36.

25. Lionel Casson, "Ancient Naval Technology and the Route to India," in Vimala Begley and Richard Daniel De Puma, eds., *Rome and India: The Ancient Sea Trade* (Madison: University of Wisconsin Press, 1991), 10.

26. Grant Parker, "*Ex oriente luxuria:* Indian Commodities and Roman Experience," *Journal of the Economic and Social History of the Orient* 45, no. 1 (2002): 40–95.

27. Michael Cook, *A Brief History of the Human Race* (New York: W. W. Norton, 2003), 163.

28. Robert B. Jackson, *At Empire's Edge: Exploring Rome's Egyptian Frontier* (New Haven and London: Yale University Press, 2002), 88.

29. Ibid., 87.

30. Vimala Begley, *The Ancient Port of Arikamedu: New Excavations and Researches, 1989–1992* (Pondicherry: École Française d'Extrême-Orient, 1996), 23.

31. Elizabeth Lyding Will, "The Mediterranean Shipping Amphoras from Arikamedu," in Begley and De Ouma, eds., *Rome and India,* 151–52.

32. M. P. Prabhakaran, *The Historical Origin of India's Underdevelopment: A World-System Perspective* (Latham, MD: University Press of America, 1989), 15.

33. Haraprasad Ray, *Trade and Diplomacy in India-China Relations: A Study of Bengal during the Fifteenth Century* (London: Sangam Books, 1999), 105.

34. I. C. Glover, "Early Trade between India and Southeast Asia: A Link in the Development of a World Trading System" (University of Hull, Centre for South-East Asian Studies, Occasional Papers 16, 1989).

35. Eric R. Wolf, "The Social Organization of Mecca and the Origins of Islam," *Southwestern Journal of Anthropology* 7 (Winter 1951): 329–56.

36. G. A. Wainwright, "Early Foreign Trade in East Africa," *Man* 47 (November 1947): 143–48.

37. Milo Kearney, *The Indian Ocean in World History* (New York: Routledge, 2004), 64.

38. George F. Hourani, *Arab Seafaring in the Indian Ocean in Ancient and Early Medieval Times* (Princeton, NJ: Princeton University Press, 1951), 64.

39. Michael McCormick, *Origins of the European Economy: Communications and Commerce, A.D. 300–900* (Cambridge: Cambridge University Press, 2001), 585.

40. Jerry H. Bentley, "Hemispheric Integration, 500–1500 C.E.," *Journal of World History* 9, no. 2 (1998): 237–54.

41. Hourani, *Arab Seafaring in the Indian Ocean,* 73.

42. R. W. Beachey, "The East African Ivory Trade in the Nineteenth Century," *Journal of African History* 8, no. 2 (1967): 269–90.

43. "An Arab geographer named Yaqut (1179–1229 AD) coined the word 'Malabar' by combining 'Mali' (from 'Malayalam') with 'bar' (Persian for 'country')." Bindu Malieckal, "Muslims, Matriliny and *A Midsummer Night's Dream:* European Encounters with the Mappilas of Malabar, India," *Muslim World* 95 (April 2005): 297–316.

44. Ibid.

45. Hourani, *Arab Seafaring in the Indian Ocean,* 104.

46. Frederic C. Lane, "The Economic Meaning of the Invention of the Compass," *American Historical Review* 68 (1963): 605–17. See also Amir D. Aczel, *The Riddle of the Compass: The Invention That Changed the World* (New York: Harcourt, 2001), 77–109.

47. Burke, *Connections*, 26–28.

48. This section is based on S. D. Gotein, trans. and ed., *Letters of Medieval Jewish Traders* (Princeton, NJ: Princeton University Press, 1973), 186–93.

49. Ibid., 203.

50. R. S. Lopez, quoted in Janet L. Abu-Lughod, *Before European Hegemony: The World System, A.D. 1250–1350* (New York: Oxford University Press, 1989), 10.

51. Patricia Risso, *Merchants and Faith: Muslim Commerce and Culture in the Indian Ocean* (Boulder, CO: Westview, 1995), 49.

52. Amando Cortesao, trans. and ed., *The Suma Oriental of Tomé Pires . . . and the Book of Francisco Rodrigues . . .* (London: Hakluyt Society, 1944), 286–87.

53. Anthony Reid, *Southeast Asia in the Age of Commerce, 1450–1680*, vol. 2 (New Haven and London: Yale University Press, 1993), 327.

54. Wolfgang Schivelbusch, *Tastes of Paradise: A Social History of Spices, Stimulants, and Intoxicants* (New York: Pantheon, 1992).

55. Paul Freedman, "Spices and Late Medieval European Ideas of Scarcity and Value" (unpublished paper), quoted in Joaquim Romero Magalhães, *Portugueses no mundo do século XVI: espaços e produtos* (Lisbon: Comissao Nacional para as Comemoraoes dos Descobrimentos Portugueses, 1998), 24–25; Vitorino Magalhães Godinho, *Os descobrimentos e a economia mundial*, 2nd ed., vol. 2 (Lisbon: Editora Arcádia, 1965), 159, quoting the anonymous chronicle attributed to Álvaro Velho. See also Sanjay Subrahmanyam, *The Career and Legend of Vasco da Gama* (Cambridge: Cambridge University Press, 1997), 129.

56. Philip D. Curtin, *Cross-Cultural Trade in World History* (Cambridge: Cambridge University Press, 1984), 142.

57. Serge Gruzinski, *Les quatre parties du monde: histoire d'une mondialisation* (Paris: Martinière, 2004), 46.

58. Robert Finlay, "The Culture of Porcelain in World History," *Journal of World History* 9, no. 2 (1998): 141–87.

59. Francesca Trivellato, "Trading Diasporas and Trading Networks in the Early Modern Period: A Sephardic Partnership of Livorno in the Mediterranean, Europe and Portuguese India (ca. 1700–1750)" (Ph.D. diss., Brown University, 2004). I thank Trivellato for sharing her knowledge about this period.

60. Karl Moore and David Lewis, *Birth of the Multinational: Two Thousand Years of Ancient Business History, from Ashur to Augustus* (Copenhagen: Copenhagen Business School Press, 1999).

61. Jaap R. Bruijn, "Productivity, Profitability and Costs of Private and Corporate Dutch Ship Owning in the Seventeenth and Eighteenth Centuries," in Tracy, ed., *Rise of Merchant Empires*, 190.

62. Frank J. Lechner and John Boli, *The Globalization Reader* (Malden, MA: Blackwell Publishers, 2000), 52–56.

63. Ibid.

64. Kevin H. O'Rourke and Jeffrey G. Williamson, *Globalization and History: The Evolu-*

tion of a Nineteenth-Century Atlantic Economy (Cambridge, MA: MIT Press, 1999), chap. 3.

65. Kevin H. O'Rourke, "Europe and the Causes of Globalization," in Henryk Kierzkowski, ed., Europe and Globalization (New York: Palgrave Macmillan, 2002), 74.

66. Kenneth Pomerantz and Steven Topik, The World That Trade Created: Society, Culture and the World Economy, 1400 to the Present (Armonk, NY: M. E. Sharpe, 1999), 50.

67. Ibid., 49.

68. Electronic Business, February 2006, 26.

69. D. Hummels, "Time as a Trade Barrier" (mimeo), quoted in O'Rourke, "Europe and the Causes of Globalization," 75.

70. Abu-Lughod, Before European Hegemony, 15.

71. Thapar, Early India, 198.

72. Abu-Lughod, Before European Hegemony, 16.

73. Ronald Finlay, "Globalization and the European Economy: Medieval Origins to the Industrial Revolution," in Kierzkowski, ed., Europe and Globalization, 43.

74. John H. Munro, "The Monetary Origins of the Price Revolution: South German Silver Mining, Merchant Banking and Venetian Commerce, 1470–1540," in Dennis O. Flynn, Arturo Giráldez, and Richard von Glahn, eds., Global Connections and Monetary History, 1470–1800 (Aldershot: Ashgate, 2003), 18.

75. Andre Gunder Frank, ReOrient: Global Economy in the Asian Age (Berkeley: University of California Press, 1998), 295.

76. Jan De Vries, "Connecting Europe and Asia: A Quantitative Analysis of the Cape-Route Trade, 1497–1795," in Flynn, Giráldez, and von Glahn, eds., Global Connections and Monetary History, 1470–1800, 80–81.

77. Ibid., 94.

78. M. N. Pearson, "Asia and World Precious Metal Flows in the Early Modern Period," in John McGuire, Patrick Bertola, and Peter Reeves, eds., Evolution of the World Economy, Precious Metals and India (New Delhi: Oxford University Press, 2001), 25.

79. Jeyamalar Kathirithamby-Wells, quoted in Anthony Reid, ed., Southeast Asia in the Early Modern Era: Trade, Power, and Belief (Ithaca, NY: Cornell University Press, 1993), 124–25.

80. De Vries, "Connecting Europe and Asia," 75.

81. Tom Standage, The Victorian Internet: The Remarkable Story of the Telegraph and the Nineteenth Century's On-Line Pioneers (New York: Walker, 1998), 83.

82. Ibid., 104.

83. Ibid., 151.

84. The British colony in Malaysia had plants that produced the wonder insulator Gutta-Percha, making the wiring of the world possible until sturdier synthetic material was invented.

85. O'Rourke, "Europe and the Causes of Globalization," 76.

86. Steve Lohr, "Bar Code Détente: U.S. Finally Adds One More Digit," New York Times, 12 July 2004.

87. Tim Berners-Lee with Mark Fischetti, Weaving the Web: The Original Design and Ultimate Destiny of the World Wide Web by Its Inventor (San Francisco: HarperSanFrancisco, 1999), 9–29, italics in original.

88. Frances Cairncross, *The Death of Distance: How the Communications Revolution Will Change Our Lives* (London: Orion Business Books, 1997), 30.

89. "Electronic Trading," *Britannica Book of the Year, 2000,* Encyclopædia Britannica Online, http://search.eb.com/eb/article-9342433.

90. Lowell L. Bryan, "The Forces Reshaping Global Banking: Technology and Demography Are Changing the Deep Foundations on Which Traditional Financial Services Rest," *McKinsey Quarterly* 1993, no. 2.

91. Anthony Giddens, *Runaway World: How Globalisation Is Reshaping Our Lives* (New York: Routledge, 2003), 28.

92. *Indian Express,* 1 January 2004.

93. In December 2003, Singapore Technologies Telemedia purchased a 61.5 percent equity stake in Global Crossing for $250 million; in January 2004, Reliance Infocomm of India purchased FLAG Telecom for $211 million. The $130 million purchase price for TGN translates to roughly 5 cents on the dollar, which is on par with the approximately 6 cents on the dollar that Reliance paid for FLAG. Press release, *TeleGeography,* 1 November 2004.

94. "Today India, Tomorrow the World," *Economist,* 2–8 April 2005, 54.

95. Martin Kenney with Richard Florida, eds., *Locating Global Advantage: Industry Dynamics in the International Economy* (Stanford, CA: Stanford University Press, 2004), 1.

CHAPTER 3: THE WORLD INSIDE

Epigraph: Rabindranath Tagore, *Letters to a Friend,* ed. C. F. Andrews (New York: Macmillan, 1929), 133–37.

1. "Protests Turn Ugly outside WTO Meeting," Dan Rather, John Roberts, *CBS News: Evening News with Dan Rather,* 30 November 1999.

2. K. N. Chaudhury, *Asia before Europe: Economy and Civilisation of the Indian Ocean from the Rise of Islam to 1750* (Cambridge: Cambridge University Press, 1990), 308.

3. Victor Lieberman, *Strange Parallels: Southeast Asia in Global Context, c. 800–1830,* vol. 1, *Integration on the Mainland* (Cambridge: Cambridge University Press, 2003), 145.

4. Arnold Pacey, *Technology in World Civilization: A Thousand-Year History* (Cambridge, MA: MIT Press, 2001), 23.

5. Mark Elvin, *The Pattern of the Chinese Past* (Stanford, CA: Stanford University Press, 1973), 184.

6. Lynda Norene Shaffer, "A Concrete Panoply of Intercultural Exchange: Asia in World History," in Ainslie T. Embree and Carol Gluck, eds., *Asia in Western and World History: A Guide for Teaching* (Armonk, NY: M. E. Sharpe, 1997), 812–13.

7. Kenneth Pomeranz and Stephen Topik, *The World That Trade Created: Culture, Society, and the World Economy, 1400 to the Present* (Armonk, NY: M. E. Sharpe, 1999), 17.

8. Chaudhury, *Asia before Europe,* 305.

9. Ruth Barnes, Steve Cohen, and Rosemary Crill, *Trade, Temple and Court: Indian Textiles from the Tapi Collection* (Mumbai: India Book House, 2002), 90.

10. Jasleen Dhamija, "The Geography of Textile," in *Textiles from India: The Global Trade,* ed. Rosemary Crill (Calcutta: Seagull Books, 2006), 265.

11. Chaudhury, *Asia before Europe*, 19.

12. Pomeranz and Topik, *World That Trade Created*, 226.

13. The Roman Empire was importing so much Indian textile by paying in gold and silver that a drain on the Roman treasury was feared. The Roman historian Pliny the Elder complained that trade with the East cost 550 million sesterces each year, of which a fifth was for imports from India. Although Pliny may have been criticizing the profligacy of Roman patrician society, hoards of Roman gold coins found in south India do attest to a flourishing trade. William Wilson Hunter, *Annals of Rural Bengal* (London, 1899), 42, cited in M. P. Prabhakaran, *The Historical Origin of India's Underdevelopment: A World-System Perspective* (Lanham, MD: University Press of America, 1989), 15.

14. Jack Goody, *The East in the West* (Cambridge: Cambridge University Press, 1996), 127.

15. John McGuire, Patrick Bertola, and Peter Reeves, eds., *Evolution of the World Economy, Precious Metals and India* (New Delhi: Oxford University Press, 2001), 42, 62.

16. Dharma Kumar, *The Cambridge Economic History of India* (Bombay: Cambridge University Press, 1982), 842.

17. Barnes, Cohen, and Crill, *Trade, Temple and Court*, 92.

18. "Industries: Silk-weaving," in William Page, ed., *A History of the County of Middlesex*, vol. 2, *General . . .* (Victoria County History, 1911), 132–37. Available at http://www.british-history.ac.uk/report.asp?compid=22161.

19. Peter Dicken, *Global Shift: Reshaping the Global Economic Map in the Twenty-First Century*, 4th ed. (New York: Guilford Press, 2003), 317.

20. Kumar, *Cambridge Economic History of India*, 131.

21. William Bentinck quoted in Karl Marx, *Capital*, vol.1 (Moscow: [English edition]), 406. Since Marx does not mention his source, there has been speculation about the quotation's authenticity. However, as Marxist scholar Paresh Chattopadhyay has found in the new German-language *Marx-Engels Complete Works* (*MEGA* in the German acronym), the source is the *Times*, 28 April 1863, where the text is slightly different: "the poor handloom weavers on the banks of the Ganges, whose bones, according to the Governor-General, whited the plains of India." This quotation actually cites a member of the House of Commons who made the pronouncement one day earlier—William Bushfield Ferrand —and who was Marx's original source. Private communication with author.

22. Hugh Thomas, *The Slave Trade: The History of the Atlantic Slave Trade, 1440–1870* (London: Picador, 1997), 69–570.

23. Sven Beckert, "Emancipation and Empire: Reconstructing the Worldwide Web of Cotton Production in the Age of the American Civil War," *American Historical Review* 109 (December 2004): 1405–38.

24. Grace Rogers Cooper, "The Sewing Machine: Its Invention and Development," Digital edition (Washington, DC: Smithsonian Institution Libraries, February 2004), 217, available at http://www.sil.si.edu/digitalcollections/hst/cooper/.

25. Ibid., 58.

26. Dicken, *Global Shift*, 320.

27. International Labour Organization, "Globalization of the Footwear, Textiles and Clothing Industries," news release, 28 October 1996, 6.

28. Joan Magretta, "Fast, Global, and Entrepreneurial: Supply Chain Management, Hong

Kong Style: An Interview with Victor Fung," *Harvard Business Review* 76 (September–October 1998): 102–14.

29. News release, Vietnam News Agency, 20 February 2001.

30. Mei Fong, "U.S. to Consider Curbing Imports of China Apparel: New 'Safeguard' Quotas on Certain Clothing Items Are Sought by Textile Firms," *Wall Street Journal*, 5 November 2004; John Larkin, "India Aims to Be Textile Titan," ibid., 17 December 2004.

31. Keith Yearman and Amy Gluckman, "Falling Off a Cliff," *Dollars and Sense* (September–October 2005), available at http://www.dollarsandsense.org/archives/2005/0905 yearman.html.

32. Guy de Jonquières, "Garment Industry Faces a Global Shake-Up," *Financial Times*, 19 July 2004.

33. Mark S. Henry, "How Are Rural Workers and Industries Affected by Globalization? Discussion of Papers by Jean Crews-Klein and Karen Hamrick," paper presented at conference sponsored by USDA's Economic Research Service and the Farm Foundation, 6 June 2005, Washington, DC, available at http://www.farmfoundation.org/projects/documents/Henry.pdf.

34. Marc Lacey, "Along with That Caffeine Rush, a Taste of Seattle," *New York Times*, 22 July 2005.

35. Mark Pendergrast, *Uncommon Grounds: The History of Coffee and How It Transformed Our World* (New York: Basic Books, 2000), 5.

36. Bernard Lewis, *From Babel to Dragomans: Interpreting the Middle East* (London: Orion Books, 2004), 48. After an etymological analysis of the Arabic word for coffee a scholar concluded, "There is little doubt, therefore, that Arabic *qahwah* does not derive from *Kaffa* in Ethiopic, but rather originally means 'the dark one,' i.e., 'bean' or 'brew.'" Alan S. Kaye, "The Etymology of 'Coffee': The Dark Brew," *Journal of the American Oriental Society* 106 (1986): 557–58.

37. Heinrich Eduard Jacob, *Coffee: The Epic of a Commodity* (New York: Viking, 1935), 7–10.

38. Jean de la Roque, *Voyage de l'Arabie heureuse* (Amsterdam: Steenhower, 1716).

39. Jacob, *Coffee*, 1–10. According to the *Encyclopaedia of Islam*, s.v. "Kahwa": 'Abd-al-Kadir Djaziri (fl. 16th c.) credited two different Sufi figures with having introduced coffee to Yemen. On the authority of Ahmad 'Abd-al-Ghaffar (fl. 1530), he reported that Muhammad b. Sa'id Dhabhani (d. 1470), a jurist from Aden, had become acquainted with it during a period of exile in Africa and had observed its medicinal effects, subsequently introducing it in Sufi circles, where it was drunk during night vigils for prayer.

40. Jacob, *Coffee*, 32.

41. *Encyclopaedia of Islam*, s.v. "Kahwa."

42. Jacob, *Coffee*, 33.

43. *Encyclopaedia of Islam*, s.v. "Kahwa."

44. Ralph S. Hattox, *Coffee and Coffeehouses: The Origins of a Social Beverage in the Medieval Near East*, Near Eastern Studies, University of Washington, vol. 77, no. 3 (Seattle: Distributed by University of Washington Press, 1985).

45. Pendergrast, *Uncommon Grounds*, 7.

46. Merid W. Aregay, "The Early History of Ethiopia's Coffee Trade and the Rise of Shawa," *Journal of African History* 29 (1988): 19–25.

47. *Encyclopaedia of Islam,* s.v. "Kahwa."

48. Because of a heritage involving animal herding and a long history of nourishment by animal milk, the European population seems to have been devoid of the lactose intolerance that marks most of humanity. See James D. Watson, *DNA: The Secret of Life* (New York: Alfred K. Knopf, 2003), 256–57.

49. John Crawford, "History of Coffee," *Journal of the Statistical Society of London* (1852): 50–58.

50. "La grande histoire du café," http://www.nestle.fr/enseignants/docs/histoire.doc.

51. Robert Harms, *The Diligent: A Voyage through the Worlds of the Slave Trade* (New York: Basic Books, 2002), 345–46.

52. Kenneth Davids, *Coffee: A Guide to Buying, Brewing, and Enjoying,* 5th ed. (New York: St. Martin's Griffin, 2001); Davids, "Coffee Fundamentals," http://www.lucidcafe.com/fundamentals.html#history.

53. Thomas, *Slave Trade,* 634.

54. Ibid., 788.

55. Luella N. Dambaugh, *The Coffee Frontier in Brazil* (Gainesville: University of Florida Press, 1959), 5.

56. Nicholas Tarling, ed., *Cambridge History of Southeast Asia,* vol. 1, pt. 1, *From Early Times to c. 1500* (Cambridge: Cambridge University Press, 1992), 595.

57. Fernand Braudel, *Civilization and Capitalism, Fifteenth–Eighteenth Century,* vol. 1, *The Structures of Everyday Life,* reprint ed. (Berkeley: University of California Press, 1992), 258.

58. Sidney W. Mintz, "The Forefathers of Crack," in North American Congress on Latin America, *Report on the Americas* 22, no. 6 (1989), available at http://instruct.uwo.ca/anthro/211/crack.htm.

59. Sherri Day, "Move Over Starbucks, Juan Valdez Is Coming," *New York Times,* 29 November 2003.

60. Celine Charveriat, "Bitter Coffee: How the Poor Are Paying for the Slump in Coffee Prices" (Oxfam, May 2001).

61. David Adams, "Waking Up to World Coffee Crisis," *St. Petersburg Times,* 11 August 2002.

62. News release, Reuters, 11 December 2000.

63. http://www.tws.com.sg/singapore/sin_html/directory/shopping/it_electronics.html.

64. Prbhakaran, *Historical Origin of India's Underdevelopment,* 13–16.

65. Mariá Rosa Menocal, *Ornament of the World: How Muslims, Jews, and Christians Created a Culture of Tolerance in Medieval Spain* (Boston: Little, Brown, 2002), 180. Jacob Bronowski observed: "It may be the size of the Moorish empire that made it a kind of bazaar of knowledge, whose scholars included heretic Nestorian Christians in the east and infidel Jews in the west. It may be a quality in Islam as a religion, which, though it strove to convert people, did not despise their knowledge." Bronowski, *The Ascent of Man* (Boston: Little, Brown, 1973), 168–69.

66. Bronowski, *Ascent of Man,* 168–69.

67. T. R. Reid, *The Chip: How Two Americans Invented the Microchip and Launched a Revolution,* rev. ed. (New York: Random House, 2001), 11.

68. Jeffrey Zygmont, *Microchip: An Idea, Its Genesis, and the Revolution It Created* (Cambridge, MA: Perseus, 2003), 79.

69. Alan M. Turing, "On Computable Numbers, with an Application to the *Entscheidungsproblem*," in Martin Davis, ed., *The Undecidable* (New York: Raven Press, 1965), 116–51.

70. T. R. Reid, *The Chip* (New York: Random House, 2001), 132.

71. "Jack Kilby (1923–2005), Inventor of the Integrated Circuit," *IEEE Signal Processing Magazine,* September 2005, 6.

72. Jack S. Kilby, "The Electrical Century," *Proceedings of the IEEE* 88 (January 2000): 110.

73. L. Buckwalter, "Now It's Pocket Calculators," *Mechanics Illustrated* 69 (February 1973): 69, 108–9, cited in Kathy B. Hamrick, "The History of the Hand-Held Electronic Calculator," *American Mathematical Monthly,* October 1996, 633–39.

74. William Aspray, "The Intel 4004 Microprocessor: What Constituted Invention?" *IEEE Annals of the History of Computing* 19, no. 3 (1997): 4–15.

75. Jeffry A. Frieden, *Global Capitalism: Its Fall and Rise in the Twentieth Century* (New York: W. W. Norton, 2006), 395.

76. Video footage of antiglobalization and other demonstrations is archived at http://video.indymedia.org/en/archive.shtml.

CHAPTER 4: PREACHERS' WORLD

Epigraph: "New Light from an Old Lamp: A Strategic Analysis of Buddhism" (documented researches), five lectures by Tan Beng Sin, Piyasilo, 1990 (unpublished manuscript).

1. Richard Dicker, interview with author, 2 June 2005.

2. Ibid.

3. Ken Roth, interview with author, 18 May 2005.

4. Max Weber quoted in Thomas Arnold, *The Spread of Islam in the World* (London 1886; reprint, New Delhi: Goodword Books, 2002), 1.

5. Elie Wiesel, "The Perils of Indifference: Lessons Learned from a Violent Century," Address at the Seventh Millennium Evening at the White House, 12 April 1999.

6. Karen Armstrong, *Holy War: The Crusades and Their Impact on the World* (New York: Anchor Books, 2001), 387.

7. Philip Jenkins, *The Next Christendom: The Coming of Global Christianity* (Oxford: Oxford University Press, 2002), 28.

8. Nicholas Tarling, ed., *The Cambridge History of Southeast Asia,* vol. 1, pt. 1, *From Early Times to c. 1500* (Cambridge: Cambridge University Press, 1992), 356.

9. Robert P. Clark, *The Global Imperative: An Interpretive History of the Spread of Humankind* (Boulder, CO: Westview, 1997), 66.

10. Romila Thapar, *A History of India,* vol. 1 (London: Penguin, 1966), 131.

11. Romila Thapar, *Aśoka and the Decline of the Mauryas* (New Delhi: Oxford University Press, 1997), 46–49.

12. In "Cultural Interchange between India and China," Tan Yun-Shan writes, "According to the records of a Chinese book called 'Li-Tai-Kao Seng-Chuan' or the biographies of great monks in various ages, there were two hundred Chinese monks who studied in India with great success, and twenty-four Indian sages who preached in China with mar-

velous achievement. But it must be remembered that there must have been many, many more monks and scholars who either perished on the way or disliked to leave their earthly names to posterity." Available at http://ignca.nic.in/ks_40038.htm.

13. Jonathan M. Bloom, *Paper before Print: The History and Impact of Paper in the Islamic World* (New Haven and London: Yale University Press, 2001), 36. See also Mishi Saran, *Chasing the Monk's Shadow: A Journey in the Footsteps of Xuanzang* (New Delhi: Penguin, 2005), 11–12.

14. Sally Hovey Wriggins, *Xuanzang: A Buddhist Pilgrim on the Silk Road* (Boulder, CO: Westview, 1996), 160.

15. Li Yongshi, trans., *The Life of Hsuan Tsang by Huili,* quoted in ibid., 176.

16. Ibid., 168.

17. Tan, "Cultural Interchange between India and China."

18. This is an interesting difference between Buddhism and Islam, where the Koran can be recited only in Arabic, the language God spoke.

19. Victor H. Mair, "Buddhism and the Rise of the Written Vernacular in East Asia: The Making of National Languages," *Journal of Asian Studies* 53 (August 1994): 707–751.

20. Xinru Liu, *Silk and Religion: An Exploration of Material Life and the Thought of People, A.D. 600–1200* (New Delhi: Oxford University Press, 1996), 14. Multicolored silk flags that adorned Buddhist holy places in Central Asia and India were mostly from China; Xinru Liu, *Ancient India and Ancient China: Trade and Religious Exchanges, A.D. 1–600* (New Delhi: Oxford University Press, 1988), 69. The fifth-century Indian poet Kalidasa described a wedding ceremony where the whole town was bedecked with Chinese-made silk flags (*ci-nams'ukam keto*). Interestingly, more than a millennium later China had emerged as the supplier of choice of foreign flags, including that of the United States.

21. John Kieschnick, *The Impact of Buddhism on Chinese Material Culture* (Princeton, NJ: Princeton University Press, 2003), 262. The earlier discussion of the Buddhist inspiration for producing books is based on Kieschnick.

22. Liu, *Silk and Religion,* 187.

23. Martin Baumann, "Global Buddhism: Developmental Periods, Regional Histories, and a New Analytical Perspective," *Journal of Global Buddhism* 2 (2001): 1–43, available at http://www.geocities.com/globalbuddhism/html/2/baumann011.pdf.

24. Based on Huston Smith, *The Religions of Man* (New York: Harper and Row, 1986), 425–43.

25. Michael Cook, *A Brief History of the Human Race* (New York: W. W. Norton, 2005), 222.

26. Thapar, *History of India,* 134–35; see also David Chidester, *Christianity: A Global History* (New York: HarperCollins, 2000), 452–59.

27. Daniel J. Boorstin, *The Discoverers* (New York: Random House, 1983), 122.

28. "European Exploration," Encyclopædia Britannica Online, http://search.eb.com/eb/article?tocId=25961.

29. Christopher Columbus, *The Four Voyages,* ed. and trans. J. M. Cohen (London: Penguin, 1969), 300.

30. Chidester, *Christianity,* 353–54.

31. Ibid., 412.

32. Margarita Zamora, *Reading Columbus* (Berkeley: University of California Press, 1993), 19.

33. Karen Armstrong, *A History of God: The Four-Thousand-Year Quest of Judaism, Christianity, and Islam* (New York: Ballantine, 1994), 258.

34. Serge Gruzinki, *Les quatre parties du monde: histoire d'une mondialisation* (Paris: Martinière, 2004), 49.

35. John King Fairbank and Merle Goldman, *China: A New History* (Cambridge, MA: Harvard University Press, 1998), 223.

36. Jonathan D. Spence, *The Search for Modern China* (New York: W. W. Norton, 1990), 206.

37. Lamin Sanneh, *Translating the Message: The Missionary Impact on Culture* (Maryknoll, NY: Orbis, 1989), 123.

38. Lê Thành Khôi, *Histoire du Viêt Nam: des origines à 1858* (Paris: Sudestasie, 1981), 290.

39. A. J. R. Russell-Wood, *The Portuguese Empire, 1415–1808: A World on the Move* (Baltimore: Johns Hopkins University Press, 1992), 202.

40. George Shepperson, "David Livingstone (1813–1873): A Centenary Assessment," *Geographical Journal* 139 (June 1973): 216.

41. Alvyn Austin, "Discovering Livingstone," *Christian History* 16, no. 4 (1997): electronic copy, n.p.

42. Shepperson, "David Livingstone," 217.

43. Leila Koivunen, "Visualizing Africa: Complexities of Illustrating David Livingstone's *Missionary Travels*," in *The Papers of the Nordic Conference on the History of Ideas*, vol. 1 (Helsinki: University of Helsinki, 2001). Also see T. Jack Thompson, "Images of Africa: Missionary Photography in the Nineteenth Century; An Introduction" (Occasional Paper, University of Copenhagen, Centre of African Studies, February 2004).

44. Shepperson, "David Livingstone," 216.

45. Quoted in ibid., 210.

46. Martha Lund Smalley, ed., "Communications from the Field: Missionary Postcards from Africa," *Occasional Publications*, 5 (New Haven: Yale Divinity School Library, 1994).

47. Victor Lewis-Smith, "God on the Box," *New Humanist*, 1 September 2002, available at http://www.newhumanist.org.uk/volume117issue3_more.php?id=224_0_12_0_C.

48. Efraim Karsh, *Islamic Imperialism: A History* (New Haven and London: Yale University Press, 2006), 88.

49. Amira K. Bennison, "Muslim Universalism and Western Globalization," in A. G. Hopkins, ed., *Globalization in World History* (New York: W. W. Norton, 2002), 74.

50. Arnold, *Spread of Islam*, 412.

51. Boorstin, *Discoverers*, 122.

52. R. Hunt Davis, Jr., "Teaching about the African Past in the Context of World History," *World History Connected*, http://worldhistoryconnected.press.uiuc.edu/2.1/davis.html.

53. Arnold, *Spread of Islam*, 256.

54. Romila Thapar, *A History of India*, vol. 1 (London: Penguin, 1966), 234.

55. Cook, *Brief History*, 287–90.

56. Quoted in Anthony Reid, *Charting the Shape of Early Modern Southeast Asia* (Chiang Mai: Silkworm Books, 1999), 16.

57. D. J. M. Tate, *The Making of Modern South-East Asia*, vol. 1, *The European Conquest* (Kuala Lumpur: Oxford University Press, 1971), 34.

58. Reid, *Charting the Shape*, 26.

59. Ibid., 27.

60. Gene M. Chenoweth, "Melaka, 'Piracy' and the Modern World System," *Journal of Law and Religion* 13, no. 1 (1996): 107–25.

61. M. C. Rickleffs, "Islamization in Java: Fourteenth to Eighteenth Centuries," in Ahmad Ibrahim, Sharon Siddique, and Yasmin Hussain, comps., *Readings on Islam in Southeast Asia* (Singapore: ISEAS, 1985), 40.

62. Anthony Reid, "A Millennium of Change," *Far Eastern Economic Review*, 10 June 1999.

63. Anthony Reid, *Southeast Asia in the Age of Commerce, 1450–1680*, vol. 2 (New Haven and London: Yale University Press, 1993), 144. Much of the Southeast Asia section relies on this classic study.

64. Rickleffs, "Islamization in Java," 41.

65. Sylvia Fraser-Lu, *Silverware of South-East Asia* (Singapore: Oxford University Press, 1989), 3.

66. Michael Laffan, "The Tangled Roots of Islamist Activism in Southeast Asia," *Cambridge Review of International Affairs* 16 (October 2003): 402.

67. T. N. Harper, "Empire, Diaspora, and the Languages of Globalism, 1850–1914," in Hopkins, *Globalization in History*, 148.

68. Arnold, *Spread of Islam*, 371–72.

69. Reza Aslan, *No God but God: The Origins, Evolution, and Future of Islam* (New York: Random House, 2005), 243.

70. Ibid.

71. A study in 2004 found that some fifty-seven publications originating in Saudi Arabia reportedly "state it is a religious obligation to hate Christians and Jews, and warn against imitating, befriending or helping such 'infidels' in any way." According to the Freedom House study, "they instill contempt for America" as well as "a Nazi-like hatred for Jews." John Mintz, "Report Cites 'Hate' Writings in U.S. Mosques," *Washington Post*, 6 February 2005.

72. Olivier Roy, "Why Do They Hate Us? Not Because of Iraq," *New York Times*, 22 July 2005.

73. This section relies largely on Armstrong, *History of God*, 132–69.

74. http://www.islamicity.com/mosque/default.shtml.

75. http://www.islamonline.net/English/AboutUs.shtml.

76. Anton La Guardia, "Al-Qa'eda Launches Voice of the Caliphate Internet News Bulletins," *Telegraph*, 28 September 2005.

77. Immanuel Wallerstein, *European Universalism: The Rhetoric of Power* (New York: New Press, 2006), 5.

78. Michael Wood, *Conquistadors* (Berkeley: University of California Press, 2002), 271.

79. Quoted by Martin Dugard, "Stanley Meets Livingstone," *Smithsonian* 34 (October 2003): 68–76.

80. Quoted by Dan Jacobson, "Dr. Livingstone, He Presumed," *American Scholar* 70 (2001): 99.

81. William Cobbett, *The Parliamentary History of England: From the Norman Conquest in 1066 to the Year 1803*, 36 vols. (London: T. Curson Hansard, 1806–20), 28:45.

82. Benenson quoted in Stephen Pincock, "Obituary of Peter James Henry Solomon Benenson," *Lancet,* 2 April 2005, 1224.

83. http://www.amnesty.org.uk/action/events/timeline.shtml.

84. http://www.amnesty.org.uk/action/events/biography.shtml.

85. Irene Khan, "Foreword," *Annual Report, 2005* (Amnesty International), available at http://web.amnesty.org/report2005/message-eng.

86. James M. Russell, "The Ambivalence about the Globalization of Telecommunications: The Story of Amnesty International, Shell Oil Company and Nigeria," *Journal of Human Rights* 1 (September 2002): 405–16.

87. Roth interview.

88. Dicker interview.

89. Kran, "Foreword."

90. Roth interview.

CHAPTER 5: WORLD IN MOTION

Epigraph: Laurence Bergreen, *Over the Edge of the World: Magellan's Terrifying Circumnavigation of the Globe* (New York: William Morrow, 2003), 396.

1. W. M. Spellman, *The Global Community: Migration and the Making of the Modern World* (Stroud: Sutton, 2002), 24.

2. Anthony Pagden, *Peoples and Empires* (New York: Modern Library, 2001), xix.

3. E. H. Hair, "The 'Periplus of Hanno' in the History and Historiography of Black Africa," *History in Africa* 14 (1987): 43–66.

4. This account is based on Lionel Casson, *Travel in the Ancient World* (Baltimore: Johns Hopkins University Press, 1994), 44–57.

5. "European Exploration," Encyclopædia Britannica Online, http://search.eb.com/eb/article?tocId=25961.

6. W. H. Schoff, trans. and ed., *The Periplus of the Erythraean Sea: Travel and Trade in the Indian Ocean by a Merchant of the First Century* (London, 1912).

7. Sima Qian, *Records of the Great Historian, Han Dynasty II,* trans. Burton Watson, rev. ed. (New York: Columbia University Press, 1993), 123.

8. Bin Yang, "Horses, Silver, and Cowries: Yunnan in Global Perspective," *Journal of World History* 15 (September 2004): 286.

9. David Christian, "Silk Roads in World History," *Journal of World History* 11 (Spring 2000): 1–26.

10. Hok-Lam Chan quoted by Ed Gargan, *Newsday* (New York), 19 January 2003.

11. A nineteen-year-old named Mwamaka Sharifu from an island off Kenya was invited to China to take part in the six hundredth anniversary of Zheng He's expedition. Joseph Kahn, "China Has an Ancient Mariner to Tell You About," *New York Times,* 20 July 2005.

12. Philip Snow, *The Star Raft: China's Encounter with Africa* (London: Weidenfeld and Nicolson, 1988), 22.

13. Edward Dreyer, "Review of Gavin Menzies, *1421: The Year China Discovered America,*" *Journal of the Society for Ming Studies* 50 (Fall 2004): 131.

14. Fernand Braudel, *Civilization and Capitalism, Fifteenth–Eighteenth Century,* vol. 3, *The Perspective of the World* (Berkeley: University of California Press, 1992), 106.

15. Jean Verdon, *Travel in the Middle Ages,* trans. George Holoch (Notre Dame, IN: University of Notre Dame Press, 2003), 147.

16. Maxine Feifer, *Tourism in History: From Imperial Rome to the Present* (New York: Stein and Day, 1985), 29.

17. Michael McCormick, *Origins of the European Economy: Communications and Commerce, A.D. 300–900* (Cambridge: Cambridge University Press, 2001), 227–35.

18. K. N. Chaudhury, *Asia before Europe: Economy and Civilisation of the Indian Ocean from the Rise of Islam to 1750* (Cambridge: Cambridge University Press, 1990), 134.

19. Cited in Robin Hanbury-Tenison, ed., *The Oxford Book of Explorers* (Oxford: Oxford University Press, 1993), 15.

20. Frances Wood, *Did Marco Polo Go to China?* (Boulder, CO: Westview, 1996), 160.

21. Greg Clydesdale, "European Explorers, Entrepreneurial Selection and Environmental Thresholds," *Prometheus* 23 (March 2005): 47–61.

22. A. S. Morris, "The Journey beyond Three Seas," *Geographical Journal* 133 (December 1967): 502–8.

23. Cecil Roth, "Genoese Jews in the Thirteenth Century," *Speculum* 25 (April 1950): 190–97.

24. David Whitehouse, "Maritime Trade in the Gulf: The Eleventh and Twelfth Centuries," *World Archaeology* 14 (February 1983): 328–34.

25. Ross E. Dunn, *The Adventures of Ibn Battuta: A Muslim Traveler of the Fourteenth Century* (Berkeley: University of California Press, 1986), 258.

26. D. O. Morgan, "Ibn Battuta and the Mongols," *Journal of the Royal Asiatic Society,* 3rd Ser., 11 (2001): 1–11.

27. Charles Beckingham, "In Search of Ibn Battuta," *Asian Affairs* 8 (October 1977): 268.

28. Walter J. Fischel, "David d'Beth Hillel: An Unknown Jewish Traveller to the Middle East and India in the Nineteenth Century," *Oriens* (December 1957): 240–47.

29. Prester John's realm held out prospects for valuable trade as well. In a letter of ca. 1170 that circulated in Europe, Prester John claims that all manner of precious substances (especially gems) abound in his territories. Precious stones are emphasized more than spices, for although Prester John's empire produces pepper in large quantities, the spice must still be taken from groves guarded by snakes. Cited by Paul Freedman, "Spices and Late Medieval European Ideas of Scarcity and Value" (unpublished paper), quoted in Joaquim Romero Magalhães, *Portugueses no mundo do século XVI: espaços e produtos* (Lisbon: Comissao Nacional para as Comemoraoes dos Descobrimentos Portugueses, 1998). Prince Henry was a crusader. His caravels, adorned with the cross of the Military Order of Christ and led by squires, not merchants, sailed to inflict damage to the Moors along the African coast. Clydesdale, "European Explorers," *Prometheus* 23 (March 2005): 54.

30. Daniel J. Boorstin, *The Discoverers* (New York: Random House, 1983), 168.

31. Michael Prawdin, *The Mongol Empire: Its Rise and Legacy,* trans. Eden and Cedar Paul (New York: Free Press, 1967), 510.

32. Hugh Thomas, *Rivers of Gold: The Rise of the Spanish Empire, from Columbus to Magellan* (New York: Random House, 2003), 68.

33. Abbas Hamdani, "Columbus and the Recovery of Jerusalem," *Journal of the American Oriental Society* 99, no. 1 (1979): 39–48.

34. Thomas, *Rivers of Gold*, 76.

35. Boorstin, *Discoverers*, 176.

36. Wolfgang Schivelbusch, *Tastes of Paradise: A Social History of Spices, Stimulants, and Intoxicants* (New York: Vintage, 1993), 12.

37. W. S. Merwin, "Name in the Sand," *New York Review of Books*, 27 May 2004, 36–37.

38. Henry Kamen, *Empire: How Spain Became a World Power* (New York: HarperCollins, 2003), 129.

39. Kenneth Pomeranz and Stephen Topik, *The World That Trade Created* (Armonk, NY: M. E. Sharpe, 1999), 49.

40. Leslie Page Moch, *Moving Europeans: Migration in Western Europe since 1560* (Bloomington, Indiana University Press, 2003), 147; Alan M. Taylor and Jeffrey G. Williamson, "Convergence in the Age of Mass Migration," NBR Working Paper No. 4711, April 1994; Andrés Solimano, "International Migration and the Global Economic Order: An Overview," World Bank Policy Research Working Paper No. 2720, November 2001.

41. John Torpey, *The Invention of the Passport* (London: Cambridge University Press, 2000), 92.

42. Roger Sanjek, "Rethinking Migration, Ancient to Future," *Global Networks* 3 (July 2003): 315.

43. Solimano, "International Migration."

44. Stephen Castles and Mark J. Miller, *The Age of Migration: International Population Movements in the Modern World*, 2nd ed. (Basingstoke: Macmillan, 1998), 57.

45. David Northrup, "Free and Unfree Labor Migration, 1600–1900: An Introduction," *Journal of World History* 24, no. 2 (2003): 125–30.

46. Hugh R. Baker, "The Myth of the Travelling Wok: The Overseas Chinese," *Asian Affairs* 28 (March 1997): 28–37.

47. Cláudia Rei, "The Role of Transportation Technology in Economic Leadership," paper, Boston University, Department of Economics, September 2002, available at http://people.bu.edu/cr/Rei_C_Transportation.pdf.

48. The mortality rate was extreme. In 1850, of 740 emigrants embarked on two ships for Callao, 247 died on the voyage, more than 33 percent. Baker, "Myth of the Travelling Wok."

49. Matthew Pratt Guterl, "After Slavery: Asian Labor, the American South, and the Age of Emancipation," *Journal of World History* 24, no. 2 (2003): 209–41.

50. Sanjek, "Rethinking Migration," 315.

51. Ibid.

52. K. Laxmi Narayan, "Indian Diaspora: A Demographic Perspective," Occasional Paper, University of Hyderabad, 2002, available at http://www.uohyd.ernet.in/sss/indian_diaspora/oc3.pdf.

53. Adam McKeown, "Global Migration, 1846–1940," *Journal of World History* 15, no. 2 (2004): 155–89.

54. Claude Markovits, "Indian Merchant Networks outside India in the Nineteenth and Twentieth Centuries: A Preliminary Survey," *Modern Asian Studies* 33, no. 4 (1999): 883–911.

55. *Migration in an Interconnected World: New Directions for Action* (Global Commission on

International Migration, Geneva, October 2005), available at http://www.gcim.org/attachements/gcim-complete-report-2005.pdf.

56. Howard W. French, "Next Wave of Camera-Wielding Tourists Is from China," *New York Times,* 17 May 2006.

57. Department of the Navy, Naval Historical Center, "By Sea, Air, and Land: An Illustrated History of the U.S. Navy and the War in Southeast Asia," chap. 5, available at http://www.history.navy.mil/seairland/chap5.htm; Walter J. Boyne, "The Fall of Saigon," *Airforce Magazine Online,* http://www.afa.org/magazine/April2000/0400saigon.asp.

58. David Lamb, *Vietnam Now: A Reporter Returns* (New York: Basic Books, 2002), 74.

59. Henry Kamen, *Spain's Road to Empire: The Making of a World Power* (London: Penguin, 2002), 198.

CHAPTER 6: THE IMPERIAL WEAVE

Epigraph: Quoted in A. G. Hopkins, ed., *Globalization in World History* (New York: W. W. Norton, 2002), 124.

1. Egyptian Islamist writer Sayyid Qutb, quoted by Efraim Karsh, *Islamic Imperialism: A History* (New Haven and London: Yale University Press, 2006), 212.

2. Anthony Pagden, *Peoples and Empires: A Short History of European Migration, Exploration, and Conquest, from Greece to the Present* (New York: Modern Library, 2001), 12–13.

3. William W. Tarn, "Alexander the Great and the Unity of Mankind," Raleigh Lecture on History, British Academy, 10 May 1933, 4.

4. Ibid., 27.

5. Plutarch quoted in Pagden, *Peoples and Empires,* 13.

6. Ibid., 31.

7. President Theodore Roosevelt announced that "chronic wrongdoing, or an impotence which results in a general loosening of the ties of civilized society, may in America, as elsewhere, ultimately require intervention by some civilized nation, and in the Western Hemisphere. . . . The Monroe Doctrine may force the United States, however, reluctantly, in flagrant cases of wrongdoing or impotence, to the exercise of an international police power." Niall Ferguson, *Colossus: The Price of America's Empire* (New York: Penguin, 2004), 52–53.

8. Cesare Polengh, "Hideyoshi and Korea," 25 April 2003, Samurai Archives, http://www.samurai-archives.com/hak.html.

9. Ferguson, *Colossus,* 80.

10. There are more than thirty thousand McDonald's restaurants in 120 countries, and 70 percent of Coca-Cola's sales are outside North America. Ibid., 18.

11. Robert Kaplan, "Empire by Stealth," *Atlantic Monthly,* July–August 2003, 66.

12. Cited by Ferguson, *Colossus,* 68.

13. Geoffrey W. Conrad and Arthur A. Demarest, *Religion and Empire: The Dynamics of Aztec and Inca Expansionism* (Cambridge: Cambridge University Press, 1984), 1, quotation at 129.

14. Ibid., 129.

15. Albert Hourani, *A History of the Arab Peoples* (London: Faber and Faber, 1991), 19.

16. Michael Cook, *A Brief History of the Human Race* (New York: W. W. Norton 2003), 281–84.

17. Ronald Findlay and Mats Lundahl, "Demographic Shocks and the Factor Proportions Model: From the Plague of Justinian to the Black Death," typescript, Columbia University, University Seminar in Economic History, 28, available at http://www.econ.barnard.columbia.edu/~econhist/papers/Findlay%20Justinian.pdf.

18. Karsh, *Islamic Imperialism*, 34.

19. Valerie Hansen, *The Open Empire: A History of China to 1600*, 6th rev. ed. (New York: W. W. Norton, 2000), 337.

20. Jack Weatherford, *Genghis Khan and the Making of the Modern World* (New York: Crown, 2004), 101.

21. Ronald Findlay and Mats Lundahl, "The First Globalization Episode: The Creation of the Mongol Empire, or the Economics of Chinggis Khan," 14, available at http://yaleglobal.yale.edu/about/pdfs/mongol.pdf. See also Nicholas Wade, "Scientists Link a Prolific Gene Tree to the Manchu Conquerors of China," *New York Times*, 1 November 2005.

22. Weatherford, *Genghis Khan*, 111.

23. According to a later account, when Alexander set out for Syria, Aristotle wrote to him advising him to seize Socotra and send a group of Greeks to settle there for the sake of *al-qatir* (resin) and aloe. Vitaly Naumkin, "Fieldwork in Socotra," *Bulletin of the British Society for Middle Eastern Studies* 16, no. 2 (1989): 133–42.

24. Daniel J. Boorstin, *The Discoverers* (New York: Random House, 1983), 160–61.

25. Henry Kamen, *Spain's Road to Empire: The Making of a World Power, 1492–1763* (London: Penguin, 2002), 301.

26. Anthony Pagden, *Spanish Imperialism and the Political Imagination: Studies in European and Spanish-American Social and Political Theory, 1513–1830* (New Haven and London: Yale University Press, 1998), 14.

27. Robert L. Tignor, "Colonial Africa through the Lens of Colonial Latin America," in Jeremy Adelman, ed., *Colonial Legacies: The Problem of Persistence in Latin American History* (New York: Routledge, 1999), 35.

28. Niall Ferguson, *Empire: The Rise and Demise of the British World Order and the Lessons for Global Power* (New York: Basic Books, 2002), 7.

29. James Bryce and General Stanley Maude quoted by Tony Judt, "Dreams of Empire," *New York Review of Books*, 4 November 2004.

30. Pagden, *Peoples and Empires*, xxiii–xxiv.

31. Sir William Tarn, *Hellenistic Civilisation* (London: Edward Arnold, 1927), 4.

32. Pagden, *Peoples and Empires*, 25.

33. Peter Mansfield, *A History of the Middle East* (London: Penguin, 2003), 17.

34. John Keegan, *A History of Warfare* (New York: Vintage, 1994), 212.

35. Findlay and Lundahl, "First Globalization Episode," 21.

36. Tatiana Zerjal et al., "The Genetic Legacy of the Mongols," *American Journal of Human Genetics* 72 (2003): 717–21.

37. Weatherford, *Genghis Khan*, 227.

38. Ibid., 221.

39. A. J. R. Russell-Wood, *The Portuguese Empire, 1415–1808: A World on the Move* (Baltimore: Johns Hopkins University Press, 1992), 60–62.

40. Kamen, *Spain's Road to Empire*, 354.

41. Ibid., 345.

42. Ibid., 355.

43. James D. Watson, *DNA: The Secret of Life* (New York: Alfred A. Knopf, 2003), 250–51.

44. "Britishers do not land on the shores of other people's states to become ethnic minorities and particularistic lobbies. They create states: the United States, Canada, Australia, New Zealand, South Africa. When the ancient Greeks emigrated, they ipso facto left the polis city-state; when British people emigrated, they took the state with them." Engseng Ho, "Empire through Diasporic Eyes: A View from the Other Boat," *Comparative Studies in Society and History* 46, no. 2 (2004): 210–46.

45. Stuart Mole, "From Empire to Equality? Migration and the Commonwealth," *Round Table* 358 (2001): 89.

46. Ferguson, *Empire*, 60.

47. Gregory Mann, "Immigrants and Arguments in France and West Africa," *Comparative Studies in Society and History* 45 (2003): 362–85, quotation at 364.

48. Claudia Zequeira, "A Petty Officer and Now, a U.S. Citizen," *Orlando Sentinel*, 30 July 2006.

49. Cam Simpson, "U.S. to Probe Claims of Human Trafficking," *Chicago Tribune*, 19 January 2006.

50. Hopkins, ed., *Globalization in World History*, 155.

51. Henry the Navigator heard a story of "the silent trade" in North Africa designed for people who did not know each other's language. As Daniel Boorstin tells it: "Muslim caravans that went southward from Morocco across the Atlas mountains arrived after twenty days at the shores of the Senegal River. The Moroccan traders laid out separate piles of salt, of beads from tan coral, and cheap manufactured goods. Then they retreated out of sight. The local tribesmen, who lived in the strip mines where they dug their gold, came to the shore and put a heap of gold beside each pile of Moroccan's. Then they, in turn, went out of view, leaving the Moroccan traders either to take the gold offered for a particular pile or to reduce the pile of their merchandise to suit the offered price in gold. Once again the Moroccan traders withdrew, and the process went on." Boorstin, *Discoverers*, 161.

52. Sir William Tarn, *Hellenistic Civilisation* (London: Edward Arnold, 1927), 2.

53. Pagden, *Peoples and Empires*, 36.

54. Mansfield, *History of the Middle East*, 15–16.

55. Cook, *Brief History*, 279.

56. Fernand Braudel, *A History of Civilizations*, trans. Richard Mayne (New York: Penguin, 1993), 79.

57. Mansfield, *History of the Middle East*, 16.

58. Weatherford, *Genghis Khan*, 112.

59. Macaulay's speech is available at http://www.languageinindia.com/april2003/macaulay.html.

60. Romila Thapar, *A History of India*, vol. 1 (London: Penguin, 1966), 86.

61. Romila Thapar, *Aśoka and the Decline of the Mauryas* (New Delhi: Oxford University Press, 1997), 46–49.

62. Priyatosh Banerjee, "The Spread of Indian Art and Culture to Central Asia and China," *Indian Horizons* 43, nos. 1–2 (1994), available at http://ignca.nic.in/pb0013.htm.

63. Richard Fletcher, *The Barbarian Conversion: From Paganism to Christianity* (New York: Henry Holt, 1997), 19.

64. *Catholic Encyclopaedia*, s.v. "The First Council of Nicaea," available at http://www.newadvent.org/cathen/11044a.htm.

65. Rodney Stark, "Efforts to Christianize Europe, 400–2000," *Journal of Contemporary Religion* 16, no. 1 (January 2001): 109.

66. Ibid.

67. Michael Wood, *Conquistadors* (Berkeley: University of California Press, 2002), 133–35.

68. Russell-Wood, *Portuguese Empire*, 201.

69. Ferguson, *Colossus*, 7.

70. Ibid., 49.

71. Lê Thânh Khôi, *Histoire du Viêt Nam: des origines à 1858* (Paris: Sudestasie, 1981), 371.

72. Story of Pakistan, "Khilafat Movement [1919–1924]," http://www.storyofpakistan.com/articletext.asp?artid=A033&Pg=2.

73. Bruce B. Lawrence, "In Bin Laden's Words," *Chronicle of Higher Education,* 4 November 2005.

74. Pagden, *Peoples and Empires,* 28.

75. Ernest Barker, quoted in ibid., 32.

76. Romila Thapar, *Early India from the Origins to A.D. 1300* (New Delhi: Allen Lane, 2002), 255.

77. Janet L. Abu-Lughod, *Before European Hegemony: The World System, A.D. 1250–1350* (Oxford: Oxford University Press, 1989), 198.

78. Mansfield, *History of the Middle East,* 18.

79. Abu-Lughod, *Before European Hegemony,* 170.

80. Weatherford, *Genghis Khan,* 221.

81. Michael Prawdin, *The Mongol Empire: Its Rise and Legacy,* trans. Eden and Cedar Paul (New York: Free Press, 1967), 507.

82. Weatherford, *Genghis Khan,* xxiv.

83. William H. McNeill, *The Age of Gunpowder Empires, 1450–1800* (Washington, DC: American Historical Association, 1989), 14.

84. Ferguson, *Empire,* 171.

85. Tarn, *Hellenistic Civilisation,* 250–51.

86. Kamen, *Spain's Road to Empire,* 295.

87. Ibid., 295.

88. Wood and coal store energy that can be transported, but until the discovery of the steam engine, that energy could not be used for any other purpose than heating. The crossbow and trebuchet could not store energy transferred from muscle. Gunpowder—combining saltpeter, sulfur, and charcoal—was thus the first invention in which energy could be stored, transported, and applied. Kenneth Chase, *Firearms: A Global History to 1700* (Cambridge: Cambridge University Press, 2003), 31.

89. Findlay and Lundahl, "First Globalization Episode," 32.

90. Arnold Pacey, *Technology in World Civilization* (Cambridge, MA: MIT Press, 2001), 46.

91. Alfred W. Crosby, *Throwing Fire: Projectile Technology through History* (Cambridge: Cambridge University Press, 2002), 118.

92. Chase, *Firearms,* 71–72.

93. Giancarlo Casale, "The Ottoman 'Discovery' of the Indian Ocean in the Sixteenth Century: The Age of Exploration from an Islamic Perspective," paper presented at Seascapes, Littoral Cultures, and Trans-Oceanic Exchanges, Library of Congress, Washington, DC, 12–15 February 2003, available at http://www.historycooperative. org/proceedings/seascapes/casale.html.

94. K. T. Achaya, *A Historical Dictionary of Indian Food* (New Delhi: Oxford University Press, 1999), 209.

95. Alfred W. Crosby, *Ecological Imperialism: The Biological Expansion of Europe, 900–1900* (Cambridge: Cambridge University Press, 1986), 136.

96. Jerry H. Bentley, "Hemispheric Integration, 500–1500 C.E.," *Journal of World History* 9, no. 2, citing Ho Ping-ti, "Early-ripening Rice in Chinese History," *Economic History Review,* 2nd ser., 9 (1956): 200–218.

97. Andrew M. Watson, "The Arab Agricultural Revolution and Its Diffusion, 700–1100," *Journal of Economic History* 34 (1974): 22.

98. Weatherford, *Genghis Khan,* 229.

99. Ibid., 229.

100. John Feffer, "Korean Food, Korean Identity: The Impact of Globalization on Korean Agriculture," available at http://iis-db.stanford.edu/pubs/20815/Globalization_and_ Korean_Agriculture_John_Feffer.pdf; see also Choe Yong-shik, "Historians Unearth Secret Past of Kimchi," *Korea Herald,* 3 October 2001. See also Amal Naj, *Peppers: A Story of Hot Pursuits* (New York: Vintage Books, 1992), 8.

101. Achaya, *Historical Dictionary of Indian Food,* 188.

102. Russell-Wood, *Portuguese Empire,* 154.

103. Ibid., 172.

104. Murray Hiebert, "Tin Cans and Tyres," *Far Eastern Economic Review,* 15 April 1999.

105. Rigoberto Tiglao, "Roots of Poverty," *Far Eastern Economic Review,* 10 June 1999.

106. Kamen, *Spain's Road to Empire,* 270.

107. Wade Graham, "Traffick According to Their Own Caprice: Trade and Biological Exchange in the Making of the Pacific World, 1766–1825," paper presented at Seascapes, Littoral Cultures, and Trans-Oceanic Exchanges, Library of Congress, Washington, DC, 12–15 February 2003, available at http://www.historycooperative.org/proceedings/ seascapes/graham.html.

108. Tony Ballantyne in Hopkins, ed., *Globalization in World History,* 135–36.

109. Watson, "Arab Agricultural Revolution," 21.

110. Tarn, *Hellenistic Civilisation,* 168.

111. William H. McNeill, *Plagues and Peoples* (New York: Anchor, 1977), 162.

112. Quoted by S. A. M. Adshead, *T'ang China: The Rise of the East in World History* (New York: Palgrave, 2004), 183.

113. James Morris, *Pax Britannica: The Climax of an Empire* (London: Penguin, 1968).

114. Cited in Ferguson, *Empire,* 171.

115. Ibid.

116. Nisid Hajari, "A Most Dignified Retreat with Bagpipers," *Time* (International), 14 July 1997, 22.

CHAPTER 7: SLAVES, GERMS, AND TROJAN HORSES

Epigraph: Christopher Columbus, *The Four Voyages,* ed. and trans. J. M. Cohen (London: Penguin, 1969), 58.

1. Maureen Johnson, "Another Arrest in Truck Deaths as Details of Journey Emerge," Associated Press, 20 June 2000. The account of the Dover tragedy is based on contemporary press reports.

2. Hugh Thomas, *Rivers of Gold: The Rise of the Spanish Empire, from Columbus to Magellan* (New York: Random House, 2003), 155.

3. Milton Meltzer, *Slavery: A World History,* 2 vols. (New York: Da Capo, 1993), 2:39.

4. Amy O'Neill Richard, *International Trafficking in Women to the United States: A Contemporary Manifestation of Slavery and Organized Crime* (Central Intelligence Agency, Center for the Study of Intelligence, April 2000), 3.

5. *Wall Street Journal,* 11 March 2006.

6. Mark Riley, "27 Million Slaves, and We Look Away," *Sydney Morning Herald,* 4 June 2001.

7. Amy Waldman, "Sri Lankan Maids Pay Dearly for Perilous Jobs Overseas," *New York Times,* 8 May 2005. See *Migration in an Interconnected World: New Directions for Action* (Global Commission on International Migration, Geneva, October 2005), available at http://www.gcim.org/attachements/gcim-complete-report-2005.pdf, 26.

8. Adam Smith, *An Inquiry into the Nature and Causes of the Wealth of Nations,* vol.1, ed. R. H. Campbell and A. S. Skinner (Oxford: Clarendon Press, 1976), 448.

9. David Christian, *Maps of Time: An Introduction to Big History* (Berkeley: University of California Press, 2004), 263.

10. Meltzer, *Slavery,* 1:71.

11. Ibid., 1:63.

12. Grant Parker, "*Ex oriente luxuria:* Indian Commodities and Roman Experience," *Journal of the Economic and Social History of the Orient* 45, no. 1 (2002): 50.

13. Timothy Taylor, "Believing the Ancients: Quantitative and Qualitative Dimensions of Slavery and the Slave Trade in Later Prehistoric Eurasia," *World Archaeology* 33, no. 1 (2001): 34.

14. Jose Honorio Rodrigues, "The Influence of Africa on Brazil and of Brazil on Africa," *Journal of African History* 3, no. 1 (1962): 54, 56.

15. Meltzer, *Slavery,* 2:132.

16. Chris Harman, *A People's History of the World,* pt. 3, chap. 6, "European Feudalism," 143, available at http://www.istendency.net/pdf/3_06_european_feudalism.pdf.

17. Eric R. Wolf, *Europe and the People without History* (Berkeley: University of California Press, 1982), 42.

18. Ibid., 74.

19. Ronald Findlay, "Globalization and the European Economy: Medieval Origins to the

Industrial Revolution," in Henryk Kierzkowski, ed., *Europe and Globalization* (New York: Palgrave Macmillan, 2002), 37.

20. Mustafa al-Jiddawi, "Al-Riqqfi al-Tarikh wafi al-Islam" (Slavery throughout history and during Muslim times) (Alexandria, 1963), 92–93.

21. Robin Blackburn, *The Making of New World Slavery* (London: Verso, 1997), 79.

22. Jere L. Bacharach, "African Military Slaves in the Medieval Middle East: The Cases of Iraq (869–955) and Egypt (868–1171)," *International Journal of Middle East Studies* 13 (1981): 471–95.

23. "Zanj Rebellion," Encyclopædia Britannica Online, http://search.eb.com/eb/article?eu=80343. Another important case of slave rebellion occurred nearly a thousand years later aboard a slave ship on the Atlantic. Mitra Sharafi, "The Slave Ship Manuscripts of Captain Joseph B. Cook: A Narrative Reconstruction of the Brig *Nancy*'s Voyage of 1793," *Slavery and Abolition* 24 (April 2003): 71–100.

24. Ghada Hashem Talhami, "The Zanj Rebellion Reconsidered," *International Journal of African Historical Studies* 10, no. 3 (1977): 456.

25. Patricia Risso, *Merchants and Faith: Muslim Commerce and Culture in the Indian Ocean* (Boulder, CO: Westview, 1995), 16.

26. Barbara L. Solow, "Capitalism and Slavery in the Exceedingly Long Run," *Journal of Interdisciplinary History* 17 (Spring 1987): 711–37, quotation at 715.

27. Columbus quoted in ibid., 722, italics added.

28. April Lee Hatfield, "A 'very wary people in their bargaining' or 'very good marchandise': English Traders' Views of Free and Enslaved Africans, 1550–1650," *Slavery and Abolition* 25 (December 2004): 9.

29. Fernand Braudel, *Civilization and Capitalism, Fifteenth-Eighteenth Century,* vol. 2, *The Wheels of Commerce* (New York: William Collins and Sons, 1982), 191.

30. The number of slaves brought from Africa to the New World remains contested. Historian Philip D. Curtin's estimate that between 8 and 10.5 million slaves were brought during the period of Atlantic slave trade has been challenged by others and revised upward considerably. See J. E. Inikori, "Measuring the Atlantic Slave Trade: An Assessment of Curtin and Anstey," *Journal of African History* 17, no. 2 (1976): 197–223, and Curtin's reply, Philip D. Curtin, "Measuring the Atlantic Slave Trade Once Again: A Comment," ibid. 17, no. 4 (1976): 595–605. One later estimate puts the number of slaves leaving Africa at 11,863,000, of which 10–20 percent perished during the voyage across the Atlantic, called the Middle Passage. Paul E. Lovejoy, "The Impact of the Atlantic Slave Trade on Africa: A Review of the Literature," ibid. 30, no. 3 (1989): 365–94.

31. Blackburn, *Making of New World Slavery,* 581.

32. Kevin G. Hall, "Brazilian Slaves Help Make Products That End Up in the United States through World Trade," *San Jose Mercury News,* 14 September 2004.

33. Eighteen illegal immigrants were found dead inside a refrigerated tractor-trailer in Texas; *Houston Chronicle,* 18 May 2003. As a newspaper report put it, "Nearly 150 years since slavery was officially abolished, about 27 million people around the world remain physically or economically shackled—the highest number ever, and it is growing"; "27 Million Slaves."

34. Fernand Braudel, *A History of Civilizations,* trans. Richard Mayne (London: Penguin, 1993), 381.

35. Robert Harms, "Early Globalization and the Slave Trade," *YaleGlobal Online,* 9 May 2003, available at http://yaleglobal.yale.edu/display.article?id=1587.

36. Patrick K. O'Brien, gen. ed., *Atlas of World History* (Oxford: Oxford University Press, 2002), 126.

37. Solow, "Capitalism and Slavery," 730.

38. Puangthong Rungswasdisab, "War and Trade: Siamese Interventions in Cambodia, 1767–1851" (Ph.D. diss., University of Woolongong, 1995), 148.

39. Ward Barrett, "World Bullion Flows, 1450–1800," in James D. Tracy, ed., *The Rise of Merchant Empires: Long Distance Trade in the Early Modern World, 1350–1750* (New York: Cambridge University Press, 1990), 236.

40. Harms, "Early Globalization and the Slave Trade."

41. Robert Harms, *The Diligent: A Voyage through the Worlds of the Slave Trade* (New York: Basic Books, 2002), 82.

42. Solow, "Capitalism and Slavery," 732. British capital investment in the colonies, amounting to thirty-seven million pounds in 1773, was large enough to make this a significant force. As British income grew in the eighteenth century—from higher agricultural productivity at home, which released farm labor to work in newly rising industries—demand for sugar was boosted and the system was kept functioning with the elastic supply of slave labor from Africa to the New World; ibid., 733.

43. Nicholas F. R. Crafts, "British Economic Growth," *Economic History Review* 36 (1983): 177–99.

44. Herbert S. Klein, "Eighteenth-Century Atlantic Slave Trade," in Tracy, ed., *Rise of Merchant Empires,* 289.

45. George Metcalf, "A Microcosm of Why Africans Sold Slaves: Akan Consumption Patterns in the 1770s," *Journal of African History* 28, no. 3 (1987): 393.

46. Tristan Lecomte quoted in Doreen Carvajal, "Third World Gets Help to Help Itself," *International Herald Tribune,* 6 May 2005.

47. Rachel Chernos Lin, "The Rhode Island Slave-Traders: Butchers, Bakers and Candlestick-Makers," *Slavery and Abolition* 23 (December 2002): 21–38.

48. John Richard Oldfield, "Slavery, Abolition, and Empire," *GSC Quarterly* 14 (Winter–Spring 2005), available at http://www.ssrc.org/programs/gsc/publications/quarterly14/oldfield.pdf.

49. W. G. Clarence-Smith, ed., *The Economics of the Indian Ocean Slave Trade in the Nineteenth Century* (London: Frank Cass, 1989).

50. Anthony Reid, *Charting the Shape of Early Modern Southeast Asia* (Singapore: ISEAS, 2000), 208.

51. Norimitsu Onishi, "In Japan's New Texts, Lessons in Rising Nationalism," *New York Times,* 17 April 2005.

52. Paul E. Lovejoy, "The Impact of the Atlantic Slave Trade on Africa: A Review of the Literature," *Journal of African History* 30, no. 3 (1989): 388.

53. Dinesh D'Souza, "The End of Racism," cited in "Slavery and Globalization" by Marian L. Tupy, 5 September 2003, Cato Institute, available at http://www.cato.org/dailys/09-05-03.html.

54. Klein, "Eighteenth-Century Atlantic Slave Trade," 291.

55. S. Elisée Soumonni, "Some Reflections on the Brazilian Legacy in Dahomey," *Slavery and Abolition* 22 (April 2001): 42–60.

56. Quoted in Rodrigues, "Influence of Africa on Brazil," 52.

57. Ibid., 56–61.

58. Nei Lopes, "African Religions in Brazil, Negotiation, and Resistance: A Look from Within," *Journal of Black Studies* 34 (July 2004): 853.

59. Alfred W. Crosby, Jr., *The Columbian Exchange: Biological and Cultural Consequences of 1492* (Westport, CT: Greenwood, 1972), 31.

60. Niall Ferguson, *Empire: The Rise and Demise of the British World Order and the Lessons for Global Power* (New York: Basic Books, 2002), 71.

61. John Archdale quoted in ibid.

62. Ronald Findlay and Mats Lundahl, "Demographic Shocks and the Factor Proportions Model: From the Plague of Justinian to the Black Death," typescript, Columbia University, University Seminar in Economic History, 28, available at http://www.econ.barnard.columbia.edu/~econhist/papers/Findlay%20Justinian.pdf.

63. Kenneth F. Kipple, "The Plague of Justinian: An Early Lesson in the Black Death," in Kipple, ed., *Plague, Pox and Pestilence* (London: Weidenfeld and Nicolson, 1997), 29.

64. Ole J. Benedictow, *The Black Death, 1346–1353: The Complete History* (Woodbridge: Boydell, 2004), 3.

65. Ibid., 382.

66. James Burke, *Connections* (Boston: Little, Brown, 1978), 70.

67. Ronald Findlay and Kevin H. O'Rourke, "Commodity Market Integration, 1500–2000," in Michael D. Bordo, Alan M. Taylor, and Jeffrey G. Williamson, eds., *Globalization in Historical Perspective* (Chicago: University of Chicago Press, 2003), 15.

68. Burke, *Connections*, 103–4. The technique of papermaking was picked up by Arabs when they overran Samarkand in 751 CE, just after the Chinese had sent a team of paper makers there to set up a factory. By 1050 paper was being made in Moorish Spain. In 1280 a paper mill running on waterpower was set up at Fabriano, Italy; ibid., 100.

69. Benedictow, *Black Death*, 393.

70. Rosen, George, *A History of Public Health*, reprint ed. (Baltimore: Johns Hopkins University Press, 1993), 43–45.

71. Ibid., 64.

72. Jonathan Tucker, *Scourge: The Once and Future Threat of Smallpox* (New York: Atlantic Monthly, 2001), 10–11.

73. Ferguson, *Empire*, 71.

74. Tucker, *Scourge*, 15.

75. Ibid., 16.

76. J. N. Hays, *The Burdens of Disease: Epidemics and Human Response in Western History* (New Brunswick, NJ: Rutgers University Press, 1998), 240.

77. Gina Kolata, *Flu: The Story of the Great Influenza Pandemic of 1918 and the Search for the Virus That Caused It* (New York: Farrar, Straus and Giroux, 1999), 297–98.

78. Virologist John Oxford estimated that the worldwide death from the flu was one hundred million rather than twenty to forty million. Ibid., 285.

79. Ibid., 5.

80. Rob Stein and Shankar Vedantam, "Deadly Flu Strain Shipped Worldwide: Officials Race to Destroy Samples," *Washington Post,* 13 April 2005.

81. Jong-Wha Lee and Warwick J. McKibbin, *Globalization and Disease: The Case of SARS,* August 2003, Working Paper no. 2003/16, Division of Economics, Research School of Pacific and Asian Studies, 13.

82. David Fidler, "SARS: Political Pathology of the First Post-Westphalian Pathogen," *Journal of Law, Medicine and Ethics* 31 (December 2003): 485.

83. http://www.whitehouse.gov/news/releases/2005/11/20051116-6.html.

84. David Heymann, "Preparing for a New Global Threat—Part I," *YaleGlobal Online,* 26 January 2005, available at http://yaleglobal.yale.edu/display.article?id=5174.

85. Thomas Abraham, "Preparing for a New Global Threat—Part II," *YaleGlobal Online,* 28 January 2005, available at http://yaleglobal.yale.edu/display.article?id=5191.

86. Eugene H. Spafford, "Computer Viruses as Artificial Life," *Journal of Artificial Life* (1994), available at http://www.scs.carleton.ca/~soma/biosec/readings/spafford-viruses.pdf.

87. Fred Cohen, "Computer Viruses" (Ph.D. diss., University of Southern California, 1985).

88. Xin Li, "Computer Viruses: The Threat Today and the Expected Future" (undergraduate thesis, Linköping University, 2003), available at http://www.ep.liu.se/exjobb/isy/2003/3452/exjobb.pdf.

89. Dugan Haltey, "Virus Alert, 2001," typescript, available at http://eserver.org/courses/s01/tc510/foobar/virus/printable.pdf.

90. Lee Kuan Yew, interview with author, 17 January 2004.

91. Mynardo Macaraig, "Philippine Internet Providers Admit Being 'Love Bug' Source," *Agence France-Presse,* 5 May 2000; Mark Landler, "A Filipino Linked to 'Love Bug' Talks about His License to Hack," *New York Times,* 21 October 2000.

92. John Eisinger, "Script Kiddies Beware," *Washington and Lee Law Review* 59 (2002): 1507–44.

93. Javier Santoyo, interview with author, 18 April 2005.

94. http://www.caida.org/analysis/security/code-red/coderedv2_analysis.xml#animations.

95. Li, "Computer Viruses," 42.

96. Mark Hall, "Sticky Security," *Computerworld,* 19 January 2004, 48.

97. This section on cybercrime relies on Brian Grow, with Jason Bush, "Hacker Hunters," *BusinessWeek,* 30 May 2005.

98. Cited by Marian L. Tupy, "Slavery and Globalization," Cato Institute, 5 September 2003, available at http://www.cato.org/pub_display.php?pub_id=3227.

CHAPTER 8: GLOBALIZATION

Epigraph: Jagdish N. Bhagwati, "Coping with Antiglobalization: A Trilogy of Discontents," *Foreign Affairs* 81 (January–February 2002): 2.

1. Jürgen Osterhammel and Niels P. Petersson, *Globalization: A Short History* (Princeton, NJ: Princeton University Press, 2005).

2. Although the database contains publications in dozens of languages, I consulted only the English and French publications dating back to 1971.

3. Simon Jeffrey, "What Is Globalisation?" *Guardian,* 31 October 2002.

4. Patrick Smith, "The Seven Year Stitch," *Far Eastern Economic Review,* 3–9 July 1981, 38.

5. "Representatives of Nineteen Developing Countries Have Been Meeting in Hong Kong to Coordinate Policy in the Face of EEC Demands for Tighter Control on Their Exports," *Guardian,* 23 June 1981; "Trade Talks on Multifiber Arrangement Opens Monday," *Wall Street Journal,* 10 July 1981.

6. Ted Levitt, "The Globalization of Markets," *Harvard Business Review* (May–June 1983): 92–94, 96–102.

7. "The Drive among Multi-National Companies to Create Products Which Are Global in Their Scope," *Financial Times,* 16 July 1984.

8. "The BSN of France Wishes to Expand Its Business Worldwide As It Feels Food Tastes Are Becoming Increasingly Global," *Financial Times,* 22 February 1984.

9. Quoted in Warren Brown, "Ford Earns a Record $1.87 Billion in '83," *Washington Post,* 14 February 1984.

10. Harvey Enchin, "Labor Negotiations in Auto Industry Are Facing New Threat," *Globe and Mail,* 13 August 1984.

11. Jim Ostroff, "AAMA Convention to Focus on Sourcing, Exporting Event Kicks Off Thursday in Arizona," *Daily News Record,* 3 May 1995.

12. Christopher Lorenz, "Plastic Can First Step to 'Globalization,'" *Financial Times,* 23 July 1984.

13. Douglas McArthur, "U.S. Airlines Becoming Jumpy about Trend to 'Globalization,'" *Globe and Mail,* 15 October 1988.

14. "On the Opening Day of a Conference on World Financial Futures," *Financial Times,* 29 September 1983.

15. "The Challenges Facing the Growing International Share-Dealing Market Given the Soaring Popularity of Round-the-Clock Trading," *Financial Times,* 5 November 1985.

16. David Lake, "NYSE Seeks to Gain Share of Global Equities Market," *Dallas Morning News,* 14 April 1986.

17. Stephen Kindel, "Markets Far and Wide; Global Trading Is Becoming an Efficient Way to Raise and Shift Capital," *Financial World,* 16 September 1986, 106.

18. "Regulatory Issues Arise with Globalization of Financial Markets," *American Banker,* 31 July 1987.

19. Dennis Walters, "A Worldwide Market: A Matter of Perspective," *American Banker,* 30 July 1987. Later reports said, "One marked characteristic of the crash was a wholesale dumping of foreign stocks and a retreat to home markets." The president of Credit Suisse Asset Management, a New York-based unit of Credit Suisse, Gordon Bowyer, was quoted as saying, "The Brits sold Swiss and German stocks and went home. The Swiss were pulling out of the U.K. and U.S. In that sense, globalization failed." But another banker was quoted as saying: "Globalization is going to go forward, but only slowly from now on. We had five terrific years in financial markets; now we're in the first of maybe two or three very difficult years." Michael R. Sesit, "Slowing the Global Express: World-Wide Markets May Be Inevitable, but Right Now Investors Are Wary," *Wall Street Journal,* 23 September 1988.

20. Mark W. Olson, "Globalization Raises a World of Questions," *American Banker,* 19 July 1989.

21. "Corrigan Offers Perspective on Globalization," *American Banker*, 30 July 1987.

22. Steve Lohr, "Crash Shifts Investors' Foreign Stock Plans," *New York Times*, 23 December 1987.

23. Louis Uchitelle, "U.S. Firms Shed National Identity as They Expand Abroad," *New York Times*, 24 May 1989.

24. Cynthia Barnum and Natasha Walniansky, "Globalization: Moving a Step beyond the International Firm," *Management Review*, 1 September 1989.

25. "Globalization of the Retail Industry: A Strategic Imperative," *Chain Store Age Executive with Shopping Center Age*, 15 December 1993, 6.

26. John King, "World without Borders," *Canada and the World Backgrounder* 60, no. 5 (1995): 8.

27. Carla Rapoport, "Retailers Go Global," *Fortune*, 20 February 1995, 102.

28. World Bank, *Global Economic Prospects and the Developing Countries, April 20, 1995*, cited by *Presidents and Prime Ministers* 4 (July–August 1995): 21.

29. G. Pascal Zachary, "Supercapitalism," *Wall Street Journal*, 29 March 1997.

30. Jane Fraser and Jeremy Oppenheim, "What's New about Globalization?" *McKinsey Quarterly*, 22 March 1997.

31. President Bill Clinton, address to World Bank and International Monetary Fund, 12 October 1995, Washington, DC.

32. Sue Neales, "Japan Lifts Its Bamboo Curtain," *Australian Financial Review*, 7 July 1988.

33. Klaus Schwab and Claude Smadja, "Start Taking the Backlash against Globalization Seriously," *International Herald Tribune*, 1 February 1996.

34. Donald Coxe, "Vanishing Act: Economic Crisis Threatens to Make the Complex Trade Network Known as Globalization Disappear," *Globe and Mail*, 30 October 1998.

35. Editorial, "Rethinking Globalization," *Toronto Star*, 28 December 1998.

36. President Bill Clinton quoted in E. J. Dionne, Jr., "Globalization Camps," *Pittsburgh Post-Gazette*, 25 January 1999.

37. Yashwant Sinha, address at the World Economic Forum, Davos, cited in Kamalakshi Mehta, "The G Word," *WorldLink*, March–April 1999, 25.

38. Al R. Dizon, "World Trade Organization Meeting: S Asean Watch Calm before the Storm," *Business World*, 26 November 1999, 20.

39. Mike Moore quoted in Rebecca Cook, "Protesters Launch 'Battle in Seattle' against WTO," *Associated Press*, 28 November 1999.

40. Personal communication from a World Bank official, 3 August 2006.

41. Vandana Shiva, "The Two Fascisms (Economic Globalization)," *Ecologist*, 1 May 1999.

42. Nayan Chanda, interview with President Bill Clinton, 31 October 2003, *YaleGlobal Online*, available at http://yaleglobal.yale.edu/display.article?id=2840.

43. Richard Tomkins, "Happy Birthday, Globalisation," *Financial Times*, 6 May 2003.

44. Editorial, "Who's Afraid of Globalization?" *Manila Standard*, 19 January 2000.

45. Robert E. Litan, "The 'Globalization' Challenge: The U.S. Role in Shaping World Trade and Investment," *Brookings Review* 18 (Spring 2000): 35–37.

46. "Assessing Globalization," *World Bank Briefing Paper*, undated, available at http://www1.worldbank.org/economicpolicy/globalization/documents/AssessingGlobalizationP1.pdf.

47. Naomi Klein, "Fete for the End of the End of History," *Nation*, 19 March 2001.

48. Some nine hundred NGOs, environmentalists, feminists, and government representatives gathered at the Brazilian town; "Forum de Porto Alegre," *Agence Telegraphique Suisse*, 21 January 2001.

49. "Selon un sondage Eurobaromètre, la majorité des Européens ne craint pas la mondialisation," *Agence Europe*, 19 November 2003.

50. Françoise Antoine and Marie Brandeleer, "Qui sont ces marcheurs?" *Trends/Tendances*, 13 December 2001, 42.

51. Fiona Fleck, "Antiglobalization Forces Shift to Pragmatic Tactics," *International Herald Tribune*, 21 January 2004.

52. Xavier Harel, "Les alter-mondialisation à l'heure du dialogue," *La Tribune*, 30 January 2003.

53. John Holusha, "General Motors Corp Chairman Roger B. Smith Says That Company Is Looking . . . ," *New York Times*, 14 October 1981.

54. Daniel Gross, "Why 'Outsourcing' May Lose Its Power as a Scare Word," *New York Times*, 13 August 2006.

55. Remarks Prepared for Delivery by Treasury Secretary Henry M. Paulson at Columbia University, 1 August 2006, available at http://www.treas.gov/press/releases/hp41.htm.

CHAPTER 9: WHO'S AFRAID OF GLOBALIZATION?

Epigraphs: Anne O. Krueger, "Supporting Globalization," IMF, available at http://www.imf.org/external/np/speeches/2002/092602a.htm; Susan George, "Another World Is Possible," *Khaleej Times*, 18 October 2004, available at http://www.khaleejtimes.com/DisplayArticle.asp?xfile=data/opinion/2004/October/opinion_October31.xml&section=opinion&col=.

1. Laura Carlsen, "WTO Kills Farmers: In Memory of Lee Kyung Hae," 16 September 2003, available at http://www.countercurrents.org/glo-carlsen160903.htm.

2. Sulak Sivaraksa, "Globalisation Represents Greed," *Bangkok Post*, 21 September 1997.

3. Dani Rodrick, *Has Globalization Gone Too Far?* (Washington, DC: Institute of International Economics, 1997).

4. For a summary of alter-globalization, see James H. Mittelman, "Where Have All the Protesters Gone?" *YaleGlobal Online*, available at http://yaleglobal.yale.edu/display.article?id=4637, and his book *Whither Globalization? The Vortex of Knowledge and Ideology* (New York: Routledge, 2004).

5. Nicholas Thomas, *Cook: The Extraordinary Voyages of Captain James Cook* (New York: Walker, 2004), 391–401.

6. Karl Marx and Friedrich Engels, *The Communist Manifesto* (Chicago: Haymarket Books, 2005), 44–45, italics added.

7. Karl Marx, *Capital*, vol. 1 (Moscow: Progress Publishers, 1954), 252.

8. Anthony Reid, *South East Asia in the Age of Commerce, 1450–1680*, vol. 2 (New Haven and London: Yale University Press, 1993), 7–9.

9. D. J. M. Tate, *The Making of Modern Southeast Asia*, vol. 2 (Kuala Lumpur: Oxford University Press, 1979), 93.

10. Nicholas Tarling, ed., *Cambridge History of Southeast Asia,* vol. 1 (Cambridge: Cambridge University Press, 1992), 602.

11. Blair B. Kling, *The Blue Mutiny: The Indigo Disturbances in Bengal, 1859–1862* (Philadelphia: University of Pennsylvania Press, 1966).

12. Jeffrey G. Williamson, "Winners and Losers over Two Centuries of Globalization," 2002 WIDER Annual Lecture, Copenhagen, 5 September 2002.

13. Kevin H. O'Rourke and Jeffrey G. Williamson, *Globalization and History: The Evolution of a Nineteenth-Century Atlantic Economy* (Cambridge, MA: MIT Press, 1999), 183.

14. Charles A. Price, *The Great White Walls Are Built: Restrictive Immigration to North America and Australasia, 1836–1888* (Canberra: Australian National University Press, 1974), 323. See also O'Rourke and Williamson, *Globalization and History,* 190.

15. Harold James, *The End of Globalization: Lessons from the Great Depression* (Cambridge, MA: Harvard University Press, 2001), 30.

16. Ibid., 121.

17. Jeffry A. Frieden, *Global Capitalism: Its Fall and Rise in the Twentieth Century* (New York: W. W. Norton, 2006), 396.

18. Niall Ferguson, in Strobe Talbott and Nayan Chanda, eds., *The Age of Terror: America and the World after September 11* (New York: Basic Books, 2002).

19. Bernard Gordon, "Development vs. Free Trade," *YaleGlobal Online,* 20 July 2006, available at http://yaleglobal.yale.edu/display.article?id=7850.

20. The General Agreement on Tariffs and Trade (GATT); the General Agreement on Trade in Services (GATS); and the Agreement on Trade-Related Aspects of Intellectual Property Rights (TRIPS).

21. Institute for International Economics, *US-China Trade Disputes,* Preview, Chapter 3: Textiles and Clothing, http://www.iie.com/publications/chapters_preview/3942/03iie3942 .pdf.

22. Kenneth Rogoff, "Paul Samuelson's Contributions to International Economics," 11 May 2005, paper prepared for volume in honor of Paul Samuelson's ninetieth birthday, ed. Michael Szenberg, available at http://www.economics.harvard.edu/faculty/rogoff/ papers/Samuelson.pdf.

23. *Cultivating Poverty: The Impact of U.S. Cotton Subsidies on Africa,* Oxfam Briefing Paper, 30 (London: Oxfam, 2002), 2. World cotton prices have fallen by half since the mid-1990s. Adjusted for inflation, they are lower than at any time since the Great Depression of the 1930s.

24. According to a study by International Cotton Advisory Committee, cited in ibid., 32.

25. U.N. Millennium Task Force Project on Trade, *Trade for Development* (New York, 2005), 49.

26. G. Pascal Zachary, "Africa's Bitter Cotton Harvest," *Straits Times,* 19 April 2006.

27. Ibid.

28. "'The Chief Responsibility Lies Here,' Lamy Tells G-8," *WTO News:* Speeches, DG Pascal Lamy, available at http://www.wto.org/english/news_e/sppl_e/sppl32_e.htm.

29. Jose Bové, interview with Robert Siegel, *National Public Radio,* 30 November 1999.

30. Foreign Broadcast Information Service report, Washington, DC, 20 August 2003.

31. *Kicking Down the Door: How Upcoming WTO Talks Threaten Farmers in Poor Countries,* Oxfam Briefing Paper, 72 (London: Oxfam, 2005).

32. Editorial, "Sweet Justice for EU Sugar: The WTO Has Put a Time-Bomb under an Indefensible Policy," *Financial Times,* 6 August 2004.

33. Cited in Pranab Bardhan, "Does Globalization Help or Hurt the World's Poor?" *Scientific American,* April 2006.

34. Reuters, "Soya Exporters to Stop Buying Amazon Beans," *Sydney Morning Herald, 26* July 2006.

35. Michael McCarthy, "The Great Rainforest Tragedy," *Independent,* 28 June 2003.

36. John Vidal, "The 7,000-Km Journey That Links Amazon Destruction to Fast Food," *Guardian,* 10 April 2006.

37. Matt Pottinger, Steve Stecklow, and John J. Fialka, "Invisible Export—A Hidden Cost of China's Growth: Mercury Migration," *Wall Street Journal,* 20 December 2004.

38. Tina Rosenberg, "Globalization," *New York Times Magazine,* 18 August 2002.

39. Keith Bradsher, "Vietnam's Roaring Economy Is Set for World Stage," *New York Times,* 25 October 2006.

40. Chakravarthi Raghavan, "A Theatre of the Absurd at Seattle," Third World Network, available at http://www.twnside.org.sg/title/deb3-cn.htm.

41. Thomas L. Friedman, comment, Asia Society, New York, 4 April 2005, available at http://www.asiasociety.org/speeches/friedman05.html.

42. The so-called Washington consensus is a set of ideas reflecting the consensus of 1990 and put forth in a World Bank study by John Williamson. The ten elements are: (1) fiscal discipline; (2) public expenditure priorities in education and health; (3) tax reform (the tax base should be broad and marginal tax rates should be moderate); (4) positive but moderate market-determined interest rates; (5) a competitive exchange rate as the "first essential element of an 'outward-oriented' economic policy"; (6) import liberalization; (7) openness to foreign direct investment (but "liberalization of foreign financial flows is not regarded as a high priority"); (8) privatization (based on "the belief that private industry is managed more efficiently than state enterprises"); (9) deregulation; and (10) protection of property rights. Cited by Stanley Fischer, "Globalization and Its Challenges," *AEA Papers and Proceedings* 93 (May 2003), 6.

43. Circular issued by "50 Years Is Enough," 28 September 2001, Washington, DC.

44. Rosenberg, "Globalization."

45. Stiglitz quoted in Ed Crook, "The Odd Couple of Global Finance," *Financial Times,* 5 July 5, 2002.

46. U.S. Department of Commerce, *U.S. Census Bureau: U.S. Bureau of Economic Analysis News,* 9 June 2006, reported the first-quarter trade deficit as $254 billion.

47. Steve Lohr, "A Dissenter on Outsourcing States His Case," *International Herald Tribune,* 7 September 2004.

48. David Dapice, interview with author, 18 November 2004.

49. Branko Milanovic, "Why Globalization Is in Trouble," part 1, 29 August 2006, *YaleGlobal Online,* available at http://yaleglobal.yale.edu/display.article?id=8073.

50. Andrew Grove quoted in Manjeet Kripalani and Pete Engardio, "The Rise of India,"

Business Week Online, 8 December 2003, available at http://www.businessweek.com/magazine/content/03_49/b3861001_mz001.htm.

51. India then produced 25 percent of the world's cloth, and Indian textiles paid for spices in Southeast Asia and slaves in Africa. Kenneth Pomeranz and Steven Topik, *The World That Trade Created* (Armonk, NY: M. E. Sharpe, 1999), 228–29.

52. In December 2004 GE sold 60 percent of the operation and renamed it.

53. Ashutosh Sheshabalaya, *Rising Elephant: The Growing Clash with India over White Collar Jobs* (Monroe, ME: Common Courage Press, 2005), 46.

54. "Faster, Cheaper, Better," in "Survey of Outsourcing," *Economist*, 11 November 2004.

55. Cited in Jeffrey A. Frieden, *Global Capitalism*.

56. Mike Ricciuti and Mike Yamamoto, "Companies Determined to Retain 'Secret Sauce,'" *C-NET News*, 5 May 2004.

57. Letter to the editor by an employee of a high-tech firm, *Sentinel and Enterprise*, 13 May 2006, available at http://www.sentinelandenterprise.com/ci_3819745.

58. "The Future of Outsourcing: How It's Transforming Whole Industries and Changing the Way We Work," *Business Week*, 30 January 2006.

59. Global Crossing spent 415 billion dollars to build a global fiber-optic network before entering bankruptcy. The Singapore government-controlled SemCorp bought 61 percent of that network for just 250 million dollars. Personal communication from a SemCorp executive, 2 May 2006.

60. Thomas L. Friedman, *The World Is Flat: A Brief History of the Twenty-First Century* (New York: Farrar, Straus and Giroux, 2005), 128–32.

61. Robert Fulford, "Upwardly Mobile Phone Jockey . . . or 'Cyber-Coolie'?" *National Post*, 1 November 2003.

62. Geoffrey Colvin, "America Isn't Ready [Here's What to Do about It]," *Fortune*, 25 July 2005.

63. Alan S. Blinder, "*Offshoring: The Next Industrial Revolution?*" *Foreign Affairs* 85 (March–April 2006): 113–28.

64. Philip Aldrick, "Indian Workers 'Slash IT Wages,'" *Daily Telegraph*, 26 December 2005.

65. Daniel Gross, "Invest Globally, Stagnate Locally," *New York Times*, 2 April 2006.

66. Quoted in ibid.

67. Craig Barrett, "Do We Want to Compete?" in Outsourcing Roundtable, *CNET News.com*, http://news.com.com/2009-1022_3-5198961.html.

68. Somini Sengupta, "Skills Gap Hurts Technology Boom in India," *New York Times*, 17 October 17, 2006.

69. *International Trade: Current Government Data Provide Limited Insight into Offshoring of Services* (Washington, DC: United States Government Accountability Office, 2004), 34.

70. McKinsey estimates that by 2008, 160 million jobs, or about 11 percent of total global service jobs, could be carried out remotely, but only 4.1 million of those would actually be offshored. This modest projected take-up is attributed to company-specific barriers rather than regulatory barriers. See Mari Sako's background paper "Outsourcing and Offshoring: Key Trends and Issues" (Said Business School, Oxford, November 2005).

71. Daniel W. Drezner, "The Outsourcing Bogeyman," *Foreign Affairs* 83 (May–June 2004): 22–34.

72. Thomas L. Friedman, *The World Is Flat,* expanded ed. (London: Penguin, 2006), 278.

73. Branko Milanovic, "Why Globalization Is in Trouble," *YaleGlobal Online,* 29 August 2006, available at http://yaleglobal.yale.edu/display.article?id=8073.

74. Gross, "Invest Globally, Stagnate Locally."

75. Elaine Sciolino, "French Youth at the Barricades, But a Revolution? It Can Wait," *New York Times,* 28 March 2006.

76. Stephen Roach, "China's Emergence and the Global Labor Arbitrage," 7 April 2006, Morgan Stanley home page, http://www.tribemagazine.com/board/showthread.php?t=114271.

77. Joseph E. Stiglitz, "Why We Should Worry about Outsourcing," *Miami Herald,* 9 May 2004.

78. Transcript, Conference Call on the Analytic Chapters of the Spring 2006 World Economic Outlook with Raghuram Rajan, Economic Counselor and Director of Research of IMF, 13 April 2006, available at http://www.internationalmonetaryfund.org/external/np/tr/2006/tr060413.htm.

79. David Dollar, "The Poor Like Globalization," *YaleGlobal Online,* 23 June 2003, available at http://yaleglobal.yale.edu/display.article?id=1934.

80. Barry Naughton, "The Chinese Economy: Five Snapshots," typescript, University of California, San Diego, 9 April 2006.

81. Pranab Bardhan, "Time for India to Reduce Inequality," *Financial Times,* 7 August 2006.

82. David Dollar and Aart Kraay, "Growth Is Good for the Poor," World Bank Policy Research Working Paper no. 2587, April 2001, available at http://ssrn.com/abstract=632656.

83. M. Lundberg and B. Milanovic, "Globalization and Inequality: Are They Linked and How?" (World Bank, 2000), available at http://www1.worldbank.org/prem/poverty/inequal/abstracts/milanov.htm.

84. Branko Milanovic, "Can We Discern the Effect of Globalization on Income Distribution? Evidence from Household Surveys" (Paper, World Bank, 22 September 2003), 31–32.

85. Nancy Birdsall, "Cheerleaders, Cynics and Worried Doubters," *Global Agenda,* 2003, available at http://www.cgdev.org/doc/commentary/birdsall_cheerleaders.pdf.

86. Pranab Bardhan, "Does Globalization Help or Hurt the World's Poor?" *Scientific American,* April 2006.

87. Pew Research Center for the People and the Press, "Views of a Changing World 2003," 3 June 2003, available at http://people-press.org/reports/print.php3?PageID=712.

88. "Indians along with Half the World's Consumers Buy into Globalisation: Survey," Indiantelevision.com, 23 August 2006, available at http://www.indiantelevision.com/mam/headlines/y2k6/aug/augmam106.htm.

89. Frieden, *Global Capitalism,* 436.

90. For a sober analysis, see Pranab Bardhan, "China, India Superpower? Not So Fast!" *YaleGlobal Online,* 25 October 2005, available at http://yaleglobal.yale.edu/display.article?id=6407.

CHAPTER 10: THE ROAD AHEAD

Epigraph: Quoted in Serge Gruzinski, *Les quatre parties du monde: histoire d'une mondialisation* (Paris: Martinière, 2004), 402.

1. Angus Maddison, *The World Economy: A Millennial Perspective* (Paris: OECD, 2001), 263.
2. Thomas P. M. Barnett, *The Pentagon's New Map: War and Peace in the Twenty-First Century* (New York: G. P. Putnam's Sons, 2004), 107–91.
3. *Migration in an Interconnected World: New Directions for Action* (Global Commission on International Migration, Geneva, October 2005), 11, available at http://www.gcim.org/attachements/gcim-complete-report-2005.pdf.
4. Roger Cohen, "Spreading Work around Leaves Other Work to Do," *International Herald Tribune,* 27 May 2006.
5. Henry Paulson, interview, *Der Spiegel,* 13 June 2006.
6. Gordon Brown, speech at Mansion House, London, 21 June 2006, available at http://www.hm-treasury.gov.uk/newsroom_and_speeches/press/2006/press_44_06.cfm.
7. Janet L. Yellen, "Economic Inequality in the United States," 2006–2007 Economics of Governance Lecture, Center for the Study of Democracy, University of California, Irvine, 6 November 2006, available at http://www.frbsf.org/news/speeches/2006/1106.html.
8. "Election Pushes Globalization to Forefront," *USA Today,* 14 November 2006.
9. Pascal Lamy, "The Doha Marathon," *Wall Street Journal,* 3 November 2006.
10. Cohen, "Spreading Work around."
11. Strobe Talbott, *A Gathering of Tribes: Reflections on the Unity of Nations* (forthcoming, 2007).
12. Dr. H. Mahler quoted in Jack W. Hopkins, *The Eradication of Smallpox: Organization and Innovation in International Health* (Boulder, CO: Westview, 1989), 125.
13. Nicholas Stern, *The Economics of Climate Change: The Stern Review* (Cambridge, 2006), PDF version available at http://www.hm-treasury.gov.uk/independent_reviews/stern_review_economics_climate_change/stern_review_report.cfm.

Index

Abd al-Wahhab, Muhhamad ibn, 134
Abdur, Eritrea, 10–11
Abdur Reef limestone, 11
Abu-Lughod, Janet L., 199
accountancy, development of, 60
Aceh, kingdom of, 132, 135
adaptation to climatic differences, 22
adventurers, 32, 146–47; ancestral adventurers from Africa, 9–11; Afanasii Nikitin, 155; Benjamin of Tudela, 156; Christopher Columbus, 160–61; explorers, 147–55, 159–64, 172–73; Ferdinand Magellan, 162–63; Hanno, 148; Herodotus, 148, 150; Ibn Battuta, 157–58; impact of early adventurers on human diversity, 19–23; first Jamaicans in Britain, 168; Marco Polo, 153–55; map, 149; migration, 6, 25–26, 147, 151, 161–73; Pêro da Covilhã, 160; quest for

knowledge, 157–58; refugees, 147, 170–72; religious, *see* missionaries; travelers, 147, 153–59, 228; unfree labor as adventurers, 167–68; Zhang Qian, 151; Zheng He, 152–153

Afghanistan: lapis lazuli from, 40; religion in, 194–95; terrorists in, 135

Africa: agriculture in, 280, 284, 310; ancestry of Yellow Emperor, 16; author's ancestors from, 11, 13–15; Christianity in, 124–25, 126–27; circumnavigation of, 150; coffee from, 73; cotton industry in, 79, 281; as cradle of globalization, 3, 7, 16, 20; diamond mines in, 126; European colonies in, *see specific nations;* fossils in, 5; genetic lines from, 6–7, 9; gold from, 42, 126; human rights in, 141, 142; ivory trade in, 48; languages in, 192; legal systems in, 197, 198; map,

169; trade networks in, 28, 41–42, 47, 48, 51, 59, 82, 160, 176, 198–99, 285; "unfree labor" from, 166–68; wealth gap in, 313; wheat grown in, 24

Chinese Exclusion Act (1882), 167

Christian, David, 19, 31, 214

Christianity, 110; Bible translations, 142; birth of, 119–20; Crusades, 112, 120, 185; Jesus of Nazareth, 31–32, 119–20, 195; spread of, 121–28, 142, 161, 162–63, 182, 185, 195–96

Chronology, 321–30

Clarke, Arthur C., 62

Clement VIII, Pope, 86

climate, 21–23

climate change, 23–25

Clinton, Bill, 257–58, 262

Coca-Cola, 262

cocoa, 223

coconut tree, 11; oil, 204

Coffee Exchange, New York, 91

coffee trade, 55, 82–94; café au lait, 90; *cappuccino*, 87; *coffee*, name derivation, 84; coffee-drinking ceremony, 84; coffeehouses, 73, 85–86; and fair trade movement, 92–93; freeze-drying, 91; and lifestyle statements, 87–88, 92; map, 83; mass commodity of, 90–93; price fluctuations in, 91–92; and slavery, 87, 89–90, 220, 221, 226; and sugar production, 87, 91

Cold War: military expansion in, 180; missile gap in, 100

Colombia: drug trade in, 93, 310; European migration to, 190

Columbus, Christopher, 147, 163; death of, 59, 161; diseases brought to New World by, 227; and gold, 121, 154, 185, 186, 211; and Marco Polo, 154, 155, 160; and Native Americans, 5, 211, 227; New World discovered by, 19, 54, 74, 121, 161, 164, 185, 186; and religious conversions, 121, 122, 161, 185; and San Sal-

vador, 5, 19, 121, 161, 162; ships of, 200; and slave trade, 209, 211, 219; Spanish sponsorship of, 54, 121, 159, 160–61

communication: ASCII, 64; bar code, 65; body-shopping, 67; call center services, 68–69; cave paintings, 17, 113–14, 119; clay tablets, 38, 40, 65; costs of, 63, 67–68; electronic, 64–69, 275, 293–94 (*see also* computers; Internet); and empire building, 206–7; evolution of, 65, 69; fax, 64; FedEx, 64–65, 69; fiber optics, 66–69, 102, 293; homing pigeons, 61, 62; HTML, 66; instant, 73; laser, 66; long-distance, 61–62, 206; microchips, 73–74, 94–95; outsourcing jobs in, 68; papermaking, 42, 117–18, 206; postal services, 61, 127, 206; radio transmission, 98, 99, 128; satellite, 102, 128, 136, 249; secure, 207; telecommunications, 63, 67–69; telegraph, 62–63, 97, 206–7; telephone, 63, 68; television, 302, 314, 318; and terrorism, 264, 314–15, 318; and trade, 61–69; transatlantic cable, 63–64, 68, 206–7; transistorized, 96, 98, 99, 100–102; and transportation, 62, 63; visual signaling system, 61; writing invented, 61; writing materials, 61

Communist Manifesto (Marx and Engels), 276

computers, 64, 65–66; body-shopping model in, 67; cybercrime in, 241–43; debugging, 98; integrated circuits, 100; and Internet, *see* Internet; and mathematics, 99, 100; microchips, 73–74, 94–95, 100–102; and outsourcing jobs, 67–68; PCs, 65, 69, 95; "phishing" programs in, 239, 240; Trojan horses, 237–38, 240; vacuum bulbs in, 98; viruses in, 236–43; worms, 237, 240, 241; Y2K crisis, 292

Confucianism, 124

Constantine, Emperor, 119, 195